DOUGLAS GRAY

THE CANADIAN SNOWBIRD GUIDE

Everything You Need To Know About Living Part-time in the U.S.A. and Mexico

THIRD EDITION

 McGraw-Hill
Ryerson

Toronto Montréal New York Burr Ridge Bangkok Bogotá Caracas
Lisbon London Madrid Mexico City Milan New Delhi Seoul
Singapore Sydney Taipei

McGraw-Hill
Ryerson Limited

A Subsidiary of The **McGraw·Hill** Companies

ISBN: 0-07-086047-5

1 2 3 4 5 6 7 8 9 0   MP   9 9
Printed and bound in Canada.

Canadian Cataloguing in Publication Data

Gray, Douglas, A.
    The Canadian snowbird guide: everything you need to know about living part-time in the U.S.A. and Mexico

3rd ed.
Includes index.
ISBN 0-07-086047-5

1. Canadians—United States—Retirement.   2. Canadians—Retirement.   3. Retirees—Canada—Finance, Personal.   4. Canadians—United States—Finance, Personal.   I. Title.

HG179.G73   1999   332.024'0696   C99-932105-6

Publisher: **Joan Homewood**
Editorial Co-ordinator: **Catherine Leek**
Production Co-ordinator: **Susanne Penny**
Editor: **Tita Zierer**
Electronic Page Composition: **Bookman Typesetting Co.**
Cover Design: **Sharon Matthews**

Contents

Acknowledgements

I am indebted to many individuals, too numerous to mention, who have given generously of their time and expertise in the preparation of this book. I am also grateful for the helpful assistance given to me by various federal, provincial, and state governments, medical insurance companies, financial planning and seniors' associations, and tax experts and authorities. In particular, I appreciated the excellent information provided by the Department of Foreign Affairs and International Trade Council through their superb publications and web sites. Selected parts of this information have been used in this new edition. I would like to thank John Budd, chartered accountant and tax and estate planning expert in Toronto, for his kind assistance. I would also like to express my appreciation to Richard Brunton, CPA, of Boca Raton, Florida, for all his generous feedback on cross-border tax issues. Richard is also the publisher of *Brunton's U.S. Tax Letter for Canadians,* and kindly consented to the use of some of the material in his recent newsletters.

In particular, I would like to thank the Go Camping America Committee and Christine Morrison for their permission to use material from their excellent publications, including the camping vacation planner, as briefly discussed in parts of Chapter 4 and shown in parts of Appendix A. I would also like to express my appreciation to the International Association for Financial Planning for permission to use some of the information from their customer brochure "Selecting a Financial Planner" in Chapter 8.

Thanks to David Cooper of Century 21 Carousel Realty in Phoenix for his candid and constructive suggestions. Also thanks to Bernard Rowe, CHFC, CLU, CFP and Archie Blaikie, RFP, CFP, CHFC, CLU, both professional financial planners for their manuscript critiques.

I would like to thank Laurie Sadowski for all her kind assistance in inputting the manuscript revisions in all their draft variations, with such speed, accuracy, and professionalism.

I would like to thank Leo and Arlene Hevey, of Belleville, Ontario, for their enthusiastic example of how rewarding the Snowbird lifestyle can be. They have been most helpful with feedback and suggestions on the issues and concerns of being a part-time resident in the United States. As their guest on numerous visits to the United States over the years, I have shared first-hand their activities, pleasures, friendships, and rejuvenating experiences as Canadian Snowbirds.

Last, but not least, I would like to thank the staff of McGraw-Hill Ryerson for their support and insightful and constructive suggestions.

Preface

There are many matters to deal with when you are spending up to six months in the United States or Mexico as a Canadian Snowbird. You must consider issues such as family, friends, finances, fluctuations in currency exchange rates, investments, taxes, immigration, customs, housing, travel, safety and security, and medical and other types of insurance. You also need to give thought to such important matters as money management, financial planning, wills, estate planning, and the need for reliable professionals and other advisors. All of these issues are discussed in this book or referenced in the Appendices.

The first eight chapters in this book are designed to provide practical and helpful information about the main issues of importance to Snowbirds in the U.S. Although each chapter has a separate topic, the topics of the chapters are interrelated.

All the chapters have a similar format. For example, each chapter opens with an introduction and ends with a section on tips before leaving Canada.

This new third edition has been substantially revised, updated, and expanded to include a chapter on retiring permanently outside Canada.

The appendices are very comprehensive and provide a ready reference source for further information to assist you and save you time, money, and hassle. They also include suggested additional reading and retirement, financial, and estate-planning checklists.

I hope you enjoy this book and find it practical and helpful. Best wishes for a healthy and enjoyable Snowbird retirement.

Douglas Gray
August 1999

CHAPTER

1

The Snowbird Lifestyle

A. INTRODUCTION

The thought of spending up to six months a year in a warm and sunny U.S. Sunbelt state or Mexico, during Canada's cold winter is becoming increasingly appealing to millions of Canadian retirees. This trend is increasing every year, as Canada's population ages. Because Canadians are living longer and staying healthier, retirement could last 30 years. That is why many Canadians choose to spend part or all of the winter months in a warmer climate, hence the term "Snowbirds." Another term used while you are staying in the U.S. or Mexico is "winter visitor."

With proper planning, the Snowbird lifestyle can provide the most active, stimulating, and enjoyable experience of your retirement years. It could enhance your quality of life immeasurably. About two-thirds of Snowbirds leave Canada for the United States or Mexico in late October or early November and return sometime before the end of April. The other third prefer to wait until January and stay in the South for up to three months. Snowbirds can therefore have the best of both countries during various seasons enjoying a wide range of outdoor activities.

Living in the South during the winter can also be very affordable. In fact, you may find that you come out ahead financially. This is because of the savings from the lower cost of living in the U.S. or Mexico. You can rent a mobile home/RV pad for a small amount, starting from CDN$280+ per month based on a 12-month lease. You can buy a used mobile home (fixed in place) in a park for CDN$7,000+ that could meet your needs. There are some good bargains, especially at the end of the season in April. When you amortize that cost over 10+ years, it becomes very affordable. You also have use of all the facilities and amenities at a mobile home/RV park, which is generally included in your pad lease fee.

Naturally, expenses can be higher in some parks, but you would normally select the type of park or condominium community that meets your budget as well as other needs. In addition, you are saving money on heating costs at home in Canada during the winter. Even taking into account the cost of your out-of-country emergency medical insurance, you could be breaking even or paying just a bit more than if you stayed at home in Canada all winter. It is this type of attractive economic reality that is also a contributing factor to the decision of many to winter in the South.

Many Snowbirds also have friends, relatives, and family from Canada who visit them for short periods down South. If that might occur in your case, read Chapter 5 on Insurance. Advise them why it is so critical for them to have out-of-country emergency medical insurance.

The Snowbird lifestyle also provides considerable net financial benefits to the Canadian taxpayer. Because Snowbirds can be active outdoors all year round, their physical and mental health is enhanced accordingly. In fact, some Canadians travel South in the winter because of medical conditions that are improved by a warmer climate. In many areas of Canada the weather is such that it would otherwise curtail outdoor or social activities. Living seasonally in the Sunbelt would have the effect of saving on health costs to the medical system in Canada, which overall could be very substantial, by prolonging the health and quality of life of most Snowbirds.

In addition, many Canadians establish close friendships with U.S. Snowbirds from northern U.S. states. This is because of the feeling of community that is conducive to social interaction and friendship in mobile home/RV parks, and other retirement developments. As a consequence of this friendship, many Americans visit their Canadian Snowbird friends between May and September, stimulating the economy in Canada through tourism.

Having said all that, the Snowbird lifestyle is not for everyone. It is just another retirement option. As will be discussed shortly, it is wise to try it for a month or so by renting. In other words, evolve into the lifestyle in a step-by-step fashion to see if you like it and it meets your various needs.

This chapter covers a variety of preliminary issues to consider. For example, it considers the things involved in being a Snowbird in the U.S., Mexico, or other locations such as Costa Rica. Also covered will be the rental option, where to stay, how to get there, what to do once you get there, tips on saving money, safety and security issues, pets and other issues. Another section covers using the Internet for doing your research and communicating with others, part of a personal skill development that you could find intriguing.

If you are considering the option of retiring outside Canada on a full-time basis, refer to Chapter 11.

B. SNOWBIRDING IN THE UNITED STATES

As you might expect, the U.S. is the most popular Snowbird location. A common language and culture, familiarity, proximity, and accessibility make it the destination of choice for the vast majority of Canadian Snowbirds.

This and the next eight chapters relate to the U.S. experience. Most of the Appendix reference material and sources of information are relevant to being a seasonal resident in the U.S.

Many Canadians don't realize the wide range of issues that they need to consider when being a part-time resident in the U.S. For your protection and peace of mind, you need to be familiar with these issues and the options available to you regarding tax, estate planning, legal, housing, insurance, immigration and customs issues, retirement and financial planning, and more.

C. SNOWBIRDING IN MEXICO

In response to a lot of interest on the topic, this 3rd edition of the book includes Mexico as a potential Snowbird option. Mexico is rich with culture and diversity, and over 1 million Canadian tourists visit Mexico every year. There are several locations in Mexico that are popular retirement communities for Canadian and American part-time or full-time residents.

However, there are considerable differences on some key issues when living in Mexico from what you are accustomed to in Canada or in the U.S., which are covered in Chapter 9. Sources of further information on Mexico and key contact numbers are contained in Appendix A. There is also an extensive list of newsletters and books relating to retiring part-time or full-time in Mexico in Appendix B.

D. SNOWBIRDING IN COSTA RICA

Costa Rica is an interesting, unique, and beautiful country. If nothing else, you may wish to visit as a tourist. It has become a very popular travel destination for people of all interests and ages.

A brief overview of this Snowbird retirement option is given in Chapter 10. As might be expected, Costa Rica has a small but growing community of retired Canadians and Americans. However, for a variety of obvious reasons, this Snowbird option may not be for you but is included for your interest.

You will find other chapters of this book relevant that cover issues that are generic to the U.S. or Mexico or Costa Rica—for example, Chapter 2 on Financial Planning and Money Management, Chapter 4 on Housing and Real Estate, Chapter 5 on Insurance, and Chapter 7 on Wills, Trusts and Estate Planning.

E. KEY FACTORS TO CONSIDER

Planning is very important. With research and preparation, you will maximize your enjoyment of your U.S. stay and minimize unexpected and unwanted surprises.

Here is an overview of some of the important preliminary issues you need to consider.

1. Renting to Try It Out

For your first Snowbird experience, you may wish to familiarize yourself with the area for a month or so to see if you like it. After doing your research, you should be able to shortlist where you would like to go. This way you can satisfy yourself before you buy. Rental accommodation options include renting a motor home or RV, mobile home (on a permanent foundation), manufactured home (prefabricated in many cases), apartment, condominium, or house.

2. Where to Stay

There are many possible places to stay. The most popular U.S. Sunbelt states are Florida, Arizona, Texas, and California. You might want to be based in one area and just take side trips for a day or several days to sightsee. Or you might want to use a recreational vehicle (RV) and travel through various states. There are many factors to consider in choosing where to stay, depending on your interests and needs. For example, do you prefer varied terrain, spectacular scenery, or hot weather? Do you prefer a dry or humid climate? Maybe you prefer the ocean, the mountains, or the desert. Do you like the proximity of city life or a rural ambience? Friends could also be a factor drawing you to one place or another. Refer to Appendices A and B for information about places to stay, as well as for where to obtain free state tourism booklets and information. Contact the local Chamber of Commerce for more information. Check with your local library for videos and books of the state and specific city you are considering. Also speak with other people you know who are Snowbirds from that location.

3. How to Get There

You have lots of options of how to get to your Sunbelt home. You could fly down, drive your car, or have someone else drive it for you. There are companies who will do that for a fee. Or perhaps you have an RV.

There are many sources of free and low-cost information to make your trip more enjoyable. Refer to Appendix A for contact numbers of provincial and state tourism departments. Refer to item 30 in Appendix A for the contact numbers of companies providing travel services. Item 34 lists various relevant travel web sites. Contact your local automobile club to obtain travel guides and detailed trip-planning schedules. Look at travel books for the specific areas or states you are travelling through. These can be found in libraries or your local bookstore.

If you are driving, remember that there are many discounts for seniors for accommodation, restaurants, and so on. Ask. If you are a member of a seniors' association, find out if it offers travel-related discounts. There are also seniors' discounts available if you are flying, so make enquiries.

If you are planning to fly, long hours of physical inactivity or crossing time zones can contribute to jet lag or fatigue, and it can take several days for your natural body cycle to adjust. Heeding the following advice while you are on the plane will aid the process:

- Walk around whenever it is convenient.
- Change the position of your body at least every hour, even when you are dozing.
- Wear a sweater or jacket to deal with fluctuating temperatures.
- Wear loose-fitting clothing with an expandable waistband to make movement more comfortable.
- Leave your shoes on. Since your feet tend to swell during flight, you may have trouble getting your shoes back on if you take them off.
- Drink plenty of nonalcoholic fluids, since they prevent dehydration. The air-conditioning in the cabin tends to have a dehydrating effect.
- Avoid a heavy intake of alcohol, since a drink has a greater impact during flight because of the effects of air pressurization.
- Avoid carbonated beverages and heavy meals, since they tend to cause discomfort.
- If you are going through time changes, attempt to lessen the impact by changing your sleeping schedule two or three days before you leave.

4. What to Do When You Get There

One of the many reasons the Snowbird lifestyle is so attractive is the wide range of available activities. You are bound to meet many kindred spirits and form new friendships. Some of the activities that may interest you include:

- Participating in regularly scheduled social activities at the mobile home park, RV park, or other retirement community. Refer to item 33 in Appendix A for an activity schedule of a sample mobile home/RV park.
- Participating in social activities through local social clubs that have regular events and members who are part-time or full-time Canadians in the U.S.
- Participating in recreational activities such as golfing, swimming, tennis, shuffleboard, cards, bingo, dancing, and keep-fit exercises.
- Travelling to explore new sights and scenery as part of a tour group, in your own car or RV, or in a convoy with others. Possibly taking a cruise.
- Taking continuing education courses through local university, college, or school board adult education programs for retirees. Courses are offered on almost every subject you can imagine and can be taken for credit, noncredit, or just to expand your knowledge. Also consider the many excellent programs available through Elderhostel. Refer to item 40 in Appendix A for more detail and contact numbers.
- Pursuing a hobby. There are many different types of hobbies or crafts that are inexpensive and creative or challenging.

- Keeping informed through subscribing to newspapers written specifically for Canadian Snowbirds, such as *Canada News* and the *Sun Times of Canada*. Refer to Appendix A, item 31. Also subscribe to local newspapers to find out what is happening in your community.

5. Tips on Saving Money

There are many ways of saving money as a senior. Get into the habit of asking if there is a seniors' discount, and comparison shop. Here are some other ways to save money:

- **National seniors' associations**
  Various Canadian and U.S. associations for Snowbirds or seniors have membership benefits such as discounts on travel packages, cruises, accommodation, meals, tourist attractions, and currency exchange. Refer to Appendix A, item 29 to obtain further information.

- **Long-distance discount rates**
  You can save a lot of money with various programs set up by the major long-distance companies such as AT&T, Sprint, and MCI in the United States, and your provincial telephone company, Sprint, or AT&T in Canada. Comparison shop to see who has the best rate package for your needs in each country. Check to see if rates are further reduced during the telephone company's normal long-distance discount time periods, such as between 6:00 P.M. and 8:00 A.M. and on weekends. Different companies can have different policies. Before you commit yourself to a particular company, make sure you have the program's details clearly spelled out in writing.

- **State tourism catalogues**
  Most states have incentive packages or special seasonal promotions to spend tourist dollars in their respective states. These could include discounts, dollar-at-par offers, and coupon books for use for attractions, entertainment, accommodations, meals, RV rentals, and so on. Contact the specific state tourism departments and ask for the tourist information package. See item 26 in Appendix A.

- **Transportation discounts**
  Almost every company offering bus, train, or plane transportation has seniors' discounts.

- **Discount shopping malls**
  There are many of these malls throughout the United States and especially the Sunbelt states. They offer discount prices on a wide range of name-brand products. Find out why particular items are discounted—whether they are seconds, inventory overruns or surplus, off-season items, low-demand items, and so on.

- **Seniors' guides**

  Contact Health Canada (see Appendix A, item 4) for a directory of money-saving discounts and free services for seniors in Canada for government-related amenities such as museums, parks, and trains. Many provinces also have similar discount policies for seniors for provincially owned attractions such as museums and parks.

- **Local Chamber of Commerce**

  One of the main purposes of a local Chamber of Commerce is to stimulate economic activity in the community. One way of doing this is to offer a special tourist discount package for the services and products of chamber members. Contact the Chamber of Commerce in areas where you are visiting. Refer to item 35 in Appendix A.

- **Local newspapers**

  Many local newspapers in key Sunbelt areas have special Snowbird discount subscription packages for seasonal residents. In addition, frequently there are visitor discount-package coupons for local products or services given to seasonal subscribers by the newspaper's advertisers.

- **Banks, trust companies, credit unions, and savings and loans institutions**

  Almost all of these institutions have discounts on services to seniors. In addition, many major Canadian financial institutions, as well as several U.S. ones in Sunbelt states, have developed additional discount or other unique programs especially for the needs of Canadian Snowbirds. These could include U.S.-dollar credit cards, Canadian-dollar accounts, lack of holding period on Canadian cheques deposited in a U.S. bank account, currency exchange-rate commission discounts, and mortgages for U.S. real estate.

- **Advance supply of medication**

  If you are on medication, have your doctor prescribe enough medication to cover your needs before you leave Canada so that you don't have to buy medication in the United States. Generally, you can get three months' supply at a time in most provinces. You would then need to reorder the medication for a further three months and arrange to have it sent to you.

- **Annual discount books**

  Several companies sell books listing a wide variety of discounts on restaurants, attractions, and events. The books are published annually and are generally valid from November 1 through October 31 or December 1 through November 30. If you are residing for up to six months in an area close to a major city, you may want to check into these types of books. The books generally cost about US$28. If you go out a lot, or frequently entertain visiting relatives or friends, you may find that you can save a lot of money with these books. One major company, Entertainment Publications, has a toll-free number for information: 1-800-374-4464.

6. Safety and Security

One of the main concerns of any Snowbird is safety and security. To ensure that you do not have a bad experience, you need to find out about how to safety-proof your home before you leave, travelling precautions, city travel, and special areas of risk. Here is where you can obtain free information to assist you:

- **Travel Information Service of the Department of Foreign Affairs and International Trade (Canada)**
  This service continually monitors and assesses potential risks to Canadians in all countries outside Canada. For example, a travel information report is available on Florida, including specific precautions to avoid being a victim of crime. Contact the Travel Information Service before your departure date. They can be reached 24 hours a day, seven days a week at 1-800-267-6788. If you want the free report faxed to you immediately, call 1-800-575-2500.

- **Local police department**
  You could contact the police in the place you are planning to stay to obtain crime statistics in the area and cautions to follow.

- **State tourism offices**
  These offices can provide you with travel safety tips and cautions in specific areas (e.g., Florida).

- **Travel agencies**
  Various travel agencies have free booklets and pamphlets giving general safety tips and tips specific to certain areas. For example, Grand Circle Travel in Boston has a free booklet entitled *Going Abroad: 101 Tips for Mature Travellers.* Contact them at 1-800-221-2610 or (617) 350-7500.

- **Seniors' Guidebook to Safety and Security**
  This book is published by the RCMP Crime Prevention Branch, 1200 Vanier Parkway, Ottawa, ON K1H 0R2. Tel: (613) 993-8435.

- **Travel guides**
  Your auto club (CAA or AAA affiliate offices) produces travel guides that include travel safety tips and cautions.

If you have access to the Internet, you can also obtain the information immediately. Refer to item 34 in Appendix A for web site addresses.

7. Precautions When Travelling in the U.S.

The same rules apply in the United States as at home, only more so. You are usually at greater risk than locals; as everywhere, tourists and non-locals could be targeted. Accordingly, you should follow these rules:

- Know where you are and where you are going at all times. Carefully plan road trips in advance.
- Do not pick up hitchhikers.
- Keep valuables out of sight, and never leave them in a parked vehicle.
- Leave a copy of your itinerary and proof of citizenship (for example, Canadian birth certificate or certificate of Canadian citizenship) with a family member or friend who can be contacted in an emergency.
- Phone home regularly if you do not have a fixed schedule.
- Keep a separate record of your travellers' cheques, credit cards and medical insurance, and ensure that the information is also available to someone back home.
- Do not carry your passport, tickets, identification documents, cash, credit cards and insurance papers together. Keep them separate so that in the event of theft or loss you do not lose everything.
- Use the safety deposit box at your hotel. Never leave valuables in your room.

8. Obtaining Medical Advice Before You Depart

Health Canada strongly recommends an individual risk assessment by your own family doctor or a travel medicine provider prior to travelling. Based on your health risks, vaccinations and any special precautions to take during your trip can be determined. This is particularly important if you are travelling outside the U.S. Health Canada's Laboratory Centre for Disease Control (LCDC) provides travel health information through the Internet (*http://www.hc-sc.gc.ca*) and through a fax retrieval system, FAXlink. To access FAXlink, call (613) 941-3900 using the handset of your fax machine and follow the instructions.

A listing of travel clinics in your area can be obtained through Health Canada's Travel Medicine Program at (613) 957-8739 or the Canadian Society for International Health at (613) 241-5785, or through the Internet (*http://www.csih.org/trav_inf.html*).

a) Vaccinations

Before travelling to any destination, for example Mexico or Costa Rica, find out *well in advance of your trip* if you need any special vaccinations or preventive medications for such illnesses as yellow fever, typhoid, meningitis, Japanese encephalitis, hepatitis or malaria. An International Certificate of Vaccination for yellow fever may be a legal requirement to enter certain countries. Your doctor, the local office of the Canadian Society for International Health, the LCDC FAXlink service or the LCDC web site can provide you with this information.

Start your vaccination shots *at least three months before you leave*. In some cases, you may need several inoculations with waiting periods between each injection.

Make sure that your *routine immunizations are up to date*. If you were not exposed to certain diseases as a child, or were not immunized, you could be at an increased risk of contracting diseases such as tetanus, diphtheria, polio, measles, mumps or rubella (German measles). All adults should ensure they are protected from tetanus and diphtheria by receiving a booster shot every 10 years.

b) Medication

If you take medication, be sure to pack an extra supply in case you are away for longer than expected. Carrying a duplicate of your original prescription is highly recommended—especially when travelling to a country that is particularly sensitive about drugs. Also, carry an extra prescription that lists both the generic and the trade names of the drug, in case your medication is lost or stolen. This is also a good idea if you wear glasses or contact lenses—having the prescription makes it easier to replace them.

Do not try to save luggage space by combining medications into a single container. Keep all medications in the original, labelled container to avoid problems.

Find out whether your medication is sold in the country you are visiting. Also check to see that it is legal. Some over-the-counter medications in Canada are illegal in other countries or require a prescription. Obtaining a note from your doctor that states the medical reasons for your prescription and the recommended dosage is also encouraged.

If you need syringes for a medical condition such as diabetes, it is very important that you take along an appropriate supply. As well, you should carry a medical certificate that shows they are for medical use.

If you have a pre-existing medical condition that could present a problem while you are travelling, it is wise to wear a Medic Alert® bracelet. Through the Medic Alert® Foundation, your vital medical facts become part of a database that can be accessed 24 hours a day from anywhere in the world. Call 1-800-825-3785 for membership information.

c) On Your Return

If you should become sick or feel unwell on entering Canada, see your doctor. Inform the doctor, without being asked, that you have been travelling or living outside Canada, and where. Likewise, if you were ill while travelling, see your doctor on your return and explain your travel history and any treatment you received.

If you have been in a malarial area and develop fever during the first year after return (especially in the first two months), see your doctor immediately and remind him/her that:

- Antimalarial pills do not guarantee protection against malaria
- Malaria must be ruled out by one or more thick and thin blood film examinations.

d) Supplemental Health Insurance

Do not rely on your provincial health plan to cover the total cost if you get sick or are injured while you are abroad. At best, your health plan will cover only a portion of the bill. It is your responsibility to obtain and understand the terms of your supplementary insurance policies. Some credit cards offer their holders health and travel insurance. Do not assume the card alone provides adequate coverage. Refer to Chapter 5 on Insurance.

Be sure to ask whether or not your policy:

- Has an in-house worldwide emergency hotline you can call if you are in trouble—check to see if it is open 24 hours a day, seven days a week; whether the operators are multilingual; and if nurses or physicians are on-staff
- Pays foreign hospital and related medical costs and, if so, whether it pays "up front" or expects you to pay and be reimbursed later
- Provides for your medical evacuation to Canada
- Pays for any required medical escort (doctor/nurse) to accompany you back to Canada
- Excludes pre-existing medical conditions. (If such conditions exist, notify your insurance company and get an agreement in writing that you are covered for these conditions. Otherwise, you could find your claim "null and void" under a pre-existing condition clause)
- Allows for cash advances if a hospital accepts only such payment
- Pays for the preparation and return to Canada of your remains should you die while travelling

Carry details of your insurance with you. Also, tell your travel agent, a friend or relative at home and your travelling companion how to contact your insurer.

Get a detailed invoice from the doctor or hospital before you leave the country. There is nothing more frustrating than trying to get the proper paperwork from thousands of kilometres away.

Remember to always submit original receipts for any medical services or prescriptions you received while travelling abroad but to retain a copy for your files. Most insurance companies will not accept copies or faxes.

9. Services Provided to Snowbirds by the Canadian Government

The Canadian government offers a wide range of emergency and other forms of assistance to Canadians in the U.S., Mexico, and in most countries throughout the world. Services are provided through the Department of Foreign Affairs and International Trade. In the U.S. the main Canadian embassy is in Washington, DC, but there are Canadian consulates in Miami, Los Angeles, Atlanta, Boston, Dallas, Buffalo, Chicago, Detroit, New York, Minneapolis, and Seattle. Refer to items 8-10 in Appendix A for contact numbers. There is also an honourary consul in San Juan, Puerto Rico. The Australian consulate general in Honolulu, Hawaii, will assist Canadians in an emergency.

The consulate offices provide a range of services including:

- Advice and support in the event of an accident, illness, or other emergency
- Communication with relatives and friends
- Assistance during natural disasters
- Support and assistance in the event of a death
- Identification of sources of information on local laws, regulations, and facilities
- In the event of an arrest, ensuring equitable treatment, informing relatives and friends, and assistance in making arrangements for a lawyer
- Making arrangements for friends and relatives to transfer funds in emergencies
- Interventions with local authorities if required
- Notarial services such as certification of documents
- Emergency passport replacement services

Emergency services are available 24 hours, 7 days a week. After normal business hours, calls to Canadian consular offices in the U.S. (or any Canadian consular office throughout the world) are automatically forwarded to Ottawa. Alternatively, you may call Ottawa collect directly at (613) 996-8885. The daytime Ottawa number for enquiries about Canadian consular operations and emergency services for Canadians outside Canada is toll-free at 1-800-267-6788. However, this number is only accessible from within Canada.

If you want travel information on geographic areas of potential risk to Canadians, contact the previous number. The office is open 24 hours, 7 days a week. If you want the travel information faxed to you immediately, on a 24 hour, 7 day basis, phone 1-800-575-2500. This number is only accessible from within Canada. You will have to phone collect to the (613) 996-8885 number from the U.S. if you want travel information, or alternatively, phone any Canadian consular office during or after business hours. For a list of the current consular office locations and phone numbers in the U.S., Mexico or Costa Rica, refer to items 8-10 in Appendix A of this book. Also, ask any Canadian consular office for a free copy of a booklet called *Crossing the 49th* and a list of their other excellent publications. They are available by phoning any of the above numbers.

If you want information on what you can or cannot bring back to Canada, Customs and Excise Canada has a 24 hour, 7 day telephone service to answer your questions. The toll-free number inside Canada is 1-800-461-9999. From outside Canada phone collect to (613) 993-0534.

10. Pets

Many people like to take their pets with them for an extended Snowbird stay. Check to see if the mobile home park or RV park you are considering has restrictions on pets. Secondly, there are requirements before you can leave the country with your pet, and enter the U.S. or Mexico.

You need to ensure that your pet has current rabies shots and a health certificate before you leave Canada. Your vet can give you advice regarding potential health risks in the geographic area in which you will be staying. Certain states have diseases that your pet could contract. Take a sufficient supply of any medication or special foods that your pet may require, in case they are not readily available there.

11. Mail

You will want to be able to have people communicate with you while you are away. You have several options available:

a) Canada Post

Arrange with Canada Post to do a temporary redirection. This service is available at monthly rates, but must be purchased for a minimum of three months. The cost is approximately $20 a month. Remember to account for your travel time between addresses. For example, if you're taking six days to drive home from your Snowbird address, is your mail heading south while you're heading north?

If you are going out of town for a shorter period of time, you can use a "hold mail" service instead. Sold by the week (with a two-week minimum), this service assures that your mail is held for you for a specified period of time, during which nobody can access your mail. When the hold mail period ends, the mail is delivered to your address. The cost is $10 a week.

Many people complain about the cost of mail redirection from Canada to the U.S. It could cost up to $120 for a six-month stay. This is often compared to the U.S. where there is no cost to redirect mail. The difference is that the U.S. system is operated by the government, and therefore is completely subsidized by U.S. taxpayers through the general federal treasury. In Canada, Canada Post is operated as a profit-making business. You may feel that the cost is inflated, but don't hold your breath waiting for a change.

b) Friends Sending Mail Down for You

Some people prefer to arrange for a friend, relative, or next door neighbour to bundle their mail, remove all the junk mail, and send it on to you every two to four weeks. This can provide some saving, as the cost is based on actual weight meaning that this arrangement might only cost you $40-$50. You have to consider the inconvenience factor and flexibility against cost.

c) Renting a Mail Box in U.S.

Depending on where you are staying, you might already have a mail box. If not, you can easily rent a mail box at any U.S. postal service outlet, or private mail box rental company, such as Mail Boxes, Etc.

d) Canadian Consulate Services

One of the services available to you if you are out of the country is to arrange for mail to be sent to the Canadian consulate office closest to where you are staying. This is not customary in the U.S. but it is in Mexico. You need to make arrangements to pick up the mail. It will not be sent to you.

12. Voting in Canadian Elections

In the event a federal or provincial election is called in Canada while you are down south, you are still entitled to vote by means of an absentee ballot. Elections Canada provides for enumeration and voting by mail. Reach them through Canadian embassies and consulates, or contact them at:

Elections Canada
1595 Telesat Court
Ottawa, Ontario
K1A OM6
1-800-463-6868 (within Canada only)

If you want information about a provincial election so you can do a mail-in absentee ballot, contact your provincial elections office, or the riding office of your elected provincial representative.

F. USING THE INTERNET FOR RESEARCH, INFORMATION AND COMMUNICATION

To many people, the Internet is still a mystery. They don't understand it, don't realize how easy it is to learn, or how helpful the experience could be.

A recent survey has shown that over 50 million people in North America use the Internet. Of those, 7 million or approximately 15 percent are over 50 years of age. You may already have a computer and use the Internet for sending electronic mail (e-mail) to friends, relatives and family throughout the world. Possibly you use the Internet for researching information of interest, such as travel, medical, or a wide range of other areas. You could also be searching for a house or condo in a geographic location that interests you.

The web site addresses (known as URLs) outlined in item 34 in Appendix A cover selected sites in areas such as travel, health, senior and Snowbird issues, government departments, Canadian news sources, and a lot more.

If you don't have a computer or are not on the Internet, you probably know people, such as friends or relatives who do have computers and can access the Internet. They would be pleased to show you how to use it as would staff at your public library. Once you have tried it a number of times, you will find the process very easy.

If the idea interests you further, you can take one day or longer courses on the computer or the Internet from school boards, colleges or university adult education departments. Seniors can generally either take courses free or at nominal cost. If a fee is over $100 and the course is offered by an accredited educational institution, Revenue Canada allows you to use it as a tax credit.

1. What is the Internet?

In brief terms, the Internet is an interlinking or networking of millions of computers throughout the world. The World Wide Web (Web or www) is a project that made possible the idea of accessible and attractive interconnections on the Internet. It does so by requiring you to have an Internet account and a browser. The browser's task is to display documents on the Web (known as web sites) and allow the user to select activities. A web site's URL is the "address" of the company, organization, government, or individual. Most web sites have features called "hot links," which means that a web site will cross-reference to other related web sites that may be of interest to you. You merely click the pointer on the computer to that "hot link" site reference and it immediately connects you to that site. Just like magic.

As mentioned, you need to have an account with an Internet Service Provider (ISP) which connects you to the Internet for a monthly fee. Many provincial telephone companies have a program for their long-distance customers, which gives them five hours free on the Internet each month. Beyond that you pay an hourly rate. These type of programs can change or be discontinued, so if they interest you, check them out. Other long distance companies such as AT & T and Sprint also have promotional programs from time to time. Also refer to various free computer magazines and newspapers for attractive deals for ISPs and computers.

2. How Can the Internet Benefit You?

If you have not used the Internet yet, here are just some of the features that you could use:

a) Researching Information of Interest

It is a gold mine of helpful information at your fingertips, that will save you a lot of time and energy and give you many creative ideas in terms of short-listing your search. One of the many benefits of the Internet is the ability to search for what you are looking for, and then print out the information. Some web sites also have audio and video features.

b) Electronic Mail (e-mail)

This option means that you select a personalized e-mail address, and then you can use your computer to communicate with anyone throughout the world who has their own e-mail address. You can write your letter on the computer screen and then send it electronically to the recipient. Their computer will show that there is mail for them, and will then display your letter. Instant communication! And the good news is that it does not cost you long-distance phone charges, only your monthly flat rate.

c) Newsgroups

Newsgroups are like a giant electronic bulletin board. They are not a discussion of news, as might be implied by the name. They are a collection of thoughts, opinions, and information on any subject you could imagine. Like people who write letters to the editor of a newspaper or magazine, people express themselves if they think someone else will be listening and might find their words to be of interest. People can pose a question on any topic and get hundreds of responses from all over the world! Newsgroups tend to be segmented under the specific topic areas or just general interest. Most ISPs include the ability to use newsgroups as part of your service package.

d) Chat Rooms

A most interesting area of the Internet, chat technology allows you to have a live conversation, in a typed format, with any number of people. Chat rooms tend to be divided by the area of interest, so you can go to those sites that interest you. Some people use this feature to socialize and meet people from all over the world and others use it to discuss specific medical conditions or other topics.

3. Example of Using the Internet

If you are already using the Internet, the following will be familiar to you, but if it is a new experience, here is a brief overview of the process. You need a computer, modem, software, and Internet connection, and you are ready to go. One of the first things to do is to select the list of directions. The Web browsers (Netscape Communicator, Microsoft Internet Explorer, and others) offer directions on how to use the Internet. Once you know the basics, navigating around the Net is quite easy. If you need help, you have a number of options. You can access the Help section of the Web browser, or the particular web site itself that you are looking at. You can also access the FAQ section of the browser or web site. FAQ stands for frequently asked questions.

For the purpose of this example, let's say you are interested in locating a condo to buy in Canada. There are two main ways of accessing Internet sites that interest you in the real estate area.

a) Going Directly To the Specific Web Site

This is the easiest route. If you know the web site address, you simply type it in and push enter. When you type the CREA (Canadian Real Estate Association) MLS (Multiple Listing Service) address, *http://www.mls.ca*, you will land (no pun intended) on the MLS home page. It contains a series of easy-to-understand icons or buttons to help you navigate through the system.

The next step on the CREA web site is to position your cursor over "Properties for Sale" and you will see a new page giving you a choice of residential, recreational, and other types of properties. If you are looking for a house or condo, choose residential. The next page is a map of Canada. Choose the province, either on the map or by name in a box on the side. Then, you will be given a choice of different regions within the province. You keep selecting ever smaller areas until you arrive in the city, town, or district where you want to concentrate your search.

The next selection allows you to choose the criteria for your search. You can choose a house or condo, whether you want a water view, one level, a garden, the number of bedrooms, etc. Finally, you select the price range of your home. Select the search button and after a few seconds, the computer will show you a selection of homes that meet your criteria. Click View to see them in colour.

Occasionally, you will receive a notice that no matches meet your criteria. In that case you will have to make a few adjustments to your selection. You can do this in three ways: change the location and view the maps again, change the type of property you are looking for, or change the details such as the number of bedrooms, bathrooms, lot size, and price.

After you have made any changes, press OK, and the MLS site updates the number of properties that match your search. You can change the options again, and keep looking, or you can press View when you are ready to look at the properties you have selected.

To read the details about the property, click on its picture and a larger image appears along with specific information about it. If you are interested in a particular property, it is easy to contact the realtor involved. Often there is an e-mail link directly to the realtor's computer. If not, you should find the realtor's address and phone number listed.

b) Searching the Internet for Specific Web Sites

In this example, you don't have a specific real estate web site address to go to, or you simply want to find out what web sites cover the geographic area that interests you.

There are various search engines that can assist you from large search engine companies to smaller ones. Some have more Canadian content than others. You may have heard of search engines such as Yahoo Canada or Alta Vista.

You simply type in the key words and the search engine then attempts to find web sites that match the content of those key words. The more key words you put in, the more fine-tuned the result. For example, you could type in "real estate" + "Canada" + "province" + "city" + "house" or "condo." You might only get 40 listings of web sites for example, rather than 10,000 or so if you just had "real estate." Remember to put the "+" sign between words, so the search engine will look for web sites that contain *all* those words. If you didn't put in the plus sign, the search engine will look for all sites that contain *any* of those words. The result could be overwhelming in terms of the volume of sites.

Another tip is to put a "—" or minus sign if you want to delete a city. For example, if you had a number of key words, plus Vancouver, you might wish to put "—Washington," so that the search engine would not look for web sites containing the key words "Vancouver" and "Washington" state, since there is a community called Vancouver in Washington state. In this example, you would want to restrict your search to sites dealing with Vancouver, British Columbia.

After you have looked at all the offerings available, don't forget to "bookmark" or "lock-in" to the computer memory those web sites that you want to come back to quickly and directly. Otherwise, you will have to go through the whole search process again.

TIPS BEFORE LEAVING CANADA

- Thoroughly plan your Snowbird vacation before you leave by taking the time to do your research. The more preparation time, the more the enjoyment. The appendices provide a wealth of helpful information.

- If you are planning to stay in an area you have not stayed in before, find out how safe it is before you go. Obtain information from the local police, the local automobile club, and the state tourist bureau.

- Compare various discount plans with seniors' associations and decide which ones will save you the most money. Also check into seniors' and other discounts you can use in the United States.

- If you are considering staying at a retirement community or in an RV park or mobile home park, contact the management and get names as references of others who reside there. Contact several of them and ask questions to ensure that the place is compatible with your needs.

- Arrange with Canada Post to have your mail forwarded to your address in the United States.

- If you are trying the Snowbird lifestyle for the first time, consider renting for the first year rather than buying.

- Subscribe to one or both of the weekly newspapers for Canadians to keep aware of issues and information of interest. When you are living in the United States, many popular Snowbird destinations have regular radio news reports specifically for Canadians.

CHAPTER

2

Financial Planning
and Money Management

A. INTRODUCTION

In order to achieve and maintain the Snowbird lifestyle, you need to have a realistic understanding of your present and future financial resources so that you can budget accordingly. This chapter covers the typical risk areas, the financial planning process, types of federal and provincial government pensions, employer-funded pension plans, your own tax-sheltered plans, the safety of your retirement plans and deposits, and your home as a source of additional income.

Numerous Canadian books are available on financial planning and money management issues and options. Books on these topics are becoming a Canadian growth industry. Many of these books are objective, balanced, informative, and relevant. Others are written to market the writer or his or her company or services and products and thus may be biased. It therefore pays to read selectively and to assess the credentials, credibility, and motivation of the writer. It also helps to read several books to get different perspectives and become familiar with the concepts involved. Some suggested reading is found in Appendix B.

Various educational seminars are available to further inform you about topical matters relating to retirement and Snowbird issues. The same cautions noted above relating to books apply to seminars.

In any event, you should obtain objective professional advice before you embark on any particular course of action. How to select professional advisors is covered in Chapter 8. The quality of the advice you rely on will profoundly affect your financial well-being, peace of mind, and quality of lifestyle.

B. POTENTIAL FINANCIAL AND OTHER RISK AREAS

There are 15 risk areas that could affect your financial net worth, cash flow, and lifestyle. In many cases, you can eliminate, minimize, or control each of these risk areas by knowing about them, doing research, and making prudent decisions. If you are retired, are planning retirement, or wish to become a Snowbird, these 15 key risk areas are particularly important to know. Statistically, if you retire at 55 years of age, you can expect to live to 85 and have 30 years of retirement—almost as long as your working life. Planning to have enough funds to meet your lifestyle needs is obviously critically important. Some of the potential risk areas are interrelated, but they are considered separately because they should be identified specifically as risk. By obtaining customized financial planning advice relevant to your own situation, you should be able to anticipate and neutralize many of the key financial risks.

1. Currency Risk

This is a particularly important issue for Canadian Snowbirds. If the Canadian dollar drops in value relative to the U.S. dollar, you will obviously notice an increase in the cost of living due to the reduced purchasing power of your Canadian money when you convert it to U.S. currency. The value of the Canadian dollar is dependent on many variables, both national and international. If it goes down five percent, you have lost five percent of purchasing power in the United States.

2. Inflation Risk

This is one of the most serious financial risks to those in retirement. Although both Canada and the United States currently enjoy very low inflation rates, that can quickly change. As you are probably aware, inflation eats away at your purchasing power. Inflation at five percent will reduce your purchasing power by 50 percent in less than 15 years. If you have investments that have interest rates or value that is keeping up with the rate of inflation, or if you have annuities or RRIFs indexed for inflation, then your purchasing power would at least remain constant. If you have a fixed income, the inflation issue is especially critical.

For example, with Canada Savings Bonds, inflation would erode the purchasing power of the bond as well as the interest. You also have to look at the real rate of return on your money, after tax and inflation is factored in. If you were earning 7 percent interest and were taxed at 35 percent, your net return would be 4.5 percent. If inflation were 3 percent, in real terms, your purchasing power would only be 1.55 percent.

3. Deflation Risk

If there is a severe or prolonged economic downturn or recession, the value of your assets could drop accordingly.

4. Interest Rate Risk

Interest rates in Canada and the United States have been very volatile over the past 15 to 20 years on any type of interest-sensitive financial investment. In the early 1980s the prime rate was in the double digits, up to 22 percent. This was of course attractive for people with interest income from term deposits, mortgages, or bonds. By the mid-1990s, rates had plunged to the low single digits, down to five percent. Interest rate risk can cut both ways, however. For example, if you set your lifestyle needs based on high interest rate returns, your lifestyle will be negatively affected when rates fall. Or if you lock yourself into a fixed-rate bond when rates are low and then interest rates increase, the value of the bond investment will go down when you try to sell it. Another example is if you have a locked-in annuity bought at a low interest rate. If rates go up and there is inflation along with it, your purchasing power and lifestyle will be affected.

5. Government Policy Risk

The Canadian and U.S. governments are constantly changing the tax or pension laws, depending on the political philosophy of the party in power and on economic pressures. For example, Old Age Security pension payments are reduced if the recipient's income exceeds a certain amount. This amount could become lower and lower over time. The Guaranteed Income Supplement could be reduced or the eligibility criteria tightened up. Federal and/or provincial income taxes could be increased. The $100,000 personal capital gains deduction was removed several years ago. Provincial governments could reduce out-of-country medical coverage, resulting in increased out-of-country supplemental insurance premiums. The U.S. government could bring in legislation to increase taxes paid by non-U.S. residents, or a state could increase an estate tax on death on real estate or U.S. assets that you own.

6. Repayment Risk

This type of risk comes in several forms. One form of risk is not being repaid what you are owed when it is due or when you want your money. For example, if you buy a bond, the issuer's ability to repay you determines whether you are going to get your money back. Although bonds issued by municipalities, corporations, or governments rarely default, several levels of credit risk are normally involved. Agencies such as Standard & Poor, Moody's Investors Service, and Dominion Bond Rating Service rate the credit risk of various bonds, which generally ranges from AAA to D. These ratings indicate the repayment risk you are taking with a particular bond issue.

Insurance companies are also rated by different agencies, including one in Canada called TRAC. Considering that insurance companies go under from time to time, you don't want to risk losing money you might be expecting from insurance proceeds, cash surrender value funds, disability insurance payments, or annuities.

If you place money in an institution by means of a term deposit, for example, you want to feel confident that you will get your money back, including all principal plus interest, if the institution fails.

A discussion of certain types of money protection you should be aware of is covered in Section G in this chapter.

Another form of repayment risk is receiving your invested money back sooner than you expect or want it. For example, if you lock in a bond with a eight percent yield and the rate falls four percent, you will not be able to replace that bond with a new one at the same yield if the bond issuer redeems or calls the bond earlier than anticipated. Many corporate bond issuers have this right after a certain number of years after the bond was issued. Most government bonds cannot be called.

7. Market Cycle Risk

Many markets, such as the real estate market, stock market, and bond market, are cyclic. Depending on where your investment is at any point in the cycle, it could slowly or rapidly diminish in value. If you wanted or needed to sell it, you could lose money. Generally, the longer you hold an investment, the less the risk. The shorter the term you intend to keep the investment, the higher the risk that a market correction could impair your investment return.

8. Economic Risk

The economy obviously has an effect on such assets or investments as real estate or stocks. The more buoyant the economy, the more buoyant the price of real estate and stocks, and vice versa.

9. Lack of Diversification Risk

The risk here is having all your assets in one specific kind of investment, like real estate or bonds or stocks. You are not protected if that asset drops in value and you do not have alternative assets to buffer the loss. If you spread the risk, you lower the risk. To spread the risk, you could have different types of assets as well as different kinds of investments within each type of asset.

10. Lack of Liquidity Risk

Liquidity means the speed at which you can sell your asset, either at all, or at a fair price. For example, if you need to sell your home or stocks and the market has dropped, you could still sell, but it could take much longer and you will obtain a lower price. Negative publicity about stocks and real estate can have a dramatic short-term effect on the market, as potential buyers become nervous. Less demand means lower prices.

11. Taxation Risk

This risk affects your lifestyle if increased taxation reduces your anticipated retirement income. This form of risk could come from higher levels of income tax, the taxing of part or all of your income currently exempt from taxation (e.g., Guaranteed Income Supplement), or the taxing of RRSPs or RRIFs in some fashion, other than when you take the money out. Naturally, all the above possible initiatives would result in a strong public demand to rescind them. Economic pressure on federal or provincial governments to reduce their respective debts, however, could result in all areas of personal income being subject to review for additional tax.

12. Pension Risk

This type of risk takes various forms. One form is for federal or provincial governments to reduce the net amount of pension you receive through Old Age Security (OAS), Canada Pension Plan (CPP), or Guaranteed Income Supplement (GIS), through taxation, increased taxation, clawbacks based on your other income, reduction in amount of money, or more restrictive eligibility criteria. As you may know, if your taxable income is over $53,215, your OAS is "clawed back," or reduced by the amount of your income over $53,000. As you may also know, the proposed Seniors Benefit program has been scrapped by the federal government. Another form of risk is that a pension fund manager may not invest money prudently and the return to the pension fund may be less than expected. Or an employer may not make any profit in a particular year and therefore does not contribute anything to the pension fund. Or possibly an employer reduces or eliminates some pension plan collateral benefits such as life insurance or health and dental plan coverage for cost-saving reasons. Types of employer-funded pension plans are covered in this chapter in Section E.

13. Acts of God Risk

When selecting your Sunbelt retirement location, it is important to assess the risk from natural disasters or "acts of God." These could include hurricanes, floods, fires, or earthquakes. For example, certain parts of California are prone to brush fires and earthquakes. Parts of Florida are prone to hurricanes or floods. Not only do these disasters pose a risk for your home or health and for the resale potential or value of your home, many insurance policies exclude any coverage of acts of God or specifically exclude potential risks of that nature that may be endemic to the area you are considering. Make sure you know what risks are partially or fully excluded. If you make a claim, an insurance company may require you to pay a deductible amount you cannot afford. Check with local insurance companies, real estate agents, and the local, state, or federal weather bureaus for seasonal statistics and risks in the geographic area you are considering.

14. Weather Risk

Apart from acts of God risks, when selecting your Sunbelt or retirement home consider such weather issues as average snowfall (if applicable), rainfall, and temperature at various times of the year. A very hot climate may hinder your comfort and outdoor activities and increase your air conditioning costs. Conversely, a cold, rainy climate could reduce your physical comfort and safety, as well as increase your heating bills, augment the amount of home maintenance required, and reduce outside activity. Check with the weather bureau for seasonal statistics in the area you are considering. If the weather conditions are not attractive, the resale value of a home there could be affected. Refer to item 34 in Appendix A for web site information on weather patterns in your geographic area of interest.

15. Crime Risk

Certain Sunbelt states have areas of higher crime than others. Clearly this is an important area to clarify. Apart from your own peace of mind and health, local crime could result in break-ins, theft, vandalism, muggings, or other criminal activities. It would also affect the insurance premiums you pay (based on risk and claims experience) or increase the deductibles you might have to pay on any claim. The resale value of your home would obviously be affected. Check with the local police department for crime statistics in the area you are considering.

C. THE FINANCIAL PLANNING PROCESS

Financial planning is very individual and personal. It should take into account all the psychological and financial factors that may have an impact on your financial goals and objectives. In short, comprehensive financial planning provides you with a long-term strategy for your financial future, taking into consideration every aspect of your financial situation and how each one affects your ability to achieve your goals and objectives. A financial plan can help you construct the foundation on which to build a secure financial future.

1. How a Financial Advisor Helps You

Through six distinct steps in the comprehensive financial planning process, a financial advisor helps you:

- Clarify your present situation
- Decide where you want to be by identifying both financial and personal goals and objectives
- Identify financial problem areas
- Provide a written financial plan with recommendations
- Implement the agreed-upon recommendations and
- Periodically review and revise your plan.

2. What a Comprehensive Financial Plan Contains

Your financial plan is the strategy for achieving your goals and objectives. A comprehensive financial plan should address all pertinent areas relating to your situation. Those areas that the planner does not personally address in the development of the plan should be coordinated by the planner.

You may want your plan to cover only a specific area, such as estate or investment planning. Although a plan for such a goal or objective may be appropriate for the areas covered, you should be aware that it is not a comprehensive plan.

Your financial plan document should contain not only the plan strategies but also all pertinent data relating to the development of the plan. Although the order and style of presentation may vary, the plan document should include at least the 13 essential elements described below. This does not necessarily mean that your plan will be long, since each area should be addressed so that it suits your personal situation. Completing the form in Appendix C will provide a lot of the background data for dealing with the following areas:

- Personal data
- Your goals and objectives
- Identification of issues and problems
- Assumptions used in plan preparation
- Balance sheet/net worth
- Cash flow management (e.g., income and expenses)
- Income tax strategies
- Risk management (e.g., different types of insurance)
- Investments
- Special needs, such as retirement planning
- Estate planning
- Recommendations
- Implementation.

If any area of the financial plan is not within the range of the financial planner's expertise, the planner has the responsibility to coordinate with other professionals and document such coordination in the financial plan report. Documentation of such areas can include the professional's name and when the review will be completed.

The analysis that is called for in all the elements of the plan should consist of a review of pertinent facts, a consideration of the advantage(s) and/or disadvantage(s) of the current situation, and a determination of what, if any, further action is required. The plan should include a summary statement providing the planner's comments on the analysis and his or her recommendations, where appropriate, for each element of the plan.

Once you have a plan in place, you should have it reviewed and revised from time to time to make sure you are on track and the current strategies are still appropriate for your needs.

As noted earlier, how to select a professional financial planner is covered in Chapter 8.

D. GOVERNMENT PENSION PLANS

There are many forms of federal and provincial government pension or financial assistance programs. Following is a brief overview of the key programs and guidelines that you should be familiar with. They are periodically modified, of course, so obtain a current update of regulations and criteria relevant to your circumstances. In addition, there could be exceptions in your case to the general guidelines outlined. For more information and assistance, including eligibility benefits, indexing, and payment outside of Canada, contact the Income Security Programs Branch of the Human Resources Development Canada (HRDC) office closest to you. Look in the Blue Pages of the phone book under Government of Canada. The HRDC covers all the programs described below, except for number four (covered by provincial governments) and number 10 (covered by Veterans Affairs Canada). Also contact your closest Health Canada office, found in the same Government of Canada section of the phone book (Blue Pages). Ask for their free publications, including the *Seniors Guide to Federal Programs and Services*, which will provide you with information about other government subsidized services for seniors.

Keep in mind that the OAS, GIS, SPA, and CPP benefits are *not* paid automatically. You have to apply for them. You can arrange to have these funds automatically deposited into your bank account, a convenient option for Snowbirds. A brief discussion of these pension plans follows.

1. Old Age Security Pension (OAS)

The OAS pension is a monthly benefit available, if applied for, to anyone 65 years of age or over. OAS residence requirements must also be met. An applicant's employment history is not a factor in determining eligibility, nor does the applicant need to be retired. You have to pay federal and provincial income tax on your OAS pension. Higher-income pensioners also repay part or all of their benefit through the tax system, referred to as a clawback. Contact your local HRDC office or Health Canada for the current amount of the clawback. This amount could be increased by the government over time. At present, there is a clawback if you earn more than $53,215. The government takes off the clawback amount in advance, based on your previous year's tax return.

All benefits payable under the *Old Age Security Act* are increased in January, April, July, and October of each year based on increases in the cost of living as measured by the Consumer Price Index (CPI).

Once a full or partial OAS pension has been approved, it may be paid indefinitely outside Canada, if the pensioner has lived in Canada for at least 20 years after reaching 18 years of age. Otherwise, payment may be made only for the month of a pensioner's departure from Canada and for six additional months, after which payment is suspended. The benefit may be reinstated if the pensioner returns to live in Canada.

2. Guaranteed Income Supplement (GIS)

The GIS is a monthly benefit paid to residents of Canada who receive a basic, full, or partial OAS pension and who have little or no other income. GIS payments may begin in the same month as OAS pension payments. Recipients must reapply annually for the GIS benefit. Thus, the amount of monthly payments may increase or decrease according to reported changes in a recipient's yearly income. Unlike the basic OAS pension, the GIS is *not* subject to income tax.

The GIS may be paid outside Canada for only six months following the month of departure from Canada, regardless of how long the person lived in Canada.

3. Spouse's/Widowed Spouse's Allowance (SPA)

The SPA is paid monthly. It is designed to recognize the difficult circumstances faced by many widowed persons and by couples living on the pension of only one spouse. Recipients must reapply annually. Benefits are *not* considered as income for income tax purposes.

The SPA is not payable outside Canada beyond a period of six months following the month of departure, regardless of how long the person lived in Canada.

4. Provincial Social Security Supplement Programs

Some provinces have guaranteed annual income systems. If you are 65 years of age or older and you receive the federal Guaranteed Income Supplement, you might qualify for additional benefits from your province. These benefits will ensure that your incomes does not fall below the province's guaranteed income level.

To apply for provincial assistance, contact your provincial government. For a list of addresses and telephone numbers of provincial offices for seniors, refer to item 11 in Appendix A.

5. Canada Pension Plan (CPP)/Quebec Pension Plan (QPP)

The CPP is a contributory, earnings-related social insurance program. It ensures a measure of protection to a contributor and his or her family against the loss of income due to retirement, disability, or death. The plan operates throughout Canada. Quebec has its own similar program, the Quebec Pension Plan (QPP), which is closely associated with the CPP. The operation of the two plans is coordinated through a series of agreements between the federal and Quebec governments. Benefits from either plan are based on pension credits accumulated under both, as if only one plan existed.

Benefits paid by the CPP are considered income for federal and provincial income tax purposes. You must apply for all CPP benefits, and you should apply for your retirement pension at least six months before you want to receive it.

A CPP retirement pension may be paid at age 60. However, the contributor must have wholly or substantially ceased pensionable employment. Contributors are considered to have substantially ceased pensionable employment if their annual earnings from employment or self-employment do not exceed the maximum retirement pension payable at age 65 for the year the pension is claimed. After turning 65, a pensioner is not required to stop work to receive a retirement pension.

All CPP benefits are adjusted in January each year to reflect increases in the cost of living as measured by the Consumer Price Index.

All benefits under the CPP are payable no matter where the beneficiary lives — whether in Canada, in the United States, or abroad.

6. CPP Disability Pension

To receive a disability pension, a contributor must have been disabled according to the terms of the CPP legislation, must have made sufficient contributions to the plan, must be under the age of 65, and must apply in writing.

A contributor is considered to be disabled under CPP if he or she has a physical or mental disability that is both severe and prolonged. "Severe" means that the person cannot regularly pursue any substantially gainful occupation. "Prolonged" means that the disability is likely to be continued for a long time and of indefinite duration, or is likely to result in death.

A disability pension begins in the fourth month after the month a person is considered disabled. It is payable until the beneficiary turns 65 or recovers from the disability (if this occurs before age 65), or until the beneficiary dies. When the recipient of a disability pension reaches age 65, the pension is automatically converted to a retirement pension.

7. CPP Surviving Spouse's Pension

A spouse of a deceased contributor or a person of the opposite sex who lived in a marital relationship with a contributor before his or her death may be eligible for a survivor's pension. To qualify, the deceased must have contributed to the CPP during at least one-third of the number of calendar years in his or her contributory period. If the deceased's contributory period was less than nine years, then at least three years' worth of CPP contributions are needed. If the contributory period was more than 30 years, at least 10 years' worth of contributions are required.

To qualify for a benefit, the surviving spouse must be 45 or older. There are some exceptions for those younger than 45 years of age.

8. CPP Death Benefit

A death benefit may be paid to the estate of a deceased contributor, if contributions to the CPP were made for the minimum qualifying period, the same as for a surviving spouse's pension. The death benefit is also paid if there is no will or estate. In this case, the benefit is usually paid to the person or agency responsible for funeral costs.

The death benefit is a lump-sum payment equal to six times the monthly retirement pension of the deceased contributor or roughly 10 percent of the year's maximum pensionable earnings, whichever is less.

9. Reciprocal Social Security Agreements with the United States

Reciprocal social security agreements allow for the coordination of two countries' social security programs and make social security benefits portable between countries. The United States is party to this agreement with Canada on the items discussed below:

a) Old Age Security

The OAS program is included in reciprocal social security agreements. Such agreements enable people who live or who have lived in the other contracting country—for example, the United States—to add those periods of residence abroad to periods of residence in Canada to satisfy the minimum eligibility requirements for the basic OAS pension and the SPA. For example, someone who has lived in Canada for less than the 10 years required to receive a partial OAS pension in Canada would be able to use periods of residence in the other country to meet the 10-year requirement. A similar provision would apply for someone who has lived in Canada for less than the 20 years needed to receive a partial OAS pension outside the country.

Under some agreements, benefits may be based only on periods of residence or contributions after specific dates. Residents who have little or no other income may receive the GIS. As noted earlier, the GIS is not payable outside

Canada beyond a period of six months, regardless of how long the person lived in Canada. Refer to Chapter 6 and to changes to the Canada/U.S. tax treaty that affect taxation of social security benefits.

b) Canada Pension Plan

Agreements are designed to avoid duplicate coverage—that is, the need to contribute to both the CPP and the comparable program of the other country for the same work.

Agreements may help people to qualify for disability, survivor's, and death benefits under the CPP. Each of the benefits has minimum qualifying conditions. An agreement may allow periods of contribution to the other country's social security system (or in some cases periods of residence abroad) to be added to periods of contribution to the CPP in order to meet these conditions. Once eligibility has been established, the amount of benefits is based on actual contributions to the CPP.

The CPP retirement pension is not included in agreements, since it is payable to anyone who has made at least one valid contribution. It is not necessary, therefore, to use periods of contribution in the other country to establish eligibility for the retirement benefit. Refer to Chapter 6 and to changes to the Canada/U.S. tax treaty that affect taxation of social security payments.

c) Provincial Social Security Programs

Canada's reciprocal social security agreements contain a provision that allows provinces to conclude understandings with other countries concerning social security programs under their jurisdiction—for example, the workers' compensation plans.

d) U.S. Social Security Programs

In many countries, nationality is an important criterion in determining eligibility for social security benefits. Noncitizens may be required to meet special conditions before they can receive a pension, and the payment of benefits to noncitizens living abroad may be severely restricted or even prohibited. Through the social security agreement between Canada and selected countries, including the United States, citizens and noncitizens become entitled to those benefits on the same conditions as the citizens of the other country. Most important, Canadian residents may start to receive benefits from the other country.

Most social security programs require contributions during a minimum number of years before a benefit can be paid. There may also be requirements for contributions in the period just before application for a benefit. People who have contributed to the programs of another country may not have enough periods of contributions to meet such requirements. Under the Canada-U.S. agreement, periods of residence in Canada and/or periods of contributions to the CPP may be used to satisfy the eligibility conditions of the other country's social security system. Refer to Chapter 6 and to changes to the Canada/U.S. tax treaty that affect taxation of social security payments.

10. Veterans' Pension

Veterans Affairs Canada provides a wide range of services and benefits to war veterans and former members of the Canadian Armed Forces in the form of disability pensions, survivors' pensions, and help with funeral and burial expenses. For more information, contact the nearest Veterans Affairs district office, listed in the Blue Pages of your telephone directory under Government of Canada. You must apply for all pensions or services provided by Veterans Affairs Canada. They do not start automatically.

E. EMPLOYER-FUNDED PENSION PLANS

You should be aware of the types of retirement plans sponsored by employers. You can make enquiries as to what exact benefits you will receive, how they will be structured, and how soon you could receive them. Some employers have more than one plan. Some employers will also include extended health and dental plan coverage as well as life insurance coverage after you retire.

1. Registered Pension Plans (RPPs)

These are the most heavily regulated by the government. The two main types of plans are defined benefit and defined contribution. The plan could be "contributory," in which you and the employer contribute payments, or "noncontributory," in which the employer pays the full amount due each year.

a) Defined Benefit Plan

This type of plan promises you a pension of a specific amount of money, based on your years of service and/or salary. There is no risk that your pension funding could be affected by economic or market fluctuations, since the employer must set aside, by law, enough money, separate from other employer funds, to capitalize the specific pension that has been promised to you. The pension fund will therefore exist even if the employer ceases to operate, though future benefits could then be restricted. If the pension fund investments do poorly, the employer must compensate by putting extra money into the fund.

There are two forms of defined benefit plans:

- **Accruing benefits plan**

  This plan can vary considerably, depending on the employer. Some offer a pension based on a percentage (e.g., two percent) of your average salary over your final three or five years of employment. This amount is then multiplied by your years of employment with the company. Other plans average all your earnings during your employment with the firm. This is not as attractive an arrangement as the previous one, which is based on your tax-earning years.

  Some employers offer a supplemental pension plan to extend the amount of pension from the RPP pension ceiling set by Revenue Canada.

- **Flat benefit plan**
  This type of plan bases the calculation of the pension on a flat amount per month for each year of employment—for example, $30 per month.

Some of these two types of plans include partial or full indexing for inflation. If this is your situation, you should verify that this provision is guaranteed, or possibly required by provincial legislation, rather than optional on the part of the company.

b) Defined Contribution Plan

These plans are sometimes referred to as "money purchase plans." The employer promises to contribute a certain amount to your pension account annually—for example, three to six percent of your annual salary. The amount of the pension, however, is not specified. You may be able to make your own contributions. In this type of plan, your employer invests the contribution on your behalf. The amount of your pension will vary, depending on the value of your pension account on retirement. If your employer invests well, you will receive a greater retirement income benefit. If not, you will get a lower amount. Your risk is related to the success of the pension fund manager and the level of interest rates when you retire.

- **Vesting**
  Vesting means that the pension credits you have earned are locked in, so you won't lose these benefits if you change your job. Ask your employer or the federal or provincial pension authorities responsible for your plan. Depending on the regulations, you might have to participate in the plan for two to five years or more before it can be vested.

If you quit your job, you can let your vested credits remain with your employer rather than taking out the amount you are entitled to in a lump sum, which would, of course, be taxable income. If the vested credits remain, you could receive a retirement pension that could net you more than you otherwise could have earned. It all depends on your needs and circumstances and what you want to do with the money. Alternatively, you could transfer the money into a locked-in RRSP. Although you can't withdraw it until your normal retirement age, you would control how it is invested. You must use the funds to provide retirement income, which would normally require you to buy a life annuity or a Life Income Fund (LIF). An LIF could allow you to wait until the age of 80, if you want, before buying a life annuity. Check what regulations and options apply in your case.

2. Deferred Profit Sharing Plans (DPSPs)

These plans are also regulated by government but are less restrictive than RPPs. They are similar to a defined contribution RPP in the sense that the amount you receive relates to the amount of the employer contribution and how effectively the money was invested.

There are some significant differences, however, from RPPs. The employer is only permitted to contribute half the amount of a defined contribution plan. If there is an annual profit, the employer is obligated to make a minimum contribution. No contribution is required if the company shows a loss that year. Another difference is that you may not have to wait until retirement to withdraw money from the plan.

3. Group RRSPs

Some employers prefer not to have the regulatory controls of an RPP or DPSP but still provide an employer-sponsored pension plan. A common approach is for the employer to contract with a professional money manager to establish an RRSP for each employee, with the administration fee normally borne by the employer. The employer could then increase your salary and deduct the increase from your salary to put into the individual RRSP. The benefit to you is that you have a form of forced savings plan, and you will receive more net pay each month, since the employer can withhold less for tax deductions as a result of the RRSP offset. The disadvantage is that you do not normally have the freedom to select your RRSP investments. The phrase "group RRSP" is a misnomer; although it is set up for a group of employees, each RRSP is individual.

F. YOUR OWN TAX-SHELTERED PENSION PLANS

1. Registered Retirement Savings Plans (RRSPs)

a) Types of RRSPs

There are three main types of RRSPs:

- **Deposit plans**
  These are offered by banks, trust companies, credit unions, and life insurance companies, and they include term deposits or Guaranteed Investment Certificates (GICs). Terms generally range from one to five years. It is prudent to vary the dates that your money comes due to average out changes in interest rates.

- **Managed plans**
  In this type of plan, which includes mutual funds, your money is pooled with that of others in a diversified portfolio of stocks, bonds, real estate, and other assets. Alternatively, you may have a singular plan managed just for your investments. The value of the assets can vary, of course, depending on the market.

- **Self-directed plans**
  With these plans, you are responsible for managing your own portfolio, subject to various restrictions. The funds are held by a trust company. You can buy and place in your plan a wide variety of assets, such as stocks, bonds, or mortgages.

Many retired people prefer to opt for the deposit plan or managed plan in conservative investments so that preservation of capital is foremost.

b) Types of RRSP Withdrawal Options

At some point you will have to decide what to do with the money you have built up in an RRSP—in other words, turn retirement savings into retirement income. If you have RRSP funds transferred from a pension plan, you may be subject to pension legislation. For example, you may be required to purchase only life annuities with your funds. Some provinces have approved various alternatives to life annuities. They are called Life Income Funds (LIFs) and/or Locked-in Retirement Income Funds (LRIFs). You basically have three RRSP withdrawal options:

- **Lump-sum withdrawal**
  Since all the money you withdraw is taxable in the year you receive it, most people don't choose this option unless there is an urgent need. Depending on the amount you take out, the tax liability could be high. Conversely, you may prefer to take out smaller amounts with low taxable consequences for specific purposes. Keep in mind that the more you take out, the less money is available for future retirement income and future potential growth in your retirement plan.

- **Registered Retirement Income Fund (RRIF)**
  This option is covered in more detail below. It means you can keep deferring tax on your money, as with an RRSP.

- **Annuities**
  Annuities provide regular income for life or for a specific period. This option is covered in more detail in Section 3.

2. Registered Retirement Income Funds (RRIFs)

An RRIF has become a very popular retirement income option because it provides the flexibility to control your retirement income and investments. It is like an RRSP in that you can select the investments you want, adjust your income payments, or take lump-sum withdrawals at your pleasure. You can have a self-directed RRIF if you want. Like an RRSP, an RRIF can grow tax-free, if you have income or growth types of investments. An RRIF is like an RRSP in reverse. Instead of putting in a certain amount of money each year, you withdraw money that is taxable. You have to draw a minimum mandatory amount, but there is no maximum amount. Obviously, the higher the payments you make to yourself, the sooner your funds will be depleted. RRIFs can continue for the lifetime of the holder or the spouse. You have to make a conversion from an RRSP to RRIF by the end of your 69th year, although you can do it at age 65 if you prefer—for example, if you need to qualify for the Pension Income Credit.

Your choice of RRIF will have an important impact on meeting your retirement needs. The key factors to consider include the amount of income you anticipate you will require in the short term and long term, and how long your savings will last.

a) Types of RRIF Withdrawal Options

Since you are permitted to have more than one RRIF, you might want to combine your withdrawal options to suit your needs. Not all institutions provide the options listed below. Obtain professional advice in advance.

- **Level payout**
  Payments are the same each month, for example, over a 25-year period. Although it is similar in some aspects to an annuity, you have control at all times.

- **Fixed-term payout**
  This is used by people who want to use up the funds in a shorter period of time—for example, 10 to 15 years—frequently because of ill health.

- **Minimum payout**
  This option maximizes your investment by allowing the funds to grow in a compounding tax-free environment. You can set up your RRIF at the end of your 69th year, but, for example, with payments to commence at the end of your 70th year. You don't have to take any payments in the calendar year it is funded. If your spouse is younger, you can set the formula based on his or her age, since there are advantages to this. Obtain further information for your situation.

- **Interest-only payout**
  In this case, you would receive interest only until the deadline arrives for minimum withdrawals. At this point your capital will start eroding, and therefore growth will not occur. In the meantime, though, you would have preserved your capital.

- **Indexed payout**
  Payments are increased annually based on a projected inflation rate—for example, five percent.

- **Smoothed payout**
  Payments are adjusted so that you receive higher payments in the early years and lower payments in the later years. The schedule of payments is calculated according to actuarial projections.

b) Factors to Consider When Making Your RRSP or RRIF Selection

You can continue making RRSP payments up to your 69th year if you want, when you have to convert to an RRIF or an annuity or to take a lump-sum withdrawal. With both RRSPs and RRIFs, you can place your funds in different types of investments, from no risk to high risk. In choosing the type of investment you want, you should take into account the following considerations:

- **Safety**
  Since you are retired or nearing retirement, preservation of capital is a primary consideration, followed by income or growth strategies that will at least neutralize inflation. You don't want to speculate. Spread any risk by diversifying your portfolio, unless you simply want to have money market funds such as GICs, Canada Savings Bonds, or term deposits. Don't invest in any product that could result in your losing money, which you can ill afford. Such an occurrence would negatively affect your retirement lifestyle or impair your peace of mind.

- **Diversification**
  As you mature, you want to move into more stable and secure investments. Equity-based mutual funds or actual stocks tend to be too risky for most people. Either they don't understand the market or feel anxious about the potential risk of eroding their capital, with little time for recovery. Conversely, if you have some "extra" money, you may wish to place some of it in more growth-oriented investments. There are many issues to consider, however.

- **Rate of return**
  There is a direct correlation between risk and potential return. The lower the risk, the lower the return; the higher the risk, the higher the potential return. Since you want to preserve your capital, you will probably opt for safety and certainty. By actively considering your options and thoroughly checking out the competition, however, you could still get one to four percent more money without any risk of impairing your capital. Over time, this extra percentage could make a considerable difference as it is compounded tax-free in your RRSP or RRIF.

- **Liquidity**
  This refers to how quickly you can access your money. You want to have access to a certain amount of money when you need it, or if interest rates start increasing considerably, you want to take advantage of that opportunity.

- **Fees**
  Normally fees are not an issue for people with deposit funds, such as GICs and term deposits. However, if you have a self-directed RRSP or RRIF, a managed plan such as a mutual fund, or a personally managed portfolio, the issue of fees for management is a consideration.

3. Annuities

An annuity involves putting a lump sum of money into a plan that provides a regular income for life or for a specified period. There are some limitations to be aware of related to RRIFs. With an annuity, you have no income payment flexibility or opportunity to manage investment options so that you might increase your retirement income. You may also have little or no inflation protection unless the annuity is indexed for inflation. Some policies permit this. The amount an annuity pays is determined by your age and the interest rates at the time of purchase. For some, annuities are a viable option if they cannot or prefer not to manage their own money, as you can with an RRIF. There are other considerations and potential benefits as well.

Term certain annuities are sold by various institutions, including banks, trust companies, credit unions, and insurance companies. Life annuities are sold only by life insurance companies. Ask about deposit insurance protection, estate preservation, and fees on any RRIF or annuity before you invest.

Here are the two main types of annuities:

a) Term Certain Annuity to Age 90 (TCA90)

This annuity provides regular periodic payments, which can continue until your 90th year. Payments are normally level but can usually be indexed for inflation. If your spouse is younger than you are, you can purchase the TCA90 to continue after your death until your spouse's 90th year. If you die before 90 and do not have a spouse, you can make arrangements for the payments to go to your estate. Some issuers offer a TCA90 with an alternative to a fixed rate of return. In this option, the yield and payments are adjusted periodically to interest rates. You can obtain a TCA100 if you want.

b) Life Annuity

A life annuity provides regular payments that will continue for the rest of your life, no matter how long you live. When you die, however, any money left in the annuity goes to the issuer, not your estate. The exception is if you arrange an annuity that has a guaranteed payment period.

There are various types of life annuities:

- **Straight life annuity**
  This type of annuity is for an individual only and provides you with the highest amount of income for each dollar of premium in monthly or annual payments. However, it only lasts for your lifetime, when the annuity payments stop, unless you have a guaranteed period. This type of plan might be suitable for people who have no dependents.

- **Life annuity with a guaranteed period**
  This provides a guarantee that you or your beneficiary will receive back all of your investments, plus full interest if you wish, even if you only

live for a short time. Alternatively, you may have the guarantee period set up to provide income payments for a fixed time frame, such as five, 10, or 15 years from the start of payments to you, or until you or your spouse reach a certain age, such as 90. The longer the guaranteed period, the lower the payments.

- **Joint and last survivor annuity**
  This annuity provides a regular income as long as either spouse is living. Payments can continue at the full amount to the surviving spouse, or they can be reduced by any stipulated percentage on the death of either spouse or specifically at your death. If you select the reduction option, this will result in higher payments while both spouses are alive, since it is necessary to have a higher income stream for two people than one. Although this type of plan results in less income for each dollar invested in the annuity, to many people the additional benefits are worth it.

- **Instalment refund annuity**
  If you die before you have received as much money as you paid for the annuity, this annuity will continue income payments to your beneficiary until they equal the amount you originally paid.

- **Cash refund annuity**
  With this plan, instead of receiving continued income payments, as in the above example, your beneficiary receives a lump-sum payout.

- **Indexed life annuity**
  This provides for annuity payments that automatically increase each year, from one to five percent, for example, based on the return of a specified group of assets. Although this plan provides you with some protection against rising living costs due to inflation, it will also reduce your payments in the early years.

- **Integrated life annuity**
  If you wish, you can integrate your Old Age Security (OAS) payments with your annuity. With this plan, you would receive substantially increased annuity payments until age 65, at which time the payments would be reduced by the maximum OAS entitlement at the time you purchased the annuity.

G. ARE YOUR DEPOSIT MONIES, RRSPS, RRIFS, AND ANNUITIES PROTECTED AGAINST DEFAULT?

Depending on how and where you invest your money, it may or may not be partially or fully protected. Making sure your retirement investments and insurance benefits are protected is naturally a matter of concern. Some banks, trust companies, credit unions, and savings and loans institutions in the United States, and insurance companies in Canada and the United States have ceased to operate. Verify all the information in this overview section to ensure that it is current, accurate, and relevant to your situation.

1. Protection of Deposit Monies, RRSPs, RRIFs, and Annuities in Canada

- **Deposits in a bank or trust company**
  These are protected by the Canada Deposit Insurance Corp. (CDIC) up to a certain amount. In Quebec, the plans are protected by the Quebec Deposit Insurance Board. Your RRSP deposit or RRIF, regular savings or chequing funds on deposit, or term deposits are automatically insured for up to $60,000 for each separate account. Each deposit (in the form of an RRSP or otherwise) must mature in five years or less. If you have more than $60,000, you can divide your funds among several CDIC members who are separate financial institutions. Some banks and trust companies have subsidiaries that are separate CDIC members, resulting in a ceiling of $60,000 each. For information and confirmation, contact CDIC at 1-800-461-2342. On May 20, 1999, CDIC launched an interactive deposit insurance calculator on its web site *http://www.cdic.ca*. You can determine the extent of your coverage by answering the questions posed.

- **Deposits in a credit union**
  These are protected by a provincial deposit insurance plan. Each province varies in its protection for deposits—savings, chequing, or term deposit, or RRSP or RRIF with term deposits or GICs less than five years. Depending on the province, the protection can range from $60,000 to unlimited protection—that is, 100 percent. Contact a credit union in your province to enquire, or phone the CDIC at 1-800-461-2342 to obtain contact numbers for the credit union deposit insurance head office in your province.

- **Deposits in a life insurance company**
  These are covered by an industry-operated protection plan called CompCorp up to certain limits and in certain situations, depending on the nature of the investment. The limit for policies registered under the *Income Tax Act*, such as RRSPs, RRIFs, and pension policies, is $60,000. The limit is also $60,000 for nonregistered policies, such as cash value of a life insurance policy. For information and confirmation, contact CompCorp directly at 1-800-268-8099.

- **Managed funds**
  Generally, these funds are protected if they are in an RRSP in the form of deposit funds—for example, term deposits or GICs under five years. Mutual funds have no protection as such, because of the nature of the pooled investment. The funds' investments are segregated from the assets of the fund manager, however, in case the fund manager ceases to operate.

- **Self-directed plans**
  These plans are not protected as such against the default of the institution holding them. Certain investments in the plan, however, such as term deposits or GICs under five years, could be protected. The amount of the protection depends on whether the institution is a bank, trust company, credit union, or brokerage firm. Refer to the deposit ceilings discussed earlier for these types of institutions.

  If a brokerage firm ceases to operate, there could be protection for certain investments in your self-directed plan up to $500,000 under an industry plan called the Canadian Investor Protection Fund. Only members, such as a Canadian stock exchange (Vancouver, Alberta, Toronto, and Montréal), the Toronto Futures Exchange, and members of the Investment Dealers Association of Canada, are covered by this fund. No mutual fund companies or investment advisors not associated with a member broker are covered by this particular fund.

  For further information and confirmation, contact your broker or the CIPF office in Toronto at (416) 866-8366.

- **Life insurance companies**
  If a company that is a member of the CompCorp protection plan makes promises in a life insurance, health insurance, money-accumulation, or annuity policy to pay either a fixed or a minimum amount of money to a person or on a person's death, and that company goes under, you could be protected up to a certain amount. If you have life insurance protection, the limit is $200,000; for life annuity and disability income policies with no options of a lump-sum withdrawal, the limit is $2,000 a month; and for health benefits other than disability income annuities, the limit is $60,000 in total payments.

  For further information and confirmation, contact CompCorp at 1-800-268-8099.

- **Creditor-proofing**
  If you have personally guaranteed loans for an incorporated company, or if you operate an unincorporated business, you could be exposed to claims from potential creditors. Funds placed with certain types of products from life insurance companies or with trust companies in Quebec could be protected from creditors. Obtain advice from the institution involved and verify it with your lawyer.

2. Protection for Deposit Monies in the United States

- **Deposits in U.S. federal or state banks, trust companies, and savings and loans institutions**
  These are covered by the Federal Deposit Insurance Corporation (FDIC) up to $100,000 for each individual account.

If you want further information, consumer brochures on deposit insurance, or confirmation that the institution is covered by FDIC, contact FDIC at 1-800-934-3342 (Canada and the U.S.), or call (202) 393-8400.

- **Deposits in U.S. credit unions**
  These are covered up to $100,000 by the National Credit Union Share Insurance Fund (NCUSIF) for each individual account.

For further information, a consumer brochure on deposit insurance, or confirmation that the credit union is covered by NCUSIF, contact the fund at 1-800-755-5999 (U.S. only), or call (703) 518-6300.

H. USING YOUR HOME AS A SOURCE OF ADDITIONAL INCOME

Many Canadian seniors prefer to remain in their own homes as long as possible for a variety of reasons, including the support network they have built up over the years, through neighbours, friends, church, or other regular social activities. Many seniors are unable to pay to remain at home, however. It is not uncommon for seniors to be house-rich and cash-poor.

There are many reasons why a senior may need extra cash or income to supplement existing financial resources. Even if contributions have been made to several savings programs, such as private pension plans, government pensions, or RRSPs, there could still be insufficient financial resources for the senior's needs or wants. Being a Snowbird and living in the U.S. Sunbelt states for up to six months a year could be one reason for lack of financial resources. Other seniors may not have the savings income mentioned and may rely only on federal Old Age Security (OAS) income, perhaps along with a federal Guaranteed Income Supplement (GIS). Some of these federal or provincial programs involve a means test. This means the government sets a maximum income level to be eligible. If you exceed this income, you do not get the funding. Many seniors who have fixed savings have had their purchasing power eroded by inflation. The home is the single largest form of "savings" for seniors, especially if they can tap into the equity that has accumulated, for lump-sum and/or continuous income, without having to make monthly payments.

Many seniors think that a home cannot readily be converted into a source of income unless the home is sold. This can be a very stressful scenario to some. In contrast, there are seniors who, by circumstance or choice, sell their homes, buy a condominium (in many cases in a retirement area) and have a considerable amount of cash left over. For information about housing and real estate for Snowbirds, see Chapter 4.

There are options for seniors who want to stay in their own homes but need or wish to supplement their income. One option is to rent out a self-contained basement suite to provide income. Another option is to rent out spare rooms in the house, taking in boarders who share common kitchen facilities and washrooms. In many cases the income is not taxable, either because the income can be offset against a percentage of the house expenses or because of the low amount of income involved. These options may provide additional benefits in the form of companionship and the feeling of security. This latter benefit could be particularly attractive, especially if the owner is a Snowbird, or often away on trips. For other seniors, these options may not be attractive because of the loss of privacy. There could also be municipal bylaw regulations that could technically restrict having tenants. In many cases these regulations are flexible, depending on various factors, current municipal policy regarding enforcement, and extenuating circumstances of the owner.

Keep in mind that the following plans vary from province to province and are constantly changing. Obtain a current update. Also contact your local Canada Mortgage and Housing Corporation (CMHC) office for information about their wide range of programs and publications for seniors. Look for the local contact phone number for CMHC in the blue pages your phone book under Government of Canada.

1. Deferred Payment Plans

This type of plan involves the postponement of certain expenses until a fixed time in the future or until the house is sold. Generally, the expenses, along with any interest applicable, constitute a debt, with the equity in the home as security. This is the simplest form of equity conversion. Under these plans, you maintain ownership and possession of the home, as well as any equity appreciation. Here are some examples of deferred payment plans:

a) Deferment of Property Taxes

There are many people who are mortgage-free but who spend a significant amount of their net income on property taxes, even after a provincial homeowners' property tax grant is deducted. In addition to property taxes, there are other recurring expenses that further erode disposable income, including costs of maintenance, lighting, heating, water, or garbage removal.

Although property taxes are collected by and for the municipality, in most cases some provincial governments have established property tax deferment plans. Under this arrangement, a senior is entitled to delay payment of property taxes and accrued interest until the home is sold or the senior's estate is settled. Check with your local property tax department to see if such a program is available or is being considered.

b) Deferment or Subsidy of Home Rehabilitation Expenses

This arrangement is similar to the previous example in that any loans approved for improvement or rehabilitation of the home may be deferred until your home is sold, until your estate is settled, or until a fixed date in the future. In some cases, there is an outright subsidy that does not have to be repaid. There are several variations of this type of program, depending on whether funds are obtained through a federal CMHC or provincial government program. Find out what current programs are available. The advantage of this type of home rehabilitation expense deferment is that it allows you to improve your standard of living without eroding your income.

If you are considering either of the above deferred payment plan programs, there are several key questions that you should ask:

- Is there a limit on the income of applicants to be eligible?
- Is there a subsidy of the deferral plan?
- Is there a limit on the amount of payment due (e.g., property taxes) that can be deferred?
- Is there a limit on the time that an amount will be deferred?
- What is the interest charge on the amount deferred?
- How often is the interest rate adjusted, if at all, on the deferred payment?
- What is the formula used for determining the interest rate and how frequently is it compounded?
- If the amount of payment deferred and accrued interest eventually exceeds the value of the home, will you be obligated to sell the home?

Keep in mind that although property taxes can increase every year and that interest rates over time, especially compounded rates, can eat away the equity in the home, these effects should be partially offset by an increase in the value of the home as a result of inflation and market demand.

2. Reverse Mortgages

Reverse mortgages, reverse annuity mortgages (RAMs), and home equity plans are similar concepts that are becoming increasingly popular among seniors or early retirees across Canada. Over the years, many people can build up considerable equity in their houses, townhouses, or condominiums. Many Canadians have decided to turn their largest asset into immediate cash and/or regular revenue and still remain in the home.

The basic concept behind these various plans is simple. You take out a mortgage on part of the equity of your home (the debt-free portion of your home), and in exchange receive a lump-sum amount of money and/or a monthly income for a fixed period, for your life, or for the life of the surviving spouse. When you sell the home, when you die, or when your surviving spouse dies, the mortgage and accrued interest must be repaid. You do not have to make any payments in the meantime. If there is any balance left in residual equity in the home after the sale, it belongs to the senior or his or her estate.

The various reverse mortgage options have different features. Here are some of the main ones:

• Reverse mortgages, RAMs, and other home equity programs are readily available through a variety of agents and brokers. This permits you to compare and contrast in a competitive marketplace and end up with a plan that has features customized for your specific needs. Look in the Yellow Pages under Financial Planning Consultants and Mortgages for companies that offer these home equity plans.

• The main home equity type of plans that are available have obtained an opinion from Revenue Canada that the lump-sum payment and monthly annuity payments are tax free, as long as you live in your home. If you have selected a monthly income annuity that continues after you have moved out of your home, the income from the sale may be subject to favourable prescribed annuity taxation rules. The current ruling on the various means-tested programs, such as the federal Guaranteed Income Supplement (GIS), is that receiving the annuity will not interfere with your eligibility for, or cause a reduction in, the GIS. As tax laws and regulations change, make sure you obtain current independent advice from a tax accountant and Revenue Canada on this issue.

• Since you retain ownership, you benefit from an appreciation in the value of your home over time—that is, you get an increase in equity. For example, if your property goes up 10 percent a year in value, and you locked in the mortgage on your property for the reverse mortgage or RAM at eight percent, then you are technically ahead in the interest differential. In reality, because you are not making regular payments on your mortgage, the interest on it is being compounded and therefore, in practical terms, is ultimately eroding the increasing equity. The reduction could be substantially offset by an attractive average annual appreciation in property value.

Although many of the reverse mortgages, RAMs and related plans operate in similar ways among various companies, interest rates and other specific conditions vary. Here are some of the points to consider in choosing a plan:

• What are the age requirements to be eligible for the lump-sum or annuity plan?
• Do you need to have clear title on your home?
• Can you transfer the mortgage to another property if you move?
• What percentage of your home equity is used to determine the reverse mortgage or RAM, and what percentage of that is available for a lump-sum payment and annuity?

- Is the interest rate on the mortgage fixed for your lifetime or duration of the annuity, or is it adjusted, and if so, how regularly and using what criteria?

- If the reverse mortgage and lump sum is for a term period, what are the various terms available?

- What if the equity of the home on sale is insufficient to pay the mortgage and accrued interest? Are you or your estate liable for the shortfall?

- Can the agreement of the term be extended if the home has appreciated in value?

- Can you move out of the house, rent it, and still maintain the home equity plan?

- What if you already have a mortgage on the house?

- If the annuity is for life, is there a minimum guaranteed period of payment, or will payments stop immediately upon the death of the recipient and/or the surviving spouse?

- How will the income received under the proposed plan be taxed, if at all?

- Will the income received affect your eligibility under any federal or provincial housing or social programs?

The process of obtaining a reverse mortgage or RAM takes about four to six weeks on average, including home appraisal, annuity calculations, and other matters. It is essential that you obtain independent legal and tax advice in advance and thoroughly compare the features and benefits.

3. Renting Out Part of Your Home in Canada or the United States

If you choose to rent out a basement suite, you are entitled to offset the rental income you receive against a portion of your house-related expenses. For example, if you received rent of $300/month ($3,600 a year) from the rented area and the total house-related expenses were $14,400 a year, and the rented area comprised 25 percent of the total square footage of the home or $3,600 of the total expenses ($14,400 $\times$ 25 percent), then the income would be offset by expense, leaving a zero taxable income. House-related expenses would include a portion of any mortgage interest, property tax, utilities (hydro, water, telephone, etc.), insurance, and maintenance costs. In all instances you should obtain tax advice from a professional accountant to make sure you are doing the calculations correctly.

If you are renting out part of your home, check with your provincial government to obtain information about your obligations and rights as a landlord; you will be governed and regulated by that legislation. For example, some provinces have rent control, and others do not. Ideally, you want to have a tenancy agreement that supplements the provincial legislation and deals with such issues as your policy on smoking, pets, noise, and the number of people living in the suite.

Your municipality has the authority to regulate zoning and determines whether a residence is zoned for single families. Technically, therefore, you could contravene a municipal zoning bylaw by renting out a part of your home to a nonrelative. In effect, you would be operating as if your home were multifamily, which it wouldn't be zoned for. If you hear the term "illegal suite," it simply means it technically contravenes the existing municipal bylaw on the issue. The contravention has nothing to do with provincial legislation (dealing with landlord-tenant matters) or federal legislation (dealing with income tax). Each level of government is independent of the other.

Check with your local municipality. It could be that certain areas in the municipality are encouraged to have rental suites. Alternatively, the municipality may have the technical restriction but does not actively enforce it unless there is a complaint by a neighbour. If a municipal inspector does investigate, you normally have a right to appeal. One of the grounds of appeal is economic hardship for you, the owner, and serious inconvenience for the tenant. Some municipalities have a moratorium (temporary freeze) on enforcing the bylaw because of a shortage of rental accommodation and/or general recessionary hardship of property owners, who need a "mortgage helper" to meet payments.

Some provincial governments have programs to encourage home renovation in order to create rental suites. In addition, the CMHC has some programs for renovation to accommodate handicapped or elderly people.

Make enquiries. The tax aspects of renting your U.S. Sunbelt home are covered in Chapter 6.

4. Operating a Business Out of Your Home

Many people, at some point, intend to start part-time or full-time businesses out of their homes. There is a growing trend to do this for various reasons, including eliminating daily commuting to work, fulfilling a lifestyle choice, creating retirement opportunity, supplementing salaried income, testing a business idea, or saving on business overhead and thereby reducing financial risk by writing off house-related expenses. There are many different types of home-based businesses. If you are interested in operating out of the home, refer to Appendix B for many publications on operating a small business. You need competent tax and legal advice before you start up. The last thing you want is potential risk, since that could deplete your retirement funds and hamper your lifestyle. You need a GST number if you have over $30,000 in income in your business or are paying GST on items you purchase and want to offset it against GST you are charging. Check with your accountant and closest GST office (Revenue Canada).

Expenses may be claimed for the business use of a work space in your home if:

- The work space is your principal place of business for the part-time or full-time self-employed aspect of your career (you could have a salaried job elsewhere; it is not required that you meet people at your home) or

- You only use the work space to earn income from your business and it is used regularly for meeting clients, customers, or patients, in which case, you could also deduct expenses from an office outside the home.

Basically, you write off a portion of all your home expenses based on the portion of the home you use for business-related purposes (e.g., office, storage, etc.). Refer to the previous discussion of renting out your home. It is the same type of formula.

You may be able to claim 100 percent of the cost of business purchases or a depreciated amount over time, depending on the item. To clarify what you can deduct and how to do it, as well as other home business tax issues, speak to your accountant. You should also speak with your lawyer about the various types of legal issues when starting a business. See Chapter 8 for information about selecting advisors.

The tax and legal aspects of working in the United States are covered in the chapters on tax (Chapter 6) and immigration (Chapter 3).

5. Keeping Records

If you are going to be renting out part of your principal residence or Sunbelt condo to a tenant, or if you intend to have a home-based business, make sure that you keep detailed records of all money collected and paid out. Purchases and operating expenses must be supported by invoices, receipts, contracts, or other supporting documents.

You do not need to submit these records when you file your return, but you need to have them in case you are ever audited.

TIPS BEFORE LEAVING CANADA

- Investigate and evaluate the various potential financial and other risks discussed in Section B in this chapter and make the appropriate decisions before your departure.

- Review your government, employer, or personal pension plans and make arrangements to have your pension or other income (e.g., dividends, tax refunds) deposited directly into your bank account during your absence.

- Make sure that your funds will receive the best interest rate, depending on your liquidity and safety of principal needs. For example, if your direct deposit goes into a low interest or chequing account, arrange to have a regular transfer of the funds (e.g., monthly) into an investment that provides you with a higher return (e.g., GIC, term deposit, Treasury bill). Always make sure your Canadian account funds are receiving interest.

- If you foresee that you will need some of your Canadian funds during your absence, have your financial institution forward the desired funds directly to your Sunbelt bank. Always confirm your instructions in writing and keep a copy.

- Keep an accurate record of when any GICs, term deposits, or Treasury bills come due during your absence so that appropriate arrangements can be made.

- Estimate how much money you will need while you are away and how to readily access it. Check your credit card and line of credit limits. If they are not high enough for possible emergencies, arrange to have them increased.

- With Automated Banking Machines (ABMs), you do not need to carry a lot of cash. But check on your bank cash card withdrawal limit. For example, you may be limited to $100 a day, so arrange to have that increased before you leave, if you want to access a higher amount.

- You can arrange to have your monthly bank statements forwarded to your Sunbelt address.

- You can pay your Canadian bills personally, on your Canadian chequing account, by having your mail forwarded to your Sunbelt address. It can be more convenient and efficient, however, to arrange for automatic debiting of your Canadian bank account. Alternatively, you can arrange to have the bills sent to your financial institution to pay on your behalf. If you choose this alternative, put your instructions in writing. Bills that can be paid this way include utility bills, cable, house taxes, condominium maintenance fees, and quarterly income tax instalments.

- You may have other investments your financial institution can deal with in your absence—for example, reinvestment of income, deposit of coupons, rollover of maturing deposits, or purchase and sale of securities. Make sure your instructions are in writing and any required documentation is signed in advance. Ask for copies of all transactions dealt with on your behalf to be sent to you at your Sunbelt address.

- If you plan to purchase real estate in the United States, many American financial institutions and some Canadian ones will lend you money. Find out whether your Canadian financial institution will lend money for a Sunbelt property based on your Canadian or U.S. assets. If you have sufficient equity in your Canadian property, can debt-service the mortgage for the U.S. property, and your credit rating is good, you should have no problem getting financing in Canada.

- Take enough money in traveller's cheques to meet your needs for the first month. Many American financial institutions put a hold on a cheque from a Canadian account until it has cleared. This could take over three weeks. After you have established a relationship, however, many U.S. financial institutions will credit your U.S. account the same day you deposit your Canadian cheque.

- If you do not already have an existing U.S. bank account, you can facilitate "no hold" chequing privileges by planning before you leave Canada. Ask the manager of your Canadian financial institution whether it has a correspondent banking relationship with a U.S. financial institution or what special Snowbird features are available. This will facilitate a "no hold" policy. Refer to Appendix A, items 38 and 39.

- Ask your bank manager to provide you with a letter of introduction to give to a U.S. bank. Such a letter confirms your good banking track record and creditworthiness and personalizes you. If you have any hassles, there are many other financial institutions that would be delighted to have your business.

- Consider the benefits of having a U.S. dollar chequing and/or savings account at a Canadian financial institution. These cheques are generally designed to clear through the U.S. clearing system. Also, consider a U.S. dollar credit card from a Canadian financial institution.

- Most major Canadian financial institutions have a special toll-free telephone access for you to pay bills in Canada or the United States in Canadian or U.S. dollar funds, as well as to make balance enquiries.

- Always arrange to have a trusted friend or relative know how to contact you quickly in case of an emergency or to advise you of economic conditions that could affect your investments during your absence.

- Subscribe to one or both of the weekly newspapers for Canadian Snowbirds so that you can be kept aware of news, or issues in the United States or Canada relevant to Snowbirds. You can have the publications sent to your Canadian or U.S. address or both, depending on the duration of your Snowbird stay. Refer to item 31 in Appendix A.

CHAPTER
3

Immigration and Customs

A. INTRODUCTION

Many people don't know what regulations apply when they are living in the United States for an extended stay each year. Each country has different regulations that will affect you, and you need to know what they are. Under the *Canada-U.S. Free Trade Agreement* (FTA), and its successor, the *North American Free Trade Agreement* (NAFTA), there is reciprocity of goods that are exempt from duty or have reduced duty when crossing the border, if the goods were made in the United States, Canada, or Mexico. The NAFTA also permits Canadians to stay in the United States longer for business or employment reasons.

This chapter provides an overview of the information about immigration and customs that you need to know, including documentation options, being prepared before you enter the U.S., working part-time in the U.S., and implications of being a U.S. citizen but having a Canadian primary residence.

B. PERSONAL DOCUMENTATION OPTIONS

When travelling outside Canada, make sure that you have appropriate documentation to be allowed entry into other countries. Many people assume that they can just cross the border into the U.S. without any ID being requested. That might be the experience. However, the U.S. has been tightening up its customs procedures and you could be refused entry if you don't have the appropriate ID, such as a passport and driver's licence. You don't need the inconvenience of being turned away when heading down south. The request of a customs officer for specific documentation may be discretionary, but it is recommended that you have more rather than less documentation than you think you might require.

If you are going to Mexico or other countries, or taking a cruise to a foreign country, a passport is a necessity. If you are a naturalized Canadian citizen, it could be wise to take a citizenship card.

It's a good idea to carry an extra copy of your birth certificate, as well as to keep a record of your passport number. Make two photocopies of your passport identification page, tourist card (if travelling to Mexico) and other personal documents before leaving home. Leave one set with a relative or friend back home, whom you could contact in case of a loss. Carry the other set with you in a separate place from your actual documents. It will be easier to replace any lost or stolen passports if you have this documentation.

Here is an outline of the key types of personal documentation that are available that you should consider for your needs.

1. Birth Certificate

You should have an official wallet-size version of this certificate. If you were born in Canada but outside Quebec, contact your provincial department of vital statistics. The contact number would be in the Blue Pages of your telephone book. If you were born in Quebec, you should get a wallet-size baptismal certificate.

2. Passport

Your passport is good for five years; make sure that it does not expire during your absence from Canada. If that does happen, you can contact the closest Canadian consulate office in the country you are in, eg. U.S. or Mexico. Refer to Appendix A for contact addresses. The consulate office can arrange for a passport in an emergency situation.

Otherwise, you can get a passport from the federal government passport office. Look in the Blue Pages of your phone book for the closest office. Alternatively, you can send away for it. You can pick up a Canadian passport application form from a post office, many travel agents, etc. The cost is $60 and it takes several weeks to process. If you need it more urgently, it can be done in a number of days.

To obtain your passport, you need to have proof of citizenship, such as a birth certificate or baptismal certificate (Quebec). You will need a Canadian citizenship card (either the actual certificate or laminated card) if you were born outside Canada. You will also need two recent passport photos taken by someone familiar with the format required.

3. Citizenship Card

If you were born outside Canada and became a naturalized Canadian, you might want to obtain a wallet-size laminated citizenship card. It costs $75 and is good for life. You would need to return your original large certificate you received before the government would process the wallet-size card. You are only permitted to have one or the other, for obvious security and control reasons.

Contact your closest federal government citizenship office. Look in the Blue Pages of your phone book. You will need two other acceptable pieces of personal identification, such as a passport, driver's licence, health card, social insurance card, etc. You will also need two passport type photos. You have to book an appointment with the citizenship office. Expect a delay of from four to six months before you receive the card, so plan ahead.

4. Driver's Licence

This is frequently requested by customs officials, if you are in an accident, or if you want to cash cheques, etc. Remember to renew your licence before you depart, if it expires while you are away. Also make sure that you have proper vehicle registration documentation. You also want to check that your auto licence plates do not expire while you are away.

5. Provincial ID Card

Many people have not heard of this card. It is issued by provincial motor vehicle departments. Look in the Blue Pages of your telephone directory to make enquiries. Basically, you would go through the same photo process and end up with a laminated wallet card that looks like a driver's licence, but is called a provincial ID card.

The card is available for the many people who do not drive, but are frequently asked for ID to do any financial transactions. Fees vary depending on the province.

6. International Driver's Licence

You can obtain this document, which has your photo on it, from various sources, including your local CAA auto club. Refer to item 36 in Appendix A for a list of CAA offices. All you need to do is show your current licence, and other ID. The cost is nominal.

You do not need this licence for the U.S., but it is advisable for Mexico and other countries. It is considered acceptable evidence of your right to drive in most countries of the world. Your provincial driver's licence would not be acceptable in most countries, as they are not familiar with it.

C. BE PREPARED WHEN ENTERING THE U.S.

Entering the U.S. has particular steps and protocols you need to know. Here are the key ones to avoid frustration and delay.

1. Identification

The most important formality on entering the United States is giving proof of citizenship. In the past, U.S. officials have been willing to accept anything from a driver's licence or birth certificate to a Canadian Tire credit card. Increasingly, however, Canadians are being required to show identification that includes a photo and proves their right to re-enter Canada.

Every Canadian should carry a valid Canadian passport for all trips outside Canada, including those to the United States. Your passport is the most widely accepted form of identification available.

Travelling Canadians may find it difficult to enter, pass through or return from the United States if they do not have valid photo identification and proof of citizenship. All carriers (noticeably airlines, but also Amtrak and Greyhound) have become much stricter about requiring proof of admissibility to Canada as a result of the heavy fines they face for carrying inadmissible passengers. Since birth and baptismal certificates, for example, do not have photographs, they are no longer accepted by airline companies without accompanying valid photo identification. Even carriers taking Canadians from Canada to the United States on round-trip tickets have refused to return them to Canada without valid photo identification and proof of Canadian citizenship. As a result, many travellers have had to contact Canadian consulates in the United States for assistance. When this happens, the consulate has to verify documentation with provincial and federal authorities, which involves further delay. Carrying your Canadian passport is recommended for all visits to the United States.

2. Dual Nationality

Some Canadians may have U.S. as well as Canadian citizenship through birth in the United States or through naturalization or descent. Although this is not likely to create problems—and in fact may solve some—it is wise for you to understand your status under U.S. law.

Canadians who are also U.S. citizens should always identify themselves as U.S. citizens when entering the United States. For information on dual nationality and a range of other relevant issues for U.S. citizens, dial 1-800-529-4410. This is the American Consular information line for American citizens. With your touch-tone phone choose English or French and then listen to the choices—press #1 for the menu of services, then #2 for citizenship information, and then #3 for information on dual nationality.

3. Criminal Records

If you have a criminal record, no matter how minor or how long ago, you likely are not eligible to enter the United States. There may also be problems in transit through U.S. airports.

Admitting you have committed a criminal offence may also make you ineligible to enter the United States. Under U.S. law, a Canadian pardon does not cancel a criminal conviction.

If you have ever been refused entry to the United States, regardless of the reason, you are most likely ineligible to enter without special permission.

It is strongly recommended that if you have a criminal conviction, or previously have been denied entry, you should contact one of the U.S. Immigration and Naturalization Service (INS) ports of entry well in advance of your travel to the United States. If you are ineligible to enter the United States and wish to apply for a waiver of ineligibility, you will be asked to complete Form I-192, Advance Permission to Enter the United States. It may take several months to process your application. Ordinarily, a Canadian citizen convicted of an impaired driving violation need not file Form I-192.

If you left the United States to avoid military service during the Vietnam war and have not since regularized your status, there might be an outstanding warrant for your arrest or you might be ineligible for U.S. entry. If you are in doubt, check with the nearest INS port of entry.

U.S. ports of entry are computerized and connected to a centralized database. Information is readily available on criminal convictions in both Canada and the United States. Even though you may have entered the United States without hindrance in the past, you could now run into difficulty if your record shows either a criminal conviction or a previous denial of entry.

4. Travel with/by Children

U.S. and Canadian authorities and transportation companies are increasingly vigilant in questioning persons travelling with children. If you are planning to travel to the United States with a child, for example a grandchild, you should carry documentation such as a custody order or a letter certifying that you have the legal right to bring the child with you. Also, persons under the age of 18 who are travelling on their own should carry documentation showing that they have the permission of custodial parents.

As well, if there is a possibility of a custody dispute developing while you are away with your child, you should talk to a Canadian lawyer before leaving home. A special publication, *International Child Abductions: A Manual for Parents*, is available from the Department of Foreign Affairs and International Trade.

5. Drugs

The U.S. Government *Zero Tolerance Policy* legislation imposes severe penalties for the possession of even a small amount of an illegal drug. Even prescription drugs and syringes used for legitimate medical purposes come under intense scrutiny.

- Never carry a package or luggage for someone else unless you have been able to verify the contents completely.

- Choose your travelling companions wisely. Never cross the border with a hitchhiker. Though you may not be carrying anything illegal, your companions might be and you could be implicated.

- Be equally careful about who and what you carry in your vehicle. As the driver, you could be held responsible for the misdeeds of your passengers, even if committed without your knowledge or involvement.

6. Admissibility and Entry

As soon as you stop at the U.S. border or at an inland port of entry, you are subject to U.S. law. U.S. Immigration can refuse entry to persons with criminal records or persons who cannot demonstrate that they have a legitimate reason to enter the United States.

Generally, the criteria for admissibility include citizenship, residence (permanent home or reason to return), purpose of the trip (legitimate reasons for entry), intended length of stay (against the backdrop of the individual's situation at home) and proof of financial support while in the United States. In a nutshell, this "test" helps tell whether you are travelling for legitimate reasons, have the financial resources for your travel and living expenses, and intend to return home. The American official at the point of entry is the sole judge of your admissibility. Under U.S. law, as an alien detained at the border by Customs or Immigration, you do not have the right or privilege of contacting your lawyer.

The permanent U.S. record created when a Canadian has been refused entry to the United States becomes part of a computerized database readily available at all pre-clearance offices in Canada, and border and inland ports of entry. If you attempt to enter at another location, you could be fined or your vehicle seized, or both. There are appeal procedures but they are prolonged, costly and unlikely to reverse the original decision.

At a pre-clearance facility in Canada, you may choose to withdraw your request to enter the United States if border officials are questioning your application. This step can be taken before you are interviewed further, or your belongings searched. Despite your taking this approach, U.S. officials may, nonetheless, make a record of your attempted entry on the U.S. Immigration database. The option to withdraw your application for entry is rarely available at land border or inland ports of entry, since at that point you are already on U.S. soil.

What you say in answer to questions by Immigration or Customs officers can be used against you if you are considered to be inadmissible. Many persons have had their vehicles or vessels seized because they pretended to be Canadian citizens when they were actually landed immigrants or visitors to Canada. Others have lost vehicles or vessels because they carried passengers who pretended to be Canadian citizens, or who did not admit to having a criminal record (no matter how long ago the conviction or how minor the offence) or who pretended to be visitors while planning to look for work in the United States. As a driver, you can be held responsible for the wrongdoings of your passengers regardless of knowledge or association.

7. Expedited Removal

Canadians travelling to the United States should take note of a new U.S. Immigration procedure. As of April 1, 1997, "expedited removal" allows an Immigration agent, with the concurrence of a supervisor, to bar non-citizens from the United States for five years if, in their judgment, the individuals presented false documentation or misrepresented themselves. Canadians should be aware that lying to a border official is a serious offence.

Expedited removal is part of comprehensive reforms intended to control illegal immigration. There is no formal appeal process under expedited removal but, if you believe the law has been misapplied in your case, you can request a supervisory review by writing to the INS district director responsible for the port of entry where the decision was made. Cases of possible misapplication should also be brought to the attention of the Consular Affairs Bureau of the Department of Foreign Affairs and International Trade in Ottawa, at 1-800-387-3124 or (613) 943-1055 or at the nearest Canadian consulate.

8. Pre-clearance

Under a Canada-U.S. agreement, U.S. Immigration has pre-clearance facilities at seven Canadian airports: Vancouver, Calgary, Edmonton, Winnipeg, Toronto, Montréal (Dorval) and Ottawa. To allow sufficient time for the pre-clearance process when you are travelling to the United States from these airports, you should be at the U.S. Immigration desk at least one hour before your flight. Pre-clearance facilities are also available at the Victoria, British Columbia, ferry terminal for travel to Port Angeles in Washington state. Again, you should allow extra time for this process.

As a Canadian using American pre-clearance facilities, you are still required to meet American entry requirements. American officials here are authorized to inspect your luggage and can refuse your entry into the United States. While you are on Canadian soil, you have rights under the *Charter of Rights and Freedoms,* subject to Canadian law, including those laws governing drugs and guns. Refusal to co-operate with American officials may result in your being refused entry to the United States.

9. American Border Fees

American border officials collect a US$6 per-person fee, payable only in American dollars, to issue an Arrival/Departure Document, Form I-94. This form is distributed to Canadian citizens and landed immigrants from member countries of the Commonwealth and Ireland who are entering the United States to study or work and to visitors from other countries. The fee does not apply to Canadian citizens and landed immigrants from member countries of the Commonwealth and Ireland who are entering the United States on temporary visits for business or pleasure, or to travellers arriving in the United States by air.

D. IMMIGRATION REGULATIONS

The following is a summary of the immigration regulations for people travelling or living in the United States.

1. Moving to the United States Part-time

Many Canadian Snowbirds live in the U.S. Sunbelt states for up to six months a year, during Canada's coldest months. There are tax and other considerations if you wish to stay longer. If you intend to stay only up to six months and you are a Canadian citizen, you will have no difficulty with U.S. immigration regulations as long as you have the proper documentation. The process is very simple. You simply declare your intention at a U.S. point of entry. Remember to bring your passport, of course, as well as other photo ID.

As a separate issue, you could be considered a U.S. resident for tax purposes only, even though you are still a Canadian citizen, if you stay in the United States for more than a set number of days a year over several years. This topic is discussed in Chapter 6.

2. Moving to the United States Full-time

There are many implications of moving to the United States full-time. You have to consider issues such as tax, estate planning, financial planning, pensions, housing and health costs, cost of living, as well as possibly leaving friends and family. There are different implications, depending on whether you are living full-time in the United States, permanently or temporarily, and the nature of your stay—for example, whether you are retired, working, or investing in the country. There are also distinct societal and governmental differences between Canada and the United States that become more apparent if you are living in the United States full-time.

Refer to Chapter 11 for a detailed discussion of the factors to consider when retiring outside Canada full-time.

Here are the steps to take if you want to explore the process of emigrating to the United States, remaining there over six months, working as a business visitor or professional, or entering under a trader or investor category:

- Contact the closest U.S. Immigration and Naturalization Service (INS) to get information and find out if you are eligible and the procedures to follow. Refer to item 23 in Appendix A.

- Contact the closest U.S. Consulate or U.S. Embassy if you wish to enter the United States under a trader or investor category. They will advise you as to your eligibility. Refer to item 16 in Appendix A for U.S. Consulates in Canada.

- Contact the U.S. Internal Revenue Service (IRS) to determine the tax implications of living full-time in the United States. The IRS is equivalent to Revenue Canada and has an office in Ottawa. Refer to item 21 in Appendix A.

- Contact Revenue Canada to determine the tax implications if you are leaving Canada to live full-time in the United States. Refer to item 1 in Appendix A.

- Contact Health Canada (item 4 in Appendix A) and your provincial office for seniors (item 11) to determine the implications for federal pensions or federal and provincial medicare coverage.

- Contact your employer/union/association retirement benefit plan to determine the implications of living full-time in the United States.

- Contact a lawyer in Canada who specializes in immigration law relating to emigrating to the United States or living there full-time. Contact your local lawyer referral service or look in the Yellow Pages of your phone book under Lawyers. You may also want to obtain a second opinion from a U.S. immigration lawyer. Ask your lawyer to give you a referral for U.S. lawyers who are experts on wills and estate issues, real estate, and so on so that you can have your interests looked after for continuity before departure and after your arrival in the United States. Refer to Chapter 8 for information about selecting professional advisors in both Canada and the United States.

- Contact a professional accountant in Canada who specializes in tax to obtain customized advice for your situation. Most major international chartered accountancy firms have experts on the tax issues of Canadians living part-time or full-time in the United States. You may also want to have a second opinion from a U.S. Certified Public Accountant (CPA) who is an expert on cross-border tax issues. Arrange to have a referral to a U.S. accountant in the area where you will be living who is a tax expert. You want to have continuity of advice before leaving Canada. Refer to Chapter 8 for further information.

- Contact an objective, professional financial planner to give you customized assessment and advice after you move to the United States full-time. Again, refer to Chapter 8 for further information about selecting a financial planner. If you are staying in the United States full-time on a temporary basis—in other words, if you still have a cross-border connection with Canada—you will want to maintain a relationship with a professional financial planner in Canada.

- Read *Immigrating to the U.S.A.*, written by two U.S. immigration lawyers, Dan Danilov and Howard Deutsch, and published by Self-Counsel Press. Make sure you have the most current edition. This book will give you a good overview of the key concepts and regulations.

- Read the booklets on the tax aspects for Canadians working or doing business in the United States that are available free from international accountancy firms. Refer to item 4 in Appendix B.

- Subscribe to the newsletter published by Richard Brunton, CPA, called *Brunton's U.S. Tax Letter for Canadians.* For information, contact (561) 241-9991 or 1-800-325-2922. Write to him at 4710 N.W. Boca Raton Blvd. #101, Boca Raton, Florida, 33431, U.S.A.

3. Different U.S. Immigration Categories

You can become a citizen or lawful permanent resident of the United States through derivative citizenship, family, employment, investment, or business. Immigration procedures are highly technical, so you should retain an immigration lawyer experienced in U.S. immigration to assist you.

a) Derivative U.S. Citizenship

This concept means that you are entitled to obtain U.S. citizenship through ancestry. Perhaps you have ancestors or distant relatives who were U.S. citizens before their death. If you think you do, research your family tree and archival documents and records. You can hire professionals who do this type of research. After you have all the documentation and facts available, speak to a U.S. immigration lawyer.

b) Family-Based Immigration

There are various ways that U.S. citizens or lawful permanent residents can bring their relatives into the United States under the family category. Some of the categories have an annual numerical limit and others don't.

- **Immediate relative**
  There is no limit on the number of people who can be sponsored under this category. It includes the children, spouse, and parents of a U.S. citizen. The U.S. citizen must be at least 21 years of age. Children are defined as unmarried persons under 21 years of age who are legitimate or legally legitimized children, adopted, or stepchildren.

- **Nonimmediate relative**
  This category has annual quotas, and members of this category are ranked in order of preference. There are four preference levels. First is an unmarried son or daughter over the age of 21 of a U.S. citizen. Second is a spouse of a lawful permanent resident alien or an unmarried son or daughter of a lawful permanent resident alien. Third is a married son or daughter of a U.S.

citizen. The fourth preference level is a brother or sister of a U.S. citizen who is over 21 years of age.

c) Employment-Based Immigration

This form of immigrant visa has four levels of preference. There are annual quotas in each category except for returning U.S. legal permanent residents or former U.S. citizens seeking reinstatement of citizenship.

The first preference is for priority workers, that is, people of extraordinary ability, outstanding professors and researchers, and multinational executives and managers. The second preference is for a professional with an advanced degree or exceptional ability. The third preference is for a professional without an advanced degree, a skilled worker, or an unskilled worker. The last and fourth preference is for what is called special immigrants, including religious workers and returning U.S. legal permanent residents or former U.S. citizens seeking reinstatement of citizenship.

d) Investor Immigration

The U.S. government wants to attract investors from other countries and, if the conditions are met, will give them an immigrant visa. The reason is to stimulate economic activity and employment. Canada has the same type of foreign investor interest, as do most other countries. Canadians wishing to make a business investment in the United States may qualify for this immigrant visa. It is referred to as a fifth preference category (E-5) and has an annual limit. In addition, the Canada-U.S. *Free Trade Agreement* (FTA), which has been superseded for the most part by the *North American Free Trade Agreement* (NAFTA), gives Treaty Trader (E-1) and Treaty Investor (E-2) status to Canadian nonimmigrant investors.

A Canadian may qualify under the E-5 category of immigrant visa if certain criteria are met. These could include establishing and investing in a business and employing at least 10 U.S. workers full-time. Depending on the location and need, the financial investment required could range from $500,000 to $1 million.

e) Business Travellers Under the Canada-U.S. *Free Trade Agreement* (FTA) and the *North American Free Trade Agreement* (NAFTA)

The FTA became effective on January 1, 1989, and was designed to facilitate trade and travel between the two countries. The agreement respecting various categories of business travellers is designed for nonimmigrants who could be living full-time in the United States. The FTA affects only temporary entrants into the United States. It is possible, however, that a history of operating under one of these categories could facilitate a subsequent application for an immigrant visa under another category. Spouses and children accompanying business travellers must satisfy normal admission requirements and cannot work or study (as full-time students) in the United States without prior authorization.

NAFTA became effective on January 1, 1994 and was designed to facilitate trade and travel between Canada, the U.S., and Mexico. It incorporated, for the most part, the provisions of the previous FTA.

There are several categories, the four main ones being:

- **Business visitor (B-1 status)**
  Canadian citizens who visit the United States on business for their Canadian company and receive remuneration from their Canadian employer.

- **Intra-company transfer (L-1 status)**
  A person who has been employed continuously for at least one year by a Canadian firm, as executive, manager, or specialist. This person can render services temporarily to the same firm (or its subsidiary or affiliate) in the United States. The position has to be in an executive or managerial capacity, or in a position of special knowledge.

- **Professionals (TC-1 status)**
  A Canadian professional, with an approved occupation, travelling to the United States to work temporarily in the profession for which they are qualified.

- **Traders and Investors (E-1 and E-2 visas)**
  A trader who works in a Canadian-owned or -controlled firm in the United States that carries on substantial trade in goods or services, principally between Canada and the United States. The position must be supervisory or executive, or involve skill essential to the operation of the U.S. firm.

  An investor who has invested, or is in the process of investing, a substantial amount of capital in the United States, must develop and direct the operation of the business in the United States.

4. Are You Unknowingly a U.S. Citizen?

U.S. citizens are taxed differently than citizens of other countries, and must file U.S. income tax returns regardless of where they live in the world, unless their income is below the minimum filing amount. Also, they are subject to U.S. gift and estate tax on their worldwide property regardless of where they live.

Many Canadians are U.S. citizens without knowing it. They may not realize they may have a birthright claim to citizenship. Refer to the previous discussion on derivative citizenship. Alternatively, some believe erroneously they have lost their U.S. citizenship. If you were a U.S. citizen and think you have lost your citizenship, here is what you need to know.

To lose U.S. citizenship, you must perform an "expatriating act" (for example, taking out Canadian citizenship), and as a result, obtain a Certificate of Loss of Nationality (CLN) from the U.S. Department of State. Therefore, even if you *think* you have lost U.S. citizenship, perhaps by becoming a Canadian citizen, you have not necessarily. You have not lost your U.S. citizenship unless you actually requested and received a CLN.

If you are a "former" U.S. citizen who took out Canadian citizenship and do not wish to be a U.S. citizen, make certain that you get a CLN, or you may be subject to unexpected U.S. income, gift, or estate tax. You can apply now for your CLN and it will be retroactive to the day you performed an "expatriating act."

On the other hand, if you were issued a CLN but now regret losing your U.S. citizenship, it may be possible for you to reclaim it. Prior to November 14, 1986, U.S. law did not allow dual citizenship, and a CLN may have been issued to you simply because you became a Canadian citizen, even though you had no desire to give up U.S. citizenship.

But the law was changed in 1986. Now dual citizenship is allowed and people do not automatically lose their U.S. citizenship unless they voluntarily give up U.S. citizenship. Further, if you previously lost your U.S. citizenship, you can apply to have it restored on the basis you did not intend to give up U.S. citizenship when you performed the expatriating act. If your application is allowed, your citizenship is restored retroactively, and you are considered to have been a U.S. citizen from your date of birth or original naturalization.

However, in the above case, you would want to thoroughly check out the U.S. tax implications of having your citizenship restored, before you commence the process. For example, would you need to retroactively file U.S. tax returns for all those prior years? Obtain expert professional tax advice on the effects, in advance.

5. Renouncing U.S. Citizenship

Occasionally a U.S. citizen residing outside the United States with no plans to return to live there, may decide that renouncing U.S. citizenship is preferable to the continuing tax and other regulatory obligations to which he/she is subject. A person may voluntarily give up U.S. citizenship by performing one of the following "expatriating acts" with the *intention* of relinquishing U.S. nationality:

- Becoming naturalized in another country
- Formally declaring allegiance to another country
- Serving in a foreign army
- Serving in certain types of foreign government employment
- Making a formal renunciation of nationality before a U.S. diplomatic or consular officer in a foreign country
- Making a formal renunciation of nationality in the United States during a time of war or
- Committing an act of treason.

If you wish to formally renounce U.S. citizenship you must execute an oath of renunciation before a consular officer, and your citizenship is nullified, effective on the date the oath is executed. In all other cases, your citizenship is revoked effective on the date the expatriating act was committed, even though it may not be documented until later. The U.S. State Department will document loss of citizenship in such cases when you acknowledge to a consular officer that the expatriating act was taken with the requisite intent.

To officially document your loss of citizenship you must apply for a Certificate of Loss of Nationality (CLN), and the consular officer will submit it to the State Department in Washington for approval. Before issuing the CLN the State Department will review the file to confirm:

- You were a U.S. citizen
- An expatriating act was committed
- The act was undertaken voluntarily
- You had the intent of relinquishing citizenship when the expatriating act was committed.

6. Working Part-time in the U.S.

If you want to earn some income while you are enjoying your Snowbird lifestyle, be wary. To work in the U.S., you need to have a green card. There are various ways that you may be eligible to apply for it, for example, if your spouse or one of your parents are U.S. citizens. Another way of being able to work in the U.S., is under provisions of the Canada/U.S. *Free Trade Agreement*. There are provisions which allow Canadians to work in the U.S. under that agreement if you adhere to certain strict criteria, for example, if you have a business in Canada and want to start a U.S. division.

If you work in the U.S. illegally, that is, work there without conforming to the above requirements, the penalties are heavy and not worth the risk. The U.S. Immigration and Naturalization Service (INS) can turf you out of the country and, depending on how seriously they view the infraction, they could deny entry for one to 10 years, or even permanently.

If you wish to explore the work option, even part-time, the best thing to do is to speak to a U.S. immigration attorney about your wishes. Most initial consultations are free, but ask in advance. Simply look in the Yellow Pages of your local telephone directory for lawyers specializing in immigration matters. Make sure that you receive at least three opinions from these experts before you decide on your next step. You want to ensure that the customized advice that you are getting is consistent. In addition, there are potential tax implications, so you would need to speak to a cross-border tax specialist as well.

E. CUSTOMS REGULATIONS

1. Travelling to the United States

If you are a resident of Canada on a visit to the United States as a Snowbird for up to six months, your U.S. customs status is that of a nonresident. There are various regulations involved, exemptions permitted, and privileges allowed.

If you are arriving in the United States by land, air, or sea, a simple oral declaration that the allowed exemptions from duty apply to you is generally sufficient. In certain situations you might be requested to fill out a written declaration. Make sure you bring your passport with you.

The following is a discussion of the main areas you need to know. Contact the U.S. Customs Service for further information and free explanatory brochures. Refer to item 22 in Appendix A. Since regulations can change, make sure you have current information from the U.S. Customs Service.

a) Exemptions

Here are some of the main federal exemptions for nonresidents of the United States:

- *Personal effects* are exempt from duty if they are for your personal use, are owned by you, and accompany you to the United States.
- *Alcoholic beverages* are free of duty and internal revenue tax if they are for personal use and do not exceed one litre. Some state alcoholic beverage laws may be more restrictive than federal liquor laws.
- *Vehicles* can be temporarily imported to the United States for one year or less if they are used for transportation for you, your family, or your guests.
- *Household effects* are free from duty if they are for your personal use and not for another person or for sale.

b) Gifts

There are several exemptions under this category:

- *Gifts you bring with you* are free of duty or tax if you are remaining in the United States for at least 72 hours and if the gifts do not exceed US$100 in retail value. This $100 exemption can be claimed once every six months. Alcoholic beverages are not included. Articles bought in so-called duty-free shops are subject to U.S. Customs duty and restrictions if they exceed your exemption.
- *Gifts sent by mail* are free of duty if they are mailed from Canada to the United States, and do not exceed US$50 in retail value. You may send as many gifts as you wish, but if they are all sent to the same U.S. addressee, there will be duty payable if the daily receipt of gifts exceeds $50. Packages should be marked "unsolicited gift" with the name of donor, nature of the gift, and fair retail value of the gift clearly written on the outside of the package.

c) Items Subject to Duty

If you import items to the United States that cannot be claimed under the allowed exemptions, they will be subject to applicable duty and tax. After deducting your exemptions and the value of any duty-free articles, a flat rate of duty of 10 percent will be applied to the next US$1,000 worth (fair retail value) of merchandise. If you exceed $1,000 worth, you will be charged duty at various rates, depending on the item. The flat rate of duty applies only if the items are for personal use or for gifts.

d) Shipping Goods

You do not need to accompany personal and household effects to the United States that are entitled to free entry. You can have them shipped to your United States address at a later time if it is more convenient. You do not need to use a customs broker to clear your shipment through Customs. You may do this yourself after you arrive in the United States or designate a friend or relative to represent you in Customs matters. If you take the latter route, you must give your representative a letter addressed to the Officer in Charge of Customs authorizing that person to represent you as your agent on a one-time basis in clearing your shipment through Customs. You have five working days to clear your shipment through Customs after its arrival in the United States; otherwise, it will be sent, at your expense and risk, to a storage warehouse.

e) Money

There is no limit on the total amount of money you can bring into or take out of the United States. If you are carrying more than US$10,000 into or out of the country at any one time, however, you must file a report with U.S. Customs. This rule applies to currency, traveller's cheques, money orders, and so on.

f) Prohibited and Restricted Items

Because U.S. Customs inspectors are stationed at ports of entry, they are frequently required to enforce laws and requirements of other U.S. government agencies in order to protect community health, to preserve domestic plant and animal life, and for other reasons.

There are several prohibited or restricted categories that you should be aware of. Here are a few of them:

- **Medicine and narcotics**

  Narcotics are normally prohibited entry and are tightly regulated. However, if you require medicines containing habit-forming drugs or narcotics (e.g., cough medicine, diuretics, heart drugs, tranquillizers, sleeping pills, depressants, stimulants), you should:

  - have all drugs, medicines, and similar products properly identified;
  - carry only the quantity that might normally be used for the length of your stay in the United States for health problems requiring such drugs or medicine; and
  - have either a prescription or a written statement from your personal physician that the medicine is being used under a doctor's direction and is necessary for your physical well-being while travelling or staying in the United States.

- **Pets**
  Cats and dogs can be brought in, but they must be free of evidence of communicable diseases. If you plan to bring your pet, obtain a copy of the leaflet, *Pets, Wildlife.* Refer to item 25 in Appendix A.

- **Wildlife and fish**
  These are subject to certain import and export restrictions, prohibitions, permits, and so on. Any part of certain types of wildlife or fish, or products and articles manufactured from them, could be affected, especially endangered species, which are prohibited from being imported or exported. If you are in doubt as to whether certain leather goods, skins, or furs are governed by the regulations, contact the U.S. Fish and Wildlife Service. Refer to item 25, Appendix A for a contact address and brochure.

- **Food products**
  Certain food products might be restricted. If you are in doubt, contact the U.S. Department of Agriculture Animal and Plant Inspection Service. Refer to item 24 in Appendix A.

- **Fruits, vegetables, plants**
  Every fruit, vegetable, or plant being brought into the United States is supposed to be declared to the Customs officer in case it is a restricted item.

2. Returning to Canada

When you return to Canada after your U.S. Snowbird stay, there are various regulations that you must comply with. As far as the Canadian government is concerned, if you have not been out of the country for more than six months, you are still a resident Canadian citizen. If you have been out of the country more than six months or you are a U.S. citizen resident in Canada, other customs regulations could apply. These customs regulations cover such matters as bringing back goods and vehicles. For vehicles, Transport Canada's regulations also must be considered. For further information, refer to the Canada Customs contact numbers and free explanatory publications outlined in item 2, Appendix A. Also refer to item 3 for information about Transport Canada. Obtain current information, since regulations can change.

Here is a summary of the key regulations:

a) Bringing Back Goods Purchased in the United States

The *North American Free Trade Agreement* (NAFTA) continues to gradually eliminate the duty that applies to goods you acquire in the United States. Your goods qualify for the lower U.S. duty rate under NAFTA if they are:

- for personal use; and
- marked as made in the U.S. or Canada; or
- not marked or labelled to indicate that they were made anywhere other than in the U.S. or Canada.

If the goods you acquire in the U.S. are marked "Made in Mexico," the Mexican duty rate will apply. Refer to Chapter 9 on Snowbirding in Mexico.

If you do not qualify for a personal exemption or if you exceed that limit, you will have to pay the goods and services tax (GST) over and above any duty or other taxes that may apply on the portion not eligible under your personal exemption.

- **Personal exemptions**
  You are entitled to your basic duty-free and tax-free exemptions of CDN$750 after a seven-day absence outside Canada, and CDN$200 after 48 hours. The 7 day rate was increased as of July 15, 1999. In addition, you can also benefit from the low special duty rate which applies to the next $300 worth of goods beyond your personal exemption, as long as these goods accompany you and are not alcohol or tobacco products. However, you still have to pay the GST. The special duty rate of 1.4 percent on eligible goods imported from the United States, works out to 8.5 percent when combined with the GST. Because it is constantly changing, check the current duty rate. Pick up a copy of the Revenue Canada brochure called *I Declare* for more information on personal exemptions.

- **Prohibited, restricted, or controlled goods**
  Canada limits or prohibits the importation of certain things. These can include cultural property which has historical significance in its country of origin, animals on the endangered species list (and any products made from them), certain food and agricultural products, and goods considered harmful to the environment.

  There are also limits on the amounts of certain food products you can bring into Canada at the low duty rates or that you can include in your personal exemption. If you bring back quantities of these products above the set limits, you will have to pay a very high rate of duty (from 150 to 350 percent), and may also need an agricultural inspection certificate. The following are some examples of the limits that apply:

— two dozen eggs;
— $20 (Canadian funds) worth of dairy products, such as milk, cheese, and butter;
— three kilograms of margarine; and
— 20 kilograms of meat and meat products, including turkey and chicken. Within the 20-kilogram limit, further restrictions apply as follows: a maximum of one whole turkey or 10 kilograms of turkey products; and a maximum of 10 kilograms of chicken. All meat and meat products have to be identified as products of the United States.

- **Alcohol and tobacco**
  You can import alcohol and tobacco products if the quantity is within the limits set by the province or territory. You cannot import alcohol products

duty-free and tax-free unless you have been outside Canada for at least 48 hours and qualify for a personal exemption. If you do not qualify for a personal exemption, or if you exceed the limit, you will have to pay the import duties and the provincial or territorial taxes that apply on the portion not eligible under your personal exemption.

- **Making your declaration**
  Prepare a list of all the goods you bought in the United States, and keep sales receipts. This will make it easier and faster to declare all these goods when you return to Canada. You will also find it easier to claim any personal exemption to which you are entitled. When you present your list and receipts, the customs officer may then work out your personal exemption and any duties you owe in the way that benefits you most. Don't forget to have your identification ready, showing your name and address.

- **Paying duties**
  You can pay by cash, travellers' cheque, VISA, MasterCard, or by personal cheque if the amount is not more than $500. In some cases, Revenue Canada may accept a personal cheque for up to $2,500 as long as you can produce adequate identification.

- **Value of goods**
  Revenue Canada will include any state taxes you have paid on your goods when determining their value, and will use the *prevailing* exchange rate to convert the total to Canadian funds. The customs officer will calculate duty on this Canadian value.

- **Goods and services tax (GST)**
  If you buy goods beyond your personal exemption, GST applies to them, just as if you had purchased them in Canada. GST is payable on the "value for tax," which is made up of the value (see previous explanation), plus the duty, plus any excise tax which applies.

- *General Agreement on Tariffs and Trade* **(GATT)**
  New provisions under GATT became effective on January 1, 1995. Customs duties on a wide range of products originating in non-NAFTA countries were eliminated or will be reduced to zero over a period of time (up to 10 years). NAFTA goods also qualify for the GATT rate, so if the rate of duty payable on the goods you are importing is lower under GATT than under NAFTA, customs officers will automatically assess the lower rate.

  There was also a change affecting the quantities or the dollar value of certain food products that you can import into Canada. As of January 1, 1995, you can import meat, dairy, and other products beyond the set limits, but, as mentioned earlier, a very high rate of duty will apply (ranging from 150 to 350 percent of the value of the product). If you do not want to pay the applicable import duty, you can either return the goods to the U.S. or leave them at a Revenue Canada customs office.

For more information on GATT and its impact on duty rates, contact the nearest Revenue Canada customs office.

- **Provincial sales tax (PST)**

  Depending on the agreements between the provinces and Ottawa, Revenue Canada may collect any PST for goods you import that do not qualify under your duty-free and tax-free exemption. In addition, in most provinces and territories across Canada, Revenue Canada collects special provincial or territorial assessments on alcohol and tobacco products that do not qualify under your duty-free and tax-free exemption.

- **Duty-free items**

  Duty-free (regardless of origin)

Aluminum baseball bats	Fax machines
Automatic toasters	Indoor smokeless barbecues
Binoculars	Irons (household)
Cameras (instant-print, video)	Microwave ovens (household)
Cameras (35-mm single lens reflex)	Rice cookers
Camera lenses	Sewing machines
Clothes dryers	Software (diskettes/CD-ROMs)
Compact disc players (audio)	Squash, racquetball racquets
Computer printers	Telephone answering machines
Curling irons	Television converters
Electronic flash apparatus	Tennis racquets
Electronic games (hand-held, video)	Typewriters (electric)
Electronic organizers	VCRs

  Duty-free (if eligible for the U.S. duty rate)

Coffee-makers (domestic)	Furniture
Computers (laptop, processing units, and input/output units)	Motorcycle body parts
	Pet food (dogs, cats, etc.)
Electric blankets	Silverware (cutlery, dishes)
Jewellery (gold, silver)	Tableware (ceramic, porcelain)
Leather bags, handbags, wallets	Telephones (including cellular)

As mentioned earlier, if the goods you acquire in the United States are marked "Made in Mexico," the Mexican duty rate will apply.

b) Bringing Back Cars, RVs, Trucks, and Other Vehicles Purchased in the United States

Special restrictions and import procedures apply to motor vehicles. For more information, see the Revenue Canada brochure, *Importing a Motor Vehicle into Canada*. Also contact the Registrar of Imported Vehicles in advance at 1-800-511-7755, toll-free from Canada and the U.S.

If you bought a new or used car, truck, trailer, or motor home in the United States, you will have to pay import assessments when you return to Canada.

These include duty and excise tax if the vehicle is air-conditioned, or if it is a passenger vehicle weighing over 4,425 pounds (2,007 kg). In addition, you would have to pay the federal goods and services tax (GST) of seven percent and any applicable provincial sales or other taxes. Check with your provincial government.

The duty rate for eligible vehicles imported from the United States that fall under the Canada-U.S. *Free Trade Agreement* (NAFTA), that is, vehicles made in the United States or Canada, is reduced every year. If the vehicle was not made in the United States or Canada and therefore does not fall under the NAFTA, then the duty is higher. Check on the current rates.

To determine the value of the vehicle for duty purposes, the original U.S. purchase price, including state sales tax and other applicable costs, will be converted into Canadian funds. That amount will vary, of course, depending on the exchange rate at the time. If you import a new vehicle within 30 days of the date it was delivered to you, the above formula applies, with no deduction for depreciation. If you purchased a new vehicle and imported it within one year of the date of delivery to you, however, you can deduct an amount for depreciation of the value of the car. Make enquiries. You can't obtain depreciation for a car that was purchased used. For a used car, the fair market value will be set according to vehicle values from a neutral source—for example, the U.S. or Canadian *Automobile Red Book*. If you have traded your old car in for a different car, the value of the new car will be a used value.

Make sure you have all receipts with you and any bill of sale. Ideally, have a current fair market value done on dealership letterhead, if you bought the vehicle from a dealership. You do not want to declare an artificially low value for the vehicle or have receipts that are clearly way below market value. The reason: if you underestimate the vehicle value, Canada Customs can seize the vehicle and impound it until you pay a penalty of 40 percent of the correct value of the vehicle. In that event, you have a 30-day period to make a written appeal, but it could take up to a year or more to adjudicate, and in the meantime you are out your car or penalty money. To avoid any stress or uncertainty, contact Canada Customs beforehand if you have any questions or doubts in your particular circumstances.

For further information about determining vehicle value for Customs purposes, contact the Canada Customs office closest to your expected point of entry or phone 1-800-461-9999 (toll-free in Canada only). Do this before you arrive at Customs. Refer to item 2 in Appendix A.

c) Transport Canada Vehicle Prohibitions

As of January 1, 1993, as a result of the FTA, and subsequently NAFTA, there are no longer any Customs prohibitions on bringing a vehicle into Canada from the United States. There are restrictive importation rules for vehicles under Transport Canada regulations, however. Because of strict Canadian safety and emission standards, you may be prohibited from importing a vehicle that only meets U.S. standards, unless it is brought up to full Canadian compliance standards.

To satisfy yourself that the vehicle you want to import is eligible and to find out what documents you require, contact 1-800-511-7755 before you buy the vehicle. This number is for the Registrar of Imported Vehicles and is toll-free from Canada and the United States. Their web site is http://www.riv.com. The registry was formed by Transport Canada in April 1995, although it is operated independently of government. There is an administrative charge of approximately $195–$245, plus GST, depending on your port of entry. This fee is to process the necessary approval documentation. Refer to item 3 in Appendix A for a list of free explanatory publications.

TIPS BEFORE LEAVING CANADA

- Take your passport and birth certificate with you if you are having an extended stay in the United States.
- If you are considering staying in the United States more than six months in the year, check with the U.S. Immigration and Naturalization Services (INS) and with an experienced cross-border tax accountant on the tax implications. Also check with a Canadian immigration lawyer experienced in U.S. immigration matters before you depart. Refer to Chapter 8, on selecting professional advisors.
- Check with U.S. Customs for the current policy on items you think might be prohibited or restricted in the United States. Ask about exemptions, shipping goods, and items that could be subject to duty.
- If you are considering buying a vehicle in the United States, check Customs and Transport Canada regulations for returning to Canada with the vehicle. Do this before you buy the vehicle. Also check with the Registrar of Imported Vehicles.
- Check with Canada Customs on the current policy for bringing back goods purchased in the United States. What items are duty-free and what items are not?
- Take receipts for items that have a high dollar value, in case you are challenged on your return to Canada. It is good to have proof that you bought a camera or expensive jewellery in Canada.

CHAPTER

4

Housing and Real Estate

A. INTRODUCTION

There are many towns and RV or mobile home parks built specifically for retired people and Snowbirds in selected locations in the United States. Some of the advantages include the opportunity to live and socialize in a homogeneous community; planned social activities such as bingo, dancing, crafts, card games, trips, and educational programs; recreational facilities such as tennis courts, exercise rooms, a swimming pool, and golf and shuffle-board areas; services such as maintenance services and shopping and transportation facilities; and religious services. Security is another reason for the popularity of retirement communities. Many have 24-hour security services, which keep watch on the residences and check all visitors when they enter or leave. Refer to item 33 in Appendix A for a schedule of activities of a sample mobile home/RV park.

Retirement communities have some drawbacks, however. For example, some communities are becoming crowded and increasingly costly. Some people don't enjoy planned activities and lessons. Others feel too isolated in communities that are far away from urban centres.

By identifying your own needs and wants, speaking to others, and doing your research, you will quickly determine what choice is the right one for you.

This chapter provides an overview of the considerations you should keep in mind when buying a house, apartment, condominium, townhouse, timeshare, mobile home, or recreational vehicle in the United States. Also covered is an overview of the home purchase process in the U.S., including terminology, types of property ownership, and obtaining a U.S. mortgage. The perils of selling your own home yourself is also discussed. Refer to Chapter 6 for a discussion of the tax consequences of renting or selling your house or condo and of owning real estate in the United States if you die. In addition, refer to Chapter 8 for how to select a realtor.

For more detailed information on issues related to real estate, refer to my other books published by McGraw-Hill Ryerson, including *Canadian Home Buying Made Easy* (2ⁿᵈ edition), *Condo Buying Made Easy* (2ⁿᵈ edition), *Mortgages Made Easy, Mortgage Payment Tables Made Easy*, and *Making Money in Real Estate*.

B. THE PURCHASE PROCESS

1. Overview

When a potential buyer and seller wish to conclude a transaction, they will normally finalize the agreement by jointly signing a "contract for sale and purchase." In Canada, this document is often referred to as an "agreement of purchase and sale." Whatever terminology is used, the document describes the details and terms of the transaction, such as which party will pay the various expenses involved and when the contract will be finalized.

The transaction is usually finalized at the closing, when both parties normally approve and sign the settlement statement prepared by the closing agent. The settlement or closing statement, (often referred to as the statement of adjustments in Canada) summarizes the financial aspects of the transaction. It lists the sale price, the expenses included, the prorations, and it displays the net amount of money due from the buyer to the seller.

The closing agent, sometimes referred to as an escrow agent, is the individual or business, usually a lawyer (or attorney in the U.S.) or title insurance agent, who organizes and conducts the closing. Closings are often conducted entirely by mail.

The expenses of the transaction include the documentary stamps, (a government land transfer tax), intangible tax (a tax on any mortgages involved), title insurance or abstract fees, as applicable, legal fees, real estate commission, fees to record documents, and other expenses. The buyer often receives title insurance to ensure clear title to the property. In some counties and states, as an alternative to title insurance, the chain of title (abstract of title) will be examined to ensure the title is clear.

The prorations are the apportioning of direct property expenses between the buyer and seller for the portion of time the property is owned by each. This includes expenses such as the current year's property taxes and the current period's condominium or homeowner's association maintenance fees, where applicable. At the closing the seller will also sign a deed to formally transfer the property to the buyer. The closing agent will then send the new deed to the county for recording, after which it is sent on to the buyer.

If you are thinking of selling your home, the individual you engage to sell your real estate is generally referred to as a real estate agent or broker or, if he/she belongs to the National Association of Realtors, may also be referred to as a Realtor. There are brokers for both sellers and buyers. It can be helpful to be aware which type is assisting you so you can better evaluate their objectivity.

If you wish to offer your real estate for sale through a broker, you will likely sign some form of listing agreement with them. It will state the terms under which your property will be offered for sale, including the rate of the commission.

2. U.S. Terminology for Real Estate Transactions

Here is more detail on the process and jargon used in the U.S. Although there may be different terms used in some states, the concepts are similar.

a) Escrow Agent

The escrow agents' function is to serve as the depository of both funds and documents. They are responsible for processing and coordinating their flow, as well as for obtaining approvals from both parties, as required. They secure title insurance, and prorate and adjust for taxes, insurance and rents. They record the deed and loan documents and are accountable for collecting and disbursing the monies to the appropriate parties.

b) Title Insurance

When a property is conveyed from one party to another, title insurance will be required. Two types of title insurance are generally issued, for the owner and the buyer. The owner's policy, which is paid for by the seller, ensures the buyer that they are receiving clear or "marketable" title to the property. A marketable title is one reasonably free of encumbrances and from risk of legal dispute over defects. The buyer's policy ensures the lender's loan position.

One of the first things an escrow agent will do after escrow instructions are completed, is begin searching the title, to assure that there are no claims or liens, and to check for restrictions, or reconveyances on the property, that have not been disclosed by the seller. A thorough evaluation and search of public records will be conducted by the title company, to ensure that no future claims arise.

Once all of the data are collected, and examined, a preliminary title report will be prepared for both the buyer and seller, along with a copy of the legal description of the property. The search continues through escrow, and prior to closing a commitment of title will be issued.

c) Seller's Disclosure

In some states, the law requires that sellers complete a property disclosure and deliver it to the buyer for review and approval within a set number of days after contract acceptance. It is on this document that the seller must disclose any known defaults of the property and indicate any work that has been done to it. Many provinces in Canada have a similar type of disclosure statement. The buyer has a set period from receipt of the disclosure to accept or disapprove it. Should you find any problems or have concerns about the information presented, address the matter immediately with the seller, their agent, or your lawyer.

d) Appraisal

The lender will demand an appraisal of the property by a certified appraiser, to prove that the sales price of the home is reasonable. The appraisal fee may be paid by either the buyer or seller, or split. Should the appraisal show that the sales price is too high, the buyer will have to either come up with the difference in cash or renegotiate with the seller. The appraisal will be sent directly to the lender for review, during their underwriting and loan processing.

e) Identity Statements

During the escrow process in some states, both the buyer(s) and seller(s) will be asked to complete a confidential identity statement. The purpose of this is to eliminate inaccurate data involving parties with the same or similar names. A name search will be run on both parties with state and federal authorities for tax liens, judgements, and bankruptcies.

f) Settlement Charges

The escrow agent will prepare a settlement statement of charges and send a copy to both the buyer and seller about a week before closing. This important financial statement summarizes the costs for both the buyer and seller, accounts for funds to be deposited and disbursed, makes adjustments, and indicates the amounts necessary to close escrow. Included within this statement are the prorations for taxes, interest and insurance. The total adjusted amounts to be paid by the borrower and the seller are shown, along with the amount of the net proceeds to be disbursed to the seller, after costs are paid.

g) Insurance

Prior to closing, you will need to make arrangements for homeowner insurance coverage and have proof of coverage sent to the escrow agent or lender. The escrow agent will generally collect for at least one year's premium in advance. If your down payment is less than 20 percent, you will need another type of insurance, called mortgage insurance. We have the same concept in Canada if you are putting less than 25 percent as a down payment. The lender requires that mortgage insurance to protect them against you defaulting on the loan, in which case, the insurance will cover the lender for any shortfall. The lender will instruct the escrow agent to collect the premium for this insurance through the escrow.

h) Final Inspection

Prior to close of escrow, you will be asked to conduct a final walk through, to assure that the property is in the same condition as when purchased, and that everything is in good working order. If it was agreed that something was to be repaired or added and you find that the work has not been done, advise your agent immediately so that it can be corrected, *before* you close escrow and take occupancy. In Canada this concept is not common. You don't customarily have the opportunity to approve the condition of the home before funds are released and possession occurs.

i) Closing Documentation

The date of closing is set in your contract, but may change due to a number of factors. For example, there can be delays due to title problems, the loan, the appraisal, inspections, insufficient funds in escrow, and missing signatures or documents. The final step in the escrow process is the recording of the documents, copies of which are sent to both the buyer and seller.

j) Trust Deeds

The principal instrument used to secure real property in many states is the trust deed, which is similar to a mortgage. The escrow agent will prepare the deeds, according to escrow instructions or the purchase contract. Signatures will be required by the parties at, or prior to, closing. Copies of the recorded documents will be sent to the seller, buyer, and lender.

k) Closing

All documents must be signed by the parties, proof of appropriate insurance provided, all inspections satisfactorily completed and all funds deposited into escrow to finalize a closing. Once everything is complete, the escrow agent will take the paperwork to the county registry office for recording, and the funds will be disbursed to the proper parties.

3. Types of Property Ownership

When a sales contract is written, the buyer is asked to choose how he/she wishes to take title to the property, or they may elect to determine this in escrow. In either case, the buyer must tell the escrow agent, and the information will be in all final escrow documents.

It's helpful to have an understanding of the forms of ownership available to you as an owner of real property. Depending on the state, there can be different terminology, but the concepts are similar. Ask about the options in the state you are purchasing property.

Select the type of ownership that best meets your needs. Consult your lawyer and professional accountant prior to making your selection, as there may be tax and estate consequences associated with each.

a) Severalty

This is an individual ownership by a person or a corporation.

b) Community Property

Not all states have community property laws, but Arizona and California, for example, do. There, if a husband and wife do not specify otherwise, it will be assumed that they are taking title as community property. This form of ownership is available only for a husband and wife, with each as equal partners, with a half interest in the property.

c) Joint Tenants With Right of Survivorship

This type of ownership is between two or more persons who take title with the right of survivorship. A single title is issued including all of the tenants' names, and each has equal ownership shares of the property. In the event that one party dies, their interest automatically goes to the other joint tenant(s). It therefore does not become an asset of the deceased's estate.

d) Tenants in Common

This form of ownership is for two or more individuals or entities, who take title without right of survivorship. The difference here, is that they do not have to have equal shares and that each party has its own separate title showing their portion of ownership. In the event that someone dies, their property interest becomes an asset of their estate. If they have a will, the will sets out what is to happen to that asset. If they don't have a will, the legislation of the state or province sets out the formula for dealing with assets of the deceased's estate.

4. Obtaining a U.S. Mortgage

Many mortgage companies provide loans for Canadians on the same basis as for U.S. citizens. Canadians receive "special" consideration because of the quality of the documentation that can be provided on the borrower's income and credit standing. Canadian tax returns are relatively easy for U.S. lenders to understand and analyse and Canada is one of the few places in the world where a resident's credit history is computerized and readily available to those authorized to make credit enquiries.

In many cases, Canadians can borrow up to 80 percent of the purchase price, at the same rates available to U.S. citizens. Canadian borrowers must provide the lender with their two most recent tax returns and evidence that they have sufficient cash on hand to complete the purchase. With some lenders, alternative documentation is acceptable. For example, a Canadian—particularly a self-employed individual—has the option of confirming his or her income with an accountant's letter, indicating taxable income for each of the last two years. Also, sometimes an employed individual can provide an employer's letter. In some cases, a letter of credit from your Canadian bank is acceptable.

The process of applying for a loan is quite simple. You are required to provide copies of the appropriate income confirmation discussed above, the contract to purchase the property and two month's bank statements showing where the needed funds are deposited. If you want a smaller amount of money, you could be eligible for a no income verification loan, which does not require you to provide documentation to verify your income. Obviously, excellent credit and substantial assets would need to be shown.

You do not have to be present in the U.S. to close. The deed and loan documents can be sent to you in Canada and executed in the presence of an appropriate notary or lawyer, and then returned to the U.S. for funding and recording.

C. BUYING A HOUSE

You may wish to buy a house in the U.S. Sunbelt that you intend to live in while you are there and leave vacant or possibly rent out the rest of the time. Maybe you hope to move to the United States at some point to live there full-time.

Whatever your motivation, there are some key steps to follow. You have probably already owned a house at some point, but the following tips and cautions bear repeating as a reminder. Many of these are equally applicable when selecting a condo.

1. Where to Find a Home for Sale

There are some preliminary considerations you need to work through before starting your search:

- Be clearly focused on what type of real estate you want in order to save time and stress.
- Target specific geographic area or areas. This means restricting your choices to specific communities or areas within a community. This makes your selection much easier and gives you an opportunity to get to know specific areas thoroughly. Obtain street maps of the areas.
- Know the price range that you want based on your funds and real estate needs.
- Determine the type of ideal purchase package that you want (e.g., price and terms) as well as your bottom-line fall-back position. What is the maximum you are willing to pay?
- Make comparisons and shortlist choices. That way you can ensure that you get the best deal.

There are various methods of finding out about what real estate is for sale. The most common methods are: word-of-mouth, using a real estate agent, reading local or real estate newspaper ads, or driving through the preferred neighbourhood and looking for For Sale signs.

2. General Tips When Looking for a Home

a) Location

One of the prime considerations is the location. How close is the property to cultural attractions, shopping centres, recreational facilities, community and religious facilities, and transportation? How attractive is the present development of the area surrounding the property? What is likely to happen in the future? Is there ample access to parking? Heavy traffic can be a noise nuisance as well as a hazard.

b) Pricing

The pricing of the property you are considering should be competitive with that of other, similar offerings. This can be difficult to determine unless you are comparing identical homes in a subdivision or condos in the same complex. If you are purchasing a condominium unit, for example, it is sometimes difficult to compare prices accurately without taking into account the different amenities that may be available in one condominium complex that are not available in the other—for example, tennis courts, swimming pool, and recreation centre. You may decide that you do not want these extra facilities, in which case paying an extra price for the unit because it has these features would not be attractive. At the same time, you have to look at the resale potential.

c) Knowledge of the Home and Neighbourhood

Surveys have shown that the average home buyer spends 17 minutes looking at the home before making the purchase decision, often making a decision on an emotional basis. Seventeen minutes is not enough time for anything other than a superficial look. Look at the property on several occasions to obtain a fresh perspective. Look at it in the day and evening. Look at the house when the owner is not present so that you can examine it thoroughly and at a leisurely pace. Bring a friend or relative with you. Take pictures outside and inside, if necessary, to enhance your recall if you are serious about buying the place. Drive around the neighbourhood to get a feeling for the appearance and conditions of other homes in the vicinity. If you wish to place an offer, remember to include a condition relating to inspection by a professional home inspector.

d) Reasons for Sale

An important factor to determine is why the property is for sale. Maybe the vendor knows something you don't that will have a bearing on your future interest. Or maybe the vendor is selling the home because of a desire to move to a larger or smaller home or a condo, because of loss of employment, or because of a serious illness or disability.

e) Property Taxes

Compare the costs of property taxes in the area that you are considering with those of other, equally attractive areas. Different municipalities have different tax rates, and there could be a considerable cost saving or expense. Also enquire as to whether there is any anticipated tax increase and why. For example, if the area is relatively new, there could be future property taxes or special levies to establish schools or other community support services.

f) Transportation

If you drive a car, how much traffic is there and how long would the commute take at various times of the day? Is public transportation available within walking distance? How reliable and frequent is it? Whether it is a bus, subway, rapid transit, freeway, ferry, or other mode of transportation, the quality of transportation will affect the quality of your life, as well as the resale price.

g) Crime Rate

Naturally this is an important issue. Check with the local police department for crime statistics in your area, and talk with neighbours on the street. Ask if there is a block watch or neighbourhood watch program in the area.

h) Services in the Community

Depending on your needs, you will want to check on the different services available in the community. A community will often be characterized by the local services. Is there adequate police, fire, and ambulance protection? Is there a hospital in the area? Are there doctors and dentists located in the vicinity? How often is garbage collected and streets maintained? Is mail delivered to your door or to a central mailbox location on your street or in your neighbourhood? If you wish to join an organization or club, is it close? Does the area cater to seniors or Snowbirds? Are there community centres or public parks nearby? Is there a place of worship of your faith in the neighbourhood? If the house or condo is proximate to a commercial development, are noise and traffic a problem? What types of businesses, stores, or services are nearby?

i) Climate

If you are buying for personal use, the issue of climate is important. Certain areas of your city or community may have more rain and higher wind than others, depending on climate patterns. Check with a local, state, or national weather bureau.

j) Parking

Is parking outdoors, in a garage, in an open carport, or underground? Is there sufficient lighting for security protection? Is it a long walk from the parking spot to your home? Is there parking space available for a recreational vehicle or second car? Is there ample parking for visitors in the lot or on the street? Is there a private driveway or back lane connected to the garage or carport? Is street parking restricted in any fashion (e.g., residents' parking only)? Is the restriction enforced? Do you need to buy a permit?

k) Topography

The layout of the land is an important consideration. If there is a hill along the property, water could collect around the base of the house, causing drainage problems. If water collects under the foundation of the house and there is only soil under the foundation, the house could settle.

l) Condition of Building and Property

Obtain an objective and accurate assessment of the condition of the property. Have an independent building inspector look at it. You can find a building inspector in the Yellow Pages of the phone book. In addition, the vendor should answer specific questions, posed by either the building inspector or you. You also want to make sure you include appropriate conditions in your agreement of purchase and sale for obtaining or confirming information.

m) Type of Construction

Is the building constructed of wood, brick, concrete, stone, or other material? Is this important for fire safety concerns you might have?

n) Common Elements and Facilities

If you are buying a condominium unit, review all the common elements that make up the condominium development. Consider whether these elements are relevant to your needs as well as what maintenance or operational costs might be required to service these features.

o) Noise

Thoroughly check the levels of noise. Consider such factors as location of highways, driveways, parking lots, playgrounds, and businesses. If you are buying a condominium, also consider the location of the garage doors, elevators, and garbage chutes, as well as the heating and air-conditioning plant or equipment.

p) Privacy

Privacy is an important consideration and has to be thoroughly explored. For example, you want to make sure that the sound insulation between the walls, floors, and ceilings of your property is sufficient to enable you to live comfortably without annoying your neighbours or having your neighbours annoy you. If you have a condominium or townhouse unit, such factors as the distance between your unit and other common areas, including walkways, parking lot, and fences, are important.

q) Storage Space

Is there enough closet and storage space? Is the location and size suitable? Are the kitchen, hall, and bedroom closets big enough for your needs? Are the basement or other storage areas large enough for sports and other equipment, tools, and outdoor furniture?

r) Heating/Cooling

How is the house heated or cooled—directly and indirectly? Is the system efficient for your needs (e.g., does it use natural gas, oil, forced air, hot water, radiators, electric baseboard, wood-burning stove, or fireplace)? How old is the furnace? Has it been serviced regularly and is it still covered by warranty? Do you have any air-conditioning or ceiling fans? Is there a heat exchanger system in the fireplace? What are the annual heating/cooling bills?

3. Questions to Ask

Address these common questions to your lawyer, real estate agent, vendor, and building inspector.

a) Questions of a General Nature

- Does the property contain unauthorized accommodation?
- Are you aware of any registered or unregistered encroachments, easements, or rights of way?
- Have you received any notice or claim affecting the property from any person or public body?
- Are the premises connected to a public water system?
- Are the premises connected to a private or a community water system?

b) Questions About the Structure of the Dwelling

- Are you aware of any infestation by insects or rodents?
- Are you aware of any damage due to wind, fire, or water?
- Are you aware of any moisture and/or water problems in the basement or crawl space?
- Are you aware of any problems with the heating and/or central air-conditioning system?
- Are you aware of any problems with the electrical system?
- Are you aware of any problems with the plumbing system?
- Are you aware of any problems with the swimming pool and/or hot tub?
- Are you aware of any roof leakage or unrepaired damage?
- How old is the roof?
- Are you aware of any structural problems with the premises or other buildings on the property?
- Are you aware of any problems related to the building's settling?
- Are you aware of any additions or alterations made without a required permit?
- Has the wood stove or fireplace been approved by local authorities?
- To the best of your knowledge, have the premises ever contained urea formaldehyde insulation (UFFI)?
- To the best of your knowledge, have the premises ever contained asbestos insulation?
- To the best of your knowledge, is the ceiling insulated?
- To the best of your knowledge, are the exterior walls insulated?

c) Questions Regarding a Condominium Property

- Are there any restrictions on pets, children, or rentals?
- Are there any pending rules or condominium bylaw amendments that may alter the uses of the property?
- Are there any special assessments voted on or proposed?

D. BUYING A CONDOMINIUM OR TOWNHOUSE

Living in a condominium is not right for everyone since it involves not only individual ownership of the unit and shared ownership of other property but also adherence to rules and regulations and shared rulership. But many people prefer condominium living over the alternatives, especially since many condominiums are adult oriented and don't permit children unless they are just visiting. Other condominium projects are geared specifically to retired people, providing security and social activities, for example.

Condominiums may be detached, semi-detached, row houses, stack townhouses, duplexes, or apartments. They can even be building lots, subdivisions, or mobile home parks. The most familiar format for a condominium is an apartment condominium, that is, one level, or a townhouse condominium, which is two or more levels. Whatever the style, a residential unit is specified and is owned by an individual in a freehold (owning the land) or leasehold (leasing rights to the land only) format. The rest of the property, including land, which is called the common elements in most provinces and states, is owned in common with the other owners. Common elements generally include walkways, driveways, lawns and gardens, lobbies, elevators, parking areas, recreational facilities, storage areas, laundry rooms, stairways, plumbing, electrical systems and portions of walls, ceilings and floors, and other items. An owner would own a fractional share of the common elements in the development. If there are 50 condominium owners, then each individual owner would own one-fiftieth of the common elements as tenants in common. The legislation of each province or state can vary, but it is always designed to provide the legal and structural framework for the efficient management and administration of each condominium project.

The part of the condominium that you own outright is referred to as the unit in most provinces and states. You have full and clear title to this unit when you purchase it (assuming you are buying a freehold, not a leasehold, property), and the property is legally registered in your name in the land registry office in the province or state. The precise description of the common elements, and exactly what you own as part of your unit, may differ from development to development, but it is stipulated in the documents prepared and registered for each condominium. Part of the common elements may be designated for the exclusive use of one or more of the individual unit owners, in which case they are called limited common elements. In other words, they are limited only for the use of specific owners. Examples include parking spaces, storage lockers, roof gardens, balconies, patios, and front and back yards.

A condominium development is administered by various legal structures set out in provincial or state legislation. Snowbirds who purchase a recreational or resort condominium tend to own it outright and leave it empty when not in use. They may also rent it by using the condominium corporation or management company as an agent, a real estate agent, or they may rent it independently.

In any situation of shared ownership and community living there are advantages and disadvantages. An overview of these follows:

1. Advantages

- Ready availability of financing, similar to a single-family home
- Range of prices, locations, types of structures, sizes, and architectural features available
- Availability of amenities such as swimming pool, tennis courts, health clubs, community centre, saunas, hot tubs, exercise rooms, and sun decks
- Benefits of home ownership in ability to participate in the real estate market and potential growth in equity
- Freedom to decorate interior of unit to suit personal tastes
- Enhancement of security by permanence of neighbours and, in many cases, controlled entrances
- Elimination of many of the problems of upkeep and maintenance often associated with home ownership, since maintenance is usually the responsibility of a professional management company or manager
- Often considerably cheaper than buying a single-family home because of more efficient use of land and economy of scale
- Reduction of costs due to sharing of responsibilities for repair and maintenance
- Enhancement of social activities and sense of neighbourhood community by relative permanence of residents
- In many cases, the residents are other Snowbirds
- Elected council that is responsible for many business and management decisions
- Participation of owners in the operation of the development, which involves playing a role in setting and approval of budget, decision making, determination of rules, regulations, and bylaws, and other matters affecting the democratic operation of the condominium community

2. Disadvantages

- May be difficult to assess accurately the quality of construction of the project.

- A loss of freedom may be experienced through restrictions contained in the rules and bylaws (e.g., restriction on the right to rent, on pets, on duration of stay of visitors, or on use of a barbecue on the patio).
- People live closer together, creating problems from time to time; problem areas include the five Ps: pets, parking, personality, parties, and people.
- One could be paying for maintenance and operation of amenities that one has no desire or intention to use.
- Management of the condominium council is by volunteers, who may or may not have the appropriate abilities and skills.

Condominiums are a popular form of housing, especially for older or retired Canadians. The many benefits will ensure that the demand for this type of housing will grow. Make sure you obtain objective legal advice from a real estate lawyer before you make a final decision to purchase a condominium.

E. BUYING A TIMESHARE

Resort time-sharing originated in Europe in the 1960s, when high costs and demand for limited resort space created the need for a way to ensure accommodation for a certain period of time each year. Timeshares are usually sold by the week and include fully furnished accommodation with maintenance and maid service. The concept was adopted in Florida in the 1970s to revive the sluggish condominium industry. Since then, timeshares have grown rapidly, with thousands of this type of resort throughout the world. These resorts range from Ontario cottage country resorts to Florida condos to Mexican beach villas. Hundreds of thousands of people have purchased timeshares. At some time or another you have probably seen the ads: "Luxury Lifestyle at Affordable Prices!" "Vacation the World!" "Trade for Exotic Climes!"

Other frequently used terms that are synonymous with time-sharing include resort time-sharing, vacation ownership, multiownership, interval ownership, and shared vacation plan. The timeshare concept has been applied to numerous other areas, such as recreational vehicle and mobile home parks.

There are two main categories of timeshares: fee simple ownership and right-to-use.

1. Fee Simple Ownership

There are different formats. One option is to own a portion of the condominium, such as one-fiftieth of the property. Each one-fiftieth portion entitles you to one week's use of the premises per year. Other people also buy into the property. Frequently you are allocated a fixed week every year. In other instances, you could have a floating time, with the exact dates to be agreed upon according to availability. In some cases, you might purchase a quarter- or half-interest. If the complete property is sold, you would receive your proportional share of any increase in net after-sale proceeds. You would also normally be able to rent, sell, or give your ownership portion to anyone you wished.

2. Right-to-Use

This concept is much like having a long-term lease, but with use for just a one-week period every year. This arrangement is similar to prepaying for a hotel room for a fixed period every year for 20 years in advance. In other words, you don't have any portion of ownership in the property; you only have a right to use it for a fixed or floating time period every year. Condominiums, recreational vehicle parks, and other types of properties offer right-to-use timeshares.

The opportunity for return on your money in a right-to-use timeshare is limited or nonexistent. This is because there is generally very little demand in the after-sale market, as well as other restrictions on resale or pricing of the resale.

In practical terms, time-sharing is primarily a lifestyle choice. Here are some of the disadvantages and cautions to be aware of:

- You may tire of going to the same location every year, since your needs may change over time.

- The timeshare programs that include an exchange option (e.g., switching a week in a different location) are not always as anticipated in availability, flexibility, convenience, or upgrade fee.

- Make sure you know what you are getting. Some people who purchase the right-to-use type think they are buying a fee simple ownership portion.

- Be wary of hard-sell marketing. In most instances, the dream fantasy is heavily reinforced, and "free" inducements, such as a buffet dinner or an evening dinner cruise with a large group of other people, are used to entice you to hear a sales pitch first. High-pressure sales pitches, with teams of salespeople, can go on for hours. The sales representatives can be very persuasive, if not aggressive, and often use very manipulative techniques to get you to sign a credit card slip as a deposit. The "freebies" would generally cost you from $10 to $25. It is an illusion to think you are going to get something for nothing. At best, you will be subjected to an intense one-on-one sales approach. At worst, you will be out your deposit money if you change your mind, unless there is a time period during which you may cancel. Trying to get your money back if you suffer from buyer's remorse, is extremely difficult, if not impossible, especially if the timeshare is outside Canada.

- Timeshare sales in Canada and some U.S. states are sometimes covered by consumer protection, ensuring your right to get your money back by rescinding (cancelling) the contract within a certain time period.

- There is usually a regular management fee for maintaining the premises.

Timeshares are a dream for some but a nightmare for others. Speak to at least three other timeshare owners in the project you are considering to get their candid opinion before you decide to buy. Never give out your credit card as a deposit, and don't sign any documents requested of you without first speaking with a local real estate lawyer. You can obtain a lawyer's name from the local lawyer referral service or provincial or state bar association; refer to Chapter 8. You might also want to check with the local Better Business Bureau before you make a decision. Don't let yourself be pressured. Sleep on the idea for a while, and if the deal seems too good to be true, it probably is.

If you want more details on timeshares in Canada, contact the Canadian Resort Development Association (CRDA) in Toronto at 1-800-646-9205 or (416) 960-4930. Ask for their free publication, *A Consumer's Introduction to Internal Ownership and Vacation Club Membership.* Also ask if a particular development is a member of CRDA and if there have been any complaints.

If you are buying in the United States, contact the American Resort Development Association in Washington, DC, at (202) 371-6700. Ask for their free publication, *A Consumer's Guide to Resort and Urban Timesharing.* If you are interested in RV or mobile home timeshare options in the United States, refer to items 41-44 in Appendix A. Most of these companies will permit you to stay at their locations for a nominal fee to see if you like them.

F. BUYING A MOBILE HOME/MANUFACTURED HOME

Mobile homes, now frequently referred to as manufactured homes, are a very popular form of housing for Canadian Snowbirds. Some people live in a mobile home in Canada as well as one in the United States. The term mobile home can be confusing. It is not an RV and has no wheels, though it is manufactured to be moved by a large truck and set up on a permanent foundation, referred to as a pad. It is meant to be like any other house, except that it can be readily moved to a new location if desired. In some cases, a basement is built and the mobile home is set on top.

Mobile homes generally come in two widths. The single width is about 10 to 16 feet (3 to 5 m) wide and sometimes as long as 64 feet (19.5 m). The double homes are built in two sections and when combined are approximately twice as wide as a single. This type of unit can be very spacious and in many respects have the rooms, features, and appliances of a regular house. You can either buy a mobile home and have it put on the location of your choice or buy one already on a site. When selecting a mobile home, you must make sure it meets safety standards. Some older mobile homes contain flammable materials or are poorly designed and may not even be insurable, so check with your insurance company beforehand. Most mobile homes are in parks that are set up as permanent communities, even though many of the residents may be Snowbirds who only live there for six months a year. These private parks provide water, sewer, and electricity hook-ups and frequently have other features, such as a recreation and social centre, a swimming pool, tennis courts, a golf course, and security personnel. Some parks may have from 200 to 1,000 or more mobile homes.

Some parks are restricted to retired people, others to Snowbirds; some combine seasonal and permanent residents. RVs are permitted in some parks and not in others. There is a variety of different formats for these parks, which are regulated by local and/or state bylaws. In some rural locations there are few restrictions; in urban settings separate parks are established specifically for mobile homes. Some have communities that are independent and include their own facilities, whereas others use the facilities of the closest community.

Before deciding to buy a mobile home, you may want to rent one for a season to see if you like the concept and the area. Talk to other mobile home owners to get their advice on makes and models. Check with the Association of Mobile Home Owners. Refer to item 26 in Appendix A for Sunbelt state associations. These associations can provide you with invaluable information, insurance, and the names of mobile home parks in their state. They also lobby for the interests of mobile homeowners in their respective states. Also refer to item 27 for state travel park associations.

Finally, before you sign any documents to buy a mobile home or rent a park location, check with a real estate lawyer in the area for your protection. Your lot lease and mobile home warranty and contract can be reviewed for clauses or exclusions that you might not understand or want.

G. BUYING A RECREATIONAL VEHICLE (RV)

Owning an RV is a growing trend, especially among people aged 55 and up. Nearly half of the nine million RVs on the road in the United States are owned by people over 55. People in this age group have the time, discretionary income, and desire to see and experience the small towns, big cities, popular attractions, and natural beauty of North America. RVs provide an enjoyable, comfortable, and economical way to take it all in and provide an opportunity to meet new people on the road. RVs can be kept packed with essentials and ready to travel at a moment's notice. Comfort is another factor. RVs can have complete living, dining, sleeping, and bathroom facilities to provide travellers with all the amenities of home while on the road, as well as slide-out rooms for expansion.

An RV is defined as a motorized or towable vehicle that combines transportation and temporary living quarters for travel, recreation, and camping. RVs do not include mobile homes. There are many types of RVs, with a wide range of prices for new RVs, from CDN $2,000 for the least expensive folding camping trailer to over CDN $200,000 for a customized motor home. Used RVs of course cost less, and if you buy off season, you can get better deals. Here is a description of some of the specific types of RVs and the current average retail price in Canadian dollars.

1. Types of RVs

There are two main categories of RVs—towables and motorized:

a) Towable RVs

A towable RV is designed to be towed by a motorized vehicle (auto, van, or pick-up truck) and is of such size and weight as not to require a special highway movement permit. It is designed to provide temporary living quarters for recreational, camping, or travel use and does not require permanent on-site hook-up. The following are types of towable RVs:

- **Folding camping trailer (average price, CDN $6,500)**
  This is a recreational camping unit designed for temporary living quarters that is mounted on wheels and connected with collapsible sidewalls that fold for towing by a motorized vehicle. It provides kitchen, dining, and sleeping facilities for up to eight people. Some larger models come with full bathroom and heating/air-conditioning options.

- **Truck camper (average price, CDN $13,000)**
  This recreational camping unit is designed to be loaded onto or affixed to the bed or chassis of a truck and is constructed to provide temporary living quarters for recreational camping or travel use. Most provide kitchen, sleeping, and bathroom facilities for two to six people, heat, air-conditioning, and running water. The unit can be easily loaded onto a truck bed in a few minutes.

- **Conventional travel trailer (average price, CDN $17,000)**
  This unit typically ranges from 12 to 35 feet (3.6 to 10.6 m) in length and is towed by means of a bumper or frame hitch attached to the towing vehicle. It provides temporary living quarters for four to eight people, with kitchen, toilet, sleeping and dining facilities, electrical and water systems, and modern appliances. The unit is available in conventional and two-level fifth-wheel models.

- **Fifth-wheel travel trailer (average price, CDN $26,600)**
  This unit can be equipped the same as the conventional travel trailer but is constructed with a raised forward section that allows a bi-level floor plan. This style is designed to be towed by a vehicle equipped with a device known as a fifth-wheel hitch.

b) Motorized RVs

- **Custom van conversion (average price, CDN $35,000)**
  This refers to a complete or incomplete automotive van chassis that has been modified by the RV manufacturer to be used for transportation and recreation. Modifications may include the addition of windows, carpeting, panelling, seats, sofas, reclining captain's chairs, closets, stereo systems, and accessories.

- **Van camper (average price, CDN $56,000)**
  This is a panel-type truck to which the RV manufacturer has added any two of the following conveniences: sleeping, kitchen, or toilet facilities. The

truck also includes 100-volt hook-up, fresh water storage, city water hook-up, and a top extension to provide more head room.

- **Motor home (compact) (average price, CDN $42,000)**
  This unit is built on an automotive manufactured cab and chassis having a gross vehicle weight ratio (GVWR) of less than 6,500 pounds (3,000 kg). It may provide any or all of the conveniences of the larger units.

- **Motor home (mini-low profile) (average price, CDN $56,000)**
  This unit is built on an automotive manufactured van frame with an attached cab section having a GVWR of 6,500 pounds (3,000 kg) or more, with an overall height of more than 8 feet (2.4 m) (low profile is less than 8 feet). The RV manufacturer completes the body section containing the living area and attaches it to the cab section.

- **Motor home (high profile) (average price, CDN $89,000)**
  The living unit has been entirely constructed on a bare, specially designed motor vehicle chassis. Kitchen, sleeping, bathroom, and dining facilities are easily accessible to the driver's area from inside. Three types—conventional motor homes, mini-motor homes, and van-campers—range from 17 to 40 feet (5 to 12 m) long. Motor homes sleep up to eight people.

If you are buying an RV in the United States, check to make sure that it is endorsed by the Recreational Vehicle Industry Association (RVIA). This endorsement shows that the RV has complied with applicable national safety standards, such as those of the American National Standards Institute. The address for the RVIA is located in item 42 in Appendix A. If you are buying an RV in Canada, make sure that it is endorsed by the Canadian Recreational Vehicle Association (CRVA), showing that it has received Canadian Standards Association (CSA) safety approval. Ask about warranty coverage in the United States and Canada. The CRVA is based in Toronto and can be contacted at (416) 971-7800. Also contact the state or provincial RV dealers' association. Refer to item 42 in Appendix A.

You should also check on various Canadian government regulations or legal implications if you buy an RV or car in the United States and wish to take it home with you to Canada. Refer to items 1, 2, and 3 in Appendix A.

You may not be sure if you want to buy an RV right away, so consider renting one to see if you like it. If you have some friends with RVs, ask to go along on a short trip with them. Also ask them about their RV experiences and tips they could give you. Refer to item 43 in Appendix A for U.S. RV rental companies. Check with your local RV dealer in Canada about rentals in Canada.

2. Where to Get Further Information

There is an immense amount of information available to assist you. Request the excellent free material from the Recreational Vehicle Industry Association (RVIA) in the United States. The association's phone number is 1-800-47SUNNY (78669) or (703) 620-6003 and web site is http://www.rvia.org.

Ask for their information kit and *Go Camping America Vacation Planner*. You can write to the association at the address given in item 42 of Appendix A.

Appendix A contains many contact sources for RV information. Refer to items 41–52, which include information about RV campground directories and chains, clubs, resorts, publications, associations, rental sources, retail shows and scenic trips. Also refer to item 12 for provincial tourism offices, item 26 for state travel offices in the United States, and item 27 for state travel park associations. All this free information will help you plan your trip. Contact your automobile association as well for information, and refer to Appendix B for books on travel in the United States.

H. PERILS OF SELLING YOUR OWN HOME YOURSELF

When the time comes to sell your U.S. or Canadian home, you may be tempted to sell it yourself. Aside from a personal challenge or learning experience, there is primarily only one reason for doing so—to save on a real estate commission. You may indeed save money. On the other hand, the saving could be an expensive illusion.

There are some general disadvantages of selling a home yourself, as opposed to using a carefully selected and experienced realtor. The following remarks are not intended to dissuade you from attempting to sell your own home, but to place the process in realistic perspective. You will have to balance the benefits and disadvantages, and decide what is best. The comments apply whether you are selling your own home or an investment property, but the examples given relate primarily to a house or condo.

1. Inexperience

If you don't know all the steps involved, from the pre-sale procedures and strategies to completing the deal and receiving the money, you could and probably would make mistakes that could be costly to you.

2. Emotional Roller Coaster

Many people, especially with their own home, tend to get emotionally involved in the sale process because of the direct interaction with the prospective purchasers. For example, frustration can be experienced due to rejection of the house, negative comments or fault-finding people whose personality you don't like, or people who negotiate toughly on the price. These one-on-one direct dynamics or comments can sometimes be taken personally, and therefore be a cause of stress.

3. Time Commitment

You have to have open houses as well as show your property at times that may not necessarily be convenient to you. In addition, you are going to be spending time preparing the ad copy and staying at home to respond to telephone calls or people knocking on the door.

4. Expense, Nature, and Content of Advertising

Costs include all the daily or weekly newspaper classified and/or box ads, as well as a lawn sign. In addition, you may not know what specific types of advertising would be appropriate for your type of property; how to write ad copy that would grab the attention of a reader and prospective purchaser; nor how to identify and emphasize the key selling features of your property.

5. Limited Market Exposure

There are considerable differences in market exposure in terms of advertising by yourself and the types of advertising and promotion a realtor could do for you. There is obviously a direct correlation between the nature and degree of market exposure and the end price. Clearly, limited market exposure means limited prospective buyers.

6. Potential Legal Problems

The prospective purchaser may supply you with his own agreement of purchase and sale. This contract may have clauses and other terms in it that could be legally risky, unenforceable, unfair, or otherwise not beneficial to you. You may not recognize these potential problems or risks. In addition, you could end up agreeing to take back a mortgage (vendor-back mortgage) when it would not be necessary or wise, or to accept a long-term option or other legal arrangement that could be risky.

7. Lack of Familiarity With Market

You may not have a clear or objective idea of exactly what a similar property in your market is selling for, or the state of the real estate market at that point in time. This can place you at a distinct disadvantage. For example, if you are being unrealistic in your pricing, along with limited advertising exposure, you could literally price yourself out of the market. Prospective purchasers may not even look, let alone make an offer. You may eventually sell your property, but only after several price reductions and after a long period of time. Naturally, of course, this depends on the market and the nature of your property. Conversely, you could have a property with unique features or potential that could justify a higher sale price than you might realize.

8. No Pre-screening of Prospective Purchasers

You would not generally know the art of pre-screening prospects in terms of questions to ask them over the phone. The end result is that you could waste your time talking to people over the phone or showing them through the house, who are not and never will be serious prospects. You could also end up accepting an offer from someone who does not realistically have a chance of financing the house, or who asks for unrealistic time periods for removing purchaser conditions, which effectively would tie up your property during that time.

9. Offer Price Not Necessarily the Best

You may think the offer is the best offer from that prospective purchaser, or any purchaser, and therefore may accept it. That price may not be the best price at all. You may have started too low or too high for your initial asking price, based on emotion or needs, not on reality; you may have received a low-ball offer from a prospective purchaser that was never intended to be accepted but was designed to reduce your expectations; or you may be subjected to effective closing skills on the part of the prospective purchaser.

10. Lack of Negotiating Skills

You may lack essential negotiating or sales skills and feel very uncomfortable or anxious in a negotiating context. As a consequence, the price and terms you eventually settle for may not be as attractive as they otherwise could be.

11. Purchaser Wanting Discount in Price Equal to Commission Saved

It is not uncommon for the prospective purchaser to determine what the fair market value is and then ask to have an additional discount equal to the real estate commission you are saving. The primary reason why prospective purchasers are attracted to a For Sale by Owner is the prospect of getting a better deal than a property listed with a realtor, due to the commission otherwise built into the sale price. The primary reason why you are selling the property yourself is to save the full amount of any commission otherwise payable. Hence the problem. A compromise may be possible whereby the price is further reduced by a percentage of the commission saved. Again, in practical terms, it is normally an illusion to think that you will save the full or even a substantial amount of the commission. You may have netted more if it was listed with a realtor.

12. Tough to Sell in a Buyer's Market

Buyers in this type of market are very price sensitive, negotiate toughly because they want the best deal, and have the time to be selective after comparing what is available in the market. You are at a disadvantage if you don't receive all the exposure possible and use all the negotiating and selling skills available. You could wait a long time before finally selling, and the market could go down further by that time in a declining sale market, due to an oversupply of homes, limited demand and reduced exposure.

As you can see, there are distinct advantages to utilizing the services and skills of a professionally trained and experienced realtor. Of course, there are exceptions in certain situations where you may choose to sell yourself, but you have to be very aware of the potential disadvantages. The vast majority of homeowners realize the benefits of using a realtor and do so, whether for buying or selling real estate.

TIPS BEFORE LEAVING CANADA

- If you are thinking of purchasing U.S. real estate, speak to your financial institution before you leave regarding their policy on financing U.S. property.
- Be wary about buying timeshares before leaving Canada without knowing their advantages and disadvantages. Always check out some of the resorts you are thinking of using, without further financial obligation. Speak to others who have bought timeshares from the company selling them.
- If you are thinking of buying a house or condo or a mobile home in a specific location, have a real estate professional, agent, or owner send material to you to review before you depart. The more research you do before you leave, the more objective and realistic your final decision will be.
- If you want to be certain you like a particular area or type of housing, consider renting a house, condo, or mobile/manufactured home or RV in your first Snowbird season. This is a low-risk and highly effective way of making your decision. You can make all your enquiries, thoroughly review information, and speak to references before you leave.

CHAPTER

5

Insurance Needs and Options

A. INTRODUCTION

Adequate insurance is necessary for your peace of mind and financial health. As a Snowbird, you need to understand all the options, benefits, features, and rates, as well as the exclusions, exemptions, and deductibles, but it is very important to understand the terms and concepts. Take the time to do your research so that you can make the right decisions to meet your needs and protect yourself from potential risks.

It is also important to shop around for comparable rates and coverage. The insurance market is highly competitive, and you will find considerable differences in price and in the quality of coverage offered by different insurance companies. Obtain a minimum of three competitive quotes. For out-of-country insurance coverage, you need more of a comparison than that. You want to check out as many Canadian insurance programs as you can that offer the type of coverage you are seeking to evaluate the relative strengths and weaknesses. The type of selection criterion to apply will be discussed later in this chapter. These comparisons will provide you with an objective basis for selection and make your final decision much less stressful. To eliminate misunderstanding, get confirmation in writing of any requests made by you to your insurer or insurance company, or of representations made by an insurance company representative to you. Keep copies of all correspondence between you and your insurance company, as well as any receipts for items to be claimed for reimbursement.

This chapter covers the various types of insurance you should consider, depending on your circumstances: out-of-country medical insurance, homeowner insurance, home office insurance, mobile/manufactured home insurance, automobile insurance, RV insurance, automobile roadside assistance, and life insurance.

B. OUT-OF-COUNTRY EMERGENCY MEDICAL INSURANCE

If you have a serious injury or illness in the United States and require emergency medical attention, you will be financially devastated unless you have out-of-country medical insurance. Provincial health insurance plans vary by province, but each provides you with the necessary protection when travelling within Canada. Coverage by provincial plans outside Canada is nominal, however—maybe $75 to $400+ Canadian funds per day for hospital care. Payments for doctors' services outside Canada, in Canadian funds, will not exceed the amount payable had you been treated in your own province. This is a very low amount compared with U.S. rates. This would generally represent less than 10 percent of the hospitalization cost in the U.S.

Health coverage in the United States is very different from the medicare coverage we are accustomed to in Canada. We are not accustomed to being personally billed, so we don't appreciate the real cost of treatment, which is paid by the government. In the U.S. system, private hospitals and doctors operate in a profit-oriented environment, and costs are much greater. In the United States, the average hospital stay often exceeds US$1,500 a day and can run as high as US$10,000 a day for intensive care. Certain emergency surgical operations can cost $100,000 or more. So who pays the shortfall if you have a medical emergency in the United States? You do. Unless, of course, you have wisely purchased supplemental health insurance *before* you leave Canada, for the duration of your U.S. stay, be it a day or six months. Keep in mind that this supplemental insurance covers emergency treatment for injury or illness only. It does not cover nonemergency treatment or services. It is not a substitute for Canadian medicare.

Premium rates vary greatly between insurers. The rate depends on factors such as the nature of the coverage, your age and existing medical condition, policy exclusions and limitations, the deductible portion of your policy, whether you have a preferred (for healthy people) or standard rate plan, and the duration of your stay in the United States. The premium range for a six-month extended-stay plan could range per person from $500 to $3,000 or more, depending on the above variables. Rates are normally set by the insurer between June and September each year for extended-stay Snowbird coverage. For competitive reasons, the insurer might drop the market rates after you have taken the policy out, but such a reduction should be passed on to you. Do not choose a plan based on price alone but consider such factors as benefits, limitations, exclusions, and deductibles.

For information about your provincial health department coverage and policy for out-of-country claims, refer to item 13 in Appendix A. Refer to item 14 for a detailed listing of companies in Canada providing out-of-country medical insurance. To obtain a comparison of the numerous insurance plans available to Canadians, refer to item 31 for the two newspapers produced for

Canadian Snowbirds. They generally provide this comparison between June and October, when the various plans announce their policies and premiums for the Snowbird season.

1. Claiming Tax Credits

On the positive side, some financial relief might be available from the tax credits you can earn when you purchase medical insurance. Many people overlook this substantial saving, which could effectively reduce your premium by up to one-quarter. You earn credits of approximately 27 cents for each dollar of medical expenses (i.e., 27 percent) in any consecutive 12-month period that exceed either 3 percent of income or $1,614, whichever is less. This is a good reason to make sure you keep receipts of all your medical expenses.

For example, let's say a retired couple, through careful professional financial and tax planning, have split their retirement income so that they are both earning $20,000 a year. By doing this, they have lowered their marginal tax rates (rather than one spouse having a higher taxed income) and minimized the risk of reaching the clawback threshold on their Old Age Security (OAS) pension, which occurs after approximately $53,215 of individual net income. They can each claim credits for medical expenses exceeding $600 (calculated by taking 3 percent of $20,000) in any consecutive 12-month period, at the rate of approximately 27 percent. To clarify, this 27 percent figure consists of a combined federal and provincial tax credit benefit. The federal tax credit is 17 percent, but this results in a reduction and, therefore, a savings in provincial tax payable, since provincial tax is a portion of federal tax. Provincial tax rates vary.

Returning to the retired couple, if they are each paying, for example, $1,400 in insurance premiums, they would be eligible to claim credits of $216 each for a total savings of $432 ($1,400 – $600 = $800 x 27 percent). If the couple were earning a lower income than $20,000 a year each, they would have a larger credit and save even more money. Other eligible medical expenses, such as prescription drugs, dental work, or eyeglasses, may also be claimed, as well as:

- Twenty percent of the cost to adapt a van for transporting an individual using a wheelchair—up to a maximum of $5,000;
- A maximum allowance of $2,000 to cover expenses incurred when moving to accessible housing;
- Fifty percent of the cost of an air-conditioner prescribed by a medical practitioner as being necessary to assist an individual in coping with a chronic illness or disorder—to a maximum of $1,000;
- The amount eligible for the tax credit for part-time attendant care of $10,000;
- No limit on the deduction from income for attendant care expenses that are necessary to allow the disabled individual to work.

2. Understanding Insurance Options

Many insurance plans are available, and it can be very confusing and frustrating trying to understand which plan is right for you. Keep in mind that one plan can't be all things to all people. You want to determine your needs and then shortlist two or three plans that meet your needs. Only then do you consider the issue of premium cost.

It is helpful to understand how the insurance system works, since several parties are involved. Insurers are the people you deal with directly. They are the companies or organizations that package a plan and arrange for an insurance company to underwrite it, or pay the claims. The companies that pay the claims are called underwriters. Sometimes the underwriters sell directly themselves or through travel agents. Sometimes underwriters insure plans for various insurers, which could be competing with each other. In that case, each plan tends to be customized for each insurer, so they are slightly different from each other. In a medical emergency, the underwriter or insurer contracts with an emergency medical assistance company to provide information, guidance, and coordination of your medical care. In other words, the company helps deal with your emergency medical needs, telling you which hospital or doctor to go to and so on. Such companies have a 24-hour, 7-day hotline, generally toll-free, or they accept collect calls from anywhere in the United States. They also monitor your treatment and make other arrangements as required. Always keep a record of who you spoke with when phoning this emergency medical number.

To keep costs down, many underwriters have negotiated reduced rates with specific hospitals and doctors, and therefore you might be referred specifically to them. If your condition is safely stabilized, they will likely send you back to Canada by air ambulance to save themselves money, since your treatment would then be covered by Canadian medicare.

Here are the main issues and options you need to know about:

a) Full Disclosure of Personal Health Information

The issue of full disclosure of health information in your initial policy application cannot be overemphasized. If the insurer denies your claim, your explanation that you made a mistake, misunderstood, or didn't know will bear no weight. As far as the insurer is concerned, you could have been deliberately misleading the company in order to save money on premiums or to get the coverage in the first place. So don't be tempted to play with the facts. Insurers are entitled to see all your past medical history records, and they know what to look for.

Money is money, and the fine print of the policy governs. No insurer is going to pay out a lot of money if it technically and legally doesn't have to.

b) Extended-Stay and Multitrip Plans

An *extended-stay plan* is intended to cover you for the duration of your Snowbird stay in the United States for a continuous period. The premium is based on the duration of your stay—for example, up to six months. You pay for the exact number of days you need. Refer to item 14 in Appendix A for companies offering extended-stay coverage.

A *multitrip plan* is designed for shorter-term stays in the United States. You arrange coverage for a packaged number of days—for example, a maximum single-duration stay not exceeding 90 days. This means you can travel and stay in the United States as many times as you like within the length of your policy coverage (say, up to six months), as long as any one trip does not exceed your maximum number of days per trip (e.g., 15, 30, or 90 days). As soon as you return to Canada for at least a day, the cycle starts again. For example, some people purchase a plan for 90-day periods and stay in the United States for six months but break up the stay by flying back to Canada before the first 90-day period expires—for example, at Christmas. A few weeks later they return to the United States for another period not exceeding 90 days. There could be some savings on insurance premium if this type of arrangement suits your lifestyle, even after taking the airfare into account. However, there could be a risk of loss of coverage if your medical condition changes or if you need to take new medication after you return to Canada and before you return to the United States. Check this out thoroughly.

These multitrip plans are usually based on an annual premium, for example, covering a calendar year or 12 months from the time you take it out. If the plan is based on a calendar year, some companies prorate the premium; others don't. One of the main benefits of a multitrip plan is that it covers spontaneous trips any time you go back and forth across the Canada-U.S. border. You can obtain multitrip plans through travel agents, banks, and some credit card companies or insurers directly. Refer to item 14 in Appendix A for a list of out-of-country insurance companies. Many of these companies do not provide multitrip plans but only extended-stay plans.

c) Top-up Insurance

This concept means that you acquire additional supplemental emergency medical coverage to "top up" an existing out-of-country medical plan. This existing plan could be coverage you get as a retiree from a government plan, other employer plan, union or association plan, or credit card plan. There are risks, however, with the top-up approach. Some plans don't permit top-ups. There can be great differences in plan policies. There could be a lapse in time periods or amounts between coverage, or disputes between different insurers as to the issue of coverage. For example, if your basic medical plan coverage has a ceiling cap of $50,000 and lasts for a maximum number of days, and your top-up plan kicks in at the end of that time period, what happens if you have a catastrophic injury before the first plan lapses? You are only covered for $50,000, and your expenses could be $200,000. You would be out the difference. Another example is if the top-up company decides that your illness was pre-existing if you make a claim with your first insurer first. An alternative is to coordinate a basic plan and top-up plan from the same insurer.

The other reality is that generally it is less expensive and less risky to have just one plan cover everything. It certainly eliminates the uncertainty. It also saves the inconvenience and frustration of having to deal with two different claims procedures.

d) Add-on Insurance

If you want to stay longer outside Canada than your current insurance policy covers, you can, in many cases, request an extension while still outside the country. You need to make these arrangements *before* the expiry of your current coverage. You can charge the extra premium to your credit card. Always ask for a confirmation number and particulars of who you spoke to and when. Ideally, have the confirmation faxed to you or sent to you for your records. Check out the terms of the policy as well. For example, if you have developed any medical conditions while outside the country, ask whether that will be excluded from coverage under the extension plan. Get it in writing.

e) Subrogation Clause

If you take out Snowbird insurance with one insurer, and the company finds out that you have existing insurance coverage through an employer or pension health plan, the Snowbird insurer can, in some cases, make a claim against that plan. This process is called subrogation. Most insurance policies state the right to do this. You may not want that to happen, since such a claim could dilute your fixed health benefits under your employer/union/association pension plan coverage.

If this is an issue to you, make sure you discuss the matter with your prospective Snowbird insurer. Get an agreement in writing to avoid any misunderstanding. Some insurers will waive any claim, some will do so for a premium surcharge (e.g., 10 to 15 percent), and others will limit their subrogation claim to a certain ceiling (e.g., $3,000).

Ask if the insurer is a member of the Canadian Life and Health Insurance Association (CLHIA). CLHIA has adopted a recent member policy that members will not claim against your pension plan coverage, by means of subrogation, under $50,000. Check with your insurer (get it in writing) and with CLHIA at 1-800-268-8099.

f) Payment of Deductibles

To reduce the risk, many insurance companies will offer you premium discounts if you agree to pay a deductible up to a certain amount—for example, from $100 to $10,000. The larger the deductible, the larger the saving in premiums, perhaps 25 to 40 percent. You have to determine your own financial comfort level and the risk you are willing to take. Check to see if the deductibles are paid in U.S. or Canadian dollars. When comparing premium rates, take into account your net deductible outlay. If you have an employee retirement health benefit plan, check to see if it covers any deductibles.

g) What Is Included in Your Insurance Policy Coverage?

You want to make sure you know what protection you are getting for your money, so compare the same types of benefits when you are comparing policies. The main types of emergency-related (injury or illness) coverage paid for by the insurer in many policies include ambulance, hospital care, special nursing care, doctor and dental services, and necessary medication. In addition, reimbursement of emergency-related expenses that you have incurred, payment for transportation of a relative to your hospital, return of your car or RV to Canada, and return of your body to Canada if you die are frequently included. If you require further treatment but can safely be returned to Canada, the insurer will normally cover the cost of an air ambulance (medically equipped jet) or regular airline to take you back home.

h) What Is Excluded From Your Insurance Coverage?

Certain medical or surgical treatment or diagnostic expenses are not covered by your medical emergency insurance in the United States. Some of the common expenses are pre-existing conditions (refer to the next item); unnecessary diagnostic procedures; treatment that can safely wait until you return to Canada; rehabilitative or continuing care treatment for substance abuse (e.g., drugs or alcohol); chronic conditions (e.g., diabetes, emphysema); cancer that was diagnosed before you left Canada; and elective nonemergency treatment such as treatment by a chiropractor, podiatrist, optometrist, or physiotherapist.

i) Pre-Existing Conditions

This issue is an important one for insurers, since it relates to risk. For example, if you had previous signs of angina, you might already be on medication. The risk to an insurer is that you could have a heart attack in the United States, resulting in medical treatment that could cost the insurer $100,000 or more. It's a calculated risk for the insurer, and different insurers deal with the risk in different ways.

For example, some insurers will simply refuse to cover you. Others would cover you except for any emergency medical condition relating to your pre-existing condition. Some offer a co-payment plan. This means if emergency medical treatment is required in the United States for a pre-existing condition, then the insurer will share the expense. For example, the insurer might pay 70 percent of the cost and you would pay the remaining 30 percent. Another variation is that the insurer agrees to pay up to a maximum amount in the event of such a claim—for example, $50,000. You would pay the rest. This could be a crippling expense financially. Some insurers will accept a pre-existing condition if it has been stabilized, with or without medication, for three, six, or 12 months. Ask your insurer if seeing your doctor for monitoring a condition is considered treatment and has to be disclosed on your application or before you leave Canada. Find out from your doctor if changes in medication are really necessary for your health, since they could impair your Sunbelt insurance coverage. For example, some insurance companies will not insure you if you are on medication before you depart, unless that was disclosed and approved in advance of your departure. Obviously, you don't want to risk your health. Also find out whether you have to notify your insurance company if you pay for nonemergency medical treatment in the United States.

j) Reasons for Rejection of a Medical Emergency Expense Claim

There are situations in which your insurance company could refuse to pay your claim. You could therefore be stuck with the bill, which could be massive. The reasons for rejecting a claim include pre-existing conditions that you have not disclosed; medical exclusions set out in the policy; failure to make a formal claim before a deadline; failure to notify the insurer by calling the medical emergency number within the policy time period (e.g., before entering the hospital or within 24 to 48 hours afterwards); refusal to go to a hospital or doctor of the insured's choice; refusal to be returned to Canada for continuing treatment after your condition was medically stabilized; lapse of your policy coverage period; or dispute with an insurance company if you are using two companies for coverage.

If you are treated for an illness during a short trip home to Canada, and you subsequently have emergency medical treatment for that ailment in the United States, you could be deemed to have a pre-existing illness that the insurer was never advised about. As a result, the insurer could deny the claim. Before you decide on an insurer and before you leave Canada, check out all these issues and get answers to your questions in writing to avoid any misunderstanding.

3. Key Questions to Ask

Here is a checklist of key questions to ask before deciding on the insurance coverage. Not all of them are necessarily applicable in your situation, but you should have them all answered to determine whether you can be covered adequately as well as to determine the benefits or drawbacks of the coverage.

- What are the age restrictions?
- What pre-existing conditions are permitted and how long must they be stable?
- Are there different policy plans and options available and what are they?
- What restrictions and limitations does the policy have?
- Are there any sports activities I cannot participate in, such as scuba diving or mountain climbing?
- What exactly does the policy cover in detail?

- What is the amount of the policy coverage limit (e.g., $1 million, $2 million, or unlimited)?
- Is the insurance paid out in U.S. or Canadian dollars?
- May I select the doctor and hospital of my choice or does the insurance company make that choice?
- If I wish to select my own hospital and doctor despite restrictions, will the insurance company still pay a portion of the bills, and if so, what percentage?
- Do I (or a spouse or family member) have to notify the insurance company within a certain time of my illness or injury to be eligible for coverage (e.g., before I enter a hospital, or within 24 or 48 hours), and if so, what is the time period? Is this position waived if I am unconscious or incapacitated?
- If I forget to comply with the above deadline but could have complied with it, what is the penalty? Does the insurance company only pay a portion of the cost, or a certain maximum dollar amount?
- Does the insurance company have a toll-free or collect telephone number to coordinate my emergency treatment and care that can be reached from anywhere in the United States? Do the representatives speak English, French, and other languages (depending on your needs)?
- Does the insurance company submit the claim directly to my provincial health insurance plan, or do I have to do it myself?
- Is there a limited time period for submitting claims after the emergency treatment has been completed, after which the claim could be denied? What is that period? With respect to insurer? With respect to provincial health department? What documentation is required, and what invoices or receipts for expenses am I required to keep and submit?
- Do I have to pay up front for any hospital and medical treatment and then seek reimbursement from my provincial health plan and insurance company later, or do the U.S. hospitals and doctors bill my provincial health insurance plan and/or insurance company directly? If I have to cover minor expenses, up to how much and what types of expenses?
- Do I have to notify the insurer of any monitoring of my existing condition, treatment for illness, or change in medication after I have been approved for coverage but before I leave Canada? Will these circumstances affect my coverage? What if I pay for such nonemergency treatment or medication change after I leave Canada for the United States? If I see my doctor during a short visit home to Canada at Christmas, do I need to notify the insurer before I return to the United States about any existing condition, monitoring, medication change, or treatment for an illness? Will that affect my coverage?
- Does the insurer offer full payment for emergency expenses for a stabilized medical condition, or only a part of the expense (e.g., co-insurance), and would

I have to pay the rest? What percentage or maximum dollar amount would the insurer pay in this instance (e.g., 50 to 90 percent, or $25,000 to $100,000)?

- If coverage is from an employer, government, or union pension health plan, who is the contact person to determine my benefits? Can coverage details be obtained in writing?

- Does my existing out-of-country medical emergency plan from a past employer, union, or other source permit me to top it up with other insurance? Does the top-up insurer immediately take over after the basic policy reaches the maximum number of days or amount of coverage? Is there a subrogation clause, and if so, what does it say?

- Will a basic out-of-country emergency medical plan allow secondary top-up insurance coverage, if required?

- Will the use of a basic plan mean that the top-up plan will consider the treated condition a pre-existing one and refuse to pay?

- Does my existing retiree/government/union health plan restrict the amount of coverage (e.g., $100,000 maximum) or days (e.g., 30 days)?

- Will the insurance company completely waive any claim for subrogation against my retiree/employee/union health benefit plan and put that in writing? If not, will the insurer waive a subrogation claim for a premium surcharge and what is that surcharge (e.g., 10 to 15 percent), or will the insurer limit a subrogation claim to a certain ceiling (e.g., $3,000)?

- If I have extended-stay coverage rather than a multitrip plan, will it impair my coverage in any way if I return to Canada for short periods during my six-month stay in the United States?

- If credit card medical coverage is being obtained, does it start on the day of departure and how long is the maximum coverage? Can I obtain all the plan benefits in writing?

- If I die, does my coverage include the expense of returning my body to Canada? My RV or car? My spouse?

- Am I reimbursed for certain additional medical/travel-related expenses, such as accommodation, meals, or transportation of my automobile back to Canada, if I have an accident or illness that is deemed by the insurer to be an emergency?

- If I am ill or injured, will the insurance company pay the air fare for an immediate family member, relative, or friend to visit me?

- Does the insurance company restrict the nature of the relationship of the person to visit me—for example, immediate family only?

- If I have to return to Canada because of my illness or injury, will the insurance company pay to have a person of my choice accompany me?

- If I am being treated for an injury or illness and the insurance company deems it safe for me to travel, can the insurance company arbitrarily arrange for me to fly back to Canada in a commercial plane or air ambulance jet so that medicare can take over?

- Will I have to pay a deductible if I have a claim? How much? In U.S. or Canadian dollars? And under what circumstances?

- Will I have to join an organization to access the medical insurance coverage, and how much will the annual dues be?

- Does the insurance policy cover any trip cancellation costs, baggage loss, or other losses?

4. Before You Leave Canada

- Take your provincial health care card.

- Take your out-of-country medical insurance policy and number and related documents.

- Take your emergency assistance phone number for your out-of-country medical insurance and carry it in your wallet or purse at all times.

- Take two photocopies of all your important papers before you go, leaving a copy with a relative and keeping a copy yourself. These papers include such items as your current prescriptions, medical history, birth certificate, passport, driver's licence, credit cards, provincial health care card, out-of-province emergency assistance policy, and emergency assistance phone number.

- See your doctor for a thorough examination before you leave Canada. Apart from having a current assessment of your condition, you then also have a reference date for verifying that you did not have a pre-existing illness in case you have a later dispute with your insurance company.

- You should maintain a record of medical and personal data, which will be helpful if you have a medical emergency in the United States. These data should include your name, address, home phone number, spouse's name, and doctor's name and phone number; the person to be notified in case of an emergency and that person's phone number; and your birth date, social insurance number, provincial health insurance number, out-of-province supplementary insurance plan number, blood type, drug allergies, immunization details, existing conditions, and current medications.

- If you are currently taking medication covered by your provincial health plan, supplemental health plan, or previous employer health plan, ask your doctor to prescribe enough medication before you leave Canada so that you won't run out while you are in the United States.

- If you have friends or relatives who are going to visit you in the United States, make sure you caution them to obtain out-of-country medical insurance to cover them while they are in the United States. Many people going there for only a day or even for several weeks don't think of getting additional insurance protection. A medical emergency could therefore turn into an economic nightmare. A single or multitrip type of plan coverage might be appropriate.

• Check to see what potential health risks you should be aware of before you go to a specific area—for example, intense sunlight, air pollution, strong water currents, or infectious or poisonous insects, reptiles, or plants.

C. HOMEOWNER INSURANCE

If you own a house or condominium in Canada, or in the United States as well, you should have a comprehensive homeowner policy that covers you for replacement cost if your home burns down. Your policy should also cover a range of potential risks, such as theft; vandalism; water damage due to frozen pipes, sewer back-up, or snow and ice build-up; or acts of God such as floods, earthquakes, tornadoes, or hurricanes. Check with your insurance company about the types of optional coverage available. The lower the deductible amount, the higher the insurance premium, so you can save some money by increasing your deductible. Deductibles can range from $200 to $2,500. Or you may prefer to have a lower deductible and pay a slightly higher premium for it. It all depends on how much you can afford to pay if you have to make a claim. Some insurance companies give premium discounts to people over 50, or if smoke detectors and/or fire or burglar alarms are installed in the home. Make enquiries.

1. Ensuring That You Are Fully Covered

If you are going to live in the United States for up to six months, check with your insurance company beforehand to ensure that you are fully covered during your absence. Different insurance companies have different policies. For example, your coverage might require you to notify the company in writing that you will be gone and who your local contact person is, turn off and empty all your water taps before you go, have the house maintained at a certain temperature so that freezing won't occur, and have your home checked once a week (or more often, depending on your policy) by a friend or neighbour or someone else you select. That person should have your house key, information on how to contact you in case of a home emergency, and the name and contact person of your homeowner insurance company. If you don't have anyone who you can ask to check your home regularly during your absence, you do have other options. You can contact the Canadian Corps of Commissionaires, which has offices throughout the country and can monitor your home while you are away. You can arrange for them to visit your home once a week if you like, or whatever is required by your insurance company, to check on the inside of the house, water your plants if you wish, and remove any junk mail. There is a nominal cost of about $15+ a visit. Refer to item 37 in Appendix A. Another option is to contact a bonded private company that has offices throughout Canada called The Housesitters, which will perform the same type of service for a fee. They can be reached at 1-800-268-9513.

2. Home Security Tips

Here are some home security tips to consider before you leave Canada. Many of these are equally applicable if you have a home in a Sunbelt state:

- Keep a current inventory list of your belongings and other personal possessions.
- Keep receipts for valuable articles, such as cameras, jewellery, art, stereo equipment, and furniture.
- Take photographs or a video of your rooms and belongings for additional support if you have to make a claim.
- Mark your valuable assets for identification in case they are stolen. You can generally borrow a marker from your local police department.
- Keep a copy of your inventory list, receipts, and photographs in your safety deposit box in case your home burns down.
- Get extra coverage for expensive items such as jewellery, since the limit may be $2,000 for any claim.
- Don't leave a message on your answering machine that you are out of the country for six months.
- Cancel newspaper delivery while you are away.
- Arrange with Canada Post to forward your mail or hold it until your return.
- Arrange for a neighbourhood friend or student to clear away advertising flyers.
- Have a reliable neighbourhood friend or student clear the snow from your sidewalk or at least tramp it down.
- Store small valuables in a safety deposit box. Store expensive items (e.g., TV or stereo) with a friend or relative while you are away, or move them out of sight if they can be seen from a window.
- Use clock timers to activate lights and radios.
- Keep garage doors locked and windows covered.
- Secure air-conditioners and other openings into your home.
- Change your locks if keys are lost or stolen.
- Make sure door hinge bolts are inside the house; hinges can easily be removed if they are on the outside.
- Install one-inch deadbolt locks on exterior doors. Doorknob locks are unreliable and easily forced.
- Insert a metal piece or fitted wood into sliding glass-door tracks.
- Reinforce basement windows with bars.

D. HOME OFFICE INSURANCE

If you have a part-time or full-time home-based business in Canada, you want to make sure you are protected in case you have to make a claim for a loss or injury that is related to your business use. This coverage is added on to your existing homeowner coverage, and is very reasonably priced. Otherwise, your current policy would likely not cover any such claims. Most basic homeowner policies specifically exclude business use of the home without additional coverage. For example, if a business-related computer or other business equipment were stolen, or if someone visiting you on business were injured on your property or in your home, your basic insurance policy would not cover you.

E. MOBILE/MANUFACTURED HOME INSURANCE

If you have this type of dwelling, either in the United States or Canada, you can get insurance to cover the risks that are unique to these types of homes—for example, damage caused by faulty blocks or jack, damage to tie-down equipment, damage to adjacent structures (e.g., storage area), or damage from falling objects, such as tree branches. You also want to consider replacement cost coverage in case the whole dwelling is destroyed. Deal with an insurance company that specializes in this type of insurance protection. In the United States, check with a state association of mobile/manufactured homeowners to get names of recommended companies. Refer to item 28 in Appendix A.

F. AUTOMOBILE INSURANCE

This type of insurance covers you for losses you might suffer due to damage to your car, car theft, vandalism, or fire. It also covers claims made against you if you have a car accident and damage someone else's car or property or injure other people.

You can reduce your insurance premiums by increasing the deductible portion of your policy. That is the portion you pay first if you make a claim with your insurance company. This amount ranges from $100 to $2,500. The lower the deductible amount, of course, the higher the premium. Another way of reducing your insurance premium is to have an accident-free claims history.

Here are some further points:

- It is prudent to carry a minimum of $1 million third-party liability coverage, and ideally more (e.g., $2–3 million). Third-party coverage means that you are covered if you cause an accident to a third party who then makes a claim against you. The premium difference between $1 million and $3 million is relatively small. If one or two people are seriously injured or die as a consequence of an accident that you were responsible for, the award against you could be millions of dollars, especially in the United States. You should have adequate insurance coverage for your peace of mind.

- Obtain underinsured motorist coverage (UMP). This type of coverage protects you in case you or your car is hit by a driver of a car with inadequate or nonexistent insurance coverage. You or a passenger could be seriously injured or permanently disabled or killed. In that event, you are covered for any claim up to the limit of your own third-party liability insurance coverage (e.g., $1–$3 million), subject to any state or provincial ceilings. If someone with inadequate or nonexistent insurance hit you and you didn't have the UMP coverage, you would have no protection. You could sue the driver of the other car, but most likely that person would have no assets and you would be totally out of luck. The premium for underinsured motorist coverage is low, e.g., $20 to $40 a year. That's cheap for the peace of mind.

- If you bought your car in Canada, you would obtain your insurance in Canada. This insurance covers you against any claims you make as a consequence of car accidents, damage, or theft in the United States. If you buy a car in the United States, however, you need U.S. insurance, which you would cancel and replace with Canadian insurance when you arrive back in Canada. You can get this U.S. insurance through your local automobile travel club in the United States (e.g., AAA) or through other private carriers.

- If any personal possessions are stolen from your car, other than a car radio, for example, your car insurance would not cover it. You would have to make a claim under your homeowner insurance policy, which normally has a deductible that you have to pay first. This deductible could be from $100 to $500 or more, depending on your policy.

- If you are travelling to Mexico, your Canadian auto insurance will not cover you. You need to obtain a separate insurance policy for the duration of the trip. This policy can be obtained from a local auto club (AAA) branch close to the Mexican border. This is covered in more detail in Chapter 9.

- If you were the cause of a car accident and your car is damaged so badly that it is considered a write-off, the insurance company can pay you either the depreciated or book value of the car or the replacement cost. Clarify with your insurance company the type of coverage you have. Generally, it is optional coverage with an additional premium if you want to receive replacement market value of the vehicle. The older the vehicle, the higher the replacement cost premium.

- If you have a part-time or full-time home-based or small business in Canada, make sure you have additional insurance coverage for business use of your personal car. It doesn't cost much extra. Otherwise, if there is an accident and the car was being used for business-related purposes, the insurance company will reject the claim.

G. RECREATIONAL VEHICLE (RV) INSURANCE

If you have an RV of any type, make sure you have adequate coverage. Check with your current auto insurance company, RV dealers, and your local CAA auto club for names of insurance companies that specialize in this type of coverage. You want to consider coverage for such occurrences as hitch failure and collision with a low-hanging tree, as well as coverage for replacement of the RV.

H. AUTOMOBILE ROADSIDE ASSISTANCE AND OTHER COVERAGE

This is an essential type of coverage, especially if you are travelling in the United States. Most people have auto coverage with a local branch of the CAA (Canadian Automobile Association). Refer to item 36 in Appendix A for contact numbers. There are many benefits of membership, including roadside assistance if your car won't start or if you are locked out of your car, for example. The plan also covers towing your car to a service station for repair if necessary, paying for hotel accommodation for a reportable accident up to a maximum amount, and paying a court bond up to a maximum amount if you have committed a traffic offence that requires a bond. There is a toll-free 24-hour CAA and AAA emergency phone number you can phone from anywhere in the United States or Canada for roadside assistance. You can also obtain free travel books, maps, and customized route destination guides by being a member of a CAA club. Your membership is recognized by all AAA club members in the United States. Ask for a free U.S. AAA club directory with contact numbers. Most CAA auto clubs have optional coverage packages over and above the basic membership benefits.

I. LIFE INSURANCE

You may not require any life insurance if you have sufficient life savings, investments, and pensions to meet your needs and your spouse's needs. Depending on your age and medical condition, you may not be eligible for life insurance in any event, or if you are, it could be at a very high premium rate with a low amount of coverage. Insurance companies base premiums on risk—the higher the age, the greater the risk.

The most common type of insurance for those over 55 is term insurance, which insures a person for a specific period of time or term and then stops. If you are a nonsmoker, the premium is lower. There are several companies that specialize in insuring those over 60 years of age, regardless of medical condition. The coverage tends to be low—for example, a maximum of $10,000—with an annual premium that is generally increased every year. If you require additional money to meet financial obligations on death, such as funeral expenses, you may want to consider that option. Most auto clubs provide coverage for accidental death from motor vehicle accidents. These premiums are generally very low.

You may already be covered by an insurance policy you had with your previous employer, even in retirement. In addition, your estate does receive death benefits from your government CPP, OAS, and Veterans' pension plans.

J. TRAVEL INSURANCE

Consider obtaining insurance to cover you for travel-related risks. For example, loss or damage of luggage or personal possessions; missed flights due to weather, delay, illness or death; repatriation (return) of your body to your home city in the event of your death; and other protections.

TIPS BEFORE LEAVING CANADA

- Refer again to the tips in Sections B-4 and C-2 in this chapter.
- Thoroughly compare the premiums of at least three insurance companies in each area that you want coverage. Check on exclusions, limitations, deductibles, and coverage.
- Make sure that you fully understand the nature of your coverage and that it is confirmed in writing before you depart.
- Make sure that you have left your United States forwarding address with family or friends and a telephone contact number in case you need to be reached in an emergency.
- If you do not have a fixed address because you have a transient RV lifestyle, set up a routine of phoning home the first or middle of the month, or more frequently. This way, your key contact people in Canada know when you will be communicating.

CHAPTER

6

Tax Issues and Options

A. INTRODUCTION

Tax issues can be very confusing to many Canadians. When you also live in the United States part-time and own property or other investments there, it can become quite complex because you can be affected by the tax laws of both countries. In the United States, for example, you could be liable under certain circumstances for income tax, capital gains tax, estate tax, and gift tax.

This chapter attempts to answer the common questions about tax that arise out of being a Snowbird. The following overview provides general guidelines only; competent professional tax advice is essential. Topics covered include determining if U.S. tax laws affect you, types of U.S. residency, renting U.S. property, selling U.S. property, U.S. gift tax, paying U.S. and Canadian taxes on death, and the Canada-U.S. tax treaty. Also covered are strategies for reducing taxes on U.S. vacation property, filing deadlines with the IRS, the tax impact of cross-border marriages, tax information exchange between the U.S. and Canada, tax credit for out-of-country medical insurance, where to get tax advice and information, tips before leaving Canada, and other topics.

B. DO U.S. TAX LAWS APPLY TO YOU?

Even though you are a Canadian citizen and only living in the United States part-time, you could still be subject to U.S. taxation. Even if you are not required to pay U.S. tax, you could be subject to various U.S. filing requirements. In addition, the recent Canada-U.S. tax treaty includes substantial changes that will affect you, many of them beneficial revisions. Some of the main changes are discussed in Section J in this chapter. Since more changes can occur at any time, be sure to get current professional tax advice.

If you are a U.S. citizen, however, or have been granted lawful permanent resident status (a green card) by the U.S. Immigration and Naturalization

Service, the discussion in this section will not apply to you. If you are a citizen of a country other than Canada or the United States, or are a Canadian citizen working full-time in the United States under the Canada-U.S. *Free Trade Agreement,* and its successor, the *North American Free Trade Agreement* (NAFTA), some of the following comments may apply. If you fall into any of the categories just noted, contact the Internal Revenue Service (IRS) in Ottawa (refer to item 21 in Appendix A), or if you are in the United States, the IRS office in your area. If you are in the United States on business or for employment, contact Revenue Canada—Taxation and obtain a copy of the pamphlet *Canadian Residents Abroad* (refer to item 1 in Appendix A).

1. Resident vs. Nonresident Alien Tax Status

If you are a Canadian resident who spends part of the year in the United States, the IRS considers you a resident alien or a nonresident alien for tax purposes. It is important to know which category you fall into, since there are considerable tax implications. For example, resident aliens are generally taxed in the United States on income from all sources throughout the world, including, of course, Canadian income. Nonresident aliens are generally taxed only on income from U.S. sources. Not all nonresident aliens have to file, as will be discussed shortly.

2. Resident Alien Under the Substantial Presence Test

The IRS considers you a resident alien of the United States if you meet the substantial presence test. Here is a brief overview:

- If you were in the United States for 183 days or more in the current year, you meet the substantial presence test and are considered a resident alien of the United States.
- If you were in the United States for 31 to 182 days in the current year, you may meet the substantial presence test.
- If you were in the United States for less than 31 days in the current year, you don't meet the substantial presence test and are considered a nonresident alien of the United States.

The substantial presence test uses the number of days you have spent in the United States over the last three years, including the current year, to determine your tax residency status. If you regularly spent over four months (122 days) a year in the United States, and you have done so for the past three years, you would be a U.S. tax resident under the substantial presence test and you don't need to do the following calculation:

- Each day in U.S. in the current year counts as a full day
  (no. of days × 1)   = _____

PLUS

- Number of days in U.S. in the preceding year counts as
  one-third of a day (no. of days × 1/3)   = _____

PLUS

- Number of days in U.S. in the second preceding year
  counts as one-sixth of a day (no. of days × 1/6)   = _____

  Total number of days   = _____

When totalling all the days for each of the above three years, remember that the days don't have to be consecutive, and a part of a day constitutes a full day.

If the total is more than 182 days, you have met the substantial presence test and are considered a resident alien for tax purposes for the current year. If the total is 182 days or less, you are considered a nonresident alien for tax purposes for the current year.

3. Exemptions From the Resident Alien Status

If you meet the substantial presence test and want to be exempted from being considered a resident alien—in other words, be considered a nonresident alien—there are two possible exemptions you can claim:

a) Exemption under the Closer Connection Category of the U.S. Internal Revenue Code

You can avoid being considered a U.S. resident for tax purposes by meeting certain criteria:

- You must have spent less than 183 days in the United States in the current year and you must not have applied for, or received, permanent resident status (a green card). When calculating the days, you can claim exemptions for days that you had to remain in the United States because of a medical condition or days spent in transit between two foreign countries, for example. Enquire about other acceptable reasons for deleting days.
- Your tax home is in Canada. If you are not employed or self-employed, your tax home is where you regularly live, as shown by owning or renting a house, condo, apartment, or furnished room there. Your Canadian home must be available to you continuously throughout the year at all times, and not just for the period that you are not in the United States.

  If you are employed or self-employed, your tax home is the location of your principal place of business or employment, regardless of where you maintain your family home.

- You had a closer connection to Canada than to the United States during the current year. Various factors demonstrate that you maintain more significant ties to Canada than the United States. These factors include the location of the following:
  - Your permanent residence
  - Your family
  - Your personal belongings, such as cars, furniture, clothing, and jewellery
  - Your bank
  - Where you carry on business (if applicable)
  - Social, cultural, religious, or political organizations to which you belong and participate
  - The jurisdiction where you vote
  - The jurisdiction where you hold a driver's licence

b) Filing Requirements for Closer Connection Exemption

You need to file Form 8840 with the IRS by June 15 of the following year. Each person claiming the Closer Connection exemption must file, each year. The form, called the Closer Connection Exemption Statement, sets out the number of days you spent in the United States, states that your tax home is in Canada, and lists the factors that establish your closer connection with Canada. After you file this form, the IRS will stamp it "certified received" and return it to you. There is usually no tax cost to filing. Keep this form in a safe place with your other records, since it will be the only proof that you have filed.

If you fail to file Form 8840 by the due date, you could be required to file a U.S. tax return if the IRS subsequently determines that you have met the substantial presence test. You would therefore be subject to penalties by the IRS for nondisclosure. Penalties could be $1,000 or more for each category of income involved, even though you could claim treaty protection from U.S. tax, as discussed in (c) below. You could be considered a resident alien for tax purposes and would not be able to claim the Closer Connection exemption.

To obtain Form 8840, contact the closest IRS office in your area, if you are in the United States. In Canada, contact the closest U.S. consulate office in your area, phone the IRS international office at (787) 759-5100 or check out the IRS web site at http://www.irs.ustreas.gov.

c) Exemption Under the Canada-U.S. Tax Treaty

If you are a resident alien because you met the substantial presence test and you cannot claim the Closer Connection exemption, you may still be able to be treated as a nonresident alien under the Canada-U.S. tax treaty. You could be considered a nonresident alien if you are considered a resident of both the United States and Canada under each country's tax laws, your permanent home is in Canada, and your personal and economic ties are closer to Canada than the United States.

To determine if the above exemption applies to you, contact any Revenue Canada income tax office or the International Taxation Office. Refer to item 1 in Appendix A for the toll-free number. Also contact the closest IRS office if you are in the United States or the other IRS sources noted in the previous section.

d) Filing Requirements for Canada-U.S. Tax Treaty Exemption

You must file a U.S. income tax return on Form 1040 NR for the year in question. The deadline is June 15 of the following year. You must report all U.S. source income, which might include interest, dividends, and rent. These are normally subject to withholding tax. You must file a statement, Form 8833, showing any income and taxes withheld. And you must explain that you are a resident of Canada and are not subject to regular income tax rates under the Canada-U.S. tax treaty.

4. Summary of Guidelines for Filing a U.S. Tax Return

a) Resident Alien

Generally, resident aliens have to file a U.S. tax return reporting worldwide income for the year. If you cannot be considered a nonresident alien under the Canada-U.S. tax treaty or the Closer Connection exemption, you need to file; contact the IRS.

b) Nonresident Alien

If you are a nonresident alien, your income that is subject to U.S. income tax is divided into two categories:

- Income that is effectively connected with a trade or business in the United States, including income from the sale or exchange of U.S. real estate property. This income, after allowable deductions, is taxed at the same rates that apply to U.S. citizens and residents.
- Income that is not effectively connected with a trade or business in the United States but is from U.S. sources, such as interest, dividends, annuities, and rents. This income is taxed at a flat rate of 30 percent or lower.

As a nonresident alien, you must file a U.S. tax return if you have income that is effectively connected, or not effectively connected, which did not have sufficient tax or had too much tax withheld at source.

C. TYPES OF U.S. RESIDENCY

A discussion of U.S. rules and regulations is often made more complicated because of a misunderstanding of the words that are used. One such word that often causes confusion is the word "resident."

The word resident is used in many different contexts and may have a different meaning and definition in each context. A few examples of the use of the word "resident" are as follows:

- To describe whether a person has the legal right to live in a country
- To compute an individual's income tax liability
- To compute an individual's estate tax liability
- To determine what jurisdiction's laws apply to a contract agreement
- To determine an individual's rights to certain health benefits
- To determine what jurisdiction's divorce laws apply and
- To determine whether certain assets of an individual are exempt from attack by creditors.

The most relevant types of "resident" are the first three types mentioned above—namely, U.S. residency for U.S. immigration purposes, U.S. residency for U.S. income tax purposes, and U.S. residency for U.S. estate tax purposes.

1. Immigration

A non-U.S. individual can be a U.S. "resident" for immigration purposes, and thus acquire the right to live in the United States, only if that person obtains that right under U.S. immigration laws from the U.S. Immigration and Naturalization Service (INS). The INS has its own criteria, entirely separate from tax law, to determine if you will be permitted to live in the United States. Further, the fact you have the *right* to live in the United States does not mean you are a resident of the United States for income tax or estate tax purposes, although special rules apply to individuals with green cards. Apart from the possession of a green card, examples of U.S. visas that permit you to live in the U.S. are: E-2 (Investor), L-1 (Corporate Transferee), and H-1B (Work Permit) visas.

2. Income Tax

As discussed in the previous section, the U.S. has two separate tests to determine whether an individual is a U.S. resident for income tax purposes, namely the green card test and the substantial presence test. The latter test was discussed in the previous section. Except for individuals who have green cards, the immigration status of an individual does not affect his/her status for income tax purposes. In other words, you may be considered a resident of the U.S. for income tax purposes even though you do not have the right to live in the United States.

3. Estate Tax

Individuals who are *nonresidents* of the U.S. for estate tax purposes are subject to U.S. estate tax only on their U.S. property. Individuals who are *residents* of the U.S. for estate tax purposes are subject to U.S. estate tax of their *worldwide* property.

The rules that apply to determine U.S. residency for income tax purposes do not apply to determine residency for estate tax purposes. Determining residency for estate tax, often referred to as your place of "domicile," is not as clearly defined as determining residency for income tax. Also it appears you can have only one domicile at a time, whereas you can be a resident of two countries simultaneously for income tax. It is possible to be a resident of the U.S. for income tax purposes without being domiciled in the United States.

D. CROSS-BORDER MARRIAGES CREATE NEW ISSUES RELATING TO RESIDENCY

Suppose you are a retired Canadian who has always lived in Canada and you marry a retired U.S. citizen who has always lived in the United States. The two of you then spend approximately six months annually in Canada and approximately six months in the United States. Of which country are you resident for income tax purposes? Are you resident in both? Is one spouse resident in one country and the other spouse resident in the other country?

It appears likely these questions will arise with increasing frequency in the years ahead and the answers may be complex.

Canada and the United States each have their own domestic tax law to determine residency of an individual in their country for income tax purposes. The rules are completely different in each country, and each country initially makes its determination under its domestic law without regard to whether the individual is a resident of another country. The U.S. determination of residency involves application of the two tests—the green card test and the substantial presence test. In Canada, an individual can either be "ordinarily" resident in Canada, or a "deemed" resident of Canada. Consult your Canadian tax advisor for the Canadian rules. In the example of a hypothetical cross-border marriage, suppose the Canadian spouse wishes to remain a resident of Canada for medical insurance purposes, but the U.S. spouse does not wish to be a resident of Canada because of a potentially higher Canadian tax liability. Can the spouses each consider themselves a resident of different countries even though they live together throughout the year?

1. Domestic Law Rules

Although each country's rules are different, it appears that if an individual spends more than 182 days in either country he/she will generally be a resident of that country for income tax purposes under the domestic law of that country. Therefore if the Canadian spouse wishes to qualify for Canadian medical insurance and the spouses wish to live together throughout the year, the U.S. spouse might be considered a resident of Canada because of presence in Canada for more than 182 days.

Of course, the U.S. spouse could live apart from the Canadian spouse for a few days to reduce the number of days present in Canada and thus attempt to avoid being classified as a "deemed resident" of Canada. However, since the U.S. individual is married to a Canadian resident who spends more than 182 days in Canada, and since they live together *almost* the entire year, it is possible the U.S. spouse would be considered to be a factual resident of Canada. Canada appears to have an informal "couples in tandem" guideline, whereby both spouses may tentatively be considered residents of Canada if either one is resident in Canada.

2. Tax Treaty Rules

Each country's domestic law, as noted above, can be overridden by the tax treaty. Under the tax treaty's residency "tie-breaker" rules it is possible to pay your taxes in one of the countries "as if" you are a nonresident of that country even though you would be classified as a resident of that country under its domestic law. Thus the U.S. spouse, in this example, may be entitled to pay Canadian taxes as a nonresident of Canada even though he/she spends more than 182 days annually in Canada, and despite Canada's "couples in tandem" guideline. In cases where a U.S. spouse is a deemed resident of Canada but wishes, and is eligible, to be taxed in Canada as a nonresident of Canada, pursuant to the tax treaty residency "tie-breaker" rules, it may be possible for the U.S. spouse to file a "protective" tax return in Canada. This protective return can perhaps be used to commence the statute of limitations in Canada and thus limit the time period in which the U.S. spouse is exposed to attack from Revenue Canada.

E. U.S. TAX NUMBERING SYSTEM FOR CANADIANS

The IRS recently introduced a new U.S. tax numbering system to assist in tax administration. The new system was generally effective beginning January 1, 1997, and earlier for estates.

Assuming the individual involved is a nonresident alien without a U.S. social security number, the following describes some circumstances in which a Canadian must obtain a U.S. Individual Taxpayer Identification Number (ITIN).

1. When Do You Require an ITIN?

- If you are filing a U.S. tax return for yourself. For example, if you sell U.S. real estate, you want to claim a tax refund, or you have U.S. real estate rental income or U.S. business income, you must obtain an ITIN.

- If you are claiming your spouse as a dependent for deduction purposes on your U.S. tax return, an ITIN must be obtained for your spouse, even if your spouse has no connection with the U.S.

- If you are claiming children (or others) as dependents on your U.S. tax return, an ITIN must be obtained for each dependent. For example, if you are a nonresident alien filing a U.S. tax return for U.S. real estate rental income and you wish to claim a deduction for your children, you must obtain an ITIN for each child, even if they are all minors living in Canada. Similarly, if you are a U.S. citizen or green card holder living in Canada, the same requirement exists when you file your U.S. tax return.

- If you are the spouse of a U.S. person and you elect to file a joint U.S. tax return with that person, you must obtain an ITIN.

2. How to Obtain an ITIN

You apply for an ITIN on IRS Form W-7 which you can obtain from the IRS by calling 1-800-829-3676 (in the U.S.), by calling a U.S. Consular Office in Canada, or by writing to the IRS at: EADC P.O. Box 25866, Richmond, VA 23286-8107. The form is then submitted to the IRS, ITIN Unit, P.O. Box 447, Bethleham, PA 19020.

Some Canadian individuals were previously issued a U.S. taxpayer identification number (IRSN) by the IRS because they filed a U.S. tax return or claimed a refund. *These numbers will no longer be valid.* You must obtain a new ITIN if you meet the requirements for an ITIN described above.

3. IRS Shares Information with Revenue Canada

The ability of the IRS and Revenue Canada to exchange data on Canadian and U.S. taxpayers by computer will now increase dramatically as a result of the new requirements for certain Canadians to have a U.S. taxpayer identification number (ITIN).

As mentioned, you apply for your ITIN on IRS Form W-7, at which time you must provide some brief but very personal information to the IRS. Of course you must provide your name, and your name at birth, if different. In addition, Form W-7 requires you to provide your address in Canada. Post office boxes and care-of addresses are not allowed. Your date and place of birth are asked for, along with your sex, your father's complete name, and your mother's maiden name. In addition, you are asked for your passport number and U.S. visa number, if any.

You are also asked for your Canadian social insurance number. You can imagine the potential cooperation between the IRS and Revenue Canada this will facilitate. Now, the IRS will have a fast, computerized cross-referencing capability between your U.S. and Canadian taxpayer numbers. Information on certain U.S. tax-related activities in which you are involved, such as the sale or rental of U.S. real estate, or your claim for a U.S. tax refund on U.S. investment or pension income, can be transmitted to Revenue Canada by computer, giving Revenue Canada your name, your Canadian address and your Canadian social insurance number.

F. RENTAL INCOME FROM U.S. REAL ESTATE

You may be renting out your U.S. property part-time or full-time. As a nonresident alien, you are subject to U.S. income tax on the rental income.

1. Tax on Gross Rental Income

The rents you receive are subject to a 30 percent withholding tax, which your tenant or property management agent is required to deduct and remit to the IRS. It doesn't matter if the tenants are Canadians or other nonresidents of the United States, or if the rent was paid to you while you were in Canada. The Canada-U.S. tax treaty allows the United States to tax income from real estate with no reduction in the general withholding rate. Since rental income is not considered to be effectively connected, it is subject to a flat 30 percent tax on gross income, with no expenses or deductions allowed. The 30 percent withholding tax therefore equals the flat tax rate.

You need to file Form 1040 NR, U.S. Non-Resident Alien Income Tax Return, showing the gross rental income and withholding tax. Your tenant or property management agent must complete Form 1042, Annual Withholding Tax Return for U.S. Source Income of Foreign Persons, as well as Form 1042-S, Foreign Persons' U.S. Source Income Subject to Withholding. For more information, contact the IRS and request publication 515, *Withholding of Tax on Non-Resident Aliens and Foreign Corporations,* and publication 527, *Residential Rental Property.* Refer to item 21 in Appendix A.

2. Tax on Net Rental Income

Since a tax rate of 30 percent of gross income is a high rate, you may prefer to pay tax on net income, after all deductible expenses. This step results in reduced tax and possibly no tax. The Internal Revenue Code permits this option if you choose to permanently treat rental income as income that is effectively connected with the conduct of a U.S. trade or business. You are then able to claim expenses related to owning and operating a rental property during the rental period—for example, mortgage interest, property tax, utilities, insurance, and maintenance. You can also deduct an amount for depreciation of the building. However, the IRS only permits individuals (rather than corporations) to deduct the mortgage or loan interest relating to the rental property if the debt is secured by the rental property or other business property. If you borrow the funds in Canada, secured by your Canadian assets, you would not technically be able to deduct that interest on your U.S. tax return. Obtain strategic tax planning advice on this issue.

To make this election, you need to file Form 1040 NR, U.S. Non-Resident Alien Income Tax Return, each year. In addition, attach a letter stating that you are making the election. You also need to include the following information:

- A list of all of your real estate located in the United States
- The extent (percentage) of your ownership in the property
- The location of the property
- Any major improvements in the property and
- Any previous applications you have made of the real estate net income election.

After you have made the election, it is valid for all subsequent years, unless approval to revoke it is requested and received from the IRS. You need to file an annual return, however.

If you want to be exempt from the nonresident withholding tax and are making that election, you have to give your tenant or property management agent Form 4224, Exemption from Withholding Tax on Income Effectively Connected with the Conduct of a Trade or Business in the U.S. Contact the IRS for further information and request the publications 515 and 527.

When you file your annual return, show the income and expenses, as well as the tax withheld. If you end up with a loss, after deducting expenses from income, you are entitled to a refund of the taxes withheld. The due date of your return is June 15 of the following year. It is important to file on a timely basis. If you fail to file on the due date, you have 16 months thereafter to do so. If you don't do so, you will be subject to tax on the gross income basis for that year—that is, 30 percent of gross rents with no deduction for any expenses incurred, even if you made the net income election in a previous year. This is an important caution to keep in mind. Many people don't arrange to have tax withheld at source or to file any U.S. tax forms on the premise that their expenses exceed the rental income and the net income election is always available.

G. SELLING OF U.S. REAL ESTATE

If you are a nonresident alien, any gain or loss that results from a sale or disposition of your U.S. real estate is considered to be effectively connected with a U.S. trade or business. The purchaser or agent of the purchaser is generally required to withhold 10 percent of the gross sale price at the time the sale transaction is completed and the balance of payment is made. The 10 percent holdback is to be forwarded to the IRS.

1. Waiver of Withholding Tax

If you anticipate that the U.S. tax payable would be less than the 10 percent withheld, you can apply to the IRS in advance to have the withholding tax reduced or eliminated by completing a withholding certificate. If the 10 percent had already been paid, you would still be entitled to a refund after you filed your U.S. tax return if the 10 percent was greater than the amount due.

You may be exempt from withholding tax if the purchase price of your property is less than US$300,000 and the buyer intends to use the property as a residence at least half of the time it is used over the subsequent two-year period. The buyer does not have to be a U.S. citizen or resident or use the property as a principal residence. To obtain this type of exemption, the buyer must sign an affidavit setting out the facts related above. If the purchase price is over US$300,000 or the buyer is unwilling or unable to sign the affidavit, you can request the waiver from withholding discussed in the previous paragraph.

2. Filing Requirements

You are required to report the gain or loss on sale by filing Form 1040 NR, the U.S. Non-Resident Alien Income Tax Return. You would have to pay U.S. federal tax on any gain (capital gain). If you own the real estate jointly with another person, such as your spouse, each of you must file the above form. For more information, contact the IRS and ask for publication 519, *U.S. Tax Guide for Aliens.* Refer to item 21 in Appendix A.

In addition, you must report any capital gain on the sale of your U.S. property in your next annual personal tax return filing with Revenue Canada. Remember, you must report your worldwide income and gains and pay tax on 75 percent of any capital gain, converted to the equivalent in Canadian dollars at the time of sale. As you may already know, the $100,000 lifetime capital gains exemption (LCGE) is no longer available as an offset against any gains payable in Canada. The last tax year that you could use the LCGE was 1994.

H. U.S. GIFT TAX

One might think that as a nonresident alien of the U.S. you could give anything to your spouse, children or other family members, and the IRS would not have any jurisdiction. The laws, however, are not that simple. You may have U.S. gift tax to pay if you give real property or tangible personal property located in the United States to another person.

There is a $10,000 annual exemption per recipient. In other words, you can give $10,000 per year to as many different people as you wish, without being subject to gift tax. If the recipient is your spouse, the annual exemption is $100,000. If the recipient spouse is a U.S. citizen, as a general rule you can give unlimited amounts without gift tax—but exceptions apply for both exemptions. Do not proceed without consulting your tax advisor.

The gift tax rates are the same as the estate tax rates, but the actual amount of the gift tax may be higher than estate tax because there generally are no tax credits or deductions for gift tax purposes.

Subject to the foregoing exemptions, the rules are as follows:

1. Real Estate

If you own U.S. real estate directly and give it to another person, U.S. gift tax will generally be payable. Alternatively if you buy real estate jointly with another person (other than your spouse) and the two of you make unequal contributions to the purchase price, gift tax may be payable.

If you purchase real estate jointly with your spouse and make unequal contributions, you must beware when you sell the property. If the sales proceeds are not distributed to the two of you in proportion to your original contributions, gift tax may apply.

Suppose, at the time of purchase, the title to the property is placed entirely in the name of your spouse (or other family member) but the funds to make the purchase come solely from you. Gift tax may apply since you bought the property for the other person.

Personal property (as distinguished from real property such as real estate), can be classified into one of two types: tangible or intangible.

2. Tangible Personal Property

Tangible personal property includes things such as residence furnishings, cars, boats, and jewellery.

You are subject to U.S. gift tax on your gifts of tangible personal property located in the United States. However, in this case, as a general rule your property is only considered located in the U.S. if its *normal* location or domicile is the United States. For example, if you give a car to a family member while both you and the car are in the U.S., the gift tax position may depend upon whether the car was normally based in Canada or the United States.

3. Intangible Personal Property

Normally a nonresident alien is not subject to U.S. gift tax on the gift of intangible property (eg. stocks and bonds) regardless of where the property is located. In other words, as a general rule, you can give U.S. stocks or bonds to another person regardless of whether the securities are located in a U.S. or Canadian brokerage firm. However, an exception applies if you are subject to the expatriation rules (exit tax rules). For example, those rules apply to certain U.S. citizens renouncing U.S. citizenship. Check with an accountant.

I. U.S. AND CANADIAN TAXES ON DEATH

If you are a Canadian nonresident living part-time in the United States, you will be taxed at your death for any assets in the United States. You will be taxed by both U.S. and Canadian authorities. Assets might include real estate, stocks in a U.S. corporation, debt instruments issued by a U.S. corporation such as bond or debenture or interest in a partnership if the partnership is doing business in the United States.

1. U.S. Estate Tax

U.S. federal estate tax is based on the fair market value of the U.S. asset on the date of death. There may be state estate taxes as well, depending on the state. These can be up to 10 percent or more of the federal estate tax. Under the new changes to the Canada-U.S. tax treaty discussed in more detail in Section J, your estate can claim foreign tax credits on U.S. estate tax paid, against deemed-disposition capital gains income taxes owed in Canada. Naturally, you would convert the amount paid in U.S. dollars to the Canadian equivalent. In the past, you could not do this, therefore effectively being subjected to double taxation on the same assets by each country.

2. Canadian Capital Gains Tax

Canada does not have an estate or death tax as such. But Revenue Canada considers that you have disposed of your assets at the time of your death and taxes you on any capital gains on your assets, whether they are in Canada or the United States. As already mentioned, under the proposed changes to the Canada-U.S. tax treaty, you would be able to offset any U.S. federal tax paid against any Canadian capital gains tax due relating to those same assets in the United States. The benefit of this change should be kept in perspective, however. Canada only taxes on 75 percent of the capital gains of the U.S. property; that is, on 75 percent of the difference between the purchase price and the deemed value of the property or asset at the time of death. If the amount of the appreciation of the U.S. property is small, the benefit of applying the U.S. tax paid will be equally small. This is because U.S. estate taxes can go up to 55 percent and are applied against the gross value of the property. If a complete exemption from U.S. tax was not possible and you had to pay U.S. estate tax, the amount paid could significantly exceed the offset against Canadian tax due, resulting in a large but unusable U.S. tax credit.

With proper tax planning, Canadian residents can defer Canadian capital gains tax on death by leaving the property to a spouse or spousal trust.

J. THE CANADA-U.S. TAX TREATY

There are significant tax savings to most Canadian Snowbirds in the recent changes to the Canada-U.S. tax treaty, as well as estate planning opportunities. Before the changes, Canadians were subject to the risk of double taxation on the death of a Canadian resident with U.S. property and other assets. For example, the combined U.S. and Canadian tax liability at the time of death could, in certain situations, exceed 80 percent or more of the value of the asset. This would greatly reduce the assets left available in the estate.

The recent changes will benefit most Canadians in many ways. Make sure you obtain advice about the most current status and any changes from a professional tax expert familiar with cross-border tax issues. The following discussion is intended to raise your awareness of key issues that may affect you.

1. U.S. Estate Tax Eligible for Foreign Tax Credit

Under the old rules, Canada did not recognize U.S. estate tax assessed and paid as a foreign income tax eligible for a foreign tax credit in Canada. Under the new rules, Canada will provide a credit for any U.S. tax paid to be applied against Canadian tax payable in the year of death on U.S. source income or capital gains.

2. Tax Credit of US$600,000

Before the new changes were ratified, Canadian citizens (non-U.S. residents) with U.S. property having a value of more than US$60,000 were subject to estate taxes. In contrast, U.S. citizens or residents were entitled to a US$600,000 base exemption. U.S. federal tax is calculated on the gross value of the estate value at death, less any allowable deductions or credits. Credits included any state death taxes and a "unified credit," which was to exempt a certain base amount from tax, as noted above. Under the recent tax treaty changes, the unified tax credit has been raised from US$13,000 to US$192,800. This effectively raises the estate tax exemption from $60,000 to $600,000 on assets.

A portion of the exemption you will be allowed will depend on the percentage of your "gross estate" that is located in the United States at the time of your death, according to a formula:

$$\frac{\text{Gross U.S. estate}}{\text{Gross worldwide estate in US\$}} \times \text{US\$600,000 exemption} = \underline{\hspace{2cm}}$$

Your gross worldwide estate includes assets in the United States and Canada, including the value of RRIFs, RRSPs, and certain life insurance proceeds.

For example, let's say a person has a U.S. condominium worth US$200,000 (gross U.S. estate) and a gross worldwide estate of US$500,000. Applying the formula just described, the credit would cover two-fifths of the $600,000 exemption, that is $240,000:

$$\frac{\$200,000}{\$500,000} \times \$600,000 = \$240,000$$

If the above individual's worldwide estate is US$1 million, the credit would cover one-fifth of the $600,000, or $120,000 of the U.S. gross estate:

$$\frac{\$200,000}{\$1,000,000} \times \$600,000 = \$120,000$$

The balance, $80,000 ($200,000 − $120,000), would be subject to U.S. estate tax.

You could be eligible for a higher exemption than the US$600,000 under certain circumstances. For example, you could also receive a marital tax credit of the same amount, as well as a limited exemption for personal property.

3. Marital Tax Credit

If a property is left to a non-U.S. citizen spouse, a second tax credit may be available, based on the previous calculation. The basic exemption is effectively doubled if all of the U.S. property is left to the surviving spouse. In this scenario, it is assumed that both spouses are citizens and residents of Canada and are seasonal residents in the United States. If the U.S. property did not all go to the surviving spouse, the additional exemption would be prorated accordingly.

4. Exemption for Personal Property

If a Canadian resident's gross estate is less than US$1.2 million, U.S. estate tax will apply only to a small range of assets, basically real estate. Therefore, other U.S. assets, such as stocks, bonds, boats, cars, and personal use home furnishings, are excluded from U.S. estate tax. Certain U.S. personal business property or stocks in U.S. real estate holding companies are included in U.S. estate tax calculations.

5. Social Security Benefits

If you are a Snowbird, you are still considered a permanent Canadian resident as far as Canada is concerned, so no withholding tax is deducted for social security payments sent to you in the United States during your Snowbird stay. If you intend to eventually live full-time in the U.S. or other country, refer to Chapter 11 for a discussion of the impact on social security payments.

6. Withholding Tax on Interest

The general rule of withholding tax on interest income from U.S. sources is 10 percent for individuals as well as corporations. Withholding taxes on most cross-border direct dividends is five percent.

7. Gambling Winnings

If you have ever bet on a horse race, gambled in a casino, or entered a lottery in the United States, a U.S. withholding may have been deducted from your winnings. Winnings are subject to a 30 percent withholding tax, except for blackjack, baccarat, craps, roulette and big-six wheel, referred to as exempt games.

Under recent changes to the Canada-U.S. tax treaty, you can now deduct your losses against winnings in all other types of U.S. gambling and pay U.S. tax only on your net winnings. You can only deduct U.S. losses. You cannot deduct losses from exempt games. To obtain your refund you must file a U.S. tax return.

On the tax return you must be able to substantiate the losses you are deducting. Therefore you should keep an accurate record of your bets or other gambles, including the date, type, location, other persons present and, of course, details of the actual amount bet and the results.

Some specific documents you should retain are:

a) Horse Racing and Dog Racing

A record of the actual races, numbers, date and times, the details and results of each bet, and payment records from the racetrack.

b) Lotteries

The lottery name, ticket dates, unredeemed tickets, and details of each ticket including the amount paid and the result.

c) Slot Machines

Record the slot machine number, and keep a record of winnings by date and time.

d) Poker and Other Table Games

Record the table number where you played, and casino credit card data, if applicable, indicating whether credit was issued in the pit or at the cashier's cage.

In the case of slots, poker and other games, you can get a gambling card for the asking from most casinos. You insert this card in the slot machines or give it to the casino staff prior to a table game. Minimum bet limits could be required to record the bet, depending on the house policy. This card automatically records your wins and losses on a computerized data bank. You can obtain a printout of your gambling history at the end of the year from the locations you gambled. This could be used for tax filing purposes.

Do not destroy or throw away your tickets from losing bets. These tickets may be required to document your loss to the IRS to obtain your refund. You should attach proof of the U.S. tax withheld to the back of your U.S. tax return.

8. Tax Information Exchange Between the U.S. and Canada

The purpose of exchange of information is to ensure a correct and speedy application of domestic tax legislation, to assist in the application of tax treaties, and to prevent tax avoidance and evasion.

There are three main types of information exchange between countries:

a) On Request

For example, Revenue Canada could *request* from the IRS specific information about a U.S. real estate sale by a particular Canadian resident.

b) Automatic

For example all information available to the IRS on U.S. rental income received by Canadians or U.S. real estate sales by Canadians, could be sent *automatically* to Revenue Canada by the IRS.

c) Spontaneous

For example, in the course of an IRS tax audit of a Canadian for a U.S. real estate sale, the IRS might spontaneously decide to send the information to Revenue Canada if it believes the information may be of interest to Revenue Canada.

9. What Does the IRS Know About You?

The IRS potentially has a wide variety of information available on individuals having U.S. income, U.S. property, or involved in a U.S. financial transaction. For example:

- If you *purchase* U.S. real estate, your name and address is recorded in the local county property records. When you sell your U.S. real estate, another entry is made in the county records. Information on both of these transactions is readily available to the IRS if it wishes to obtain it.
- If you *sell* U.S. real estate, the closing agent (e.g., the lawyer, title insurance agent, etc) must complete IRS Form 1099-S and submit it to the Internal Revenue Service along with a copy to you. This form includes your name, address, and the sale price of your property. The IRS can use the form to determine if you have filed a U.S. tax return.
- If you *sell* U.S. real estate to a U.S. person and take back a mortgage, a notation of the interest paid to you must be made on the U.S. person's tax return.
- If you *rent* out your U.S. real estate, another IRS form may be generated. The rental agent is required to complete IRS form 1042S and submit it to the Internal Revenue Service along with a copy to you. The form lists your name, Canadian address, and the rental income you received. Again, the IRS can use this form to determine if you have made the proper U.S. filing.
- If you *receive* certain types of interest or dividends from U.S. sources, IRS Form 1042S is also filed with the IRS.
- If you *receive* pension income from U.S. sources, similar IRS forms may also be generated and sent to the IRS.

As mentioned, all the information available to the IRS can also be given to Revenue Canada.

10. Mutual Assistance in Collection Efforts

The recent tax treaty changes included a provision that Canada and the United States will assist each other in collecting revenue owing for taxes, interest, penalties, and costs. In practical terms, it will be much easier for the other country to collect taxes owing and harder for the taxpayer to avoid collection efforts from the other country. This issue has been covered in other sections of this chapter.

K. YOUR U.S. BANK INTEREST WILL BE REPORTED TO REVENUE CANADA

The IRS has issued new rules for U.S. bank interest paid to Canadians. If you receive U.S. bank interest, your bank will be required to advise the IRS of your name and address and the amount of interest paid to you. This will be required even if you use a U.S. address on your account. The bank will be able to identify you as a Canadian from IRS Form W-8 which you must file with the bank. Normally, you must file IRS Form W-8 at the bank when the account is opened, and every three years thereafter. If you do not do so, the bank is required to deduct U.S. withholding tax on your interest.

It would appear that the purpose of this reporting is to enable the IRS to forward the information to Revenue Canada, thus indicating a new, higher level of cooperation against tax avoidance between the two countries. This is because the new rules only affect interest paid to residents of Canada, not other countries.

This new rule, which commenced on January 1, 1997, will be phased in over a three-year period. The U.S. banks will be required to identify Canadian account holders as new Forms W-8 are filed with the banks after that date. Since existing Forms W-8 are valid for three years, it will take up to three years to recycle all existing account holders.

L. STRATEGIES FOR REDUCING U.S. ESTATE TAX ON U.S. VACATION PROPERTY

The previous section discussed the changes in the Canada-U.S. tax treaty with respect to U.S. estate tax. These changes will probably eliminate the U.S. estate tax problem for most Snowbirds. For example, in spite of the changes there could be a situation where some people might still be paying an excess of U.S. estate tax over what they can offset in Canadian tax payable. For example, if you own an estate with a very high net worth, and a small percentage but high dollar value of the estate is in the United States, the recent Canada-U.S. tax treaty changes will be of limited benefit to you. The foreign tax credit changes will only have an effect if there are considerable capital gains on U.S. assets at the time of death. If you think this is your situation, you should consider some estate planning options to reduce any estate tax liability. Obtain expert professional tax advice customized to your situation, since the best solution may be complex.

To lower your Canadian tax liability, you may also be able to claim the principal residence exemption on the sale of your U.S. property. This is assuming you were eligible to claim it—in other words, that it was a principal residence at least for part of the year. This claim, however, will reduce your ability to benefit from the full amount of your foreign tax credit for the U.S. estate tax paid, since you may have reduced your Canadian liability to be lower than your U.S. tax credit. You may therefore want to consider claiming only a portion of the principal residence exemption in order to maximize your foreign tax credits. Most of your exemption will therefore still be available for your Canadian home. This strategy and the calculations could be complicated, so make sure that you obtain tax advice from an expert familiar with both U.S. and Canadian taxes.

1. Joint Ownership of Property with Spouse or Family Members

The advantage of this option is that it splits the estate tax liability on death. Only your portion of the fair market value is taxed if you die. Because the value is reduced as a result of shared ownership, the tax liability is less. The owners of your property must show that they contributed to the purchase of the property in proportion to their ownership interest, unless you already own the property and wish to give a portion of it to your spouse or family members. There is an annual U.S. exemption of $100,000 for gifts to spouses, and you would only be giving a portion of the property value to your spouse. The gift would also reduce the amount of property value held by your spouse, thus reducing future taxable estate liability in the United States. You could also expand the annual gift exemption strategy by giving a part of the property each year beneath the annual exemption ceiling, if the property is of high value.

Canadian capital gains tax (CGT) would apply, however, to any gift of your U.S. second property (nonprincipal residence) to someone other than your spouse. The CGT is based on 75 percent of the proportional amount of the gain in current fair market value from the original acquisition price. The gift would be considered by Revenue Canada a "deemed disposition" of part of your U.S. property gain. For example, if the home went up in value by $100,000 in Canadian funds, and you were making a gift of half of the property, that would be a gain of $50,000 (half of the total gain). You would have to include 75 percent of that gain, or $37,500, in your tax filing for income in that taxation year. You would be paying Canadian tax on an artificial income from your second property.

In addition, if you decided to sell part of your U.S. property to friends or relatives, the U.S. capital gains tax would apply to that sale at fair market value. As mentioned in Section G, at the time of sale, you are required to remit 10 percent of the fair market value or purchase price to the IRS as a credit towards any U.S. capital gains tax that you may be required to pay when you file a U.S. tax return. Any excess amount paid would be refunded to you. If you receive payment from the buyer in instalments, however, you can spread the gain in both the United States and Canada over the number of years involved. You want to synchronize the payment structure to minimize the capital gains paid in both countries. There are foreign tax credits available for U.S. capital gains tax paid, to enable you to apply them against your Canadian tax payable.

2. Sale and Leaseback

If you want to avoid estate tax but continue living in your U.S. residence, you can sell the property at fair market value and then lease it back for a certain number of years with options for renewal. This would minimize or reduce taxes, such as Canadian and U.S. capital gains tax on any profit from the sale, U.S. estate tax on the value of any mortgage you receive from the purchaser as part of the purchase price package, and U.S. withholding tax for future U.S. income tax liability on any interest income you receive from a mortgage you accepted as part of the purchase price. Since everyone's situation is unique, make sure you get specific tax advice from a professional accountant.

3. Disposing of U.S. Property Prior to Your Death

This strategy may be desired if you want to defer selling the property right now, and thereby defer any U.S. and Canadian capital gains tax until a future time. At the same time, you could avoid any U.S. estate tax by having an option to purchase your U.S. property exercised before your death, if possible.

For example, you may wish to grant an option, for a fee, to a family member to purchase the U.S. property before or on a certain date. The price could be fixed at the time of the written option or a price formula could be included in the option document. You can include in the option that you have the power to nullify the deal if you wish. You need to have legal advice to ensure that the option is considered valid, including the payment of money for the granting of the option—for example, a nominal sum such as $100—from the person receiving the option. You should also grant a power of attorney (PA) to the person who has the option to purchase, or to another party, depending on the circumstances. The PA would be specific to the sale and transfer of the property, pursuant to the terms of the option. You need to be in good mental health when you grant the PA. Make sure you see a local U.S. lawyer experienced in these matters. If you suddenly become ill or incapacitated, prompt action could be taken by the option holder to transfer the real estate out of your name to the option holder's name, thereby avoiding U.S. estate tax. The exercise of the option prior to your death subjects you to U.S. and Canadian capital gains tax (CGT). You pay Canadian CGT whether your property is transferred before your death or triggered by your death (deemed disposition). However, the U.S. CGT would most likely be creditable against Canadian CGT. Therefore, the combined amount of U.S. and Canadian capital gains taxes could be significantly less by the property being transferred before your death by the exercising of the option, than the combined amount of U.S. estate tax and Canadian capital gains tax that would arise on your death, if it wasn't transferred out beforehand.

If you suddenly die, however, no action could be taken under the option agreement and PA. There could therefore be estate tax payable on the value of your U.S. real estate property in your name, subject to any of the changes to the Canada-U.S. tax treaty discussed in Section J. Refer to Chapter 7 for more discussion on PAs.

4. Buying Term Life Insurance

This is an option to help pay for any future estate tax liability shortfall. For many Snowbirds, however, it is not a realistic option, because it is either impossible to acquire or too expensive. Even if you could afford to acquire enough coverage, you would need to increase the face value, since the value of your estate goes up every year, along with the cost of your insurance premium. You should attempt to buy a policy that enables you to increase the face value up to a certain amount, without having to undergo a medical exam each time. If you can't obtain term life insurance, you may want to consider the cheaper accidental death insurance.

There are other strategies that may or may not be beneficial or necessary in your individual situation to reduce or eliminate U.S. estate taxes—for example, selling the U.S. property outright and renting, renting and not buying any U.S. property in the first place, holding the U.S. property in a sole purpose Canadian holding corporation, or taking out a non-recourse U.S. mortgage on the U.S. home. A nonrecourse mortgage means a lender can only take legal action against the property. They have no recourse against you personally. These options have advantages and disadvantages. Make sure you obtain tax advice from a tax expert skilled in U.S.-Canada tax strategies.

M. DEADLINES FOR FILING WITH THE IRS

Here is a summary of some key deadlines you should be aware of. Depending on your situation, there could be other forms to complete and file with the IRS.

1. Closer Connection Statement

Form 8840 must be filed within 5½ months after the end of your tax year, unless you received an extension. Thus, it is generally due June 15 for the previous tax year. Failure to file a required 8840 will likely result in your being considered a U.S. resident for U.S. income purposes unless you can demonstrate you tried to comply.

2. Qualified Domestic Trust Election

Canadian estates wishing to defer U.S. estate tax on U.S. property through the use of qualified Domestic Trust must generally make an election no later than one year after the normal due date for the return (including extensions). The due date (without extensions) is normally nine months after the date of death. If the election is not made in time, the trust could not be used in most cases, and hence the tax deferral is forfeited.

3. Estate Marital Tax Credit Claim

Canadian estates desiring to reduce their U.S. estate tax liability by claiming a marital tax credit under the Canada-U.S. tax treaty have an important deadline to meet. The estate will generally be disqualified from obtaining this important tax reduction if the proper waiver and claim are not made by the same deadline described above for the qualified Domestic Trust election.

N. TAX CREDIT FOR OUT-OF-COUNTRY EMERGENCY MEDICAL INSURANCE PREMIUMS

Revenue Canada will permit you to claim, as a tax credit, up to 27 percent of the amount of your insurance premium, as long as it is deemed to be a qualifying medical expense. Refer to Chapter 5, Section B-1 for a more detailed discussion.

O. WHERE TO GET TAX ADVICE AND INFORMATION

Many sources of information and assistance are available to help you understand the tax issues and improve your decision making.

- **Revenue Canada—Taxation** has many free guides, pamphlets, and interpretation bulletins covering a wide range of issues. They will also provide you with assistance on your tax return questions and on international tax issues, such as being a Snowbird in the United States. Refer to item 1 in Appendix A for a list of publications and contact numbers. Also, refer to the Revenue Canada Internet site for taxation and customs. See item 34 in Appendix A.
- **Revenue Canada—Customs** has information brochures and will answer your enquiries relating to any taxes, such as duties and so on when you are bringing goods back to Canada. Refer to item 2 in Appendix A and Chapter 3.

- **The U.S. Internal Revenue Service (IRS)** has many free publications and a toll-free enquiry number for assistance with the tax implications and filing requirements of being a Canadian nonresident alien of the United States or another category of temporary resident. Refer to item 21 in Appendix A.

- **Independent professional advisors** such as chartered accountants (Canada) or certified public accountants (United States) and lawyers who specialize in tax matters and are familiar with cross-border Canada/U.S. tax issues. Refer to the IRS Internet site. See item 34 in Appendix A. As mentioned before, it is prudent to obtain two opinions, at least one from a Canadian expert and one from a U.S. expert. The more extensive and complex your investments or assets in the United States, the more important it is to satisfy yourself that the advice you are getting is consistent. If you are considering moving to the United States permanently, it is imperative that you receive opinions from tax experts on both sides of the border. For suggestions on what to look for in a professional tax accountant or lawyer, refer to Chapter 8.

- ***Brunton's U.S. Tax Letter for Canadians*** is available by subscription. It contains a lot of helpful information and analysis. Contact Richard Brunton, CPA, at 4710 N.W. Boca Raton, Florida, 33431, U.S.A. Tel: (561) 241-9991 or 1-800-325-2922. It is published three times a year.

TIPS BEFORE LEAVING CANADA

Here are some reminders of tax-related steps you should take before leaving on your extended vacation in the United States. Or make arrangements for these matters to be dealt with while you are away. There are significant deadlines that have negative tax or financial consequences if they are not met.

- If you pay the current year's income tax in quarterly instalments, make arrangements to have your December 15 and March 15 instalments paid on time.

- If Revenue Canada has not yet notified you of acceptance of your previous year's income tax return self-assessment, make sure you are notified of any ruling while you are gone. You only have 90 days to file a notice of objection if Revenue Canada rejects your return and does a reassessment. If you are staying in one place for the duration of your Snowbird vacation, you probably have mail forwarded to you regularly. If you have no fixed address because you are an RV nomad, have someone monitor your mail and notify you when you next communicate with that person.

- Remember some key deadlines that may occur while you are away. For example, December 31 is the deadline for an annual withdrawal from a Registered Retirement Income Fund (RRIF). March 1 is the deadline for any contributions to a Registered Retirement Savings Plan (RRSP).

- If you turn 69 in the current calendar year, make your RRSP contribution by December 31 of the current year, rather than by 60 days after the end of the year.

- Pay safety deposit fees, RRSP administration fees, accounting fees, investment counsel fees, charitable donations, and moving expenses by December 31 if you intend to claim them as deductions or credits in the tax return filing for the current year.

- If you have spent at least 31 days in the United States in the current calendar year and have spent substantial periods in the United States in the previous two years, you may be required to fill a treaty disclosure return or a Closer Connection statement before April 15 or June 15, respectively, of the following year, to avoid significant penalties.

- Before you leave Canada, select a professional accountant who can assist you, before you depart, on the cross-border tax issues you need to know. Leave your U.S. contact address and phone number with the accountant in case he or she needs to reach you, and contact the accountant before the end of December to see if there are any tax-related matters that have to be dealt with before the end of that month or in the next quarter of the following year.

CHAPTER
7

Wills, Trusts, and Estate Planning

A. INTRODUCTION

Over the course of your life you will sign many documents. Your will is the most important one you will ever sign. With very few exceptions, everybody should have a will. A will is the only legal document that can ensure that your assets will be distributed to the beneficiaries of your choice, in the way that you wish, instead of by a government formula in the absence of a will. A will also ensures that your estate will be settled in a timely and efficient manner, rather than in a delayed fashion that will be a burden for your family. Combined with effective estate planning, a will can ensure that the least amount of tax is payable. There are no estate taxes or succession duties in Canada at this time. There are tax implications for dying in the United States, however, if you own property there; this is discussed in Chapter 6. As a Snowbird living in the United States for an extended period, you should deal with your will, power of attorney, and estate planning matters before your departure.

It is estimated that only one out of three adults has a will, meaning that two-thirds of the time when people die their wishes are not met and the government has to become involved. There are various reasons for the failure of people to prepare a will. Some people just procrastinate by nature or have busy lives and simply never make writing a will a priority. Others do not appreciate the full implications of dying without a will or even put their mind to the issue. And some people simply resist the reality that they are mortal. The contemplation of the finality of death is discomfiting to many people, and therefore they resist dealing with issues connected to death. Preparing a will and dealing with estate planning means facing the issue of mortality in a direct way.

Of those who do have a will, many do not review it regularly or modify it according to changing circumstances. Typically, people first think of their will at predictable stages of their lives, such as when they get married, when their first child is born, the first time they fly without their children, or upon news of the sudden death of a friend or relative. After the will has been completed, they forget about it. Not updating it can be as bad as not having a will at all. It can cause the beneficiaries a lot of grief, stress, time, and expense when these problems are easily avoided by regular review and updating of the will. Other people do their own will, with potentially serious implications if it is not done properly.

Your will comes into effect only after your death and is strictly confidential until that time. You can rewrite or amend the will at any time. In fact, the need to keep your will up to date cannot be overemphasized, since circumstances can change at any time. A will should be reviewed every year, ideally at the same time—for example, on the first day of the new year or on some other special event or another set date. For example, your family needs or marital status may have changed, your assets may have increased or decreased, you may have moved to a new province or bought a U.S. Sunbelt condo or house, or new government tax or other legislation may have been introduced that should prompt you to look at your estate plan again. When the federal government changed the tax laws in the 1992 and 1994 budgets, it removed the $100,000 personal capital gains exemption offset against real estate investment and other capital gains. People who owned second properties, such as a cottage or a second home, were affected. Those who did not revise their strategies quickly could lose money on the sale of the cottage or house after any capital gains tax, or the deceased's estate could pay a higher tax on the capital gain in the property at the time of death.

As a caution, this chapter provides general guidelines only. The laws and terminology relating to will preparation or estate planning can vary from province to province and state to state and can change from time to time. Federal and provincial income tax legislation continually changes. Seek professional advice. Refer to Appendix C for assistance in planning.

For a more detailed explaination of will and estate planning, refer to the recently released book I co-authored with John Budd. It is called, *The Canadian Guide to Will and Estate Planning* and is published by McGraw-Hill Ryerson.

B. WHAT'S IN A WILL?

Depending on the complexity of your estate, your finances, and personal affairs, your will can be short and simple, or long and complex. Here is an outline of the main contents of a basic will:

- Identification of person making the will
- Statement that the current will revokes all former wills and codicils (a codicil is a supplementary document to a will that may change, add to, or subtract from the original will)
- Appointment of an executor and trustee (this is discussed in more detail later)

- Authorization to pay outstanding debts including funeral expenses, taxes, fees, and other administrative expenses before any gift of property can be made
- Disposition of property
- Special provisions (such as trusts or alternative beneficiaries) and
- Funeral instructions.

C. WHAT HAPPENS IF THERE IS NO WILL?

If you don't have a will, or don't have a valid will, the outcome could be a legal and financial nightmare and an emotionally devastating ordeal for your loved ones. Not having a will at the time of death is called being intestate. It means you have not left instructions for how you want your assets to be dealt with on your death and you have not appointed anyone to be legally in charge of your estate. Accordingly, provincial and state (if you are a Snowbird with assets in the United States) legislation covers that situation. The court eventually appoints an administrator. If no family member applies to act as administrator, the public trustee or official administrator is appointed. Your estate will be distributed in accordance with the formulas of the laws of your province or state, which are inflexible and may not reflect either your personal wishes or the needs of your family or loved ones. Although the law attempts to be fair and equitable, it does not provide for special needs. For example, a home or other assets could be sold under unfavourable market conditions in order to effect the necessary distribution of assets that the law requires. In addition, the settling of your estate could be a long and expensive matter.

If you have assets in both Canada and the United States, you will have two separate probates governed by the laws of the province and state where you had assets. Your heirs could end up paying taxes that might easily have been deferred or reduced. There may not be enough worth in the estate to pay the taxes. Your family could be left without enough cash for an extended period of time. During this period, your assets may suffer a loss because of a lack of proper safeguards. There may be a delay in the administration of your estate and added costs such as an administrator bond. A bond is similar to an insurance policy in case the administrator makes a mistake.

The consequences of not having a will are not the type of memory or legacy most people would choose to inflict on their children, spouse, or relatives. At the time of a death and during the natural grieving process, the survivors do not want the stress and uncertainty of there not being a will. You should leave them cherished memories, including the foresight, consideration, and love shown by having a valid will that reflects current realities and your wishes. Simply put, there is no logical reason not to have a will.

D. WHAT IS A LIVING WILL?

A living will is designed for those who are concerned about their quality of life when they are near death. It is a written statement of your intentions to the people who are most likely to have control over your care, such as your family and your doctor. Have a copy of the living will where it can be readily obtained—for example, in your wallet or purse. Give a copy to your spouse and family doctor. You should also review your living will from time to time.

The purpose of a living will is to convey your wishes in the event that there is no reasonable expectation of recovery from physical or mental disability. Such a will requests that you be allowed to die naturally, with dignity, and not be kept alive by artificial means or "heroic medical measures." In some provinces, a living will is merely an expression of your wishes only and is not legally binding on your doctor or the hospital in charge of your care in Canada. However, other provinces have legislation on the issue of living wills. These provinces officially endorse the concept, if your written instructions are correctly done. Contact the Centre for Bioethics below for further information.

1. Canada

To obtain a sample living will with instructional booklet and/or videotape, contact:

Centre for Bioethics
University of Toronto
88 College Street
Toronto, ON M5G 1L4
Tel: (416) 978-2709
Web site: *http://www.utoronto.ca/jcb*

The cost of the booklet on living wills is $5, or $24.95 for two booklets plus a videotape.

2. U.S.

In the United States, most states recognize a properly drawn living will. Except for Michigan, New York, and Massachusetts, all the U.S. states, including the Sunbelt states, have some form of legislation dealing with living wills. For further information and to obtain a living will and health care proxy form customized for the Sunbelt state you reside in, contact:

Choice in Dying
1035-30th Street N.W.
Washington, D.C. 20007
Tel: (202) 338-9790
Tel: 1-800-989-9455
Web site: *http://www.choices.org*

The living will and health care proxy package is $US3.50. Various videos are available as well at an average cost of $US19.95.

If you are a Snowbird, you should consider two living wills. One should be recognized in Canada and comply with any provincial legislation; it should also be generic enough for provinces in Canada without legislation. The other living will would be prepared for your extended stay in the United States and comply with appropriate U.S. state legislation or be generic enough to express your wishes for the three states that do not have specific living will legislation. You may also wish to consult a lawyer in Canada and, if you are living in the United States as a Snowbird, a U.S. lawyer as well, if you desire further information on this issue. Refer to Chapter 8.

E. PREPARING A WILL AND SELECTING A LAWYER

There are basically three ways to have your will prepared: write it yourself, have a lawyer do it for you, or have a trust company arrange a lawyer to do it for you. A brief overview follows. When you read the section on the reasons for seeing a lawyer, you will see the compelling need to protect your estate and personal wishes by doing so.

1. Writing Your Own Will

This is the poorest choice, because it could have many defects and inadequacies that could result in legal, financial, and administrative grief for your family, relatives, and beneficiaries. How you expressed your wishes may very well be legally interpreted differently from what you intended because of ambiguity. Worse still, any ambiguous clause in the will could be deemed void or the whole will could be considered void for various technical reasons. Some people do their own will by drafting it from scratch or by using a standard form for a will purchased in a bookstore or stationery store. The risk is very high when you try to save money and do it yourself rather than using a skilled professional. It is false economy, and depending on your situation, you could have a lot to lose. Many people assume that a simple will that they complete will suffice. What may appear to be simple to a layperson, however, could require more complex decisions and wording. Each person's situation is unique. There are better and inexpensive alternatives to provide you with peace of mind, as outlined in the next two subsections.

2. Hiring a Lawyer and Other Specialists

Wills, in almost all cases, should be prepared by a lawyer who is familiar with them and is qualified to provide legal advice and is knowledgeable about how to complete the legal work required in drafting a will. If your will is properly and professionally drafted, it will be valid in the United States and will cover your

U.S. assets. If you have assets in both the United States and Canada, there will be a probate in both countries on your death. Your estate will require a lawyer in each country. Probate is governed by the laws and taxes of the province and state in which you have assets.

Depending on the complexity of the estate, however, a lawyer may not have the expertise to advise you on other, nonlegal issues, such as tax, investments, and retirement. If that is your situation, you should enlist the expertise of the other specialists, such as a professionally qualified accountant who specializes in tax, specifically a chartered accountant (CA) or certified general accountant (CGA). A lawyer specializing in wills could recommend a tax expert. You can also look in the Yellow Pages of the telephone book for accountants with these designations. Ask to speak to a tax specialist.

If you are selecting a financial planner as well to help manage your finanacial affairs, make sure that you check that person's credentials, expertise, and reputation. Ask for referrals from your lawyer or accountant and have any advice verified for the tax, legal, and administrative implications by your lawyer, accountant, and trust company.

For a discussion of how to select a lawyer, accountant, or financial planner, see Chapter 8.

The legal fee for preparing a basic will is very modest, generally between $100 and $200 per person. If your estate is complex, of course, this fee could be higher because of the additional time and expertise required. A "back-to-back" will is a duplicate reverse one for husband and wife and is generally a reduced price.

3. Main Reasons for Consulting a Lawyer When Preparing a Will

To reinforce the necessity of obtaining a legal consultation before completing or redoing a will, just look at some of the many situations in which legal advice is specifically required because of the complex legal issues and options involved. By not dealing with these issues, there could be serious legal and financial problems on your death.

- You want to live in the United States or elsewhere for extended periods of time—for example, to retire and travel south in the winter months. The issue of your technical domicile, or permanent residence, at the time of your death has legal and tax implications for your will. This is discussed in detail in Chapter 6.
- You own or plan to own foreign real estate, in the United States or elsewhere.
- You have a will that was signed outside Canada or plan to do so.
- You are separated from your spouse but not divorced.
- You are divorced and want to remarry.

- You are divorced and paying for the support of your former spouse and your children.

- You are living common-law, will be entering a common-law relationship, or are leaving an existing one.

- You are in a blended family relationship, with children of each spouse from previous relationships.

- You have children from a previous relationship and an existing one.

- You own your own business or partly own a business with other partners.

- Your estate is large and you need assistance with estate planning long before your death to reduce, delay, or eliminate taxes on your death.

- You have a history of medical problems and so someone could attack the validity of your will on the basis that you did not know what you were doing when you signed the will or were not capable of understanding the financial matters covered in the will.

- You want to have objective, unbiased, and professional advice rather than making choices in a vacuum or possibly being in an environment where you could be influenced by others who have a vested interest in the contents of the will, or you do not want to feel under duress or pressure from relatives or family members when preparing your will.

- You want to forgive certain people for debts they owe you, or make special arrangements for the repaying of debts or mortgages to your estate should you die before the debt or mortgage is paid back to you.

- You want certain events to occur that are complicated and have to be carefully worded, such as having a spouse or friend receive a certain income or use a home until he or she remarries or dies, at which time the balance of the money or the house would go to someone else.

- You want to set up a trust arrangement to cover various possibilities. Trusts are discussed later in this chapter.

- You want to make special arrangements to care for someone who is incapable of looking after himself or herself, or who is unable to apply sound financial or other relevant judgement—for example, a child, an immature adolescent, a gambler, an alcoholic, a spendthrift, or someone who has emotional, physical, or mental disabilities or limitations or who is ill.

- You wish to disinherit a spouse, relative, or child. There are several reasons for disinheriting someone. For example, you may have lent a lot of money to one child out of several, the money was not repaid, promises were broken, and a serious estrangement occurred. The unpaid money substantially reduced your estate, and to keep peace with the rest of the family you may want to remove the debtor child from sharing in the proceeds of your estate or reduce that child's portion by the amount of the debt. Another, more positive reason might be that all your children are now wealthy on their own and don't need your money at all. You may therefore want to give the majority of your estate to charitable causes that interest you.

- You wish to appoint a guardian to look after any children you are responsible for, in case you and your spouse die together.
- You have several children and you want to provide the opportunity for one specific child to buy, have an option to buy, or receive in the will the house, business, or farm or a specific possession or asset of your estate, and you want to set up the appropriate procedures and wording to enable your wishes to occur.

When viewing your own situation at this point, or where you project your circumstances might be in the near future, there could be at least one, if not many different reasons to consult with a legal expert on the topic of wills customized for your needs and wishes.

4. Using a Trust Company

A trust company can offer extensive services related to wills and estate planning, generally in conjunction with a lawyer of your choice or one recommended by the trust company. Always make sure that you obtain independent legal advice. A trust company can administer a trust set up as part of your estate planning or act as your executor. Everyone's needs vary, and after obtaining advice you may not require a trust company. Compare a minimum of three trust companies before deciding who to deal with. The decision is a critically important one, and you want to feel confident in your choice. Look in the Yellow Pages of your phone book under Trust Companies.

5. Make Sure Your Canadian Will Is Valid in Your Snowbird State

The following explanation is general in nature. You should seek professional advice customized to your specific situation, from a U.S. and a Canadian lawyer skilled in wills, to ensure that there is no conflict of wills. In particular, when you are dealing with the issue of more than one will, the situation is fraught with potential perils, unless your U.S. and Canadian lawyers coordinate the contents of each will and any amendments to them.

In general terms, if you have a valid will which is legally enforceable in your province, it would probably also be valid in the U.S. state that you have assets.

There could be a serious problem if you have two wills. Because there are different legal jurisdictions between Canada and the U.S., there could be, in theory, a challenge about the contents of the will by a beneficiary (or someone who would like to be one), in one will jurisdiction but not in the other one. Another point is that standard boilerplate clauses in wills state that the most recent will automatically revokes any and all previous wills. You can imagine the problem in that case, if you inadvertently included that clause in a U.S. will. It would automatically nullify your Canadian will!

There are other options to consider for your Snowbird assets that might be more appropriate for your needs. One option is for your Canadian lawyer to include specific terms in your Canadian will relating to your U.S. Snowbird property, and have affidavit attestation of the witnesses of your will at the same time. All this must be done in conjunction with feedback from a U.S. lawyer expert in will matters in your Snowbird state. Another option is to have a U.S. lawyer transfer your U.S. property and other assets into joint names, with right of survivorship, so that your assets in your Snowbird state would automatically go to your surviving spouse and bypass probate. A further option to consider is to have your Snowbird property in a living trust or revocable trust. This bypasses your estate, and therefore probate procedures, as the trust is not in the deceased's name, but a trustee's name. Check into the pros and cons of these options in your personal situation.

As mentioned earlier, if your will has been correctly executed in your provincial jurisdiction and has the appropriate clauses, then it should be valid for your assets under the laws of your Snowbird state. It could then be admitted to probate, once the court has been satisfied that the will has been properly witnessed. If you do not have any assets in the U.S. because you are renting, the issue of a valid U.S. will is not applicable, as there would be no U.S. probate procedures on death.

F. GRANTING POWER OF ATTORNEY

Many lawyers draft a power of attorney at the same time that they prepare a will. The purpose of a power of attorney is to designate a person or a trust company to take over your affairs if you can no longer handle them because of illness or incapacitation, for example. This is normally referred to as an "enduring power of attorney." Another reason is that you may be away for extended periods on personal or business matters or on a vacation. You may want to give someone the authority to sign documents on your behalf regarding the sale of your home while you are away. This is normally referred to as a "specific power of attorney," which is limited in scope and time. Considering the benefits of a power of attorney is important if you have substantial assets that require active management. You can revoke the power of attorney at any time in writing.

If you do not have a power of attorney and are unable to manage your financial affairs because of illness, accident, or mental infirmity, an application has to be made to the court by the party who wishes permission to manage your affairs. This party is referred to as a committee. If another family member does not wish to take on this responsibility, a trust company can be appointed, with court approval. Committee duties include filing with the court a summary of assets, liabilities, and income sources, along with a description of the person's needs and an outline of how the committee proposes to manage the accounts or structure the estate to serve those needs. In addition, continuing asset management is required to meet any changes in circumstances or needs, as well as record-keeping and accounting functions, all subject to the direction of the court.

1. Make Sure Your Power of Attorney is Valid in Your Snowbird State

How valid your Canadian power of attorney (PA) is in your Snowbird state, if you suffer a stroke or are otherwise incapacitated, depends on the terminology of the PA. There are two main types of PAs. One type would not be recognized in Florida, for example, and the other one might be. If you have a PA that gives someone a specific right to act on your behalf within a certain time period (e.g., selling a house in Canada for you), that is one type of PA. If you have a PA that gives someone authority to look after all your affairs if you are incapacitated, that is another type of PA. It is the second type that you have to be careful of, in terms of the terminology in any Snowbird states.

If it is a contingent (or nonenduring) PA, that is it only takes effect when and if you become incapacitated, it is *not* recognized in Florida. If you have a "durable" PA, sometimes referred to in Canada as an "enduring" PA, then that type of PA *could* be valid in Florida. In that type of PA, you are appointing someone to be an attorney now, but it survives incapacity or disability. The premise being that if you give someone the right to act on your behalf, you have to have the right to revoke that if you are mentally capable, unless the specific terminology in the PA deals with the issue of incapacity (e.g., enduring or durable). Naturally, all PAs terminate at death, when your will takes over.

Even if your Canadian PA is technically acceptable in Florida, it may not be functionally useable. That is because the people who are being asked to accept the PA (e.g., transfer or sell property), will be naturally concerned and cautious about its validity and could refuse to recognize it because they are not familiar with the terminology or the content of the document. The more remote the area, the greater the chance of rejection. For example, if you have a Florida PA, dealing specifically with your Florida property and assets, and it is on a statutory form, accepted and approved by the Florida government (the standard form came out in 1995), then naturally that will make a huge difference in acceptance. It costs approximately CDN $200-$300 to have a Florida PA drawn up by a lawyer.

Although this example referred to Florida, the guidelines and cautions would be pertinent to consider for other popular Snowbird states, such as Arizona, Texas, or California. You can see why you need to get legal advice from a lawyer in the U.S. state in which you have assets. You also want to check with your Canadian lawyer to make sure there is no conflict between your PAs in each country.

G. SELECTING AN EXECUTOR OR TRUSTEE

One of the most important decisions you will make is your choice of executor to fulfill your instructions in your will. Your executor acts as your personal representative and deals with all the financial, tax, administrative, and other aspects of your estate, including assembling and protecting assets, projecting future cash needs, handling all tax requirements, distributing the assets of the estate, and acting as a trustee for the continuing management of the assets of your estate. As you can see, it would be difficult to find a layperson or family member who would have the range of skills and expertise needed to adequately fulfill all the functions that might be required. An executor should either be an expert or retain specialists in potentially diverse areas such as law, income tax, real estate, asset evaluation and management, accounting, financial administration, and insurance. Not only can the process be time-consuming and complicated, it can also expose the executor to personal legal liability if errors are made. The executor is accountable to all beneficiaries.

1. Selecting an Executor

A will takes estate planning only so far. It is up to the executor to settle the estate to the satisfaction of the beneficiaries. Generally, there are two kinds of executors. One type is the professional executor, such as a lawyer, accountant, or trust company. The other type is the inexperienced layperson, generally a relative or family friend familiar with your personal life.

Many people consider being asked to be an executor an honour, a reflection of the trust and respect in the relationship. Unfortunately, in the emotional context of a death, however, conflicts can and do occur between executors and beneficiaries. The conflicts can arise if the executor is perceived as being overzealous or indifferent, being authoritarian or showing favouritism, lacking necessary knowledge, making decisions too hastily, or lacking tact, sensitivity, or insight in dealing with people.

An executor can retain the services of a lawyer, of course, and use a trust company as an agent. Another possibility is to appoint a co-executor. If the will names more than one person to administer the estate, they are referred to as co-executors. They have equal rights and responsibilities in administering the estate. For example, you could consider having a spouse and a trust company as co-executors. In addition, if you are naming an individual as an executor or a co-executor, make sure you have an alternative executor in the event the first one is unwilling or unable to act.

2. Selecting a Trustee

You may want to set up trusts that are operable during your lifetime. These are generally called *inter-vivos* trusts. You need to have a trustee manage the trust. Another type of trust is one that is operable upon your death, as outlined in your will. This is generally referred to as a testamentary trust.

Through your will, you can appoint an individual or trust company to administer assets of your estate that you identify for later distribution. For example, you may wish to appoint a trustee to manage a portion of your assets for an extended period of time. If you are selecting a layperson to be the executor, you may not want the same person to be the trustee. There could be a potential conflict of interest for various reasons, and different skills could be required.

You can also set up trust funds in a variety of ways, depending on your objectives. You may wish the beneficiaries to have regular monthly payments of the income generated from the original capital of trust money. This could be the situation if you are leaving money to an educational or charitable organization. Conversely, you could have that monthly payment provision in favour of a surviving spouse, with the stipulation that payments cease if he or she remarries. The remaining capital goes elsewhere. If you are setting up a trust for young children, payments are usually made to parents or guardians for the maintenance and education of the child. For such a trust, there should be a provision allowing the trustee to deplete the capital of the trust fund, as required, to meet the needs set out in the trust provisions. Another option is to invest the trust funds until a specified time and then release the total funds. For example, if a child has been financially irresponsible, you may wish to have the funds held until he or she is more mature, say, 35 or 40 years old. If you wish to keep a gift in your will secret, there are various ways of doing that. Speak to a lawyer who is experienced in dealing with trusts.

Trustees are normally given the power in the will to undertake many duties, including taking in money, investing money, selling assets, and distributing the estate proceeds in accordance with the trust terms. It is important the trustee maintain a balance between the interests of income beneficiaries and beneficiaries subsequently entitled to the capital. In addition, a trustee should maintain accounts and regularly issue accounting statements and income tax receipts to beneficiaries, make income payments to beneficiaries, and exercise discretion on early withdrawal of capital where permitted, to meet special needs of beneficiaries. Finally, the trustee makes the final distribution of the trust fund to beneficiaries on the death of the income beneficiary and/or when beneficiaries reach a certain age designated in the terms of the will, or based on other conditions in the will.

You can see why trust companies perform a vital role. An individual may not have the long continuity required, because of death or lack of interest or ability, for the 10, 15, 20, 25 or more years required. It is an onerous role to place on an individual. The benefits of using a trust company are discussed in Section H of this chapter.

3. Fees and Expenses

There are various fees associated with probating a will, settling an estate, or dealing with a trust. If you die in the United States and have assets there, such as a condo, you would have probate in both countries with a duplication in costs. The main costs are as follows:

a) Compensation for Executors/Administrators

In most cases an executor or administrator is entitled to a fee for his or her time and services provided. The maximum fee is normally 3 to 5 percent of the value of the estate. The beneficiaries or the court must approve the accounts prepared for compensation, and the amount comes out of the estate. An executor who is also a beneficiary could be denied a fee unless the will makes it clear that the gift to the executor is given in addition to, not instead of, executor's fees.

b) Legal Fees

A lawyer can assist in locating and collecting assets, make any necessary application to court and prepare related documents, get the assets transferred into the name of the executor or administrator, prepare accounts, distribute funds, obtain releases, and file tax returns.

Legal fees are considered a proper expense and may be paid out of estate funds, subject to approval of the court or the beneficiaries. A lawyer may charge a fee for itemized services rendered or a lump-sum fee of generally up to 2 percent of the value of the estate for certain basic services. This is a maximum percentage, not a standard rate. If any legal issue arises, such as the validity or meaning of a will, or if an application to the court is made, legal fees will be extra and are normally billed out at the lawyer's hourly rate. This could be between $150 and $200 or more an hour.

c) Probate Fees

These are also known as court fees. They are established by provincial or state legislation. They do not form part of the executor's compensation, nor do they include legal fees associated with administering the estate. The probate fees can range from low to high, depending on the province or state. Check with a Canadian and a U.S. lawyer. The value of the estate is used as a base when determining the probate fee. It is paid to the provincial and/or state government.

d) Trustee Fees

These would generally be negotiated separately, especially if a trust company is involved, and confirmed in writing. The services involved in managing a trust were discussed earlier.

e) Additional Fees and Costs

Naturally, income-tax-related costs and financial costs are extra.

If a beneficiary of the estate thinks that the administration fee charged by an executor is excessive, he or she can ask the executor to "pass accounts" in a court of law. The executor must present an accounting of the work done to the court and ask a judge to set the fees. The final fee may be higher or lower than the fee that the executor initially requested. When beneficiaries are infants or children, the executor may be required to pass accounts because minors cannot give their approval for the actions of the executor. If the executor or beneficiary believes that the legal fees are excessive, they can be challenged. This is called "taxing" a lawyer's account. The account is generally taxed before the registrar at the courthouse. Procedures may differ in your community.

Selecting the right executor for your needs will enhance the smooth disposition of your assets and the administration of your estate. It will also reduce the stress your family will be under. Selecting the wrong executor for your needs will result in the opposite outcome. To be on the safe side, use a professional to act as an executor or trustee, or appoint a family member to be a co-executor or co-trustee if the circumstances warrant it or you wish that to occur. Remember to shortlist three prospects and/or trust companies before you decide who will act as your executor and/or trustee.

H. BENEFITS OF USING A TRUST COMPANY AS EXECUTOR OR TRUSTEE

Many people prefer to name a trust company in the will as their executor for a variety of reasons. Compare these benefits to the capabilities of a personal friend, relative, or family member acting as an executor in your given situation.

1. Experience and Expertise in Will and Estate Planning

A large portion of any trust company's operation involves acting as an executor. A trust company's staff can regularly advise you about coordinating the contents of your will with the other financial affairs, needs, and personal changes in your life, since they are closely interrelated, and in conjunction with your legal and tax advisors. This broad expertise should enable the trust company to administer the estate economically and efficiently. Part of estate planning involves establishing objectives for estate distribution, taking into consideration any legislation concerning provision for dependents. In addition, planning involves determining what taxes would be payable by the estate or beneficiaries and considering procedures for minimizing or providing for these taxes.

2. Continuity of Service

The appointment of a trust company ensures continuity of service during the full period of administration of the estate. This is particularly important if the estate involves a trust responsibility that might have to be administered for many years (e.g., if young children are the beneficiaries). A trust company will designate only their most experienced staff to deal with the administration of estates. The staff must combine both business ability and capacity for human understanding and empathy. These qualities enable them to deal tactfully and fairly with each beneficiary.

3. Accessibility

A trust officer is assigned a specific estate and is personally responsible for providing customized and responsive service.

4. Full Attention to the Needs of Your Estate

With a trust company as executor, the operation of estate administration is smooth, since infrastructure and continuity exists. If a layperson is an executor, that person's attention to the executor duties may be influenced by other personal interests, age, ill health, procrastination, or excessive stress due to the demands of fulfilling expectations in an area where he or she has no experience, expertise, or interest.

5. Portfolio Management

A trust company can provide expertise for your estate's investment needs, such as cash management or operating a business.

6. Ensuring Control When That is Important

There could be instances when a professional, neutral, and experienced executor or trustee must deal with issues in the will that require an element of control—for example, releasing funds over time to a child who is an adult but lacks financial responsibility. Another example is managing a business until the appropriate time to market and sell it. Trust companies have access to this type of expertise and can competently deal with any situation that might come up.

7. Confidentiality

Trust company staff are trained to treat the estate administration and related client business in the strictest confidence.

8. Sharing of Responsibility

If you decide to name a friend or relative as joint executor, the trust company assumes the burden of the administration but works together with your other executor to make joint decisions.

9. Financial Responsibility and Security

Most trust companies in Canada are well established and are backed by substantial capital and reserve accounts. Reputable trust companies also strictly segregate estate assets from general funds. In addition, a trust company is covered by insurance if there is a mistake or oversight due to negligence or inadvertence.

10. Funding Capacity

A trust company can work with your family to provide for their immediate financial requirements and needs immediately after your death.

11. Specialized Knowledge

Because of the increasingly complex nature of an estate, as well as a wide variety of options available, a trust company employs a staff of experts to review and advise on matters that arise. Specialists offer expertise in tax, legal, insurance, investment, and other areas.

12. Ability to Act as a Trustee

This means that the trust company protects your interests after you die. For example, the company might manage your investments or capital and make payments to designated beneficiaries as required over time. If there are minor children, children from a previous marriage, or situations in which the estate assets have to be controlled for an extended period of time, for example, a trustee could be giving out necessary funds from your estate over a period of 20 years or more.

13. Group Decisions

If vital matters come up that involve a major decision, a trust company will use the collective expertise of a variety of senior staff and specialists to arrive at a decision.

14. Fees and Savings

Most trust companies will enter into a fee agreement at the time your will is prepared. Trust company fees are determined by legislative guidelines and the courts, in most provinces. The same guidelines also apply to a private executor. There can also be savings due to efficiency by having an experienced trust company perform the executor duties. This would not, of course, include fees involved in regular estate management or the maintenance of trusts set up during the will planning process and included in the will. Obtain quotes from the trust company.

15. Avoidance of Family Conflict

In any family situation there could be personality or ego conflicts, or friction due to issues dealing with control, power, money, distribution of family possessions or assets, resentment due to past financial favours to certain children or forgiveness of loans to others, unequal distribution of the estate to family members, or a multitude of other potential conflict areas. A trust company acts as a neutral, objective, and professional catalyst in pre-empting, ameliorating, or resolving potential disagreements affecting the administration or distribution of the estate. Based on practical experience, a trust company understands and anticipates the many potential personal, family, financial, emotional, and psychological dynamics that may be operating following a death and the administration of the wishes set out in the will.

16. Peace of Mind

There is a great reduction in stress to know that the estate will be administered competently, professionally, promptly, and in accord with your stated wishes.

An experienced trust company can provide this peace of mind and feeling of security.

There are clear advantages to using the services of a trust company in many situations, not only to act as an executor, but also to act as a trustee. As mentioned earlier, you may wish to appoint a spouse or family member as a co-executor or co-trustee in certain situations. Always have your own lawyer, from whom you can obtain independent legal advice on will or trust matters. Make sure your lawyer has expertise in this area.

I. ESTATE PLANNING AND TRUSTS

1. Reasons for Estate Planning

Estate planning refers to the process required to transfer and preserve your wealth in an orderly and effective manner. Trusts are often at the centre of the strategic planning process. There are many types of trusts. A living trust, referred to as an *inter-vivos* trust, is established while the creator of the trust is still alive and is a very common type of trust. Trusts are set up with various instructions and conditions that the trustee must follow. There are tax and non-tax reasons for setting up a trust. A trust enables you to set aside money for a specific person or beneficiary under specific conditions. It is a powerful instrument, and great care must be taken in setting one up, since it enables you to exercise "control from the grave." Trusts vary widely. Some give the trustee wide discretion; others are rigid. Once again, a properly drafted will is the foundation of a strategic estate plan.

From a tax perspective, your estate planning objectives include:

- Minimizing taxes on your death so that most of your estate can be preserved for your heirs and

- Moving any tax burden to your heirs to be paid only upon the future sale of the assets.

There are various techniques for attaining the above objectives. Some of these are:

- Arranging for assets to be transferred to family members in a lower tax bracket

- Establishing trusts for your children to maximize future tax savings

- Setting up estate freezes, generally for your children, meaning that you reduce the tax they pay in the future on the increased value of selected assets

- Making optimal use of the benefit of charitable donations, tax shelters, holding companies, or dividend tax credits and

- Taking advantage of special income tax options to minimize tax or payments on your present assets.

Federal and provincial governments are always looking for ways of increasing revenue. One way is to tax what has been exempted before. Proper estate planning can anticipate these events and therefore reduce, delay, or save tax.

2. Stages of Estate Planning

Estate planning is a continuing process, as your circumstances, needs, and wishes change. Regardless of your age, the issue of estate planning, in conjunction with your will, is an essential element of life planning. There are different stages in a person's life, though, when certain issues may arise that require different estate planning strategies.

In the later stages of life, you could be approaching retirement or already be retired. As you get older, there could be health concerns or medical needs that you or your spouse have. Your assets are probably at their peak. Your children may be married and may or may not need your financial support. Alternatively, you may have a child who is out of work, divorced or separated and requires financial support for him- or herself or his or her children. Here are the basic steps you want to consider:

a) Assess your financial status and your personal needs, goals, priorities, and wishes

If you are reading this book, you are probably already a Snowbird or plan to become one. You may also want to do a lot of travelling by car, RV, or other means. You may wish to sell your existing home and move to a condominium in a quiet, retirement-oriented community in Canada or the United States with activities that challenge and stimulate as well as provide a socializing dimension. Many people "cash out" by doing this; in other words, they have so much equity in their home that after their new purchase they still have lots of money left. If you are considering any of the above real estate options, refer to Chapter 4. Complete Appendix C, a checklist for retirement, financial, and estate planning.

b) Review your will

You need to balance the needs of your spouse against those of your children. You may wish to enjoy your lifestyle and retirement fully and leave whatever is left to your children. Alternatively, you may wish to leave a trust for your grandchildren or give additional money to a favourite charity or other worthwhile cause. If your children are already financially independent, these options may be attractive to consider. You may want to completely disinherit a child for other reasons. Make sure your lawyer words the will carefully to minimize the chance that it could be contested.

c) Reconsider your executor and trustee

Make sure that your executor will completely fulfill your needs. For a variety of reasons, an immediate family member or relative may not be the best choice as executor or trustee. For example, there could be personality conflicts between someone chosen as executor or trustee and other members of the family. You may therefore wish to retain a trust company to act as your executor and trustee. You could name a responsible family member as a co-executor and co-trustee, if you so wished.

d) Obtain professional advice on minimizing taxes

The issue of tax is always an important one, and the size of your estate can have considerable tax consequences. Federal and provincial income taxes are due when you die. There are tax consequences of having U.S. assets, but there are steps you can take in advance to minimize or eliminate them; refer to Chapter 6. Although Canada, unlike the United States, has no succession duties at present, several provinces have been considering them from time to time, but they have proven to be politically unpalatable and have therefore died a natural death. Unless you have taken steps to minimize taxes on your death, taxes could seriously deplete your estate. Obtain advice from your lawyer, professional tax accountant, and trust company.

3. Reducing Probate Fees and Taxes

Assets of your estate that are passed on through your will and go through the probate process are subject to probate fees. Some provinces have a ceiling, whereas other provinces do not. As a reminder, whenever an executor asks the court to confirm or validate the executor's right to deal with an estate, the executor applies for what is referred to as a Grant of Probate. This permits the executor to deal with the assets of the estate. At the time that this formal confirmation is made, the probate fees are due. If the executor did not go through this legal confirmation process, many people, regulatory or government agencies, or banks could become concerned that the will is invalid or that there could be a later will, and thus they refuse to recognize the executor's authority. Even if no will exists, the courts must formally and legally confirm the authority of an administrator to administer the estate, and a probate fee must still be paid.

You can minimize the amount of probate tax paid by removing assets from your estate. Clearly, if after professional consultation you choose to do this, you must be sure to leave enough assets or funds in your estate to pay the tax. These strategies have to be viewed, though, in the context of your overall estate plan. For example, if you have a business, part of your estate plan could be to place most of your assets beyond the reach of potential creditors. In addition, you may not want certain assets to remain in the estate, since these could be frozen pending the probate of the estate. Obtain professional advice from your lawyer, accountant, and trust company on the various issues that concern you, such as relinquishing control, your marital situation (particularly if you are separated or living common-law), whether you have children, tax consequences, legal or creditor considerations, and many other issues. There are some key techniques to move assets out of an estate before death or to automatically transfer them directly to a beneficiary at the time of death, thereby avoiding going through the will and probate. For example:

- Register property jointly so that it automatically passes to the survivor and not through the estate. In other words, the asset is not affected by the will. Examples are a joint tenancy in real estate or a joint bank account.

- Designate beneficiaries on your life insurance policies, RRSPs, RRIFs, annuity programs, and employee pension plans. If you are designating beneficiaries, check to see if you can easily change the beneficiary during your lifetime, without the consent of the beneficiary if you so wanted. This could be relevant in case of a marital estrangement. Some provinces don't allow you to name a beneficiary of an RRSP.

- Establish trusts during your lifetime to transfer title to property before your death.

The main financial purpose of an estate plan is to keep taxes and expenses as low as possible and pay as much as possible to your beneficiaries. You don't want to automatically make decisions as described just to reduce probate fees when other strategies could better suit your overall estate planning objectives. You may wish to consider other strategies, such as:

- Using a testamentary trust to split income among your beneficiaries. This type of trust operates through the provisions of your will at the time of your death.

- Using the $500,000 capital gains deduction for the sale of shares in a privately held Canadian business by selling the asset to family members and thereby crystallizing the tax-free gain while you are still alive. This is assuming you have not already used $100,000 of it as your personal tax exemption in the past. Collateral documentation for you to retain control of the operation or management of the business could be negotiated and signed, including the remuneration package. This deduction is still available, but could be changed in any federal budget.

- Using strategies to protect certain family assets, in a marital breakdown, from being deemed to be marital property. This is relevant if you have married a second time and wish to protect the interests of the children of the first marriage, as well as the rights of your second spouse.

4. Death Benefits Available Through the Canada Pension Plan

A surviving spouse will probably be entitled to two benefits under the CPP. One is called a death benefit and comes in a lump-sum payment, with a ceiling. The second benefit is called the survivor's benefit and depends on the age of the surviving spouse. There is a ceiling per month for a person over 65, and the survivor receives it for life. The survivor is also entitled to his or her own CPP benefits, but the two benefits have a ceiling. Check with your local CPP office for more information. Refer to Chapter 2.

TIPS BEFORE LEAVING CANADA

- Make sure that your will is current and reflects your wishes.
- Keep a copy of your will in your safety deposit box, as well as with your lawyer and/or trust company. Tell a close, trusted family member where your safety deposit box is located and who your lawyer is.
- Review your selection of executor and trustee, and consider the benefits of a trust company for those roles, as sole executor and trustee or co-executor and co-trustee.
- Have your Canadian lawyer confirm, or confirm with a lawyer in the Sunbelt state you live in, that according to the laws of the state your Canadian will covers any U.S. real estate assets.
- Consider the benefits of a power of attorney, either to handle specific matters during your absence or to deal with any incapacity on your part.
- Consider the benefits of a living will. Make sure you have left copies of such a will with key relatives, your spouse, and your doctor. Carry a copy in your purse or wallet and in the glove compartment of your car. If you are seriously ill or in an accident, you want the document to be accessible.
- Ensure that you have adequately arranged your estate planning needs to reduce probate fees and other taxes.
- If you do not already have a will or power of attorney, select a lawyer skilled in those areas and have the documents completed before you leave.
- If you do not already have a professional accountant who is skilled in cross-border tax issues, select one and obtain advice before you depart.

CHAPTER

8

Selecting Professional Advisors

A. INTRODUCTION

Professional advisors are essential to protect your interests. They can provide knowledge, expertise, and objective advice in areas in which you have little experience. It is important to recognize when it is necessary to call in an expert to assist you. Because of the costs associated with hiring a lawyer, accountant, or financial planner, some people are inclined to try the do-it-yourself approach, but this decision can be short-sighted and detrimental to their financial interests. For instance, the person who processes his or her own income tax return rather than hiring a professional tax accountant may miss out on tax exemptions that could save much more than the cost of the accountant's time. Or a person who does his or her own will or power of attorney could end up having the will or power of attorney deemed invalid because of a technicality. Alternatively, lack of professional tax and estate planning could mean that you pay a lot more tax during your lifetime and on your death than is necessary.

Professional advisors you may need include lawyers, accountants, financial planners, and others. They serve different functions, and you have to be very selective in your screening process. The right selection will enhance your peace of mind, reduce taxable income, and protect your legal and financial health. The wrong selection will be costly in time, money, and stress.

B. GENERAL FACTORS TO CONSIDER

There are many factors you should consider when selecting a professional advisor. The person's professional qualifications, experience in your specific area of need, and fee for services are factors you will want to consider. It is helpful to prepare a list of questions about these factors, plus others relating to your specific needs. By doing so, you won't forget them and can pose the questions to each of the prospective advisors. List the questions in order of priority in case you run out of time. You want to control the agenda. You also want to see if the advisor is proactive—that is, asks you questions—rather than being strictly reactive—that is, expecting you to ask all the questions. Some people may feel awkward discussing fees and areas of expertise with a lawyer, for instance, but it is important to establish these matters from the outset, before you make a decision to use that person's services. Some of the most common general selection criteria include the following:

1. Qualifications

Before you entrust an advisor with your affairs, you will want to know that he or she has the necessary qualifications to do the job. These may include a lawyer's or accountant's professional degree, or if you are looking for a financial planner, professional training accreditation and experience in the person's professed area of expertise. The fact that the person is an active member of a professional association or institute usually means a continuing interest in seminars and courses to keep his or her professional training current.

2. Experience

It is very important to take a look at the advisor's experience in the area in which you need assistance. Such factors as the degree of expertise, the number of years' experience as an advisor, and percentage of time spent practising in that area are critically important. The amount of reliance you are going to place on someone's advice and insights is obviously related to the degree of experience he or she has in the area. For example, the fact that a lawyer might have been practising law for ten years does not necessarily mean that the lawyer has a high degree of expertise in the area in which you are seeking advice—for example, real estate law dealing with houses, condominiums, timeshare properties, or immigration. Perhaps only 10 percent of the practice has been spent in that specific area. An accountant who has had 15 years' experience in small business accounting is not likely to have expertise in providing advice on tax planning strategies for individuals living part-time in Canada and the United States. It cannot be overemphasized how important it is to enquire about the degree of expertise and length of experience in the specific area you are interested in. If you don't ask the question, you won't be given the answer that may make a difference between satisfaction and dissatisfaction.

3. Compatible Personality

When choosing an advisor, make certain that you feel comfortable with the individual's personality. If you are going to have a long-term relationship with the advisor, it is important that you feel comfortable with the degree of communication between the two of you. You should also find out about the advisor's attitude, approach, degree of candour, and commitment to meet your needs. A healthy respect and rapport will increase your comfort level when discussing your needs and will thereby enhance further understanding of the issues. If you don't feel that there is the chemistry you want, don't continue the relationship. It is only human nature to resist contacting someone you don't like, and that could compromise your best interests.

4. Objectivity

This is an essential quality for a professional advisor. If advice is tainted in any way by bias or personal financial benefit, that advice is unreliable and self-serving. That is why you want to get a minimum of three opinions on your personal situation before carefully deciding which professional to select.

5. Trust

Trust is a vital trait in the person you select to advise you. Whether the person is a lawyer, accountant, financial planner, or other investment advisor, if you don't intuitively trust the advice as being solely in your best interests, do not use that person again. You have far too much to lose in financial security and peace of mind to have any doubts whatsoever. By having a better understanding of how to cautiously select an advisor, you will increase the odds of selecting wisely and developing a relationship with a professional you know will be guided by your needs at all times. You cannot risk the chance that advice is governed primarily by the financial self-interest of the advisor, with your interests as a secondary consideration.

6. Confidence

You must have confidence in your advisor if you are going to rely on his or her advice to improve your decision making and minimize your risk. After considering the person's qualifications, experience, personality, and style, you may feel a strong degree of confidence and trust that he or she will be totally objective. If you do not, don't use the person as an advisor; seek someone else as soon as possible.

7. Fees

It is important to feel comfortable with the fee being charged and the terms of payment. Is the fee fair, competitive, and affordable? Does it match the person's qualifications and experience? The saying "You get what you pay for" can be true of fees charged by lawyers, accountants, and financial planners. For instance, if you need a good tax accountant to advise you on minimizing taxes, you may have to pay a high hourly rate for the quality of advice that will save you thousands of dollars.

Most initial meetings with a lawyer, accountant, or financial planner are free or carry a nominal fee. Ask in advance. This meeting provides an opportunity for both parties to see if the advisory relationship would be a good fit.

8. Comparison

It is important that you not make a decision about which advisor to use without first checking around. See a minimum of three advisors before deciding which one is right for you. You need that qualitative comparison to know which one, if any, of the three you want to rely on. Seeing how they each respond to your list of prepared questions is a good comparison. The more exacting you are in your selection criteria, the more likely it will be that a good match is made and the more beneficial that advisor will be for you.

C. SELECTING A LAWYER

There are many situations in which you might require a lawyer in Canada or the United States—for example, having to do with wills, living wills, powers of attorney, trusts, estates, buying or selling of real estate, timeshares, leases, contracts, insurance or accident claims, legal disputes, or immigration matters. If you have a business, you will need a lawyer to assist you.

For the most part, you will deal with a lawyer in Canada for the above needs. There are situations, however, where you would require a U.S. lawyer — for example, if you are buying a condo or timeshare in the United States, or if you are signing legal documents in the United States. In certain situations, your lawyer in Canada would coordinate services with your U.S. lawyer.

Although your lawyer is trained to give legal advice about your rights, remedies, and options, it is you who must decide on the action to be taken.

1. Qualifications

a) Canada

Lawyers in Canada generally have a Bachelor of Laws degree (LL.B.) from a recognized Canadian university and must be licensed to practise by the provincial law society in the province where they are practising.

b) United States

Lawyers in the United States (sometimes referred to as attorneys) generally have a Bachelor of Laws degree (LL.B.) or a Juris Doctorate degree (JD) and must be licensed by the state bar association in the state they are practising.

2. How to Find a Lawyer

Methods of finding lawyers include referrals by friends, a banker, or an accountant, or through the Yellow Pages. There is also an excellent system called a lawyer referral service you should consider.

In Canada, most provinces have a lawyer referral program that is usually coordinated through the Canadian Bar Association. Simply look in the telephone directory under Lawyer Referral Service or contact the Law Society or Canadian Bar Association branch in your province. The initial meeting is usually free or carries a nominal fee (e.g., $10).

In the United States, similar lawyer referral systems are available, operated by the state or local bar association. Look in the telephone directory.

3. Understanding Fees and Costs

Whatever costs a lawyer incurs on your behalf and at your request will be passed on to you as an expense.

There are various types of fee arrangements, depending on the nature of the services provided. To avoid any misunderstanding, always ask about fees at the outset, as well as any applicable federal or provincial or state taxes that are added to those fees.

The main fee options include hourly fee, fixed fee (e.g., for routine services), percentage fee (e.g., for probating an estate up to a certain maximum), or contingency fee (e.g., for a personal injury claim in a car accident; if the lawyer attains a settlement, he or she receives a percentage of that, but if no settlement is made, there is no fee). Only some provinces allow contingency fees.

D. SELECTING AN ACCOUNTANT

You should speak with a tax accountant to advise you on matters dealing with tax and estate planning, including the possible use of trusts, in order to minimize taxes during your life and tax consequences on your death. Depending on the size and nature of your estate, there could be considerable tax issues and consequences involved.

A Canadian tax accountant will probably meet your needs, if he or she is familiar with the Canadian and U.S. tax consequences of holding U.S. real estate or other investments and dying in the United States. Many large chartered accountancy (CA) firms in Canada have tax experts who are familiar with cross-border tax and estate planning issues. They also have associate offices in the United States. However, you may wish to get a second opinion from a certified public accountant (CPA) in the United States who is a tax expert familiar with U.S. and Canadian tax consequences. To locate such a professional, as well as a CPA who is also an expert on financial planning, refer to Section E in this chapter.

1. Qualifications

a) Canada

In Canada, anyone can call himself or herself an accountant. One can also adopt the title "public accountant" without any qualifications, experience, regulations, or accountability to a professional association. That is why you have to be very careful when selecting the appropriate accountant for your needs. There are two main designations of qualified professional accountants in Canada that could provide tax and estate planning advice: Chartered Accountant (CA), and Certified General Accountant (CGA). Accountants with the above designations are governed by provincial statutes.

b) United States

In the United States, contact a certified public accountant (CPA) for tax and estate planning advice if you have assets in the United States. A CPA is similar to a CA in Canada. Some CPAs have a specialty designation in personal financial planning (PFS), which could include knowledge of U.S. and Canadian tax and estate planning issues. This is important; otherwise, decisions could be made in a vacuum, with adverse tax consequences.

2. How to Find an Accountant

One of the main purposes of having an accountant is to tailor strategic tax and estate planning to your needs. It is therefore prudent to seek advice from a professional accountant who specializes in tax matters exclusively, since tax and estate planning are highly specialized areas. Again, be sure to speak to three different tax experts before choosing an accountant. When you are phoning an accounting firm, ask which accountant specializes in tax and estate planning matters. Most initial meetings are free, without any further obligation. Keep in mind that all professional tax experts do not have the same mindset. Some are very conservative in their advice, whereas others are very bullish. Some enjoy the professional and intellectual challenge of knowing where the fine line is and adopt an aggressive approach to tax planning strategies. Others are more reluctant to do this. In all instances, we are talking about using accredited professional accountants. They have too much to lose to advise you improperly. But you will definitely find differences in style and attitude. The quality and nature of the advice could make a profound difference in the tax and estate savings you enjoy. That is why you need to compare accountants. You will have a much better idea who will meet your needs after you have interviewed three or more accountants.

You can obtain names of accountants and their specialties from their professional associations. Ask for referrals from friends, a lawyer, or a banker. Look in the Yellow Pages. Whatever sources you use, apply the preceding selection criteria.

3. Understanding Fees and Costs

Accountants' fees vary depending on experience, specialty, type of service provided, size of firm, and other considerations. The fee can range between $100 and $200 or more per hour for tax and estate planning advice.

E. SELECTING A FINANCIAL PLANNER

Some people may wonder if they need to use a U.S. financial planner as well as a Canadian one. It really depends on the circumstances. For the most part, a Canadian financial planner will meet your needs, since you are a resident of Canada and most, if not all, of your assets and investments are in Canada. If you are a U.S. citizen or plan to live in the United States full-time, however, or if you have assets or investments in the United States, then there are cross-border tax and estate planning considerations and you should obtain tax and legal advice in those areas. There are chartered accountants and lawyers in Canada who have expertise on these issues; refer to Sections C and D. Also, many Canadian financial planners have a network of tax and legal professionals who are experts in the U.S. tax implications and can advise you. The hourly rates for equivalent expertise would be comparable. However, at the current Canadian/American exchange rate you are also saving more than 30 percent in fees by using Canadian experts. Getting a second opinion can be reassuring if you get consistent advice. If not, you want to find out why not.

1. Qualifications

When you are choosing a financial planner, keep in mind that anyone can call himself or herself a planner; no federal, provincial (except for Quebec), state, or local laws require qualifications such as those imposed on other professionals, such as lawyers. Several associations and organizations grant credentials that signify a planner's level of education; since criteria can change from time to time, however, check with the association involved. Some of the most commonly recognized designations follow.

a) Canada

- **Registered Financial Planner (RFP)**
  This designation is awarded to members of the Canadian Association of Financial Planners (CAFP—Toronto) who have engaged in the practise of financial planning for a minimum of three years and who have satisfied certain educational requirements. An individual with an RFP must regularly take professional development courses and must be covered by professional liability insurance. An RFP is also governed by a professional code of ethics and can be disciplined for breaching that code. Many financial planners with an RFP also have a CFP designation (see below), as well as such credentials as CA, MBA, LL.B., CLU, CHFC, or CFA.

- **Certified Financial Planner (CFP)**
  CFP is an internationally recognized designation used in the U.S., United Kingdom, Australia, New Zealand, and Japan. It was first introduced into Canada in November 1995 by the Financial Planners Standards Council of Canada (FPSCC), a nonprofit organization with the objective to increase

consumer understanding and enhance the reputation of the financial planning industry.

To obtain a CFP, one must take various comprehensive financial planning courses. The program takes an average of two years to complete. A six-hour, two-part exam is written. Candidates must also satisfy a work requirement of at least two years in the industry. After the licence is granted, it is renewed annually, as long as the planner follows the code of ethics and completes 30 hours of continuing education each year. If complaints are received by the FPSCC about a planner, and if they prove to be valid and serious, FPSCC has the authority to revoke the CFP designation.

- **Chartered Financial Planner**
  This designation has been in use in Canada since 1971. However, as of the spring of 1999, the Chartered Financial Planner designation is no longer being granted. The Chartered Financial Planner designation required the completion of a financial planning training program covering six different modules, each with a three-hour exam. The program took approximately two years to complete. In addition, two years' experience in the industry was required. Planners holding the Chartered Financial Planning designation are not subject to any monitoring, code of ethics, or continuing education program.

b) United States

- **Registered Financial Planner (RFP)**
  The International Association of Registered Financial Planners confers the RFP title on financial planners who have had at least four years' experience in planning, a college degree in business, economics, or law, and either a CFP (Certified Financial Planner), CHFC (Chartered Financial Consultant), or CPA (Certified Public Accountant) designation, as well as a securities or insurance licence.

- **Certified Financial Planner (CFP)**
  This designation is earned by people who have been licensed by the International Board of Standards and Practices for Certified Financial Planners, Inc. (IBCFP). The majority of these licensees have taken a self-study program administered by the Denver-based College for Financial Planning. These people must then pass a certification exam over several months to prove their expertise in financial planning, insurance, investing, taxes, retirement planning, employee benefits, and estate planning. In addition to passing the tests, a CFP must possess a certain amount of work experience in the financial services industry, have a defined amount of college education, participate in a continuing education program, and abide by a strict code of ethics.

- **Registry of Financial Planning Practitioners (Registry Financial Planner)**
  The Atlanta-based International Association for Financial Planning (IAFP) has established the Registry of Financial Planning Practitioners. To become

a member of the registry, a planner must hold a CFA, CFP, CHFC, or CPA or a degree that has a strong emphasis on financial services, complete a minimum number of hours of continuing education credits every two years, possess three years of experience, and obtain letters of recommendations from clients, among other requirements.

- **Personal Financial Specialist (PFS)**
  The PFS is awarded only to people who are already Certified Public Accountants (CPAs). Within the American Institute of Certified Public Accountants (AICPA), those with a PFS concentrate on financial planning. They must be members in good standing of the AICPA, possess at least three years of personal financial planning experience and demonstrate special expertise by passing a comprehensive financial planning exam.

2. How to Find a Financial Planner

There are several ways of locating a financial planner. Referral by a friend, accountant or lawyer is one way. Looking in the Yellow Pages is another. One of the most effective ways is to contact a financial planning professional association.

There are several financial planning associations in Canada and the United States that will provide you with names and other educational information.

a) Canada

Canadian Association of Financial Planners
60 St. Clair Avenue East, Suite 510
Toronto, Ontario M4T 1N5
Tel: 1-800-346-2237
Web site: *http://www.cafp.org*

The association will give you the contact phone number for the chapter in your province. By contacting this number, you will be sent a free publication called *A Consumer Guide to Financial Planning*. You will also be sent a roster of members who have been awarded the Registered Financial Planner (RFP) designation in your province. This list shows experience, and services provided, lists any financial products sold, and states the method of payment—for example, fee for service, commission, or both.

b) United States

International Association for Financial Planning (IAFP)
2 Concourse Parkway, Suite 800
Atlanta, Georgia 30328
Tel: (404) 395-1605 or 1-800-945-IAFP (4237)
Web site: *http://www.iafp.org*

The IAFP represents financial planners, will refer you to member planners in your area and will also send you free copies of its various publications.

The Institute of Certified Financial Planners
3801 E. Florida Ave., Suite 708
Denver, Colorado 80210-2544
Tel: (303) 759-4900 or 1-800-282-7526
Web site: *http://www.icfp.org*

The ICFP represents financial planners who have passed the CFP test. They will refer you to several planners in your area as well as send you free information brochures.

National Association of Personal Financial Advisors (NAPFA)
1130 Lake Cook Road, Suite 105
Buffalo Grove, Illinois 60089
Tel: (847) 537-7722 or 1-888-333-6659
Web site: *http://www.napfa.org*

The NAPFA represents financial planners who work for fees only and collect no commissions from the sale of products. They will refer you to planners in your area as well as send you free informational brochures.

American Institute of Certified Public Accountants
201 Plaza 3
Jersey City, New Jersey 07311-3881
Tel: (201) 938-3000 or 1-888-777-7077
Web site: *http://www.aicpa.org*

The AICPA represents and maintains standards for CPAs. They can help you find a local tax-oriented accountant or an accountant who provides financial planning services and who has a personal financial specialist (PFS) designation. The AICPA will also send you a free copy of various information brochures.

3. How to Select a Financial Planner

After you've decided to seek the services of a financial planner, you may have other questions: Which professional is right for me? How do I identify a competent financial planner who can coordinate all aspects of my financial life? Just as you select a doctor or lawyer, you should base your decision on a number of factors: education, qualifications, experience, and reputation.

When selecting your financial planner, choose one you can work with confidently. You are asking this person to help shape your financial future, and you are paying him or her to do so. It is your responsibility and right to fully enquire about the planner's background, numbers of years in practise, credentials, client references, and other relevant information.

Once again, it is recommended that you meet with at least three planners before you make your final selection. To work effectively with a planner, you will need to reveal your personal financial information, so it's important to find someone with whom you feel completely comfortable.

Research shows that consumers rate "trust" and "ethics" as the most important elements in their relationship with financial advisors. In fact, survey respondents gave this response twice as often as they mentioned good advice and expertise.

By asking the following questions, you should get the information you need to make your decision on which financial planner to hire. As you think of others, add them to your list. Keep in mind how the answers fit your personal needs.

4. Questions to Ask a Financial Planner

- *How long has the planner been working with clients in the comprehensive financial planning process?*
- *What did the planner do before becoming a financial planner?*
  Most planners come from fields related to financial services. If he or she started out as a lawyer, accountant, insurance agent, or other specialist, that background will most likely affect the advice the planner gives.
- *What are the planner's areas of expertise?*
  Ideally, these should include investments, insurance, estate planning, retirement planning, and/or tax strategies.
- *What services does the planner provide?*
  Most planners will help you assemble a comprehensive plan, but some specialize in particular areas of finance. The services you should expect include cash management and budgeting; estate planning; investment review and planning; life, health, and property/casualty insurance review; retirement planning; goal and objective setting; and tax planning. Ask about each service specifically.
- *Who will you deal with regularly?*
  You might see the planner only at the beginning and end of the planning process and work with associates in between. Ask if this will be the arrangement, and ask to meet the personnel involved. Also enquire about their qualifications.
- *What type of clientele does the planner serve?*
  Some planners specialize by age, income category, or professional group.
- *Will the planner show you a sample financial plan he or she has done?*
  The planner should be pleased to show you the kind of plan you can expect when the data-gathering and planning process is complete. Naturally, any plan you are shown would not reveal client names or confidential information.
- *Does the planner have access to other professionals if the planning process requires expertise beyond the scope of the planner?*

Most financial planners are generalists and frequently consult with other professionals from related fields for added expertise in specialty areas. A good planner has a network of lawyers, accountants, investment professionals, and insurance specialists to consult if questions arise.

- *Does the planner just give financial advice, or does he or she also sell financial products?*
  As discussed earlier, there are several different types of advisors.

- *Will the planner's advice include only generic product categories or specific product recommendations?*
  Some planners will name a particular mutual fund or stock, for example. Others will advise that you keep a certain percentage of your assets in stocks, bonds, and cash, leaving you to assess which bonds, stocks, and money market funds are appropriate.

- *Will the planner spend the time explaining his or her reasons for recommending a specific product and how it suits your goals, circumstances, and tolerance for risk?*
  Ask how the planner will monitor a recommended mutual fund or investment product after you've bought it. You should feel comfortable that the planner will ensure that you understand the strategy and products.

- *Will the planner do independent analysis on the products or become dependent on another company's research? Does the practitioner have any vested interest in the products recommended?*

- *How will you follow up after the plan is completed to ensure that it is implemented?*
  A good planner makes sure that you take steps to follow your plan. The plan should be reviewed and revised as conditions in your life, tax laws, or the investment environment changes.

- *How is the planner compensated?*
  Some planners charge for the advice they give. Others collect commissions from the sale of products they recommend. Some charge both a planning fee and a sales commission. Ask for a written estimate of any fees. An explanation of compensation is covered in Section 5.

- *Will the planner have direct access to your money?*
  Some planners want discretionary control of their clients' funds, which permits the planners to invest at their discretion. You have to be extremely careful, since there is a high degree of potential risk. If you do agree to it, make sure that the planner has an impeccable track record, is bonded by insurance, and is covered by professional liability insurance. Also, limit the amount so that it is within your financial comfort zone and have it confirmed in writing.

- *Are there any potential conflicts of interest in the investments the planner recommends?*

A planner must advise you, for example, if he or she or the planner's firm earns fees as a general partner in a limited partnership that the planner recommends. If the planner receives some form of payment, frequently called a referral fee, when he or she refers you to another firm, you want to know.

- *What professional licences and designations has the planner earned?*
  Enquire whether the planner holds a RFP, CFP, CHFC, CA, CGA, CPA, PFS, LL.B., or CFA. Also find out the planner's educational background.

- *Has the planner ever been cited by a professional or governmental organization for disciplinary reasons?*
  Even if the planner says that he or she has an impeccable professional track record, you can check with the provincial or state securities office, and the provincial or state financial planning associations.

5. How a Financial Planner Is Compensated

Generally, financial advisors are compensated in one of four ways: solely by fees, by a combination of fees and commissions, solely by commissions, or through a salary paid by an organization that receives fees. It is important to understand, and be comfortable with, the way your financial planner gets paid—and ensure the planner's compensation method is suited to your particular needs. In some cases, financial advisors may offer more than one payment option. Compensation is just one among many important elements that should figure into your decision about hiring a financial advisor.

Here's how these different methods work:

a) Fee-Only

Many lawyers, accountants, and fee-only financial planners charge an hourly rate, and your fee will depend on how much time the advisor spends on your situation, including time in research, reviewing the plan with you, and discussing implementation options. Others just charge a flat amount. Such planners usually offer a no-cost, no-obligation initial consultation to explore your financial needs. Some ask you to complete a detailed questionnaire and then provide a computerized profile and assessment of your situation and options for a nominal fee that can range from $200 to $500 or more.

Fee-only financial advisors typically advise you on investments, insurance, and other financial vehicles but do not benefit from commissions if you take their suggestions. The advantage of this type of arrangement is that the planner has no vested interest in having you buy one product over another, since there is no financial gain to be made personally from any specific recommendation. Some fee-only financial planners will help you follow through on their recommendations using mutual funds and other investments, if you so wish.

b) Commission-Only

Some financial advisors charge no fee for a consultation but are compensated solely by commissions earned by selling investments and insurance plus services necessary to implement their recommendations—for example, a life insurance policy, annuity, or mutual fund. A commission-only advisor will develop recommendations for your situation and goals, review the recommendations with you and discuss ways to implement these recommendations.

In some cases, the commissions are clearly disclosed—for example, a percentage front-end-load commission on a mutual fund. In other cases, the fees are lumped into the general expenses of the product, as with life insurance, so you won't know how much your planner makes unless you ask him or her. When you interview such a planner, ask him or her approximately what percentage of his or her firm's commission revenue comes from annuities, insurance products, mutual funds, stocks and bonds, and other products. The planner's answers will give you a sense of the kind of advice his or her firm usually gives.

Not only do you pay fees in the form of an upfront charge, but you could also pay regular charges that apply as long as you hold an investment. For example, some insurance companies pay planners trailing fees for each year a client pays the premiums on an insurance policy. In addition, some mutual funds levy fees, which are annual charges of your assets designed to reward brokers and financial planners for keeping clients in a fund.

Some companies reward commission-motivated planners with prizes of free travel or merchandise if their sales of a particular product reach a target level. Other arrangements award planners who attain certain target sales goals with noncash goods and services, such as assistance in paying for investment research.

Your planner might not like your questioning his or her cash payment and other perks. It is your right to know, however, whether the products you buy generate direct fees and indirect benefits for the planner. By knowing the full extent of your planner's compensation, you will be better able to decide whether his or her advice is self-serving or objective.

c) Fee Plus Commission

Some planners charge a fee for assessing your financial situation and making recommendations and may help you implement their recommendations by offering certain investments or insurance for sale. They typically earn a commission on the sale of some of those products.

In some cases, planners are actually captives of one company, so they recommend only its product line. They may have a comprehensive product line or a small one. Other planners are independent and therefore recommend the mutual funds or insurance policies of any company with which they affiliate.

Like fee-only planners, fee-plus-commission advisors may charge a flat fee or bill you based on the amount of time they spend on your situation. Others use a fee scale, varying their fees according to the complexity of your financial situation.

Another form of compensation is called fee offset, meaning that any commission revenue your planner earns from selling you products reduces his or her fee for planning. If you buy so many products that your entire fee is covered, you should request a refund of the fee you paid for your basic plan.

d) Salary

Many banks, trust companies, credit unions, and other companies offer financial planning services. In most instances, the financial advisors on their staffs are paid by salary and earn neither fees nor commissions. There could be other incentives, however, based on the volume and value of the business done, including a raise in salary or a promotion given at an annual performance review. Alternatively, there could be quotas to be met.

All four compensation methods discussed have their advantages. You must choose the method that, combined with the other qualities of the advisor you select, best meets your needs. If you don't understand how your financial advisor is compensated, it's your responsibility and your right to ask.

An advisor who is honest and straightforward about compensation gives you the information you need to make smart financial decisions. Do not consider hiring a financial planner who will not disclose how he or she is compensated.

F. SELECTING A REALTOR

There are distinct advantages to having a realtor acting for you in buying a home. As with any profession, you can minimize the risks and benefits greatly by choosing a knowledgeable, experienced, and sincere realtor. The terms agent, broker, and realtor are often used interchangeably. You do not pay a commission fee to a realtor for assisting your purchase. Only the vendor pays the commission.

1. Qualifications

a) Canada

Real estate agents are required to be licensed by their respective provincial governments.

b) U.S.

Real estate agents are required to be licensed by their respective states.

2. Where to Find a Realtor

- Open houses provide an opportunity to meet realtors.
- Newspaper ads list the names and phone numbers of agents who are active in your area.
- For Sale signs provide an agent's name and phone number.
- Real estate firms in your area can be contacted. Speak to an agent who specializes in the type of property you want and is an experienced salesperson.

3. Selection Criteria

After you have met several agents who could potentially meet your needs, there are a number of guidelines to assist you with your selection:

- Favour an agent familiar with the neighbourhood you are interested in. Such an agent will be on top of the available listings, will know comparable market prices, and can target the types of property that meet your needs.

- Favour an agent who is particularly familiar with the buying and selling of residential and revenue properties.

- Look for an agent who is prepared to pre-screen properties so that for viewing purposes, you are informed only of those that conform to your guidelines.

- Look for an agent who is familiar with the various conventional and creative methods of financing, including the effective use of mortgage brokers.

- Look for an agent to be thorough on properties you are keen on, in terms of background information such as length of time on the market, reason for sale, and price comparisons among similar properties. An agent who is familiar with the Multiple Listing Service (MLS) system computer can find out a great amount of information in a short time, assuming the property is listed on the MLS or U.S. equivalent.

- Look for an agent who will be candid with you in suggesting a real estate offer price and explain the reasons for the recommendation.

- Look for an agent who has effective negotiating skills to ensure that your wishes are presented as clearly and persuasively as possible.

- Favour an agent who is working on a full-time basis, not dabbling part-time.

- Look for an agent who attempts to upgrade professional skills and expertise.

- Look for an agent who is good with numbers, in other words, is familiar with the use of financial calculations.

Because of the time expenditure by the agent, you should give the agent your exclusive business if you have confidence in him or her. Keep the agent informed of any open houses in which you are interested. Advise any other agents that you have one working for you. Focus clearly on your needs and provide the agent with a written outline of your specific criteria to assist in shortlisting potential prospects. If for any reason you are dissatisfied with your agent, find another agent as quickly as possible.

In addition to the MLS which can provide instant, thorough and accurate information on properties, an agent could use the Internet as a research tool to assist your search. Without an agent searching for you, you seriously minimize your range of selection and the prospect of concluding the deal at a price that is attractive to you. In many cases, realtors can refer you to a lender or mortgage broker to assist you in arranging mortgage financing.

4. Types of Realtors

In Canada, as of January 1, 1995, there is a structure for the relationship between real estate agents and home buyers and sellers across Canada. In the U.S., this type of option has been in existence for some time. The reason for this change in Canada had to do with public confusion as to the roles of a realtor representing the buyer or the vendor. Many people assumed that if they found a realtor and the house was listed on the MLS system that realtor would represent their interests exclusively when an offer was presented and candid financial and negotiating information was shared by the buyer with that realtor.

The law, however, took a different view, related to the issue of principal and agent. The agent (e.g., realtor) owed a duty of trust to the seller. Legally, the agent was bound to be completely loyal to the seller, not disclose any information to the prospective purchaser that could compromise the seller's interests, take reasonable care in his actions, etc. Any subagent, e.g., another realtor involved, was considered to be bound completely to the seller by an extension of the principal/agent law. Hence the confusion. Litigation issues could result because of this confusion, by either the buyer or the seller, against the selling or listing realtor.

The new system spells out the respective roles and responsibilities of each realtor involved. The seller still pays the real estate commission, which is shared with any other realtor involved. All disclosures of who is acting for whom is spelled out in the agreement of purchase and sale. In some cases, an agent working with the buyer may also enter into a Buyer Agency Contract. In other words, each realtor is acting exclusively for the benefit of the buyer or seller. There is no confusing perceived overlap. However, if the listing realtor is also the selling realtor (double-end deal), the agent has to enter into a Limited Dual Agency Agreement. This is agreed upon and signed by both the buyer and the seller. The agent modifies his or her exclusive obligations to both the buyer and the seller by limiting it primarily to confidentiality as to each parties' motivation and personal information.

You can get more information from any Canadian or U.S. real estate agent, real estate company, or your local real estate board.

5. Understanding Fees and Costs

In both Canada and the U.S., it is the seller who customarily pays the real estate commission. The buyer does not. If you are selling, the amount of the commission could vary, as it is negotiable in various circumstances and jurisdictions. It could range from five to seven percent on the first $100,000 purchase price and 2.5 percent thereafter. It could be lower or you could negotiate a flat rate.

G. OTHER PEOPLE PROVIDING FINANCIAL AND INVESTMENT ADVICE OR INFORMATION

Your first step is to have an objective financial planner assess your current financial situation and needs and give advice on fulfilling your long-term objectives and needs with an integrated and comprehensive financial plan. There are many other people in the financial and investment area however, that you might have dealings with or hear about at some point. Here is a brief summary.

1. Retirement Counsellor

A retirement counsellor specializes in clients who are generally over 50 years of age, that is, nearing retirement or actually retired. Types of investments sold include RRSPs, RRIFs, LIF annuities, GICs, and mutual funds. The main thrust of these investments should be preservation of capital and low or moderate risk.

2. Company Human Resource Personnel

If you have a pension plan from your employer, you should ask the people administering it to provide you with details. Also ask them to assist you in projecting the income you will receive from the plan and, after you retire, what additional benefits, other than pension income, you will be entitled to. Also ask if these benefits are guaranteed or if the employer can withdraw them at any time. Refer to the discussion of company pension plans in Chapter 2.

3. Government Pension Plan Personnel

Check with the federal and provincial governments to see what pension or financial assistance plans you may be currently eligible for, such as OAS, CPP, QPP, or GIS. Refer to Chapter 2 for more detail.

4. Bank, Trust Company, or Credit Union Personnel

These financial institutions have an extensive range of investment products including mutual funds, GICs, term deposits, Canada Savings Bonds, and so on. With mutual funds, there is generally a wide selection of money market funds, growth funds, income funds, and balanced funds to accommodate people's investment needs and risk tolerance.

The range of training and expertise of bank, trust company, or credit union personnel can vary. Staff members licensed to sell mutual funds can give very helpful advice about the nature and benefits of their particular products. Expect to get general advice, however, not comprehensive advice dealing with all your present and future needs. Many of these institutions have instructive pamphlets to give you a better understanding of general money management strategies.

Many major financial institutions in Canada are expanding into collateral financial services beyond their traditional scope. This is being done through subsidiary companies in areas such as discount stock brokerages, investment portfolio management, estate planning, trusts, and asset management and insurance.

One service provided by most major financial institutions is called private banking services, or something similar. It involves giving customized, personalized, and integrated advice about a mixture of services and products—for example, straight banking, investment, wealth management, and trust and estate planning. To be eligible, you have to meet certain criteria, such as having a minimum of net worth and/or liquid assets available for investing. The criteria vary considerably, depending on the institution involved.

5. Insurance Agent or Broker

The primary goal of these advisors is to sell life insurance and other insurance company products such as annuities or segregated mutual funds. As a consequence, you may be limited to building a financial plan around an insurance policy. An agent is a person who sells the products of only one company, whereas a broker can sell the products of any company. Thus, while the recommended solutions offered by an agent could be restricted to a small range of products, an independent insurance broker could offer a wide range of different insurance-related products.

6. Mutual Fund Broker

Since a broker makes a commission on any product sold to you, you have to satisfy yourself that it is the right type of product and the best choice of that product for your needs. A high degree of trust is necessary as you don't want to feel a broker's recommendation is based on the size of the commission or other special incentives. Be cautious, as a broker may only have a mutual fund licence but promote himself or herself as a professional financial planner.

7. Stockbroker/Investment Advisor

Sometimes stockbrokers refer to themselves as "investment advisors." Although the advice is free, the client pays for it through commissions that his or her accounts generate. Some full-service brokers offer investment advice on a broad range of financial products, such as stocks, bonds, mutual funds, and mortgage-backed securities. Some stockbrokers don't want to deal actively with small investor accounts because of the time involved, but would probably recommend a mutual fund to serve your needs instead.

Many brokerage firms offer "managed" accounts, referred to as "wrap" accounts in the industry. With these accounts, your money is invested in several pooled portfolios, depending on your risk profile, and managed generally by an outside money manager rather than a broker. You normally pay a fixed annual fee, based on a percentage of the value of the money invested.

8. Discount Broker

Although these brokers charge significantly lower commissions than do full-service stockbrokers, they only buy and sell based on your instructions. They do not give advice. Using discount brokers is only a realistic investment option if you know the stock and bond market thoroughly and can take the time to make prudent decisions by understanding and researching the market.

9. Deposit Broker

These individuals generally sell term deposits, GICs, annuities, and RRIFs; in some cases, they are licensed to sell mutual funds.

10. Investment Counsellor

This type of financial advisor generally only deals with wealthy clients wishing to invest a minimum of $250,000 to $1 million. This restriction is due to the time involved to customize and monitor an investment portfolio. Some investment counsellors will take on a lower investment portfolio. A management fee is generally a percentage, normally 1 to 2 percent, of the value of the assets in the portfolio. If the management skill results in an increase in value of the client's portfolio, the fee obtained increases accordingly.

TIPS BEFORE LEAVING CANADA

- Make sure your financial affairs are in good order before you depart.
- Select objective professional tax, legal, and financial planning advice as your situation and needs dictate before you depart.
- Seek advice on the various cross-border implications of being a Canadian citizen living part-time in the United States for up to six months.
- Obtain advice on your various retirement, pension, and investment needs before you head South.

CHAPTER
9

Snowbirding in Mexico

A. INTRODUCTION

Mexico is a very popular tourist destination and increasingly popular with Snowbirds. Naturally, there are considerable differences between being a seasonal resident in the U.S. and in Mexico. But it is precisely these differences that attract those who choose Mexico.

There are many issues to consider when selecting any foreign country as a part-time residence including language, culture and regulatory differences. If you don't speak Spanish, you can pick up key words and phrases very quickly. Also, in the popular Snowbird retirement areas, English is frequently spoken. Residing in a foreign country is not for everyone of course. Spend some time as a tourist and investigate the various locations where other Canadian and American Snowbirds reside, and make an assessment. The next step is to try it for part of a season, say a month or so, and rent housing while you are there, or you might have an RV or mobile home.

This chapter is merely the starting point in your extensive research. It includes some popular Snowbird destinations, preliminary factors to consider, entering Mexico, insurance matters and some other information.

B. POPULAR SNOWBIRD DESTINATIONS

The three most prominent areas for Canadian/American Snowbirds in Mexico are:

- Guadalajara (residential areas of Las Fuentes, Chapalita, and Ciudad Buganvilias)
- Lake Chapala (villages of Chapala, Chula Vista, and Ajijic)
- San Miguel de Allende

In addition, there are a few other retirement areas for Snowbirds.

1. Cuernavaca

Located south of Mexico City, it can be reached over a four-lane mountain highway. Its population is approximately 100,000. At an altitude of 1524m (5,000 feet), the climate of Cuernavaca is ideal. Usual average temperature is 20.5°C (69°F). Nights and early mornings are crisp and cool. There is also a large enclave of retired North Americans who lead active social lives.

2. Guadalajara

The second largest city in Mexico, with a population of over 2 million people, Guadalajara has a benign climate, a slower pace but almost as many attractions as Mexico City for the retiree. Flowering trees and shrubs, lovely old churches and residential areas contribute to its beauty. It is in the centre of the breadbasket of Mexico, so food is plentiful and inexpensive. There is a large Canadian/American colony, and living costs are substantially lower than Mexico City.

Guadalajara has many modern supermarkets, pharmacies, and small shops with a wide variety of American and Mexican products.

3. Lake Chapala

Chapala is about forty minutes by car from Guadalajara on a paved highway on the shores of Lake Chapala, the largest lake in Mexico. Originally a lakeshore resort popular among Mexicans, it has also become the locale of a large Canadian/American settlement.

Ajijic, also on Lake Chapala, is a well-known Canadian/American retirement locale. The beauty of this area has spurred the development of many retirement homes.

4. Oaxaca

The capital city of the state of Oaxaca is one of the least expensive retirement centres in Mexico. It is far from the hustle and bustle of the big cities, but has a population of approximately 130,000, at an altitude of 1524m (5,000 feet) with an average temperature of 20°C (68°F).

5. San Miguel de Allende

About a three-hour drive north from Mexico City, in the state of Guanajuato. San Miguel has a population of approximately 25,000, with a large number of tourists and retired people during the winter. It is the outstanding model of Spanish colonial architecture in Mexico and is located in a mountain setting. At an altitude of 1950m (6,400 feet), it is colder than Mexico City, with an average temperature of 17.5°C (64°F). There is a fairly active artists' colony with frequent exhibits by local painters. Living costs are considerably lower than in Mexico City.

C. PRELIMINARY FACTORS TO CONSIDER

1. Travelling to Mexico

There are direct flights to the most popular Snowbird areas from several points in the United States, or connecting flights from anywhere in the U.S. or Canada through Los Angeles, Dallas or Houston. The only documents you need to go to Mexico are a valid passport, a photo ID, such as a driver's licence, and a tourist visa which you can fill out on the plane or at the border. You can obtain a tourist visa at your entry point, at the airport, or before your departure. This visa will be valid for the length of your stay in Mexico, up to 180 days, if requested. More detail on entering Mexico will be discussed later.

Should you decide to drive, there are excellent, modern toll-roads. The older thoroughfares, used by Mexicans and foreigners, can be more time-consuming.

2. Residential Status

If you should decide you want to stay in Mexico for a longer time than permitted by a tourist visa, you have two choices. You can apply for an FM3 permit, which is a temporary residence permit that must be renewed every year, or an FM2 permit, which is a permanent residence permit and allows you to work in the country. With both, you are required to have a certain amount of income from the U.S. or Canada (currently about CDN $1000 per month for the main applicant and CDN $500 per dependant for FM3, and CDN $1700 for FM2), or to have a sufficient amount of investments in Mexico to provide this amount of income. If you own a home in Mexico, the amount is reduced by half for the main applicant.

3. Cost of Living

In general, the cost of living in Mexico is much less than in Canada or the U.S., even after devaluation and inflation. Notable items that are much cheaper are medicine (which often can be purchased over the counter without a prescription), medical, home and car (foreign-plated) insurance, fresh fruits and vegetables, wine, beer, and liquor. Foreign residents do not pay any taxes on their income in Mexico. The only tax you would pay is a modest property tax (CDN $45—CDN $150+ per year) should you buy a home.

Utility costs are also much lower. Electricity will be about CDN $30 per month because heating and air conditioning are not necessary due to the comfortable weather all year round. The tap water is used for washing and gardening. For drinking purposes most residents prefer to buy bottled water which is delivered in 23 litre (five gallon) containers right to your home. Even Canadian bottled water is available in some stores.

If you bring your Canadian or U.S. car and apply for FM2 or FM3 status, which allows you to keep your foreign-plated car legally in Mexico as long as your residence status is up-to-date, your insurance will cost you CDN $300 to CDN $450 per year. You are not allowed to sell your foreign-plated car in Mexico.

4. Health Care

You may have wondered about the quality of health care in Mexico. This is a common concern of U.S. and Canadian citizens considering a move south. Snowbirds in Guadalajara, Lake Chapala and other popular areas, can choose from a variety of health care options. For example, there is private medical care which is very personalized, and state health care (IMSS) which serves 70 percent of the population adequately and to which foreign residents can subscribe for less than CDN $300 per year. Another option is enrolling in a medical group which gives access to English-speaking doctors in several specialties.

Not only are costs lower, but the risk factor has decreased considerably with the influx of modern equipment and local doctors learning about new treatments and medications. Many doctors have also trained in the United States and speak English well.

Mexico has a nationalized health care system, and almost every town and city in Mexico now has either a national hospital or medical clinic. Before you leave home, check with your health insurance carrier to make sure that your insurance plan will cover you in Mexico. Refer to Section E on insurance. Currently no vaccinations are needed to enter Mexico from the United States or Canada.

In the event of a major medical emergency, medical jet evacuation services are available, including:

- Air Ambulance America of Mexico: Offices in Mexico City dial (95) 800-222-3564

- Air Evac: Offices in Mexico City and San Diego call (619) 278-3822

However, you want to arrange for out-of-country emergency medical insurance before you leave Canada.

5. Staying Healthy

You may find that your eating and drinking habits are initially different than back home. Altitude, climate, and time zone changes also throw your system off during your first few days.

Here are some tips to smooth the transition:

- Take it easy the first few days.
- Ease into local eating and drinking habits.
- Always wash your hands before eating.

- Drink bottled water.
- Take yogurt or papaya enzyme tablets throughout your stay to act as a buffer for stomach upset.
- When eating from open-air food stands, use discretion.
- Drink plenty of nonalcoholic fluids and do not become dehydrated.
- Take a siesta (nap) each afternoon.

If you have a problem, Mexico has pharmacies (*farmacias*) which dispense prescription drugs at a fraction of their cost back home. Anti-diarrhea drugs such as Lomotil are readily available. Obviously, you should consult your physician before taking any prescription drugs.

If you require medicines containing habit-forming drugs or narcotics, take precautions to avoid any misunderstanding. Under Mexican law, possession of illegal drugs is a federal offence. Properly identify all drugs, carry only the necessary quantity and have with you a prescription or written statement from a physician. These safeguards will also help to avoid potential customs problems upon return to Canada.

6. Consular Aid

If, for any reason, you require the aid of a lawyer or consul, there are many bilingual legal aids in Guadalajara, Chapala, and other popular Snowbird areas. As well, both Canada and the United States have consulates in or near key Snowbird areas. Refer to item 9 in Appendix A for contact listings.

7. Money Matters

All the major Mexican banks are represented in the major retirement areas. In most cases, accounts can easily be opened and deposit investments made at generally higher rates than in Canada or the U.S. Transfers of funds or money exchange can be done rapidly. Managers and many employees are bilingual and have years of experience dealing with the banking needs of retirees. Mexican bank hours are normally from 9 A.M. to 2:30 P.M., weekdays only. Some branches are open in the afternoon from 4 to 6 P.M. and on weekends.

Money is often exchanged at *casas de cambio* (currency exchange houses) that are open longer hours than banks and offer quicker service. The worst exchange rates are at hotels, the best at exchange houses. Expect a slightly lower rate for traveller's cheques. Exchange fees are generally not charged.

You can also access ATMs. For example, Bancomer ATMs are now in the Cirrus and PLUS systems, and offer Spanish/English menus. Some machines will dispense pesos or dollars. Credit cards are widely accepted, including Visa, MasterCard, and American Express. There is a sales tax of 15 percent applied to the purchase of most items and paid by everyone, residents and visitors alike. Often this tax is included in the purchase price.

D. ENTERING MEXICO

1. Mexican Customs

Tourists normally are subject to a brief and informal baggage inspection when entering Mexico. There are limitations and restrictions on what you can bring into the country. Check with your nearest Mexican Consulate (item 19 in Appendix A) for a current list. You are allowed to bring in any of the following:

- Personal items, such as clothing, footwear, toiletries, all in reasonable quantities according to trip duration
- Medicine for personal use, with medical prescription in the case of psychotropic substances
- Books and magazines
- One portable TV set, and one portable typewriter
- Used or second-hand sporting equipment
- A musical instrument
- Up to 20 records, cassettes, or CDs
- One movie camera and one regular camera, and up to 12 rolls of film
- Fishing equipment, a pair of skis, and two tennis racquets
- Three litres of alcohol or wine
- 400 cigarettes or 50 cigars

Customs declaration forms can be obtained from airlines or at border crossings. Here is how the customs inspection system works:

- Visitors complete a customs declaration form.
- Visitors declare if they are importing items beyond their allowance.
- Those declaring items have their belongings searched, and duty is collected.
- Those not declaring items are asked to push a button on a street traffic light that is mounted on a post inside the customs area. A green light allows you to pass without inspection. A red light will signal an inspection. Your odds are better than winning Lotto 649.

In the event that items are found that were not declared, heavy fines and penalties apply.

2. Documents Required

Your first stop is at Mexican Immigration (*Migración*) where proof of citizenship is inspected, and tourist cards are validated.

Visitors need three items to enter Mexico:

- A photo ID such as a driver's license

- A valid proof of citizenship, such as a passport and
- A tourist card.

3. Tourist Card

This two part document is your "permission" from the Mexican government to visit Mexico. It is available free of charge. Here are some tips:

- Do not lose the blue copy returned to you after the immigration inspection, as it must be returned on departure. Write down your tourist card number and keep it with your travel documents. If the card is lost, having the number will help greatly.
- Keep your tourist card and travel documents in a secure place.
- You can ask to have your card validated for up to 180 days.

4. Proof of Citizenship

You will need:

- A valid Canadian passport, which, of course, includes your photo. This is the most recommended document.
- Canadian naturalization papers, showing that you are a naturalized Canadian. It can be the original certificate or laminated card with your photo on it. Photocopies are not acceptable.
- Birth certificate — official original copy or laminated card. Must be original and photocopy not acceptable.

  Refer to Chapter 3, Section B, for more information on the above documents.

5. Minors

Any person under 18 years of age is considered a minor. Very strict regulations govern travel by minors into Mexico. This may not be relevant to your own children, but could be to your grandchildren or visiting friends with minor children.

- If travelling alone, the minor must have a notarized consent form signed by both parents.
- If travelling with only one parent, the minor must have a notarized letter of consent signed by the absent parent. If a couple is divorced, getting the consent of the former spouse may be difficult.
- If travelling with only one parent and the other parent is deceased or the child has only one legal parent, a notarized statement must be obtained as proof.

E. INSURANCE MATTERS

There are various important types of insurance to consider, such as auto, out-of-country emergency medical, and legal insurance.

1. Auto Insurance

Canadian automobile insurance is *not* valid in Mexico. Only a Mexican automobile liability policy is acceptable as evidence of financial responsibility if you have an accident in that country. Compare the features and limitations of various competitive insurance coverages. Arrange for a policy with full coverage issued through a reliable Mexican insurance company with complete adjusting facilities in cities throughout the country. You can get Mexican auto insurance coverage from various sources, including AAA club offices in U.S. border states, and through Sanborn's at 1-800-638-4423 (Canada and the U.S.).

Unlike the U.S. and Canada, Mexican law is based on the Napoleonic Code, which presumes guilt until innocence is proven. As a result, all parties (operators of vehicles) involved in an accident involving injury, are detained for assessing responsibility. A Mexican insurance policy is recognized by the authorities as a guarantee of proper payment for damages according to the policy terms. When presented, it can significantly reduce red tape and help to bring about an early release.

All accidents or claims must be reported before leaving Mexico. Only obtain assistance in a claim from an authorized agent or adjuster of the insurance company that issued the policy. Official release papers should be kept as evidence that the case is closed, especially if the car shows obvious damage from the accident.

The Mexican government has no minimum requirement for insurance, but you should get the maximum available, as a precaution.

2. Legal Insurance for Motor Vehicle Accidents

If detained or arrested for involvement in a traffic accident that involves injury, you should immediately contact the closest Canadian consulate in Mexico. Refer to Appendix A (item 9) for contact locations and phone numbers. Most insurance companies do not cover lawyer's fees to defend the driver against criminal charges, so it is important that you also have legal coverage. Get that phone number when you take out the policy, and keep it with you at all times.

Here are the types of legal coverage and insurance protection services that you would want:

- Legal assistance and defence before any authority until the case is closed
- Release of the driver when arrested or detained due to a traffic accident
- Bail bond provision integrated into your vehicle's liability insurance policy
- Release of your vehicle if impounded
- Your defence in case of a traffic accident in which a third party is involved
- Assistance in case of theft of your vehicle
- Court costs covered and lawyer fees without monetary limit
- Towing and roadside assistance
- 24 hour toll-free telephone number with assistance available in English

There are several companies that provide auto, RV, and legal insurance coverage. Sanborn's specializes in all types of insurance in Mexico. It is based in Texas but has offices throughout the U.S. border states, plus they provide coverage by phone to Canadians as well as Americans. For more information, phone 1-800-638-9423 (Canada and U.S.).

CAA members can obtain various types of Mexican car or RV insurance coverage from AAA border state offices. You can contact your local CAA office for further information. Refer to item 36 in Appendix A. Contact them for further information. There are also many other companies providing Mexican insurance coverage that you will see along the border routes. However, it is critical that you scrutinize any coverage closely to know exactly what the features and benefits are, and that you understand them fully. If you do not, ask. As with other important types of insurance, the limitations, deductibles, exclusions, etc. are the determining factors. If you buy based merely on low price, it could be that there are some key elements of protection missing. Do your research thoroughly before you depart, so you can make a decision without time pressure.

3. Out-of-Country Emergency Medical Insurance Coverage

This is very important coverage. In fact, don't leave home without it. Inadequate coverage could cause you massive financial loss in the event of an emergency, such as a major surgery or hospitalization outside Canada. If you are medically stabilized, it is common for your insurance company to transport you back to Canada by medical jet. The Canadian medicare system then takes over your treatment and care and the insurance company saves on that expense. Refer to Chapter 5 on Insurance Needs and Options for a detailed discussion of all the issues that you need to know.

In terms of insurance coverage for Mexico, you have a number of options:

a) Worldwide Insurance Coverage, including Mexico

You would purchase this coverage in Canada before your departure. It would cover you in Mexico as well as the U.S. if you had a stopover there and had serious medical problems requiring treatment in the U.S. You can obtain this coverage from a wide variety of insurance companies and brokers listed in item 14 in Appendix A.

b) Mexico Insurance Plus Transit Insurance Through the U.S.

In this case, you would have two separate insurance policies. One would cover you while you are in Mexico, the other while you are travelling in the U.S.

c) Air Ambulance Insurance

Both of the above options (a) or (b) have advantages and disadvantages. The most suitable option depends on your research and needs, and an objective comparison of the features, benefits, limitations, exclusions and deductibles. However, some people prefer to get insurance for air ambulance coverage, instead of, or in addition to the other options, in case they may wish to return to Canada that way. This would normally be the route that your insurance company would take, for cost saving. It would be risky for you to attempt to "save" on a regular out-of-country emergency medical insurance premium, on the premise that if you were seriously ill or injured, you would coordinate your own air ambulance return to Canada. For more information on the air ambulance insurance option refer to the companies listed in item 15 in Appendix A.

F. TRANSPORTATION TIPS

1. Gasoline

Gasoline is available at stations throughout Mexico. As in Canada, gas is sold in litres (3.78 litres = 1 gallon). Nova (blue pump) is leaded; Magna Sin (green pump) is unleaded. Prices are about the same as in Canada, but only cash is accepted, most stations close by 10 P.M., and there is no self-service.

2. Roadside Assistance

Major highways are patrolled by Green Angels (*Los Angeles Verdes*). These government-operated green pick-up trucks are driven by mechanics. They have a nationwide hotline that can be reached by calling 250-82-21 or 250-85-55, extension 314. The service is free, except for parts and gas. Make sure that your auto insurance includes roadside assistance in case the Green Angels are off duty (generally after 8 P.M.).

3. Road Travel Guidebooks

Due to the variety of highways and terrain throughout Mexico, a guidebook will help maximize your trip enjoyment. Refer to Appendix B for the names of various helpful books. Also, contact your CAA branch (item 36 in Appendix A) for AAA guidebooks on Mexico (free to members).

G. BUYING MEXICAN REAL ESTATE

1. New Regulations

Under the Mexican constitution, foreigners may not hold title to property within the restricted zone, that is within 50 kilometres of any coastline. To circumvent this limitation, the Mexican Congress has implemented a system whereby Mexican banks acquire the property and place it in trust for the sole "use and enjoyment" of a beneficiary. This includes the right to resell the property at fair market value any time during the trust. Terms of the trust usually extend to 50 years, renewable in 50-year increments.

2. Mortgages for Mexican Real Estate

Mortgage capital is now being made available to Canadians and Americans acquiring property in Mexico resort destinations. Canadian and U.S. banks have traditionally been reluctant to provide mortgage financing on trust property because of their inability to obtain title, along with potential difficulties with foreclosing in a foreign country. And Mexican banks have not entered the field due to a lack of available capital. Purchases have therefore been limited to investors with sufficient resources to buy real estate without financing.

This situation has changed recently. There are several American mortgage firms offering financing for up to 70 percent of the appraised trust amount. Interest rates vary, yet most are between two and three percent above the prevailing Canadian rate, for amortization terms up to 15 years. The trust is itself sufficient collateral and a simple notation is made on the Mexican trust to protect the lender.

Some mortgage firms require an application fee of 1.5 percent while others ask for a flat US$250 registration. Mortgage documents are signed in Canada or the U.S. and the promise to pay is considered to have originated in Canada or the U.S. for legal purposes. Documentation is in English, yet all Mexican transactions must be done in Spanish.

3. Getting Legal Advice

You should use the services of a Mexican lawyer skilled in real estate matters, before signing any documents or paying any money. This is wise even in Canada, but especially so in a foreign country with different laws and procedures.

To obtain the name of a lawyer, contact the Canadian Consulate or Mexican Tourism Office in the city you are thinking of buying real estate. Refer to Appendix A for contact addresses and phone numbers.

H. BRINGING BACK GOODS FROM MEXICO

The *North American Free Trade Agreement* (NAFTA) continues to gradually eliminate the duty that applies to goods you acquire in Mexico. Your goods qualify for the lower Mexican duty rate under NAFTA if they are for personal use and marked as made in Mexico or Canada or not marked or labelled to indicate that they were made anywhere other than in Mexico or Canada.

If you do not qualify for a personal exemption or if you exceed your limit, you will have to pay the goods and services tax (GST) over and above any duty or other taxes that may apply on the portion not eligible under your personal exemption.

1. Personal exemptions

You are entitled to the basic duty- and tax-free exemptions of CDN$750 for absence outside Canada a minimum of seven days. In addition, you can benefit from the low special duty rate if you exceed your personal exemption limit. This special duty rate applies to the next CDN$300 worth of goods when you exceed your $750 exemption, as long as these goods accompany you and are not alcohol or tobacco products. Refer to item 2 in Appendix A and pick up a copy of the Revenue Canada brochure called *I Declare* for more information.

2. Prohibited, restricted, or controlled goods

Canada limits or prohibits the importation of certain goods. These can include cultural property which has historical significance in its country of origin, animals on the endangered species list (and any products made from them), certain foodstuffs and agricultural products, and goods considered harmful to the environment.

There are also limits and restrictions on the amount of meat, and other products you can bring into Canada from Mexico. For more information, contact your Revenue Canada customs office (see item 2 in Appendix A).

3. Alcohol and tobacco

You can import alcohol and tobacco products only if you meet the minimum age requirements of the province or territory of entry, and if the quantity is within the limits the province or territory sets.

You cannot import alcohol or tobacco products duty-free and tax-free unless you have been outside Canada for at least 48 hours and qualify for a personal exemption. If you do not qualify, or if you exceed your limit, you will have to pay the import duties *and* the provincial or territorial taxes and levies that apply on the portion not eligible under your personal exemption.

4. Making your declaration

By preparing a list of all the goods you have acquired in Mexico, and by keeping sales receipts, you will find it easier and faster to fully declare all these goods when you return to Canada. You will also find it easier to claim any personal exemption to which you are entitled. When you present your list and receipts, the customs officer can then work out your personal exemption and any duties you owe in the way that benefits you most.

5. Paying duties

You can pay by cash, traveller's cheque, VISA, MasterCard, or personal cheque if the amount is not more than $500. In some cases, Revenue Canada may accept a personal cheque for up to $2,500 as long as you can produce adequate identification.

6. Value of goods

Revenue Canada will include any taxes you have paid on your goods when determining their value, and will use the *prevailing* exchange rate to convert the total to Canadian funds. The customs officer will calculate this duty.

7. Goods and services tax (GST)

With the exception of goods you include in your personal exemption, GST applies to your goods as if you purchased them in Canada. GST is payable on the "value for tax," which is made up of the value (discussed above), plus the duty, and any applicable excise tax.

8. *General Agreement on Tariffs and Trade* (GATT)

New provisions under GATT became effective on January 1, 1995. Customs duties on a wide range of products originating in non-NAFTA countries were eliminated or will be reduced to zero over a period of time (up to 10 years). NAFTA goods also qualify for the GATT rate, so if the rate of duty payable on the goods you are importing is lower under GATT than under NAFTA, customs officers will automatically assess the lower rate. For more information on GATT contact the nearest Revenue Canada customs office.

9. Provincial sales tax (PST)

In some provinces, Revenue Canada collects any PST that applies to goods you import that do not qualify under your duty-free and tax-free exemption. In addition, in most provinces and territories, the Department collects special provincial or territorial assessments on alcohol and tobacco products that do not qualify under your duty-free and tax-free exemption.

I. WHERE TO GET FURTHER INFORMATION

Whether it be for a short trip or longer Snowbird season stay, there is a tremendous amount of helpful information available.

1. Books

Refer to Appendix B for books on retiring, living or travelling in Mexico. There are a lot of books available and only some of those relevant to Snowbirds have been included. Your local public library and bookstores in your community offer many other books on Mexico, that will fascinate and inform you. Also check out the publications on Mexico published by the AAA Auto Club and available free to members through your local CAA branch. Refer to item

36 in Appendix A for a listing of Canadian branches. A list of publications on Mexico is available through Sanborn's, the company that also specializes in Mexican auto and other insurance (1-800-638-9423 Canada and U.S.). They also have a web site on the Internet. Refer to item 34 in the Appendix.

2. Newsletters

A list of the main newsletters dealing with travelling and living in Mexico is in Appendix B, Sections 2, 5 and 6. Also, look in your local library for other newsletters. Ask the publishers listed in Appendix B for a complimentary copy of their most recent issue, to help you decide if you wish to subscribe.

3. Videos

Videos give you a colourful sense of Mexico in its various forms; check with your local library. Also, check with the companies that publish the newsletters noted above. Several of them also produce videos.

4. Mexican Government Tourism Offices in Canada

These offices will be very helpful in answering any questions that you have. You can also visit them in person. Refer to item 17 in Appendix A for contact numbers and locations. You will also find a toll-free number there for the Mexican Tourism department, accessible from Canada or the U.S. They also have an excellent web site on the Internet. Refer to item 34 in Appendix A.

5. Mexican Government Consulates in Canada

You could have questions relating to obtaining tourist cards, applying to retire in Mexico under various categories, or about government policy that might affect you. Refer to item 19, Appendix A for a listing of contact numbers.

6. Mexican State Tourism Offices in Mexico

A list of all the Mexican tourism offices is shown in item 20 in Appendix A, along with a toll-free number for tourists to call while in Mexico. You can also phone this number if you have an emergency or a problem that you think Mexican Tourism might help with.

7. Canadian Consulates in Mexico

Canada has numerous federal government consulates throughout the world to represent the interests of Canadians, and assist them in a foreign country. There are several Canadian consulate offices throughout Mexico. Refer to item 9 in Appendix A. You can also use the consulate address to have mail delivered for you to pick up. Refer to point 9 in Section E of Chapter 1 for more information on Canadian consular services.

8. Department of Foreign Affairs and International Trade Canada

Refer to item 6 in Appendix A for more detail and toll-free contact numbers for this federal government department. You can obtain information about current conditions and "risk assessments" that might affect you if you are travelling in any country in the world. These include crime, political instability, weather conditions (e.g., hurricanes), natural disasters (e.g., earthquakes), general or specific tourist advisory warnings, health issues and so on. You can speak on the phone, listen to their "voice prompt" recorded messages on various countries; or you can use their fax-back service. This latter service allows you to call their toll-free fax number, punch in the countries that you want an update on, and then punch in your fax number. Within minutes a report will be faxed to you automatically. In addition, this government department has an excellent web site which is "hot-linked" to other relevant government sites. Refer to item 34 in Appendix A.

9. Internet

Refer to item 34 in Appendix A for a list of key web sites dealing with Mexico. Many of these have hot-links to other key information sites. You will find doing your research by surfing the Net very productive.

Refer to Section F in Chapter 1 for a brief overview on using the Internet.

10. Travel Agents

Travel agents familiar with travel in Mexico can be of great assistance.

TIPS BEFORE LEAVING CANADA

- The sections "Tips Before Leaving Canada" at the end of Chapters 1 through 8 contain a lot of information relevant to Mexico.
- Research the various sources of information discussed in Section I.
- Speak to other Canadians and Americans who have been seasonal residents of Mexico and ask for their opinions and suggestions.
- Contact the various social associations of Canadian and American Snowbirds or full-time retirees in Mexico. The Canadian Consulate offices throughout Mexico that have Canadian/American retirement communities will be able to provide you with that information.
- Have sufficient auto, legal, and out-of-country emergency medical insurance coverage to protect you before you leave Canada.

CHAPTER
10

Snowbirding in Costa Rica

A. INTRODUCTION

Costa Rica is often referred to as a combination of Switzerland and Hawaii because of its mountains and forests. It is a beautiful place to visit and an experience you will not forget quickly. It is situated in Central America between Panama and Nicaragua, and the Caribbean Ocean on the east and the Pacific Ocean on the west. It has the climate of a tropical paradise. Most Snowbirds and full-time residents from Canada or the U.S. tend to prefer the Pacific Coast side of Costa Rica.

Everyone has different needs and expectations when planning their Snowbird trip. Costa Rica is a very different type of destination that would not be suited for many due to its distance from Canada, and because the Snowbird or North American retirement communities are not as prevalent or large as in Mexico or the U.S. Sunbelt states. Visiting any location numerous times and speaking with other Snowbirds and residents is an important first step to any Snowbird location decision.

Before you decide to live in Costa Rica, consider an extended visit. Rent an apartment or an "*apartohotel*" and enquire about real estate prices, shop in the grocery stores, and take taxis and buses around town. Talk to foreigners about their experiences after living there. An excellent way to introduce yourself to the country is to take an introductory Spanish language course, or even better, stay with a local family.

B. TYPES OF RESIDENCE STATUS

As a tourist with a passport, you can stay in Costa Rica for up to three months. If you want to stay longer, there are three main residence status categories:

1. Annuitant Pensioner

If you have a permanent pension income, either public or private, you may be able to become an Annuitant Pensioner. Here are the conditions:

- Income of US$600 (CDN$800) per month generated abroad
- Must remain in the country for at least four months per year
- Not allowed to earn a salary
- Allowed to be a shareholder and earn profits
- Must exchange foreign currency through the National Banking System
- Final approval of the Annuitant Pensioner status given by the Ministry of Tourism of Costa Rica (ICT)

The Annuitant Pensioner status guarantees residence to family dependants.

2. Annuitant Resident

If you are not of age to get a permanent pension income, or you are economically independent, but you want to retire and move to Costa Rica, you may be able to become an Annuitant Resident. The same conditions apply as for Annuitant Pensioner, except you must have local or foreign income of CDN$1,400 per month. This can include a five-year bank deposit in the National Banking System which produces CDN$1,400 in interest per month.

3. Foreign Investor

You may be able to obtain residence status. Here are the conditions:

- Invest no less than CDN$70,000 and generate employment, foreign exchange, or new technology, within one of the priority economic sectors
- Allowed to earn a salary
- Allowed to be a shareholder and earn profits
- Must present annual investment audits
- Final approval of the status given by the Costa Rican Investment Centre (CENPRO)

The Foreign Investor status guarantees residence to the family dependants.

The application process for an Annuitant Pensioner, Annuitant Resident, or Foreign Investor, takes an average of two to four months. Once your file is "opened" you can stay legally in the country until the final decision is made by the Costa Rican Immigration department.

C. ANSWERS TO THE MOST COMMON QUESTIONS ABOUT COSTA RICA

Here are some of the common questions asked of the Costa Rican Tourist Bureau:

Q: *Do Canadians require a "visa" to visit Costa Rica?*

A: No. As a tourist entering with a passport, you are allowed to stay in Costa Rica for three months.

Q: *Do Canadians need a passport to enter Costa Rica?*

A: No, although you should always have a passport when travelling anywhere outside Canada. However, if you do not have one, you only need your birth certificate with another photo ID, such as a driver's licence. You will have to buy a tourist card from your airline (CDN$7.50). However, without a passport you will only be allowed to stay in Costa Rica for one month.

Q: *How can you get to Costa Rica, and how much does it cost?*

A: You have two ways of going to Costa Rica: commercial or charter flights.

Commercial flights

There are flights all year round. The most common direct routes are from Vancouver, Toronto, or Montréal, and cost from CDN$700 to CDN$900 return, plus taxes. These can vary of course, due to competitions, type of seating, time of year, etc.

Charter flights

They are available from any travel agency, most frequently from the end of October to the end of April. The cost of charter flights are normally one half of commercial rates.

Departure tax

At your departure you will be asked to pay US$16.15 as a departure tax.

Q: *Are you able to communicate in English or only in Spanish?*

A: It would be to your advantage to know basic Spanish, but a large percentage of Costa Ricans can speak some English. In most tourist areas, hotels and beaches, English is widely spoken.

Q: *How is the Costa Rican currency compared with the Canadian dollar?*

A: For one Canadian dollar you will receive approximately 160 CR colons (colones).

   For example, in Costa Rica one Canadian dollar can buy you:

- One litre of milk
- Two litres of gas
- One kilo of rice
- 1.5 litres of coke.

Typical prices are:

- A movie is CDN$3.
- A haircut is CDN$6.
- A full-time live-in maid is CDN$200/month.

Q: *Are there legal restrictions for foreigners buying property in Costa Rica?*

A: No. You can buy any property through a real estate agent or negotiate directly with the owner. It is recommended that a Costa Rican lawyer go through the National Registrar's Office to make sure everything is legal.

Q: *Is Costa Rica politically stable?*

A: Costa Rica is the most politically stable country in Latin America. In 1989 it celebrated the 100th anniversary of its democracy. The army was abolished in 1948, and Costa Rica has the largest per capita expenditures for health and education in Latin America.

Q: *Is Costa Rica economically stable?*

A: The majority of people in Costa Rica belong to the middle class and the economic situation is considered one of the most stable in Latin America. For example, in 1994, the Costa Rican annual income per capita was CDN$3,032, one of the highest in this region. The actual unemployment is 4.5 percent, one of the lowest in the world. In the past three years, Costa Rica has had an average of 6 percent growth in Gross Domestic Product (GDP). It has free movement of capital as well as a public and private banking system.

Q: *Do you need any vaccinations before entering the country?*

A: No. All major contagious diseases have been controlled many years ago. However, get your doctor's recommendations. Refer to point 8 in Section E, of Chapter 1 for tips on obtaining health advice before you leave Canada.

Q: *How good is the health system in Costa Rica?*

A: The health system is a priority area and Costa Rica has invested heavily in it. For example, the country spends over 30 percent of the national budget on health. Life expectancy is approximately 76 years and the social security system is considered one of the best in Latin America.

Q: *How does the health system work for foreigners who live in Costa Rica?*

A: By paying the small amount of CDN$50, you will be protected by the Costa Rican Social Security System (*Seguro Social*). This is an inexpensive medical coverage program that does not have deductibles or exclude pre-existing conditions. The insurance covers your spouse and children. However, as a Snowbird, you would want to have your own out-of-country emergency medical insurance coverage obtained in Canada.

Q: *How good is the education system in Costa Rica?*

A: Education, both public and private, has always been an important part of Costa Rican culture. The country has a literacy rate of over 90 percent. Whether you want to learn survival Spanish in a day, or plan to study in a university, you will find an educational institution to suit your purpose.

Costa Rica has four public universities and spends over 30 percent of its GNP on education. The main public universities are the University of Costa Rica in San José and National University in Heredia.

Q: *If you own a business in Costa Rica, can you take your profits out of the country?*

A: Yes, any profits made can be taken out of the country.

Q: *How expensive is it to buy a house or to rent an apartment in Costa Rica?*

A: Even though housing prices are on the rise, real estate in Costa Rica is still a bargain compared to Canada. You can get a small house in the San José suburb of San Pedro for around CDN$70,000. Houses in the elegant areas of Escazu and Santa Ana start around CDN$135,000. They are very complete new houses, with several bedrooms and bathrooms, maid's quarters and large lots. The rent on a two-bedroom apartment starts at about CDN$300 a month, and on a house, about CDN$500.

Q: *How costly is the food compare to Canada?*

A: On average, basic food items cost about two-thirds of what they do in Canada.

Q: *How do the taxes in Costa Rica compare to those in Canada?*

A: Costa Rican taxes are generally less than Canadian. For example, for an annual taxable income of CDN$40,000 you would pay approximately CDN$15,000 per year in Canadian income tax, depending on your province of residence. With the same annual income in Costa Rica, you would pay approximately CDN$6,000 per year.

For comparison purposes, here is an overview of the Costa Rican tax system. Naturally these rates are only approximate and government policies can change at any time. Check out the current status if it is relevant to you, but as a seasonal Snowbird, it is probably not.

Income tax

This tax applies only to income generated in Costa Rica. It has to be paid by persons with profit generating activities and legal entities (corporations).

The following rates are applied to taxable annual profits:

- Profits up to CDN$3,950 per year are tax-exempt
- Between CDN$3,951–$5,900 —10 percent
- Between CDN$5,901–$9,850 —15 percent
- Between CDN$9,851–$19,750 —20 percent

An annual tax credit of CNDN$15 is available for each child and CDN$20 for a spouse.

The following tax table is applicable to legal entities (corporations):

- For an annual gross income up to CDN$59,200, 10 percent on net profits
- For an annual gross income up to CDN$119,200, 20 percent on net profits
- Above CDN$119,200, 30 percent on net profits.

Corporations without any commercial activities during the fiscal year (October to September) must pay CDN$95 yearly, currently being reviewed. Losses during a fiscal year can be deducted over the next three fiscal years, and in case of agricultural activities, losses can be deducted for the following five years.

Whenever the profits are distributed to partners, 15 percent tax must be paid to the Costa Rican Tax Office. When dividends are distributed by a corporation whose shares are registered in an officially recognized stock exchange, a five percent tax must be withheld only if the shares were acquired through a stock exchange.

Land tax

This is applied to registered real estate and fixed assets, and includes land, buildings, and fixed machinery. It is calculated as follows:

- Up to CDN$1,200 of fixed assets —tax exempt
- Between CDN$1,201–$2,000 —0.36 percent
- Between CDN$2,001–$4,000 —0.63 percent
- Between CDN$4,001–$24,000 —0.90 percent
- Between CDN$24,000 —1.17 percent

D. WHERE TO GET FURTHER INFORMATION

Whether it be for a short trip or longer Snowbird season stay, here are some tremendous sources of information to consider:

1. Books

Refer to Appendix B for books on retiring, living, or travelling in Costa Rica. Only those books that are relevant to Snowbirds have been included.

Your local public library and bookstores in your community will offer many other books on Costa Rica that will excite and inform you. Also check out any publications on Costa Rica published by the AAA Auto Club and available free through your local CAA Auto Club branch if you are a member. Refer to item 36 in Appendix A for a listing of Canadian branches. You can also obtain a list of publications on Costa Rica available through Sanborn's, the company that specializes in Mexican and Central American auto and other insurance (1-800-638-9423, Canada and U.S.). Refer to item 34 in Appendix A.

2. Newsletters and Newspapers

The main newsletters and newspapers dealing with travelling and living in Costa Rica are listed in Appendix B. Also, look in your local library for newsletters or ask the publishers listed in Appendix B for a complimentary copy of their most recent newsletter issue.

3. Videos

Videos give you a colourful sense of Costa Rica in its various forms. Check with your local library and the various newsletter companies for videos.

4. Consular and Tourism Offices of Costa Rica in Canada

These offices will be very helpful in answering any questions that you have. Refer to item 18 in Appendix A to see a listing of the contact numbers and locations. You will also note a toll-free number for the Costa Rican Tourism department and their web site address. Refer to item 34 in Appendix A.

5. Costa Rican Resident's Association

This organization assists foreign residents who wish to live in Costa Rica.

Apartado 700-1011
San José, Costa Rica
Call: 333-8068 or 221-2053 inside Costa Rica and 011-506-333-8068
    outside the country
Fax: 011-506-222-7862
Address in the U.S.: Costa Rican Resident's Association
P.O. Box 025292-BC19
Miami, Florida 33102-5292

6. Costa Rican Tourism Institute

The government department in Costa Rica for tourism enquiries is:

Apartado, 777-1000
San José, Costa Rica
Call: 011-506-223-1733, Ext. 264 or 1-800-343-6332
Fax: 011-506-255-4997

7. Canadian Consulate in Costa Rica

Canada has federal government consulates throughout the world to assist and represent the interests of Canadians in a foreign country and to provide information in a wide range of areas. There is a Canadian consulate office in San José, Costa Rica. Refer to item 10 in Appendix A. You can also use their address to have your mail delivered there for pick up. Refer to point 9 in Section E of Chapter 1 for more information on Canadian consular services.

8. Department of Foreign Affairs and International Trade Canada

This federal government department can provide you with information about current conditions and risk assessments to travelling Canadians in any country throughout the world—for example, crime, political instability, weather conditions (e.g., hurricanes), natural disasters (e.g., earthquakes), general or specific tourist advisory warnings, health issues, and so on. You can ask questions on the phone; listen to their variety of voice-prompt recorded messages on various countries; or you can use their fax-back service. This means that you can phone their toll-free fax number, punch in the countries that you want a current update on, and then punch in your fax number. Within minutes a report will be faxed to you automatically. In addition, this government department has an excellent web site on the Internet, which is hot-linked to other relevant government sites. Refer to item 6 in Appendix A for more detail and toll-free contact numbers.

9. Internet

Refer to item 34 in Appendix A for a list of web sites dealing with Costa Rica. Many of these sites have hot-links to other key information sites. You will find doing your research or surfing the Net very productive. Refer to Section F in Chapter 1 for a brief overview on using the Internet.

10. Travel Agents

Travel agents familiar with Costa Rica can be of great assistance.

TIPS BEFORE LEAVING CANADA

- Refer to the Tips Before Leaving Canada sections Chapters 1 through 8. You will find a lot of generic information relevant to Costa Rica.
- Do your research as discussed in Section D.
- Speak to other Canadians and Americans who have been seasonal residents of Costa Rica and ask for their opinions and suggestions.
- Contact the various social group associations of Canadian and American Snowbirds or full-time retirees in Costa Rica. The Canadian Consulate office in Costa Rica could provide you with that information.
- Have sufficient automobile and out-of-country emergency medical insurance to protect yourself before you leave Canada.

CHAPTER
11

Permanent Retirement Outside of Canada

A. INITIAL CONSIDERATIONS

There are many implications of moving to another country full-time and becoming an official non-resident of Canada. Permanently severing ties with Canada can be a difficult decision. You have to consider issues such as tax, estate planning, financial planning, pensions, housing, health costs and the cost of living. You also need to look at the citizenship, cultural, societal, government and language issues. There could also be considerable emotional, psychological and social adjustment considerations if you are leaving family, relatives and friends behind.

This chapter gives an overview of the practical issues to consider including documentation requirements, immigration, citizenship, taxation, health and housing issues and a list of tips before you leave Canada.

1. Reasons for Retiring Outside Canada

Retiring permanently outside of Canada holds many potential pitfalls for those who choose a destination on the basis of a dream rather than on sound planning. In general, those who consider only the financial benefits of moving south or overseas are more likely to experience disappointment than those who retire abroad for lifestyle or cultural reasons. Whatever your motives, careful research is essential, and the Internet makes it more practical than ever to carry out a detailed evaluation before you leave.

If you are retiring as part of a couple, do this research together so that both of you fully understand what your choices involve. Recognizing and preparing for potential difficulties ahead of time is much easier than dealing with disappointment, or even a crisis, later.

Many Canadians who retire outside Canada full-time are surprised at the cultural isolation that they experience. This can make the normal adjustments from a career to full-time leisure even more stressful. Before you go, make sure you understand the social environment where you will be living. Are you prepared to be in a minority and to be treated as a foreigner? Do you make new friends easily? Are you open to different ways of doing things? Can you handle a much slower pace of life and a high level of bureaucracy? You need to think about all these are questions before deciding to retire permanently south or abroad.

2. Destination

Before making a final decision, spend some time in the country or countries where you are thinking of retiring before you make any major commitment. Go in the off-season to see if you are prepared to live there all year round.

If climate is one of your considerations, you can obtain reliable weather statistics on the Internet. Be sure to consider the situation year-round. Many countries with warm winters are hot and humid in the summer and the cost of air-conditioning is often prohibitive.

Immigration regulations vary greatly from one country to another. Before you leave, make sure you understand all the regulations of the country you have chosen for retirement.

3. Finances

Taxation and the cost of living are related issues. Many developing countries lack the resources to collect taxes on foreign source income, so they compensate by imposing high consumption taxes or import duties. Take into account all taxes, duties and fees, as well as the withholding taxes you will pay on income originating in Canada.

Withholding tax is the money that the Canadian government requires to be held back from income being received by Canadians who are no longer residents of Canada. In the case of money paid out by the federal government such OAS and CPP, the amount of withholding tax can vary from zero to 25 percent depending on the country involved. Refer to Item 54 in Appendix A for the withholding tax rates for OAS and CPP. The amount of holdback for other money being generated in Canada and paid out to a nonresident can vary depending on the type of income, for example, rental income, RRSP, RRIF or employer or private pension payments.

You also need to consider how much it will cost you in communications and travel to stay in touch with your family and friends in Canada.

4. Medical Advice

It is a good idea to have a medical checkup before you go and to plan carefully for your health needs once you have left Canada. Many nations have health care systems that most Canadians would consider inadequate. The cost of medical care outside Canada can be extremely high. Arrange for adequate private health care coverage before you leave Canada. Take copies of your prescriptions and an initial supply of non-prescription medicines.

As you probably know by now, there is a considerable difference between health care coverage for seasonal as compared to permanent absence from Canada. Snowbird insurance acts as a supplement to your provincial Medicare coverage and only covers you for emergency medical treatment that can't wait until you return to Canada. If you are severing your ties to Canada and living permanently outside the country, you will need to obtain full health insurance. There is a big difference in premium rates as well, as you can understand, as the latter insurance in effect replaces the Canadian Medicare program that is administered by your current home province. Refer to items 14 and 34 in Appendix A for a list of companies providing health insurance for expatriates of Canada.

Find out well in advance of your departure date if you need any special vaccinations or preventive medications for such illnesses as yellow fever, typhoid, meningitis, Japanese encephalitis, hepatitis or malaria. An International Certificate of Vaccination may be a legal requirement to enter certain countries. You can obtain this information from your doctor, from the Canadian Society for International Health at (613) 241-5785, from the web site of Health Canada's Laboratory Centre for Disease Control (LCDC) (*http://www.hc-sc.gc.ca*) or from the LCDC FAXlink service at (613) 941-3900.

5. Documentation

Once you have chosen a destination, make sure your passport, any visas you require and other travel documents are in order, including those concerning your status in your new country.

A valid passport is essential. It will expedite immigration procedures and is useful for other purposes, such as opening bank accounts and cashing traveller's cheques. If your passport will expire while you are abroad, make plans to renew it on time.

Even though you may be resident in another country full-time, you may wish to retain your Canadian citizenship and current passport. Many countries will permit you to retire permanently without taking out the citizenship of that country. Some countries permit you to have dual citizenship, such as the U.S. There are many reasons why you may want to maintain your Canadian citizenship and keep your passport current. For example, some countries, due to political differences, will not permit you to enter if you have a passport from certain countries. However, Canadians citizens are looked on very favourably internationally, so if you intend to do a lot of travelling a Canadian passport will open many doors.

Be sure that, when you leave, you have copies of all essential records. You may need these later to clarify your tax status. And keep in mind that you may come home sooner than you planned.

Make sure that you know how to contact the nearest Canadian diplomatic or consular mission in your new country in case you run into difficulties. Your rights to Canadian consulate assistance are based on your citizenship. As long as you remain a Canadian citizen, you will always have those rights anywhere in the world that you might be. However, if you relinquish Canadian citizenship through an act of renunciation, you would obviously lose all the rights of a Canadian citizen in a foreign country.

6. Travel Arrangements

The relatively low cost of travel to popular vacation destinations usually involves charter flights that originate in Canada and are available only on a seasonal basis. In addition, direct flights to Canada are not available from many popular destinations on a year-round basis.

Many countries require foreign visitors to have a valid return ticket pending formal confirmation that you have been accepted as a full-time resident—a paid ticket with a return date within the time limits allowed by immigration. A full-fare return ticket with an "open" travel date is generally acceptable, but an unused return portion of a charter flight ticket is not. You may need to purchase expensive one-way open tickets connecting through other countries to satisfy immigration authorities, even if your application for residency is pending. If you have to make an unplanned trip home for family or personal reasons, be prepared to pay several times the charter rate.

If you have special needs when travelling, make sure that before you go, you research the attitudes and facilities that you may encounter. You may have to make special arrangements to obtain amenities that you expect as a matter of right in Canada. While most developed countries can provide for many special needs, few places, however, can offer as sophisticated arrangements as Canada. And in some countries, disabled people are not expected to access travel facilities and other public places at all.

B. PERMANENT RETIREMENT OUTSIDE OF CANADA

Retiring permanently to another country is an option for Canadians who are seeking a lower tax jurisdiction, do not intend to return regularly to Canada and can obtain adequate health care protection.

The most popular destination for permanent retirement is the U.S. The popularity of other destinations depends on the motivation. For example, if you are concerned about the tax advantages elsewhere, you might be attracted to a country which is a tax haven or has low taxes. Many small countries in

Europe or in the Caribbean fall into this category. They want to attract people with money to invest. Possibly you have family ties to the country where you were born or have an extensive network of relatives. Maybe climate or recreational opportunities is a consideration, depending on your health and lifestyle.

Taking up permanent residence in another country involves establishing a legal status within the other country that goes well beyond that of an annual tourist. You may seek either permanent residency or citizenship status, or both. Either may impose a variety of conditions and requirements, and you should be very clear about their implications. Among other consequences, Canadian consular officials in your new country may not be able to help you if you run into difficulties.

As mentioned before, most Canadians would not choose to give up their Canadian citizenship. The advantages of maintaining Canadian citizenship would be sufficiently compelling in most circumstances.

1. Immigration and Citizenship Issues

a) Country of Destination Regulations for Immigrants

Immigration regulations vary greatly from country to country, and it is essential that you understand them before you go.

Most countries base their immigration system on three fundamental principles:

- Employment
- Investment
- Family connections.

Some countries also recognize retirees or people with a guaranteed minimum income as potential immigrants, but this is far from universal. For example, Mexico has a special category for retirees called *immigrante rentista*, but the United States does not recognize retirement as a valid reason for establishing permanent residency.

Countries that do recognize retirement as an immigrant category generally require proof of sufficient guaranteed income to support the retiree and any dependents. For example, Mexico requires an income of 10,000 pesos per month, and half as much for each dependent. Costa Rica requires CDN$900 per month.

Regardless of your country of destination, you will need proof of Canadian citizenship. A valid Canadian passport is the best form of proof, and is often required for entry. Many countries require prospective immigrants to apply before they leave Canada; others allow individuals to enter as tourists and then apply to immigrate. Carefully research these aspects of any destination you are considering for retirement.

b) Canadian Citizenship

Canadian citizenship can be relinquished only through a specific act of renunciation. An individual has to apply to Citizenship and Immigration Canada and complete a specific form to begin the process of terminating Canadian citizenship.

One reason for relinquishing your Canadian citizenship could be because your newly adopted country requires you to be a citizen to live full-time and/or own property and does not permit dual citizenship. Alternatively, maybe you no longer have ties to Canada in any way, and see no practical benefit in your circumstances. Possibly there could be tax or pension benefits in certain situations in relinquishing your Canadian citizenship. Countries tend to tax based on residency.

c) Dual Nationality

Many countries do not recognize a person's right to have more than one nationality (citizenship). If you were born outside Canada or, in some instances, if your parents were born outside Canada, you may be regarded as a citizen of the other country. In some cases, the laws of your country of origin may provide for the revocation of your citizenship if you become a citizen of Canada, but this is not necessarily automatic. You may have to take overt action, such as living on a permanent basis in Canada, consistently using a Canadian passport and obtaining a visa when you travel to your country of origin. In some countries, you can formally renounce citizenship.

Canadian law permits a Canadian to have more than one nationality. The Canadian government encourages Canadians to use their Canadian passport when travelling abroad and to always present themselves as Canadians to foreign authorities. Canadian officials abroad will offer consular assistance to Canadian citizens wherever they can. However, local authorities may not assist Canadians who have not specified their Canadian citizenship when entering the country.

2. Taxation Issues

a) Severing Canadian Residency

You cannot terminate your Canadian citizenship or residency simply by living in another country. Moreover, becoming a legal resident of another country does not establish nonresidence in Canada for tax purposes. You must demonstrate your intention to leave the country permanently. Revenue Canada determines nonresident status on a case-by-case basis, so you should consult a tax advisor about the necessary steps you should take. Retaining Canadian residency does not necessarily put you at a disadvantage. Depending on your situation, your actual tax liability could be lower than the nonresident withholding taxes imposed on your Canadian pensions and investment income. For example, if you have a modest income and would not have to pay much tax under Canadian tax laws, you could be further ahead tax-wise than if you relinquished your residency. The reason is that if you are a non-resident, there is a flat rate withholding tax that could be more than you otherwise would need to pay.

In general, absence from Canada for two years or longer is considered evidence of nonresidence provided that you relinquish or terminate other key connections, such as:

- Residences
- Bank accounts
- Credit cards
- Drivers' licences
- Health-plan memberships
- Club or professional memberships

If you return to Canada to live within two years, you will probably be taxed on the income you earned while you were gone. Regular visits to Canada, for example every other month or stays for extended time periods, such as several months at a time, can be regarded as evidence of continued residency. This is especially the risk if you have family connections in the country. If you retain ownership of your home, you should lease it on a non-revocable basis; if you have ongoing access to it, it may still be regarded as your residence.

Although you are not obliged to do so, as a taxpayer you may submit an NR73 Residency Determination Form to Revenue Canada to see if you are regarded as a nonresident. Further information is available from Revenue Canada's Interpretation Bulletin IT-221, Determination of an Individual's Residence Status, and its special release.

In order to determine what would be best for your situation, consider the following questions:

- Have you allowed for Canadian withholding taxes on your pension income?
- Will you be subject to double taxation in your country of destination?
- Have you arranged to file required tax returns in Canada?
- Have you made allowances for additional communications and travel costs, and import duties?

b) Nonresident Tax Returns

Once you have become a nonresident of Canada as defined by Revenue Canada, you are no longer required to file income tax returns. It may be in your interest to do so, however, if you have income subject to Canadian withholding tax. Withholding taxes are considered final if you do not file a return, but you may be entitled to a refund if you file a return and your taxable income is low enough.

c) Canadian Departure Taxes

Taxpayers who emigrate from Canada are generally deemed to have disposed of their assets at fair market value on the date they leave. Capital gains taxes, if any, are assessed at this time. Assets affected by this provision include shares in Canadian corporations, but not real estate. Deemed disposition is triggered by your declaration that you have left the country, which you make on your final income tax return, filed by April 30 of the year following your departure. Those with assets valued at more than $25,000 must file a special return.

d) Receiving Canadian Public Pensions Abroad

Canada Pension Plan/Quebec Pension Plan (CPP/QPP) and Old Age Security (OAS) benefits can be paid to you when you are living outside the country, subject to certain conditions. If you have lived or worked in a country with which Canada has concluded a reciprocal social security agreement, you may qualify for social security benefits from both countries for the duration of your lifetime.

Canada's OAS system is intended to guarantee a minimum income to retirees, and it is subject to an income test. You can receive OAS benefits outside Canada for the duration of your lifetime, but you must file an annual return reporting your worldwide income.

Refer to Chapter 2 for a more detailed discussion of pension availability and criteria.

e) Canadian Nonresident Withholding Taxes

Canada imposes a withholding tax on "passive" income paid to nonresidents from Canadian sources, including annuity payments and pension plans. As of January 1, 1996, this tax applies to CPP/QPP and OAS benefits. You are eligible for OAS payments for your lifetime, as long as you were resident in Canada for at least 20 years before you leave Canada. You are eligible to CPP payments for your lifetime as well, without a minimum residency requirement. The amount varies depending on the type of income, but it is 25 percent for pension payments. This tax may be reduced or waived according to the terms of tax treaties between Canada and other countries. For example, the withholding rate on pensions is waived for residents of the U.S. and is 15 percent for residents of Mexico. Rates vary for other countries. Refer to item 53 in Appendix A for a list of countries with which Canada has tax treaties. Refer to item 54 in Appendix A for non-resident tax rates for Canadian federal pension income, e.g. CPP and OAS.

f) Tax Treaties

The tax situation of Canadians living abroad is complicated to some extent by the fact that each country bases its income tax system on different principles. Canada and the United States both tax factual residents on their worldwide income, and also tax nonresidents on some types of domestic income. Many other countries tax only income from local sources, partly because they lack the resources to assess worldwide income. A few countries do not tax income at all, relying instead on consumption taxes and import duties.

Fortunately, the situation is simplified if you move to a country with which Canada has a tax agreement. Canada has tax conventions or agreements (commonly referred to as tax treaties) with more than 60 countries. Refer to item 53 in Appendix A. These tax treaties often eliminate double taxation for those who would otherwise have to pay tax on the same income in two countries. Generally, tax treaties determine how much each country can tax income such as salaries, wages, pensions and accrued interest.

If you move to a country that does not have a tax treaty with Canada, you may be subject to double taxation. You should carefully research the tax laws of your intended country of destination. If you will be taxed on your Canadian-source income, find out if the withholding taxes you pay in Canada will be credited against your tax liability in your country of destination.

g) Estate Tax

Canada does not levy an estate tax, but many other countries, including the United States, do. This was discussed in Chapter 6. In the United States, this tax can reach 55 percent for large estates. If you are going to become a resident of a country with an estate tax and you have substantial assets, you should consult a tax advisor in your country of destination. You may need to draw up a new will or make other strategic arrangements.

3. Health Care Issues

a) Canadian Provincial Health Care Programs

Canadian provincial health care programs provide limited coverage during temporary periods of absence from Canada, typically six months. The level of benefits, however, may be inadequate to cover costs in some locations, especially the United States. The reason for this is that the payments allowed for out-of-country treatment are comparable to the fees paid by the provincial plans to health care providers in Canada. A foreign hospital may charge several times as much as your provincial program will allow. It is therefore essential that you arrange for private health care insurance for when you are resident outside Canada. The seasonal resident aspect has been covered in some detail in Chapter 5 on Insurance. Health insurance coverage for permenent residents outside Canada is a different matter. This is discussed in the next section.

In most cases, you must be physically present in your Canadian province of residence for 183 days of each calendar year to maintain your provincial health care coverage. The rationale for this is that, when you are out of the country, you are not paying provincial sales tax or the Goods and Services Tax, both of which help to pay for medical care.

If you lose your provincial health care coverage, there is a waiting period to re-qualify after you return. In most provinces, this period is three months. Supplementary private insurance sold in Canada generally will not cover you during this period, because such policies are usually issued on the condition that you maintain eligibility under provincial plans.

In some provinces, you can avoid the re-qualification period by waiving your right to coverage while you are out of the country. This way, you will be covered immediately upon your return, even though you were out of the country for more than six months. Before leaving Canada, you should check with your provincial health care authorities to make sure you fully understand how your health care coverage will be affected, and consider the following questions:

- What will you do if you have an accident or become ill?
- Are you prepared for emergency repatriation?
- Have you checked the provisions of your provincial health care plan?

b) Health Care Programs in Your Country of Destination

Health care is a serious issue for Canadian expatriates because few countries have systems that are as comprehensive or as inexpensive for the user as Canada's. Some developed countries have comprehensive health care plans that will cover you, after a waiting period, if you immigrate. But the countries that are the major destinations for Canadian retirees generally do not offer comparable programs. Private health care in the United States presents particular problems because the Health Management Organization (HMO) system that covers the majority of Americans is generally restricted to U.S. residents with a social security number. Even then, unrestricted coverage usually ceases at age 65, when the Medicare system begins its coverage.

Many developing countries provide free universal medical care to citizens and permanent residents. Mexico, for example, has a national health care program. But most Canadians living in these countries seek private medical care, which many consider to be of a higher quality and which involves shorter waiting periods. Private health care facilities are fairly advanced in most countries, and a private hospital or clinic will usually see you immediately, for a fee approaching the cost of similar services in the United States. Faced with these trade-offs, most Canadians choose the private alternative and make sure they are well covered by insurance.

c) Private Health Care Insurance

There are two types of private health care insurance. Supplementary insurance provides supplementary benefits for people who are covered by a Canadian provincial health care plan and who are seasonal residents only in another country for up to six months a year, e.g. Snowbirds. This type of coverage has been discussed at some length in Chapter 5. Replacement insurance provides coverage for those who are ineligible for provincial plans.

d) Replacement Insurance

If you will be living outside Canada long enough to lose your provincial health care coverage, you will need full replacement coverage and not just supplementary benefits. You may elect to waive your temporary out-of-country coverage if your provincial plan allows it, since you will need replacement coverage from the date of departure anyway.

Full replacement insurance is less readily available than supplementary insurance, but there are a number of companies that provide insurance specifically designed for expatriates. An Internet search on the key words "global expatriate health insurance" produces the names of several alternative providers. Refer to items 14 and 34 in Appendix A for more information. You should arrange for replacement insurance before you leave, but be aware that you may not be able to obtain appropriate coverage from a Canadian company. Most of these policies reserve the right to repatriate you to a country for which you hold a passport in the event of serious illness or injury, and they may not pay for treatment in Canada. This is another reason for waiving your out-of-country coverage when you leave.

All such policies place some limitations on pre-existing medical conditions and have age restrictions. It is possible, however, to obtain coverage from an international provider with no forced repatriation provision that will cover you up to age 75, with limited coverage for pre-existing medical conditions. After age 75, the coverage could lapse because of the risks of illness. The premiums for such a policy are in the neighbourhood of CDN$15,000 per year for each covered person at the higher end of the age range. This would be for coverage in the U.S. However, it is important to comparison shop.

4. Real Estate Issues

For many Canadians, owning their own home is part of their dream of an ideal retirement. This is also a practical issue since good rental accommodation is expensive in many popular destinations, especially as furnished homes are often the norm for expatriates. While it is prudent to rent for a time before you decide on a particular location, purchasing a condominium or a house is an option you may want to consider.

a) Property Ownership

Purchasing property in some countries can be risky because of the difficulty in obtaining clear title. Careful research and professional legal representation are essential to prevent you falling victim to unscrupulous operators. In some countries, you can also buy title insurance.

The right of foreigners to buy certain property is restricted in some countries. In Mexico, for example, Canadians and other foreigners require special permits to buy land. They cannot own land within a 100-kilometre band along the borders or a 50-kilometre zone along the coasts. In addition, they cannot own mineral or water rights. They may, however, set up trusts to hold restricted property for them. In the U.S. there is no restriction on property ownership.

It is difficult for foreigners who are not locally employed to obtain conventional mortgage financing in most countries. If you still have Canadian residency status, your Canadian bank may extend a personal loan based on your Canadian assets and your credit rating at home, but in general the terms are not nearly as favourable as they are for mortgages. So depending on your circumstances, you might just need to pay for the property outright with your own financial resources.

b) Condominiums

In principle, condominiums offer many advantages to retirees. External maintenance is handled on a shared basis, and it is relatively safe to leave units unoccupied for extended periods. On the other hand, condominiums can entail serious risks in countries with little experience in administering the relevant laws. You cannot assume that condominium bylaws drafted by property developers will actually be enforceable. Indeed, some restrictions, such as those prohibiting occupancy by children, may contravene local laws. Condominiums in developing countries tend to be occupied by foreigners from many parts of the world, who may have very different ideas from yours about the use of common property. Many condominiums have rental units available, and leasing one before buying is a good way to check out not only the property, but also the community.

c) Real Estate Agents and Lawyers

Few developing countries regulate real estate agents and lawyers as rigorously as Canada. In most parts of Latin America and the Caribbean, for example, real estate agents require no formal qualifications or training and are not prevented from promoting sales in which they have an undisclosed personal interest. Similarly, regulations governing conflicts of interest by lawyers may be much less stringent than they are in Canada. Moreover, the authorities may not take complaints from foreigners seriously, especially if the agent or lawyer is an established member of the local community. You should therefore be very careful about accepting claims regarding property that you have not checked out yourself. Such claims as "beach access" may turn out to be fictitious and you could find yourself without any recourse. Do not sign anything that has not been carefully examined by your own lawyer. If possible, try to retain a Canadian lawyer with expertise in the laws of your country of destination. If you have trouble locating an English- or French-speaking local lawyer, the nearest Canadian diplomatic or consular mission can provide you with a list of reputable lawyers who speak English or French. You can also seek out other Canadians in the area and ask for a recommendation.

A lot of the key areas that you need to consider when looking at retiring outside of Canada on a permanent basis have been highlighted. These would involve, tax, pensions, safety, security, citizenship, health, housing, cost of living and cultural considerations. Separation from family and friends is another factor to evaluate.

Your peace of mind, health, quality of life and financial security are key factors when weighing your options. A feeling of well being and balance is so important. Statistics have shown that many Canadians who do sever their ties to Canada to live permanently elsewhere, frequently get homesick and return. A thorough and objective analysis of the motivating factors and advantages and disadvantages needs to done in advance.

TIPS BEFORE LEAVING CANADA

- Do a thorough self-evaluation of the reasons why you want to leave Canada permanently. Put the reasons in writing and include the pros and cons and implications. This would include tax, pensions, housing, cost of living, health care and quality of life. Also include the language, societal, cultural and government differences, as well as emotional, social and psychological implications of missing family, relatives and friends.

- Contact the consular office of the country that you are moving to and obtain information about eligibility for full-time residence and the tax and pension implications.

- Make sure that you are familiar with the country that you intend to move to permanently. Visit it often in advance and stay for extended periods, as a visitor to satisfy yourself that your intended decision is the right one.

- Contact Revenue Canada to determine the tax implications if you are leaving Canada permanently. Refer to item 1 in Appendix A. Speak to the International Tax Services office at 1-800-267-5177. You can obtain numerous free publications that will be helpful, including *Emigrants and Income Tax*.

- Contact Human Resources and Development Canada to determine the implications on federal government pensions if you leave permanently, eg., OAS and CPP. Refer to item 5 in Appendix A for contact numbers.

- Contact Health Canada to determine any necessary health precautions that you should consider before departure. Look in the Blue Pages of your phone directory for your closest phone number or refer to item 4 in Appendix A.

- Contact Foreign Affairs and International Trade Canada for information on the country that you are considering for permanent residence. They also have many excellent publications and helpful information on health, safety and political issues for any country in the world. Refer to item 11 in Appendix A, for more information.

- Contact your provincial office for seniors to determine the implications on any provincial pension plans that you have. Refer to item 11 in Appendix A for contact numbers.

- Contact a professional tax accountant in Canada who specializes in international tax to obtain customized advice for your situation. Most major international chartered accountancy firms have experts on the tax issues of Canadians living full-time in another country.

- If you are intending to move permanently to the U.S., refer to section D.2., Moving to the U.S. Full-time, in Chapter 3, Immigration and Customs.

- Contact the providers of your employer/union/association retirement benefit plan to determine the implications of living full-time outside of Canada.

- Read the book, *Canadians Resident Abroad*, 2nd edition, by Garry Duncan and Elizabeth Peck and published in 1997 by Carswell Publishing. It is available through bookstores, or from the publisher or authors.

- Contact a company called Canadians Resident Abroad Inc. 305 Lakeshore Road East, Oakville, Ontario, L6J 1J3. Tel: (905) 842-0080, Fax: (905) 842-9814. Their web site address is: *http: //www.cdnresabroad.com*. The President of the company is the co-author of the book by the same name. The company publishes a quarterly newsletter for Canadians living full-time outside Canada, called *Update* and provides a variety of other services.

CHAPTER

12

Answers to the Most Commonly Asked Snowbird Questions

Whether you are an experienced or novice Snowbird, there are always lots of questions involved in being a seasonal resident of the U.S., Mexico, or elsewhere. Laws and regulations that might affect you, whether Canadian or foreign, are always in a state of flux. Here is a sampling of some common questions gleaned from my biweekly *Snowbird Q & A* column in *Canada News*, and from radio or TV interviews and educational seminars.

A. RELATING TO HEALTH INSURANCE

Q: *If you had a pre-existing condition such as diabetes and got sick in the States, how adequately would your insurance cover you?*

A: It depends on the insurance company and its policy. Some policies will cover a pre-existing illness such as diabetes if it has been under control for at least three months with no change in the type or dosage of medication. If the medication changes frequently (say monthly) and the condition is therefore not stabilized, most policies will exclude coverage for it, but will cover you for everything else.

Q: *I'm a retiree with a $25,000 extended health benefits plan. I'd like to protect that plan. Where can I obtain that type of insurance that waives subrogation?*

A: A subrogation clause gives the insurance company the right to collect on any other insurance coverage you have (eg., provincial government health programs or your retiree insurance plans). Ask your insurance company if it is a member of the Canadian Life and Health Association (CLHIA). If so, it may be bound by a new system that CLHIA has adopted that its member companies will not use subrogation clauses unless the claim is over $50,000. Call CLHIA at 1-800-268-8099.

Q: *As a senior who intends to go to the States for five months, should I get insurance coverage in Canada or the States?*

A: You want to get insurance in Canada. The companies here are familiar with insuring Canadian travellers and the protocol of getting partial reimbursement from your provincial government and other issues. In addition, coverage is less costly in Canada.

Q: *I have a credit card which grants me 22 days of free out-of-country medical coverage. Can I buy eight more days to make it a month?*

A: Yes. It is easier to get it from the same credit-card insurer. Some credit-card companies require you to deal with them for extended coverage or it voids the underlying policy. Others don't care who you use, as long as that insurer knows who the primary out-of-country carrier is. It is best, though, in this type of situation to try to deal with the same company.

Q: *What insurance pitfalls should I be aware of?*

A: Be sure to disclose any pre-existing conditions and understand the terms of coverage, including deductibles, limitations, exclusions and claim deadlines. Thoroughly comparison shop and look at features and benefits. Price should be the *last* consideration. Always make sure you fully understand the terms of the coverage, or ask questions until you do. You don't want to take chances, because there is so much at stake if you have a claim.

B. RELATING TO TRAVEL

Q: *Of what planning tips should I be aware if I am considering the Snowbird option for the first time?*

A: You should start cautiously and step-by-step. Do your research thoroughly. Read up as much as you can on the areas that interest you. Look at Snowbird newspapers. Speak to other Snowbirds and ask about their experiences and what they would recommend and why. Rent a mobile home in a Snowbird retirement park, or a condo in a retirement complex or rent a RV. Just spend a month or so outside the country for a couple of years until you get a good feeling for what place is right for you. Ask lots of questions of other Snowbirds whenever you can when you are renting. Make sure you feel good about your decision before you buy any housing.

Also, set out your goals, expectations, needs and wants. Put them in writing. You want to make sure that your spouse is on the same wavelength. Take your time in decision-making.

Q: *Is there a place you recommend for novice Snowbirds?*

A: No. It is very much an individual decision. Most Western Canadians prefer Arizona (Phoenix area) first, California (Palm Springs area) second, and southern Florida last. The first two sunbelt states have a dry climate, where Florida tends to be more humid. Most Eastern Canadians prefer Florida first followed by Arizona and then California or Texas. Proximity of travel is a primary factor. Try it step-by-step. Perhaps spend just one month on your first visit and rent an RV, mobile home, condo, or apartment in an area which is popular with other Snowbirds, then ask a lot of questions.

Q: *What is the cheapest way to snowbird in the States?*

A: It depends. Travelling and living in an RV can be very inexpensive. Buying a used mobile home in a mobile home park can be very reasonable, and if you buy at the end of the Snowbird season (April), you can get good deals. At that time you could buy a mobile home for CDN$5,000 to $8,000, for example. Fees for pad rental could range from CDN$250 to $350 and more per month based on a one-year contract. Another option is to rent a mobile home, RV, or apartment.

Q: *I bought my car in Canada but use it for my Snowbird stay. Is there any additional car insurance coverage I should have to protect myself in the U.S.?*

A: It depends on the coverage you currently have. Wherever possible, obtain competitive quotes from car insurance companies in your province.

It is prudent to carry a minimum of $1 million third-party liability coverage, and ideally more (e.g., $2—3 million). Third-party coverage means that you are covered if you cause an accident and the other person makes a claim against you. The premium difference between $1 million and $3 million is relatively small. If one or two people are seriously injured or die as a consequence of an accident that you were responsible for, the award against you could be millions of dollars, especially in the United States.

Obtain under-insured motorists coverage (UMP). This type of coverage protects you in case you or your car is hit by someone with inadequate or no insurance coverage. In that event, you are covered for any claim up to the limit of your own third-party liability insurance coverage (e.g., $1—3 million), subject to any state or provincial ceilings. Without the UMP coverage, you would have no protection. You could sue the driver of the other car, but most likely they would have few assets and you would be totally out of luck. The premium for under-insured motorist coverage is low.

If you are travelling to Mexico, your Canadian auto insurance will not cover you. You need to obtain a separate insurance policy for the duration of that trip from a Mexican insurance company. This policy can be obtained from a local auto club (AAA) branch close to the Mexican border, or from Sanborn's at 1-800-638-9423 (in Canada and the U.S.), or other companies.

Q: *I have a question about insurance on a rented vehicle. If I have the correct coverage in Canada, will it cover everything the same in the U.S.? Is getting a letter from my insurance company enough? Also, if I don't have out-of-country medical coverage will I be covered for all health care costs due to an auto accident?*

A: First, check with the rental company and its insurance company. It depends on the policy of each individual company. However, most rental car companies continue all coverage whether an accident occurs in Canada or the U.S., even though you rented the car in Canada.

Secondly, check to make sure the auto insurance policy is very clear on the above point. If it is not, make sure you do get a letter from the rental company confirming coverage. Never rely on a verbal confirmation. Also make sure there is no limitation on the number of days you can stay in the U.S.

Lastly, you again want to check the coverage of the policy and obtain a separate letter from the rental company if the coverage is not completely clear. You want to check on the dollar limit of the injury coverage (in Canadian or U.S. funds), any exceptions or exclusions in the coverage, and coverage for the costs of sending you back home.

Make sure that you have out-of-country emergency medical coverage for trips to the U.S., no matter how short. You could have medical problems other than auto injuries, or as side effects of the accident (such as, a heart attack or stroke) that would not necessarily be covered by the rental car insurance. In that case, only your out-of-country coverage would protect you from a potentially massive financial outlay.

Q: *This is my first year as a Snowbird. I am renting an RV and travelling to various Sunbelt states but would like to eventually settle in one place. Where can I get information on the safety and security aspects?*

A: There are various free resources about home security, travelling precautions, and special areas of risks. By planning ahead, you will minimize the chance of a bad experience.

- **Travel Information Service of the Department of Foreign Affairs and International Trade (Canada).** This service continually monitors and assesses potential risks to Canadians in all countries outside Canada. For example, a travel information report is available on Florida, including specific precautions to take to avoid being a victim of crime. Contact the Travel Information Service before your departure date. They can be reached 24 hours a day, 7 days a week, at 1-800-267-6788. If you want the free report faxed to you immediately, call 1-800-575-2500.

- **Local police department.** You could contact the police in the place you are planning to stay to obtain crime statistics on the area and precautions to follow.

- **State tourism offices.** These offices can provide you with travel safety tips and advice about specific areas.

- **Travel agencies.** Various travel agencies have free booklets and pamphlets giving general safety tips and specific ones for certain areas. For example, Grand Circle Travel in Boston has a free booklet entitled, *Going Abroad: 101 Tips for Mature Travellers.* Contact them at 1-800-221-2610; or (617) 350-7500.
- **Travel guides.** Your auto club (CAA or AAA affiliate offices) produces travel guides that include travel safety tips and warnings.

Q: *What about the timeshare option?*

A: Time-sharing is primarily a lifestyle choice. Your needs may change, you may tire of the same place, and exchange options may not be as flexible as claimed. Beware of free dinners or evening cruises that expose you to high-pressure sales tactics. The freebie is seldom worth the hassle. If you're tempted, always seek candid opinions from at least three other timeshare owners in the project, and never put a deposit on your credit card. Don't sign any documents without speaking to a real estate lawyer. You may also want to speak with the local Better Business Bureau. Then sleep on the idea for awhile.

Q: *What about security for my home in Canada while I am away?*

A: Check with your insurance company which probably sets stringent requirements to maintain full homeowner coverage during your absence. You may need to name a contact person who will check the home at least once a week to pick up flyers and provide other security measures. And don't leave a message on your answering machine that you're out of the country for six months!

C. RELATING TO CUSTOMS

Q: *What are the current regulations in terms of bringing back goods from the U.S? I am interested for myself and also for various relatives and friends who will be visiting me in the U.S. for short periods.*

A: When you re-enter Canada you must declare everything you acquired abroad, whether you purchased goods for yourself or gifts for others. This includes anything you bought at Canadian or U.S. duty-free shops. Remember to keep all receipts and have them readily available for inspection by a Canada Customs officer.

Here are the regulations relating to the time spent outside Canada and the value of goods that are duty-free. If someone is away from Canada for only 24 hours, they can bring in CDN$50 worth of goods, excluding alcohol and tobacco, duty-free. After a 48 hour absence, the duty-free exemption is extended to CDN$200. A person may bring back CDN$750 worth of goods duty-free without restriction, (including alcohol or tobacco) after an absence of seven full days. This includes up to 1.5 litres of liquor or wine, or a case of 24 bottles/cans of beer, each containing 340 ml (12 ounces). In addition, a person can bring back 50 cigars, one carton of cigarettes, or 400 grams of tobacco.

Other goods subject to restrictions include meat or dairy products, plants, vehicles, or exotic animals or products made from their skins, feathers or bones.

If you have specific questions concerning imports, contact the closest Canada Customs office. These can be contacted 24 hours a day from inside Canada at 1-800-461-9999, or from outside Canada at (613) 993-0534.

Q: *What if I want to buy a U.S. vehicle and return it to Canada?*

A: Determine if your vehicle meets Canadian safety and emission standards by contacting the Registrar of Imported Vehicles toll-free number 1-800-511-7755 (U.S. and Canada). Expect to pay $195 to $245 plus GST for approval documentation. Before you arrive at the border, contact Canada Customs at your expected point of entry (or at 1-800-461-9999, in Canada) to find out what you will owe in import duties. You will also be required to pay seven percent GST plus provincial sales taxes.

Q: *What do you need to do to take a cat or dog across the border?*

A: Get a certificate signed by your vet confirming that the cat or dog has been vaccinated against rabies in the past three years. Make sure this protection doesn't lapse while you are away. This policy is required by both U.S. and Canadian Customs.

D. RELATING TO FINANCIAL TRANSACTIONS

Q: *What are my options for dealing with my various financial transactions while I am in the U.S.?*

A: You have lots of options available. Here are some of the main ones to consider.

- Check to make sure your funds will receive the best interest rate, depending on your liquidity and safety of principal needs. For example, if your direct deposit goes into a low interest or chequing account, arrange to have a regular transfer of the funds (e.g. monthly) into an investment that provides you with a higher return (e.g. GIC, term deposit, Treasury bill). Always make sure your Canadian account funds are receiving interest.

- You may have other investments your financial institution can handle in your absence, for example, reinvestment of income, deposit of coupons, rollover of maturing deposits, or purchase and sale of securities. Make sure your instructions are in writing and any required documentation is signed in advance. Ask for copies of all transactions to be sent to you at your Sunbelt address.

- You can arrange to have your monthly bank statements forwarded to your Sunbelt address.

- You can pay your Canadian bills personally, on your Canadian chequing account, by having your mail forwarded to your Sunbelt address. However, it can be more convenient and efficient to arrange for automatic debiting of your Canadian bank account. Alternatively, you can arrange to have the bills sent to your financial institution to pay on your behalf. In that event, put your instructions in writing. Many bills can be paid this way, for example, utility bills, cable, house taxes, condominium maintenance fees, quarterly income tax instalments, etc.

- Some Canadian financial institutions offer 24 hour, 7 day toll-free automatic access to your account.

- Consider the benefits of having a U.S. fund chequing account at your Canadian bank, with cheques encoded for the U.S. clearing system.

- If you do not already have an existing U.S. bank account, you can facilitate "no hold" chequing privileges by planning for it before you leave Canada. Some banks will hold an out-of-country cheque for up to three weeks for processing and clearing before they will release the funds. Ask the manager of your Canadian financial institution whether they have a correspondent banking relationship with a U.S. financial institution. If they do, this will facilitate a "no-hold" policy.

- Before you leave Canada, check to see what special Snowbird features are available from Canadian and American financial institutions.

Q: *I have read about various financial institutions in Canada and the U.S. having problems or going under. How do I find out what protections I have for savings or chequing deposits in a U.S. bank or savings and loans?*

A: You have good reason to feel cautious. Many people assume that their deposit funds are protected, and they may be—to a certain amount. Here is an overview of deposit money protection in the U.S. and where to get further information:

- Deposits in U.S. federal or state banks, trust companies, and savings and loans are covered by the Federal Deposit Insurance Corporation (FDIC) up to $100,000 for each individual account. For further information, consumer brochures on deposit insurance, and confirmation that the institution is covered by FDIC, contact FDIC at 1-800-934-3342 (in Canada and the U.S.), or call (202) 393-8400.

- Deposits in U.S. credit unions are covered up to $100,000 by the National Credit Union Share Insurance Fund (NCUSIF) for each individual account. For further information, consumer brochures on deposit insurance, and confirmation that the credit union is covered by NCUSIF, contact the National Credit Union Administration at 1-800-755-5999 (U.S. only) or call (703) 518-6300.

Q: *How can I stretch my dollar as a Snowbird?*

A: You can open up a U.S. dollar chequing and savings account at your financial institution in Canada. You can also obtain a U.S. dollar credit card so you can make payments from your U.S. dollar account. This savings account also acts as a buffer to average out the currency exchange rate fluctuations. Ask your financial institution for any discount programs.

Also get into the habit of looking at special discount coupons in Snowbird community newspapers. Look for seniors' specials or portions.

One of the many benefits of the Snowbird lifestyle is that fruit and vegetables tend to be much cheaper and fresher than in Canada during the winter months. Most Snowbird states are in the breadbasket areas of the U.S., so the cost of living is lower in that respect, even with the exchange rate.

E. RELATING TO TAXATION

Q: *Can I write off part of my out-of-country medical insurance premium from my annual income to reduce my income tax, and if so, how do I go about it?*

A: Some financial relief might be available from the tax credits you can earn when you purchase medical insurance. Many people overlook this substantial saving, which could effectively reduce your premium by up to one quarter. You could earn total credits of approximately 27¢ for each dollar of medical expenses (e.g. 27 percent) in any consecutive 12 month period, which exceeds the lesser of 3 percent of income or $1,614. For example, if you were earning $20,000 a year, 3 percent of that is $600. If your out-of-country emergency insurance premium was $1,400 for a six-month stay in the U.S., you would be eligible to claim a tax credit of $216 ($1,400 minus $600 = $800 × 27 percent).

Don't forget to claim other eligible medical expenses such as prescription drugs, dental work, or eyeglasses. If you have further questions, contact your accountant or closest Revenue Canada office.

Q: *Must I file a U.S. tax return?*

A: Cross-border tax issues can be confusing, especially if you have property or other investments in the U.S. Even if you are not required to pay tax, you could be subject to U.S. filing requirements if your visits to the U.S. exceed 182 days over three years, based on a formula counting the current year visits in full, the previous year as one-third days, and one-sixth of days for the year preceding that. Contact a professional accountant familiar with cross-border tax issues as well as the U.S. Internal Revenue Service.

Q: *What if I want to rent out or sell my U.S. property?*

A: Rents are subject to a 30 percent withholding tax, but owners can claim rental expenses including mortgage interest and property tax, and deduct depreciation by filing an annual U.S. tax return. If you sell, the purchaser is required to forward 10 percent of the gross sale price in the U.S. Internal Revenue Service at the time of the transaction. You would be entitled to a refund at tax time if the amount was greater than the tax due. You can request a waiver from the withholding tax if the purchase price of your U.S. property is less than US$300,000 and the buyer intends to use it as a residence for at least half of the subsequent two years.

Q: *How do I find the right professional advisor?*

A: If you already have a trusted lawyer, accountant, or financial planner, they should be able to recommend a specialist in cross-border issues. If you are starting from scratch, various professional associations will offer names as well as advice on qualifications, experience, compatibility, and fees. Trying to do it all yourself could cost you more than you have saved, and give you an ulcer in the bargain!

Q: *I am currently a Snowbird, but am seriously considering living in the U.S. full-time if I can. What information do I need?*

A: There are many implications of moving to the U.S. full-time. You have to consider issues such as tax, estate planning, pensions, housing and health costs, cost of living, as well as the problem of leaving behind friends, and relatives. Taxes and pensions will vary, depending on whether you are living full-time in the U.S., permanently or temporarily, and the nature of your stay (e.g., retired, working, or investing). There are also distinct societal and governmental differences between Canada and the U.S. which would become more apparent if you were living in the U.S. full-time.

Here are the steps to take if you want to explore the process of emigrating to the U.S., remaining in the U.S. over six months, working in the U.S. as a business visitor or professional, or entering the U.S. under the category of trader or investor:

- Contact the nearest U.S. Immigration and Naturalization Service (INS) to find out if you are eligible and the procedures to follow.

- Contact the closest U.S. Consulate or Embassy if you wish to enter the U.S. under the trader or investor category. They will advise you of your eligibility.

- Contact the U.S. Internal Revenue Service (IRS) to determine the tax implications of living full-time in the U.S.

- Contact Revenue Canada to determine the tax implications if you are leaving Canada to live full-time in the U.S.

- Contact Health Canada and your provincial office for seniors to determine how it will affect your federal pension and medicare coverage.

- Contact your employer/union/association retirement benefit plan to determine the implications of living full-time in the U.S.

- Contact a lawyer in Canada who specializes in immigration law as it relates to emigrating to the U.S. or living there full-time.
- Contact a professional accountant in Canada who specializes in cross-border tax issues to obtain customized advice in your situation.

F. RELATING TO WILLS AND ESTATES

Q: *What are the implications if I die owning U.S. property?*

A: Under changes to the Canada-U.S. tax treaty, your estate can offset the U.S. taxes against capital gains tax owed in Canada. Also, there are exemptions up to a certain amount and you can defer estate tax if your spouse is a beneficiary. With proper tax planning, Canadians can also defer Canadian capital gains tax on death by leaving the property to a spouse or a spousal trust.

Q: *Is my Canadian will valid in the U.S. if I own property there?*

A: Since laws relating to wills can change and can vary from place to place, it is essential to seek professional advice. If you have a valid and enforceable will in your province, it would *usually* be deemed valid in the state that you have property. For a comprehensive discussion of estate planning, refer to *The Canadian Guide to Wills and Estate Planning* (Gray and Budd).

G. RELATING TO A PERMANENT MOVE OUTSIDE CANADA

Q: *What are the tax implications of permanent residence in another country?*

A: There are numerous implications depending on how you go about departing. If you decide to be officially designated by Revenue Canada as a non-resident of Canada, you will have to pay a departure tax on your capital gains calculated as of the date of departure. You may also have tax withheld from any income that you continue receiving from Canada, for example, CPP, RRSP, real estate rental revenue, etc. There are various amounts of tax taken off at source, depending on the nature of the income. Depending on your personal financial circumstances, you could be further ahead to remain a technical resident of Canada for tax purposes.

There are many issues for consideration. You need professional tax advice based on where you plan to move. You need to look at the strategic pros and cons of your tax options. As your decisions make such a difference in the tax outcome, it is ideal to obtain three opinions from tax experts.

APPENDIX

A

Sources of Further Information

One of the challenges of researching information is knowing where to start. This Appendix can save you a great deal of time, energy, money, and hassle by providing you with contact numbers you may wish to phone.

Many of the numbers provided are toll-free. Those that are not toll-free may accept collect calls; there is no risk in asking. Most Canadian or U.S. government offices will accept collect calls. If you can't locate the phone number for a federal or provincial government office in Canada, phone Reference Canada at 1-800-667-3355. Its representatives are very resourceful in providing information.

1. Revenue Canada—Taxation

There could be tax implications of living, working, investing, or owning assets in the United States. Contact your closest Revenue Canada office below.

International Taxation Office
2540 Lancaster Road
Ottawa, ON K1A 1A8
Tel: 1-800-267-5177 (toll-free in Canada)
Tel: (613) 952-3741 (from Ottawa area or outside Canada)
Collect phone calls accepted from anywhere in the United States.

District Taxation Offices
Collect phone calls are accepted.

British Columbia
277 Winnipeg St.
Penticton, BC V2A 1N6
Tel: (604) 492-9200
1-800-565-5125

1166 W. Pender St.
Vancouver, BC V6E 3H8
Tel: (604) 689-5411

1-800-663-9033 (calls from Yukon and northwestern British Columbia)

1415 Vancouver St.
Victoria, BC V8V 3W4
Tel: (604) 363-0121
1-800-742-6108

Alberta
220 - 4th Ave. S.E.
Calgary, AB T2G 0L1
Tel: (403) 221-8919
1-800-332-1410
(calls from southern Alberta)
1-800-661-6451
(calls from Northwest Territories
and northeastern British Columbia)

9700 Jasper Ave., Suite 10
Edmonton, AB T5J 4C8
Tel: (403) 423-3510
1-800-232-1966
(calls from northern Alberta)

Saskatchewan
1955 Smith St.
Regina, SK S4P 2N9
Tel: (306) 780-6015
1-800-667-7555

340 - 3rd Ave. N.
Saskatoon, SK S7K 0A8
Tel: (306) 975-4595
1-800-667-2083

Manitoba
325 Broadway Ave.
Winnipeg, MB R3C 4T4
Tel: (204) 983-6350
1-800-282-8079

Ontario
11 Station St.
Belleville, ON K8N 2S3
Tel: (613) 969-3706
1-800-267-8030

150 Main St. W.
P.O. Box 2220
Hamilton, ON L8N 3E1
Tel: (905) 522-8671
1-800-263-9200
(calls from area codes 416 and 905)
1-800-263-9210
(calls from area code 519)

385 Princess St.
Kingston, ON K7L 1C1
Tel: (613) 545-8371
1-800-267-9447

166 Frederick St.
Kitchener, ON N2G 4N1
Tel: (519) 579-2230
1-800-265-2530

451 Talbot St.
London, ON N6A 5E5
Tel: (519) 645-4211
1-800-265-4900

77 City Centre Dr.
P.O. Box 6000
Mississauga, ON L5A 4E9
Tel: (905) 566-6700
1-800-387-1700
(calls from area codes 519, 705,
and 905)

5001 Yonge St., Suite 1000
North York, ON M2N 6R9
Tel: (416) 221-9309
1-800-387-1700
(calls from area codes 519, 705,
and 905)

360 Lisgar St.
Ottawa, ON K1A 0L9
Tel: (613) 598-2275
1-800-267-8440
(calls from area code 613)
1-800-267-4735
(calls from area code 819)

185 King St. W.
Peterborough, ON K9J 8M3
Tel: (705) 876-6412
1-800-267-8030

32 Church St.
P.O. Box 3038
St. Catharines, ON L2R 3B9
Tel: (905) 688-4000

1-800-263-5672

200 Town Centre Court
Scarborough, ON M1P 4Y3
Tel: (416) 296-1950
1-800-387-5229
(calls from area code 905)
1-800-387-5183
(calls from area codes 519 and 705)

19 Lisgar St. S.
Sudbury, ON P3E 3L5
Tel: (705) 671-0581
1-800-461-4060
(calls from area code 705)
1-800-461-6320
(calls from area codes 613 and 807)

130 South Syndicate Ave.
Thunder Bay, ON P7E 1C7
Tel: (807) 623-3443
1-800-465-6981

36 Adelaide St. E.
Toronto, ON M5C 1J7
Tel: (416) 869-1500

185 Ouellette Ave.
Windsor, ON N9A 5S8
Tel: (519) 258-8302
1-800-265-4841

Quebec
100 Lafontaine St., #211
Chicoutimi, QC G7H 6X2
Tel: (418) 698-5580
1-800-463-4421

3131 Saint-Martin Blvd. W.
Laval, QC H7T 2A7
Tel: (514) 956-9101
1-800-363-2218

305 René-Levesque Blvd. W.
Montreal, QC H2Z 1A6
Tel: (514) 283-5300
1-800-361-2808

165 vue de la Pointe-aux-lièvres S.
Quebec, QC G1K 7L3
Tel: (418) 648-3180
1-800-463-4421

320 St-Germain E., 4th Floor
Rimouski, QC G5L 1C2
Tel: (418) 722-3111
1-800-463-4421

44 du Lac Ave.
Rouyn-Noranda, QC J9X 6Z9
Tel: (819) 764-5171
1-800-567-6403

50 Place de la Cité
Sherbrooke, QC J1H 5L8
Tel: (819) 564-5888
1-800-567-7360

5245 Cousineau Blvd., Suite 200
Saint-Hubert, QC J3Y 7Z7
Tel: (514) 283-5300
1-800-361-2808

25 des Forges St., Suite 111
Trois-Rivières, QC G9A 2G4
Tel: (819) 373-2723
1-800-567-9325

New Brunswick
120 Harbourview Blvd., 4th Floor
P.O. Box 8888
Bathurst, NB E2A 4L8
Tel: (506) 548-7100
1-800-561-6104

126 Prince William St.
Saint John, NB E2L 4H9
Tel: (506) 636-4600
1-800-222-9622

Prince Edward Island
94 Euston St.
P.O. Box 8500
Charlottetown, PE C1A 8L3
Tel: (902) 628-4200

Nova Scotia
1256 Barrington St.
P.O. Box 638
Halifax, NS B3J 2T5
Tel: (902) 426-2210
1-800-565-2210

47 Dorchester St.
P.O. Box 1300
Sydney, NS B1P 6K3
Tel: (902) 564-7080
1-800-563-7080

Newfoundland
Sir Humphrey Gilbert Building
P.O. Box 5968
St. John's, NF A1C 5X6
Tel: (709) 772-2610
1-800-563-2600

Free Publications

General and Supplemental Income Tax Guides

- *General Income Tax Guide*
- *Emigrants*
- *Capital Gains*
- *Rental Income*
- *Business and Professional Income*
- *RRSPs and Other Registered Plans for Retirement*
- *Preparing Returns for Deceased Persons*
- *Employment Expenses*

Interpretation Bulletins

IT-29	*United States Social Security Tax and Benefits*
IT-31	*Foreign Exchange Profits and Losses*
IT-76R2	*Exempt Portion of Pension When Employee Has Been a Non-resident*
IT-95R	*Foreign Exchange Gains and Losses*
IT-120RY	*Principal Residence*
IT-122R2	*U.S. Social Security Taxes and Benefits*
IT-161R3	*Non-residents—Exemption from Tax Deductions at Source on Employment Income* (also ask for *"Special Release"*)
IT-163R2	*Election by Non-Resident Individuals on Certain Canadian Source Income*
IT-171R	*Nonresident Individuals—Taxable Income Earned in Canada*
IT-194	*Foreign Tax Credit—Part-Time Residents*
IT-221R2	*Determination of an Individual's Residence Status (also ask for "Special Release")*
IT-262R	*Losses of Non-Residents and Part-Year Residents*

IT-270R2	*Foreign Tax Credit*
IT-298	*Canada United States Tax Convention—Number of Days "Present" in Canada*
IT-370	*Trusts—Capital Property Owned on December 31, 1971*
IT-372R	*Trusts—Flow-Through of Taxable Dividends and Interest to a Beneficiary* (1987 and Prior Taxation Years)
IT-395R	*Foreign Tax Credit—Foreign-Source Capital Gains and Losses*
IT-399	*Principal Residence—Non-Resident Owner*
IT-420R3	*Non-Residents—Income Earned in Canada*
IT-465R	*Non-Resident Beneficiaries of Trusts*
IT-506	*Foreign Income Taxes as a Deduction from Income*
IT-520	*Unused Foreign Tax Credits—Carry Forward and Carry Back*

Pamphlets

- *Canadian Residents Going Down South*
- *Canadian Residents Abroad*
- *Are You Moving?*
- *How to Calculate Your RRSP Contribution Limit*
- *Gifts in Kind*
- *Tax Information for People with Disabilities*
- *Paying Your Income Tax by Instalments*

Information Circulars

- *Registered Retirement Income Funds*
- *Away-from-Home Expenses*
- *Deferred Profit Sharing Plans*
- *Canada U.S. Social Security Agreement*
- *Gifts in Right in Canada*
- *Consent to Transfer Property of Deceased Persons*

2. Revenue Canada—Customs

It is important to know your rights and obligations when coming back from a trip to the United States. To save frustration and expense, check with the customs office before you leave. Phone 1-800-461-9999 (toll-free in Canada).

Regional Canada Customs Offices:

Pacific
1001 W. Pender St.
Vancouver, BC V6E 2M8
Tel: (604) 666-0459

Alberta
220 - 4th Ave. S.E., Suite 720
Calgary, AB T2P 2M7
Tel: (403) 292-4622

Central
Federal Building
269 Main St.
Winnipeg, MB R3C 1B3
Tel: (204) 983-3771

Southwestern Ontario
Walkerville P.O. Box 2280
Windsor, ON N8Y 4R8
Tel: (519) 645-4133

Hamilton
10 John St. S.
Hamilton, ON L8N 3V8
Tel: (416) 572-2818

Toronto
2nd Floor, 1 Front St. W.
P.O. Box 10, Station A
Toronto, ON M5W 1A3
Tel: (416) 973-6433

Ottawa
360 Coventry Rd.
Ottawa, ON K1K 2C6
Tel: (613) 991-0552

Montréal
400 Youville Square
Montréal, QC H2Y 3N4
Tel: (514) 283-6632

Quebec
130 Dalhousie St.
Quebec, QC G1K 7P6
Tel: (418) 648-3401

Atlantic
6169 Quinpool Rd.
Halifax, NS B3J 3G6
Tel: (902) 426-2667

Free Publications

- *Bringing Back Goods from the United States Under the North American Free Trade Agreement (NAFTA)*
- *Importing a Motor Vehicle into Canada*
- *Importing Goods into Canada? Documentation Simplified*
- *Importations by Mail*
- *I Declare*

3. Transport Canada

There are technical requirements to consider if bringing a U.S.-purchased car or RV back to Canada (for example, emission control). Enquire before you go to the U.S., or before you buy a vehicle in the U.S. Transport Canada established a special registry in April 1995. Contact them at:

Registrar of Imported Vehicles
Tel: 1-800-511-7755 (toll-free in Canada and the U.S.)
P.O. Box 94, 260 Adelaide St. E.
Toronto, ON M5A 1N1
Web site: *http://www.riv.com*

Free Publications

- *List of Vehicles Admissable and Nonadmissable from the U.S.*

- *Your Guide to Importing a Vehicle from the U.S. into Canada*
- *Importers Checklist*
- *Vehicle Modification Requirements*

4. Health Canada

There are many forms of federal government assistance and free educational material for seniors. Contact your local office (see the Blue Pages in your telephone directory) or the number below for further information. You can call any long distance number collect.

Division of Aging and Seniors
3rd Floor, 473 Albert St.
Ottawa, ON K1A 0K9
Tel: (613) 952-7358
Fax: (613) 957-7627

Free Publications
These include the *Seniors' Guide to Federal Programs and Services*, and many other publications. Ask for a current list.

5. Human Resources and Development Canada

140 Promenade du Portage
Phase 4, Level O
Hull, QC K1A 0J9
Tel: (819) 994-6313
Fax: (819) 953-7260

Free Publications:
- *Old Age Security Pension*
- *Retirement Pension*
- *Survivor Benefits*
- *Spousal Allowance*

6. Department of Foreign Affairs and International Trade

The consular service of this Canadian government department provides invaluable services throughout the world to all Canadians. If any unexpected problems occur, you can contact the closest office to you in the U.S., Mexico or Costa Rica. If you cannot reach the local office promptly and there is an emergency, you can phone the headquarters in Ottawa collect at (613) 996-8885. It is open 24 hours, 7 days a week.

There are many publications available as well as current updates on safety and travel concerns and tips for Canadians throughout the world. This service constantly monitors and assesses potential risks to Canadians outside Canada. Contact them before you depart. They can be reached 24 hours a day, 7 days a week. If you want a free report faxed to you immediately, call the number below. For other information, contact the numbers listed below.

InfoCentre
235 Sussex Drive
Ottawa, ON K1A 0G2
Tel: 1-800-267-8376 (Canada only)
    or 1-800-267-6788 (Canada only)
    (613) 944-6788
Fax-back service: 1-800-575-2500
Web site: *http://www.dfait-maeci.gc.ca*

Free Publications

- *Crossing the 49th: A Compendium of the Bumps on the Road for Canadians Going South*
- *Bon Voyage, But: Tips for Canadians Travelling Abroad*
- *Retirement Abroad—Seeking the Sunsets*
- *Her Own Way: Advice for Woman Traveller*
- *A Guide for Canadians Imprisoned Abroad*
- *Working Abroad: Unravelling the Maze*
- *México Qué Pasa? A Guide for Canadian Visitors*
- *Country Travel Reports*—These reports offer travellers current information on conditions in over 170 countries, including safety, health and passport requirements. Services are available 24 hours a day, 7 days a week.

7. Reference Canada

Reference Canada is your telephone referral and basic information service for federal government programs and services.

With Reference Canada, you no longer need to worry about how to track down information about the federal government. All it takes is a telephone call. Information officers are available to help you in either English or French.
All regions except Manitoba and Quebec: 1-800-667-3355
Manitoba residents: 1-800-282-8060
Quebec residents: 1-800-363-1363
Persons with a hearing impairment: 1-800-465-7735

In Quebec, also contact the Communication-Quebec office closest to your area. You can locate this number in the Blue Pages of your telephone directory.

8. Canadian Consulates in the United States

If you have any problems (for example, you lose your passport) that require Canadian government assistance, contact the closest Canadian consulate in the United States. In cases of emergency when you cannot contact the local office quickly, you can phone the Ottawa office of the Department of Foreign Affairs and International Trade. The number is (613) 996-8885 (24 hours, 7 days a week). You can phone collect.

Washington
501 Pennsylvania Ave. N.W.
Washington, DC 20001
Tel: (202) 682-1740
Fax: (202) 682-7726

Atlanta
Suite 400, South Tower,
One CNN Center
Atlanta, GA 30303-2705
Tel: (404) 577-6810/577-1512
Fax: (404) 524-5046

Boston
Three Copley Place, Suite 400
Boston, MA 02116
Tel: (617) 262-3760
Fax: (617) 262-3415

Buffalo
One Marine Midland Center,
Suite 3000
Buffalo, NY 14203-2884
Tel: (716) 852-1247
Fax: (716) 852-4340

Chicago
Two Prudential Plaza
180 N. Stetson Ave., Suite 2400
Chicago, IL 60601
Tel: (312) 616-1860
Fax: (312) 616-1877

Dallas
St. Paul Place, Suite 1700
750 N. St. Paul St.

Dallas, TX 75201
Tel: (214) 922-9806
Fax: (214) 922-9815

Detroit
600 Renaissance Center, Suite 1100
Detroit, MI 48243-1798
Tel: (313) 567-2085
Fax: (313) 567-2164

Los Angeles
300 S. Grand Ave.
10th Floor, California Plaza
Los Angeles, CA 90071
Tel: (213) 687-7432
Fax: (213) 620-8827

Minneapolis
701 Fourth Ave. S., Suite 900
Minneapolis, MN 55415-1899
Tel: (612) 333-4641
Fax: (612) 332-4061

New York
1251 Avenue of the Americas
New York City, NY 10020-1175
Tel: (212) 596-1600
Fax: (212) 596-1793

Seattle
412 Plaza 600
Sixth and Stewart Streets
Seattle, WA 98101-1286
Tel: (206) 443-1777
Fax: (206) 443-1782

9. Canadian Consulates in Mexico

The following Canadian government offices are there to assist you in any way that you might require, especially in the case of an emergency or some other difficulty. If you are unable to contact a Canadian consulate in the case of an emergency, you can phone collect to the Department of Foreign Affairs and International Trade office in Ottawa, at (613) 996-8885, 24 hours, 7 days a week.

Mexico City
Calle Schiller No. 529 (Rincon del Bosque)
Colonia Polanco
11560 Mexico
D.F., Mexico
Postal Address: P.O. Box 105-05, 11580 Mexico, D.F., Mexico
Tel: 52 (5) 724-7900
Toll-free: 91-800-70629
Fax: 52 (5) 724-7980

Acapulco
Hotel Club del Sol
Costera Miguel Aleman, at the corner of Reyes Catolicos
39300 Acapulco
Guerrero, Mexico
Postal Address: PO Box 94-C, 39670 Acapulco, Guerrero, Mexico
Tel: 52 (74) 85-66-21
Fax: 52 (74) 86-74-17

Ajijic
Hotel Real de Chapala
Paseo del Prado 20
Ajijic, Jalisco, Mexico
Tel: 52 (376) 62-288
Fax: 52 (376) 62-420

Cancun
Plaza Mexico Commercial Centre
Room 312, 200 Avenida Tulum, at the corner of Agua
77500 Cancun, Quintana Roo, Mexico
Tel: 52 (98) 84-37-16
Fax: 52 (98) 87-67-16

Guadalajara
Hotel Fiesta Americana
Local 30, Aurelio Aceves 225
Col. Vallarta Poniente
P.O. Box 44100
Guadalajara, Jalisco, Mexico
Tel: 52 (3) 615-6270/615-6266/ 616-5642
Fax: 52 (3) 615-8665

Mazatlan
Hotel Playa Mazatlan
Zona Dorada
Rodolfo Loaiza 202
82110 Mazatlan
Sinaloa, Mexico
Postal Address: P.O. Box 614, 82110 Mazatlan, Sinaloa, Mexico
Tel: 52 (69) 13-73-20
Fax: 52 (69) 14-66-55

Monterrey
Edificio Kalos
Floor C-1, Room 108-A
Zaragoza 1300 Sur and Constitucion
Monterrey, N.L., Mexico
Postal Address: P.O. Box 64000, Monterrey, N.L., Mexico
Tel: 52 (83) 44-32-00/44-27-53/ 44-29-06/44-29-61
Fax: 52 (83) 44-30-48

Oaxaca
119 Dr. Liceaga, Suite 8
68000 Oaxaca, Mexico
Postal Address: P.O. Box 29, Station C, Colonia Reforma, 68050 Oaxaca, Mexico
Tel: 52 (951) 33-777
Fax: 52 (951) 52-147

Puerto Vallarta
160 Zaragoza Street, Interior 10
Colonia Centro
48300 Puerto Vallarta, Jalisco,
Mexico
Tel: 52 (322) 253-98
Fax: 52 (322) 235-17

San Miguel de Allende
Mesones 38, Interior 15
San Miguel de Allende

Guanajuato, Mexico 37700
Tel: 52 (415) 230-25
Fax: 52 (415) 268-56

Tijuana
German Gedovius No. 10411-101
Condominio del Parque, Zona Rio
22320 Tijuana
Baja California Norte, Mexico
Tel: 52 (66) 84-04-61
Fax: 52 (66) 84-03-01

10. Canadian Consulate in Costa Rica

If you need any assistance, especially in an emergency, contact the following Canadian consular office. In the event that you can not reach the office immediately, you can phone collect to the Department of Foreign Affairs and International Trade office in Ottawa, at (613) 996-8885, 24 hours, 7 days a week.

Costa Rica
La Sabana Executive Business Centre
Building No. 5, 3rd Floor, beside the Contraloria General de la Republica
San José, Costa Rica
Postal Address: P.O. Box 351-1007
San José, Costa Rica
Tel: (506) 296-4149
Fax: (506) 296-4270

11. Provincial Offices for Seniors

To learn more about provincial services available to seniors, you may wish to contact the following offices:

Office for Seniors
B.C. Ministry of Health
1515 Blanshard St., 6th Floor
Victoria, BC V8W 3C8
Tel: (205) 952-1238
Fax: (205) 952-1282

Seniors' Benefit and Special Needs
Alberta Community Development
Main Floor, Standard Life Centre
10405 Jasper Ave.
Edmonton, AB T5J 4R7
Tel: (403) 427-6358
Fax: (403) 422-5954

Corporate Policy
Saskatchewan Social Services
1920 Broad St.
Regina, SK S4P 3V6
Tel: (306) 787-3619
Fax: (306) 787-0925

Manitoba Seniors' Directorate
822 - 155 Carleton St.
Winnipeg, MB R3C 3H8
Tel: (204) 945-6565
Fax: (204) 948-2514

Ministry of Citizenship, Culture
and Recreation
Province of Ontario
77 Bloor St. W., 8th Floor
Toronto, ON M7A 2R9
Tel: (416) 327-2422
Fax: (416) 314-7458

Direction de l'intégration sociale
Ministère de la santé et
des services sociaux
Édifice Joffre
1075, chemin Sainte-Foy, 11e étage
Quebec, QC G1S 2M1
Tel: (418) 643-6386
Fax: (418) 643-9024

Office for Seniors
Health and Community Services
Province of New Brunswick
520 King St., 4th Floor

P.O. Box 5100
Fredericton, NB E3B 5G8
Tel: (506) 453-2480
Fax: (506) 453-2082

Health and Community Services
Agency
Government of Prince Edward Island
P.O. Box 2000
Charlottetown, PE C1A 7N8
Tel: (902) 368-6130
Fax: (902) 368-6136

Nova Scotia Senior Citizens'
Secretariat
P.O. Box 2065
1740 Granville St., 4th Floor
Halifax, NS B3J 2Z1
Tel: (902) 424-4649
Fax: (902) 424-0561

12. Provincial Tourism Offices

If you are travelling by car or RV to and from the United States, you may want
to plan to explore your own beautiful and diverse country on your way. Here
is a list of toll-free phone numbers for provincial tourism offices. They will
send you a detailed information package as well as an accommodations directory.

Tourism British Columbia
1-800-663-6000

Alberta Tourism
1-800-661-8888

Tourism Saskatchewan
1-800-667-7191

Travel Manitoba
1-800-665-0040

Ontario Travel
1-800-ONTARIO (668-2746)

Tourism Québec
1-800-363-7777

New Brunswick Tourism
1-800-561-0123

Nova Scotia Tourism
1-800-565-0000

13. Provincial Health Departments—Out-of-Country
Medical Claims and Information

Contact your provincial health department about coverage for out-of-country
medical expenses. You will need to obtain supplemental insurance from a private carrier. See Item 14.

Medical Services Plan
P.O. Box 2000
Victoria, BC V8W 2Y4
Tel: (205) 386-7171
1-800-663-7100
Fax: (205) 952-2964

Alberta Health
P.O. Box 1360
Edmonton, AB T5J 2N3
Tel: (403) 422-1954
1-800-310-0000
Fax: (403) 422-3552

Department of Health
3475 Albert St.
Regina, SK S4S 6X6
Tel: (306) 787-3261
1-800-667-7523
Fax: (306) 787-3761

Manitoba Health
P.O. Box 925
Winnipeg, MB R3C 2T6
Tel: (204) 786-7221
1-800-392-1207
Fax: (204) 783-2171

Ministry of Health
P.O. Box 9000
Kingston, ON K7L 5A9
Tel: (613) 546-3811
(Call your local office collect)
Fax: (613) 545-4399

RAMQ
P.O. Box 6600
Quebec, QC G1K 7T3
Tel: (418) 646-4636 (Quebec)
Tel: (514) 861-3411 (Montréal)
1-800-561-9749

Medicare
P.O. Box 2500
Fredericton, NB E3B 7J3
Tel: (506) 453-2161
Fax: (506) 453-2726

Department of Health
P.O. Box 8700
Confederation Building, West Block
St. John's, NF A1B 4J6
Tel: (709) 729-4928
Fax: (709) 729-4009

Health Services
P.O. Box 2703
Whitehorse, YT Y1A 2C6
Tel: (403) 667-5725
1-800-661-0408
Fax: (403) 393-6486

Department of Health
2nd Floor, ICC Building
Inuvik, NT X0E 020
Tel: (403) 979-7400
1-800-661-0830
Fax: (403) 979-3197

Health and Community Services
Agency
35 Douses Rd.
Montague, PE C0A 1R0
Tel: (902) 368-5858
Fax: (902) 838-2050

Department of Health
P.O. Box 488
Halifax, NS B3J 2R8
Tel: (902) 424-5999
1-800-563-8880
Fax: (902) 424-0615

14. Companies and Associations Providing Out-of-Country Medical Insurance

Many companies provide out-of-country medical insurance to supplement provincial coverage. These companies may change their insurance underwriters from year to year. Also, some insurance companies may sell coverage directly, as well as underwrite different organizations or companies with special packages. The market is very competitive, so thoroughly comparison shop and look at features, benefits, premiums, limitations, exclusions, and deductibles. These factors can change each year, usually between June and September.

Associations

Canadian Association of Retired Persons
1-888-239-2444

Western Association of Canadian Sun Seekers
1-800-830-9398

Association of Mature Canadians
1-800-667-0429

Arizona Winter Visitors Association
1-888-698-4040

Auto Clubs

CAA Travel & Medical Insurance
Contact your local auto club. Refer to item 36 in this Appendix.

National Auto League
1-800-387-2298

Banks

Bank of Montreal Travel Protection Plan
1-800-661-9060

BCI Bank
1-800-267-7557

CIBC Travel Medical Insurance
1-800-565-6010

HSBC Travel Insurance
1-800-387-5290

Royal Bank Travel Health Protector
1-800-565-3129

Scotiabank Medical Insurance Plan
1-800-387-9844

TD Bank Green Plan Travel
1-800-293-4941

Credit Unions

CUIS (Credit Union Insurance Services) Travel Insurance
1-800-263-5110

Trust Companies

Canada Trust Travel Medical Insurance
1-800-263-4008

Other

ACA Assurance Tour Med Insurance
1-800-268-9633

Administered Insurance Services
1-888-779-7977

Advantage Travel Centre Travelprotect 50 Plus
1-800-461-0730

Air Canada Travel Insurance
1-800-420-3011

ATTO & Associates
1-800-263-9683

Blue Cross Plans

B.C. (through Medical Services Association)	Tel: (604) 737-5528
Alberta & Northwest Territories	1-800-661-6995
Saskatchewan	1-800-667-6853
Manitoba	1-800-262-8832
Ontario	1-800-873-2583
Quebec	1-888-625-7653
Atlantic	1-800-561-7123

Canadian Plus Members Travel Insurance
1-800-880-0866

Canadian Travel Medical Insurance
1-800-260-6703

Citibank Visa Out of Country Travel Insurance
1-888-592-9292

Commercial Union Life Insurance
1-800-268-4102

Desjardins/Laurentian Life Travel Insurance
1-800-463-7830

Destination Travel Health Plans
1-800-337-3532

Direct Med
1-800-300-9601

Golden Age Insurance
1-800-387-0339

Good Holiday Travel Insurance
1-800-667-7267

Grey Power Health Insurance
1-888-731-6911

Ingle Life and Health Insurance
1-800-216-3588

Journeyman Travel Protection
1-888-577-7432

Liberty Health
1-800-268-3763

Maritime Medical Care
1-800-565-8785

Manulife Financial Entourage Plan
1-800-810-0187

Medicare International
1-800-461-2100

MediSecure Travel Companion
1-800-268-6703

MediSelect Advantage
1-800-567-8819

Mutual of Omaha Insurance Company of Canada
1-800-268-8825

Protection Plus Golden Age Insurance
1-800-387-0339

RV Advantage Travel Health Insurance
1-877-777-1718

Thomas Cook Quality Care Travel Insurance
1-800-482-7744

Travel Insurance Coordinators
1-800-663-4494

Travel Insurance Made Easy (TIME)
1-800-500-2947

Travel Insurance Specialists
1-800-563-0314

Travel Underwriters
1-800-663-5389

Travellers Choice
1-800-665-8553

Voyageur Travel Insurance
1-800-265-6896

Canadians Living Full-Time Outside Canada
The following is a list of some Canadian, British and U.S. insurance companies offering health insurance coverage to Canadian expatriates. Refer to item 34 for a list of web site addresses for these and other companies.

CANADA

Compass International
(A division of Wright Mogg & Associates Ltd.)
100 Regina Street South
Suite 270, PO Box 96
Waterloo, ON   N2J 3Z8
Tel: (519) 886-1690
Fax: (519) 886-8559

John Ingle Insurance
438 University Avenue, Ste. 1200
Toronto, ON   M5G 2K8
Tel: (416) 340-0100
Fax: (416) 340-2707
Toll-free: 1-800-387-4770
(within Canada and the U.S.)

The Norfolk Group
Suite 510, 940 – 6th Ave SW
Calgary, AB   T2P 3T1
Tel: (403) 232-8545
Fax: (403) 265-9425

Telfer International Consultants Inc.
Suite 200 – 59 rue St. Jacques
Montréal, QC   H2Y 1K9

Tel: (514) 284-2002
Fax: (514) 284-3203

UNITED KINGDOM

BUPA International
Russell Mews
Brighton, East Sussex, England,
BN1 2N12
Tel: 44-1273-323563
Fax: 44-1273-820517

ExpaCare Insurance Services
Dukes Court, Duke Street
Woking, Surrey, England,
GU21 5XB
Tel: 44-1483-740090
Fax: 44-1483-776620

Goodhealth Worldwide Limited
Mill Bay Lane
Horsham, West Sussex, England,
RH12 1TQ
Tel: 44-1403-230000
Fax: 44-1403-268429

International Health Insurance Danmark
64A Athol Street
Douglas, Isle of Man, British Isles,

1M1 1JE
Tel: 44-1624-677412
Fax: 44-1624-275856

PPP Health Care
20 Upperton Rd.
Eastbourne, East Sussex, England,
BN21 1LH
Tel: 44-1323-410505
Fax: 44-1323-731325

UNITED STATES

International Medical Group, Inc.
135 North Pennsylvania
Suite 1700
Indianapolis, Indiana   46204
Tel: (317) 636-4721
Fax: (317) 687-9272

15. Air Ambulance Services

UNITED STATES

Air Ambulance America
Florida-based. Fee for service.
1-800-262-8526

Air Ambulance Anywhere
Florida-based. Family plan.
1-800-327-1966

Air Response
1-800-631-6565

Care Flight Air Ambulance
Florida-based. Fee for service.
1-800-282-6878

Medical Air
Texas-based. Family plan.
1-800-643-9023

Med Jet Assistance
1-877-963-3538

National Air Ambulance
Florida-based. Fee for service.
1-800-327-3710

SkyMed International
Arizona-based. Fee for service.
Annual family membership plan.
1-800-275-9633

Skyservice Lifeguard
Canada and Florida-based. Fee for
service.
1-800-463-3482

Mexico

Air Ambulance America of Mexico
Mexico-(Mexico City) based. Fee for
service.
(95) 800-222-3564

Aeromedical Group
Mexico-(Mexico City) and U.S.-(San
Diego) based. Fee for service.
1-800-982-5806 (U.S. only)
(619) 278-3822

16. U.S. Consulates in Canada

You may have questions about travelling to the United States, in terms of any
restrictions, limitations, or documentation required. Or you may want to invest
in a business enterprise in the United States.

1095 W. Pender St.
Vancouver, BC V6E 2M6
Tel: (604) 685-4311
Fax: (604) 685-5285

#1050 - 615 Macleod Trail S.E.
Calgary, AB T2G 4T8
Tel: (403) 266-8962
Fax: (403) 264-6630

360 University Ave.
Toronto, ON M5G 1S4
Tel: (416) 595-1700
Fax: (416) 595-0051,
(416) 595-5419

100 Wellington St.
Ottawa, ON K1P 5T1
Tel: (613) 238-5335, (613) 238-4470
Fax: (613) 238-5720

2 Place Terrasse Dufferin, C.P. 939
Quebec, QC G1R 4T9
Tel: (418) 692-2095
Fax: (418) 692-4640

Suite 910, Cogswell Tower,
Scotia Square
Halifax, NS B3J 3K1
Tel: (902) 429-2480
Fax: (902) 423-6861

P.O. Box 65
Postal Station Desjardins
Montréal, QC H5B 1G1
Tel: (514) 398-9695
Fax: (514) 398-0973, (514) 398-0711

17. Mexican Government Tourism Offices in Canada

Contact the closest office to you or phone 1-800-44-MEXICO (639426) (toll-free from Canada and the U.S.) for more information, assistance and resource material about travel to Mexico or visit the Mexican Government Tourism site on the Net at *http://www.mexico-travel.com.*

Montréal
One Place Ville Marie, #1526
Montréal, QC   H3B 2B5
Tel: (514) 871-1052
Fax: (514) 871-3825

Toronto
2 Bloor Street West, #1801
Toronto, ON   M4W 3E2
Tel: (416) 925-1876
Fax: (416) 925-6061

Vancouver
999 West Hastings Street, #16010
Vancouver, BC   V6C 2W2
Tel: (604) 669-2845
Fax: (604) 669-3498

18. Consular Offices of Costa Rica in Canada

Contact the closest consular office for information about tourism questions, living part-time or full-time in Costa Rica, or investing or buying property there.

You can phone the Costa Rica Tourist Board at 1-800-343-6332. At present, this toll-free number is only accessible from the U.S., but could soon be available in Canada. You can visit their site at *http://www.tourism-costarica.com.*

Toronto
164 Avenue Road
Toronto, ON   M5R 2H9
Tel: (416) 961-6773
Fax: (416) 961-6771

Montréal
1425 Avenue Rene Levesque W.,
#602
Montréal, QC   H3T 1T7
Tel: (514) 393-1057
Fax: (514) 393-1624

Ottawa
135 York Street, #206
Ottawa, ON   K1N 5T4
Tel: (613) 562-2855
Fax: (613) 562-2582

Vancouver
789 West Pender Street, #430
Vancouver, BC   V6C 1H2
Tel: (604) 681-2152
Fax: (604) 688-2152

19. Mexican Consulate Offices in Canada

Ottawa
45 O'Connor St., Suite 1500
Ottawa, ON K1P 1A4
Tel: (613) 233-8988 or 233-6665
Fax: (613) 235-9123 or 567-9036

Montréal
2000 Mansfield St., Suite 1015
Montréal, QC H3A 2Z7
Tel: (514) 288-2707 or 288-2502
Fax: (514) 288-8287

Toronto
99 Bay St., Suite 4440
Toronto, ON M5L 1E9
Tel: (416) 368-8141 or 368-2875 or
368-2450
Fax: (416) 368-8342 or 368-0676

Vancouver
1130 West Pender St., Suite 810
Vancouver, BC V6E 4A4
Tel: (604) 684-3547 or 684-1859
Fax: (604) 684-2485

20. Mexican State Tourism Offices in Mexico
English-speaking operators are available 24 hours a day, 7 days a week, to assist visitors with questions, disputes and emergencies during their stay in Mexico. Call 91-800-90392 from anywhere in Mexico (in Mexico City the local number is 250-0123).

Aguascalientes
Edificio Torres Plaza Bosques
Av. Universidad No. 1001, Piso 8
Fracc. Prados del Bosque
20127 Aguascalientes, AGS.
Tel: (49) 12 35 11
Fax: (49) 12 19 30

Baja California
Edificio Plaza Patria, Piso 3, Zona K
Blvd. Diaz Ordaz Y Av. De Las Americas
22440 Tijuana, B.C.
Tel: (66) 81 94 92
Fax: (66) 81 95 79

Baja California Sur
Edificio Fidepaz, Apartado Postal 419
Km. 5.5. Carretera Transpeninsular
23090 La Paz, B.C.S.
Tel: (112) 4 04 90
Fax: (112) 4 07 22

Campeche
Calle 12 No. 153 Col. Centro
24000 Campeche, Camp.
Tel: (981) 6 60 68
Fax: (981) 6 67 67

Coahuila
Edificio Torre Saltillo
Blvd. Luis Echeverria No. 1560,
Piso 11
Col. Guanajuato Oriente
25286 Saltillo, Coah.
Tel: (84) 15 21 62
Fax: (84) 15 17 14

Colima
Portal Hidalgo No. 20 Col. Centro
28000 Colima, Col.
Tel: (331) 2 43 60
Fax: (331) 2 83 60

Chiapas
Edificio Plaza De Las Instituciones
Blvd. Belisario Dominguez
No. 950 Col. Centro
29000 Tuxtla Gutierrez, Chis.
Tel: (961) 2 45 35
Fax: (961) 2 55 09

Chihuahua
Edificio Agustin Melgar
Libertad No. 1300, Piso 1 Col.
Centro
31000 Chihuahua, Chih.
Tel: (14) 29 34 21
Fax: (14) 16 00 32

Durango
Hidalgo No. 408 Sur Col. Centro
Durango, Dgo. 34000

Tel: (81) 1 11 07
Fax: (81) 1 96 77

Distrito Federal
Amberes No. 54, Esq. Londres Col.
Juarez
06600 Mexico, D.f.
Tel: (5) 525 9381
Fax: (5) 525-9387

Guanajuato
Plaza De La Paz No. 14 Col. Centro
36000 Guanajuato, Gto.
Tel: (473) 2 76 22
Fax: (473) 2 42 51

Guerrero
Av. Costera Miguel Aleman No. 187
Fracc. Hornos
39350 Acapulco, Gro.
Tel: (74) 86 91 64
Fax: (74) 86 45 50

Hidalgo
Blvd. Felipe Angeles S/n
Carretera Mexico-Pachuca Km. 93.5
Col. Venta Prieta
42080 Pachuca, Hgo.
Tel: (771) 1 41 50
Fax: (771) 1 41 95

Jalisco
Morelos No. 102, Plaza Tapatia Col.
Centro
44100 Guadalajara, Jal.
Tel: (3) 6 14 01 23
Fax: (3) 6 14 43 65

Estado De Mexico
Urawa No. 100
Puerta 110 Col. Izcalliipiem
50150 Toluca, Edo. de Mex.
Tel: (72) 19 51 90
Fax: (72) 12 16 33

Michoacan
Nigromante No. 79 Palacio Clavijero,
P.b. Col. Centro

58000 Morelia, Mich.
Tel: (43) 12 37 10
Fax: (43) 12 98 16

Morelos
Av. Reforma No. 204 Col. Reforma
62260 Cuernavaca, Mor.
Tel: (73) 13 74 68
Fax: (73) 13 74 68

Nayarit
Av. De La Cultura No. 74
Col. Ciudad Valle
83157 Tepic, Nay.
Tel: (32) 14 02 14
Fax: (32) 14 80 74

Nuevo Leon
Edificio Kalos, Nivel A-1, Despacho
136
Zaragoza Sur No. 1300 Col. Centro
64000 Monterrey, N.I.
Tel: (8) 3 45 00 31
Fax: (8) 3 45 30 32

Oaxaca
Av. Independencia No. 607 Col.
Centro
CP 68000 Oaxaca, Oax.
Tel: (951) 6-0717
Fax: (951) 6-1500

Puebla
11 Oriente No. 2224, Piso 2 Col.
Azcarate
72380 Puebla, Pue.
Tel: (22) 35 81 82
Fax: (22) 34 12 24

Queretaro
Pasteur No. 4 Norte, Esq.
Palacio De Gobierno Col. Centro
77000 Queretaro, Qro.
Tel: (42) 12 13 92
Fax: (42) 12 10 94

Quintana Roo
Av. Heroes No. 622 Col. Venustiano
Carranza
77010 Chetumal, Q. Roo
Tel: (983) 2-8661
Fax: (983) 2-8682

San Luis Potosi
Alvaro Obregon No. 520 Col. Centro
78000 San Luis Potosi, S.L.P.
Tel: (48) 12 99 39
Fax: (48) 12 67 69

Sinaloa
Edificio Banco De Mexico
Paseo Olas Atlas 1300
Piso 1 Col. Centro
82000 Mazatlan, Sin.
Tel: (69) 16 51 60
Fax: (69) 16 51 66

Sonora
Edificio Sonora, Ala Norte, 3 er.
Nivel
Blvd. Paseo Canal Sur Y Comonfort
83280 Hermosillo, Son.
Tel: (62) 17 00 44
Fax: (62) 17 00 60

Tabasco
Centro Administrativo De Gobierno
Tabasco 2000 Paseo De Tabasco
No. 1504
Col. Tabasco 2000
Cp 86035 Villahermosa, Tab.
Tel: (93) 16 35 33
Fax: (93) 16 28 90

Tamaulipas
Torre De Gobierno
Rosales y 5 De Mayo No. 272
Oriente
Col. Centro
87000 Ciudad Victoria, Tamps.
Tel: (131) 2 70 02
Fax: (131) 2 57 84

Tlaxcala
Av. Juarez, Esq Lardizaval Col.
Centro
90000 Tlaxcala, Tlax.
Tel: (246) 2 53 06
Fax: (246) 2 53 06

Yucatan
Calle 59 No. 514, Entre 62 64 Col.
Centro
97000 Merida, Yuc.
Tel: (99) 24 80 13
Fax: (99) 28 65 47

Veracruz
Edificio Torre Animas
Blvd. Cristobal Colon No. 5, Piso 14
Fracc. Jardines De Las Animas
91190 Jalapa, Ver.
Tel: (28) 12 73 45
Fax: (28) 12 59 36

Zacatecas
Edificio Mar-zes
Prolongacion Gonzales Ortega S/n
Col. Centro Cp.
98000 Zacatecas, Zac.
Tel: (492) 4 03 93
Fax: (492) 2 93 29

21. U.S. Internal Revenue Service (IRS)

The IRS is equivalent to Revenue Canada. As there could be various tax implications to your stay in the United States, income derived in the United States, or assets owned in the United States, check with the IRS Canadian office.

IRS Canadian Office
Toll-free: 1-800-829-1040 (U.S. only)
Web site: *http://www.irs.ustreas.gov*

Free Publications
These publications with related forms are available from any IRS office in the United States or U.S. consulate office in Canada. Look in the Yellow Pages of your telephone directory for listings. If you are calling from the United States, you can request these forms by phoning the following toll-free number: 1-800-TAX-FORM (1-800-829-3676).

#54   *Tax Guide for U.S. Citizens and Resident Aliens Abroad*
#448   *U.S. Estate and Gift Tax Guide*
#513   *Tax Information for Visitors to the United States*
#514   *Foreign Tax Credit for Individuals*
#515   *Withholding of Tax on Non-Resident Aliens and Foreign Corporations*
#519   *U.S. Tax Guide for Aliens*
#521   *Moving Expenses*
#523   *Tax Information on Selling your Home*
#527   *Residential Rental Property*
#593   *Tax Highlights for U.S. Citizens and Residents Going Abroad*
#910   *Guide to Free Tax Services*

22. U.S. Customs Service

You will have to comply with U.S. customs regulations when entering the United States. Make enquiries before you leave Canada.

For specific information on requirements and regulations that might affect you, contact the U.S. Customs office closest to your point of entry into the United States (for example, at an airport or border station).

As there are many entry points and therefore many phone numbers, contact directory information in the location that you are going to enter the United States.

Address for Free Publications

U.S. Customs Service
P.O. Box 7407
Washington, DC 20044

Free Publications

- *U.S. Customs Directory*
- *International Mail Imports*
- *Customs Hints for Visitors (Non-residents)*
- *Tips for Visitors*
- *Pets, Wildlife*
- *Importing a Car*

23. U.S. Immigration and Naturalization Service (INS)

For further information on remaining in the United States over six months a year, working in the United States as a business visitor or professional, or emigrating to the United States, contact the appropriate INS office below before entering the United States. If you intend to enter the United States under the category of trader or investor, contact the U.S. Embassy or a U.S. Consulate office in Canada.

Ports of Entry INS Offices

Peace Arch Inspection Station
P.O. Box 340
Blaine, WA 98230
Tel: (306) 332-8511

U.S. Immigration Building
P.O. Box 165
Sweetgrass, MT 59484
Tel: (406) 335-2911

Detroit Tunnel
150 E. Jefferson Ave.
Detroit, MI 48226
Tel: (313) 226-2390

Peace Bridge
Rhode Island St.
Buffalo, NY 14213
Tel: (716) 885-3367

Thousand Island Bridge
P.O. Box 433, Road No. 1
Alexandra Bay, NY 13607-9796
Tel: (315) 482-2681

Ogdensburg Prescott Bridge
Ogdensburg, NY 13669
Tel: (315) 393-0770

65 W. Service Rd.
Champlain, NY 12919
Tel: (518) 298-3221, (518) 298-8433

P.O. Box 189
Military Rd.
Houlton, ME 04730
Tel: (207) 532-2906

One Maine St.
P.O. Drawer 421

Calais, ME 04619
Tel: (207) 454-2546, (207) 454-2547

Vancouver International Airport
P.O. Box 23046
Vancouver, BC V7E 1T9
Tel: (604) 278-2520

Air Terminal Building
2000 Airport Rd. N.W.
Calgary, AB T2E 6W5
Tel: (403) 221-1730

Edmonton International Airport
P.O. Box 9832
Edmonton, AB T5J 2T2

Tel: (403) 890-4486

Winnipeg International Airport
Winnipeg, MB R2R 0S6
Tel: (204) 783-2340

L.B. Pearson International Airport
P.O. Box 6011
Toronto, ON L5P 1E2
Tel: (905) 676-2563

Montréal International Airport
P.O. Box 518
Dorval, QC H4Y 1B3
Tel: (514) 631-2097

24. U.S. Department of Agriculture—Animal and Plant Inspection Service

Certain types of fruits, vegetables, meats, animals, plants, and seeds are prohibited entry into the United States. Make enquiries at your closest U.S. customs office, or contact:

U.S. Department of Agriculture
1400 Independence Ave. S.W.
Washington, DC 20250
Tel: (202) 720-2791

Free Pamphlet: *Travelers' Tips*

25. U.S. Fish and Wildlife Service

You are prohibited from buying, owning, or transporting certain types of live fish or animals, or products made from these animals. Ask for further information at your closest U.S. customs office, or contact:

Department of the Interior
Washington, DC 20240

Free Pamphlets

- *Fish and Wildlife*
- *Facts About Federal Wildlife Laws*

26. State Travel Offices in the United States

Use this listing of state travel offices to order free vacation information. One call, often to a toll-free number accessible from Canada as well as the United States, or a letter will let you explore a variety of American vacation destinations in the comfort of your home.

Although the quantity and variety of information available will vary from state to state, you will receive maps, calendars of events, travel guides, and information about accommodations, campgrounds, restaurants, attractions, and recreational activities.

For assistance in making specific travel arrangements, contact your local travel agent. Common Sunbelt states are noted with an asterisk (*).

Alabama Bureau of Tourism and Travel
P.O. Box 4309
Montgomery, AL 36103-4309
Tel: (205) 242-4169
1-800-ALABAMA

Alaska Division of Tourism
P.O. Box 110801, TIA
Juneau, AK 99811-0801
Tel: (907) 465-2010

* Arizona Office of Tourism
1100 W. Washington St.
Phoenix, AZ 85007
Tel: (602) 542-8687
1-800-842-8257

Arkansas Department of Parks and Tourism
One Capitol Mall, Dept. 7701
Little Rock, AR 72201
Tel: (501) 682-7777
1-800-NATURAL

* California Division of Tourism
P.O. Box 1499, Dept. TIA
Sacramento, CA 95812-1499
Tel: (916) 322-2881
1-800-TO-CALIF

Colorado Tourism Board
P.O. Box 38700
Denver, CO 80238
Tel: (303) 592-5410
1-800-COLORADO

Connecticut Department of Economic Development, Tourism Division
865 Brook St.
Rocky Hill, CT 06067
Tel: (203) 258-4355
1-800-CT-BOUND

Delaware Tourism Office
99 Kings Hwy., Box 1401, Dept. TIA
Dover, DE 19903
Tel: (302) 739-4271
1-800-441-8846

* Florida Division of Tourism
126 W. Van Buren St., FLDA
Tallahassee, FL 32399-2000
Tel: (904) 487-1462

Georgia Department of Industry, Trade and Tourism
P.O. Box 1776, Dept. TIA
Atlanta, GA 30301
Tel: (404) 656-3590
1-800-VISIT-GA

* Hawaii Visitors' Bureau
2270 Kalakaua Ave.
Honolulu, HI 96815
Tel: (808) 923-1811

Idaho Division of Tourism Development
700 W. State St., Dept. C
Boise, ID 83720
Tel: (208) 334-2470
1-800-635-7820

Illinois Bureau of Tourism
100 W. Randolph, Suite 3-400
Chicago, IL 60601
Tel: (312) 814-4732
1-800-223-0121

**Indiana Department of
Commerce/Tourism and Film
Development Division**
One N. Capital St., Suite 700
Indianapolis, IN 46204-2288
Tel: (317) 232-8860
1-800-289-6646

Iowa Division of Tourism
200 E. Grand
Des Moines, IA 50309
Tel: (515) 242-4705
1-800-345-IOWA (for ordering
vacation kit only, U.S. only)
1-800-528-5265
(special events calendar)

**Kansas Travel and
Tourism Division**
700 S.W. Harrison St., Suite 1300
Topeka, KS 66603-3712
Tel: (913) 296-2009
1-800-2-KANSAS

**Kentucky Department of
Travel Development**
500 Mero St., 22nd Floor, Dept. DA
Frankfort, KY 40601
Tel: (502) 564-4930
1-800-225-TRIP

Louisiana Office of Tourism
Attn.: Inquiry Dept.
P.O. Box 94291, LOT
Baton Rouge, LA 70804-9291
Tel: (504) 342-8119
1-800-33-GUMBO

Maine Office of Tourism
189 State St.
Augusta, ME 04333

Tel: (207) 289-5711
1-800-533-9595

**Maryland Office of
Tourism Development**
217 E. Redwood St., 9th Floor
Baltimore, MD 21202
Tel: (410) 333-6611
1-800-543-1036
(for vacation kit only)

**Massachusetts Office of
Travel and Tourism**
100 Cambridge St., 13th Floor
Boston, MA 02202
Tel: (617) 727-3201
1-800-447-MASS
(for vacation kit only, U.S. only)

Michigan Travel Bureau
P.O. Box 3393
Livonia, MI 48151-3393
Tel: (517) 373-0670
1-800-5432-YES

Minnesota Office of Tourism
121 - 7th Place E.
St. Paul, MN 55101
Tel: (612) 296-5029
1-800-657-3700

Mississippi Division of Tourism
P.O. Box 1705
Ocean Springs, MS 39566-1705
Tel: (601) 359-3297
1-800-WARMEST

Missouri Division of Tourism
P.O. Box 1055, Dept. TIA
Jefferson City, MO 65102
Tel: (314) 751-4133
1-800-877-1234

Travel Montana
Room TIA
Deer Lodge, MT 59722
Tel: (406) 444-2654
1-800-VISIT-MT

Nebraska Division of Travel and Tourism
P.O. Box 94666
Lincoln, NE 68509
Tel: (402) 471-3796
1-800-228-4307

* Nevada Commission on Tourism
Capitol Complex, Dept. TIA
Carson City, NV 89710
Tel: (702) 687-4322
1-800-NEVADA-8

New Hampshire Office of Travel and Tourism Development
P.O. Box 856, Dept. TIA
Concord, NH 03302
Tel: (603) 271-2343
1-800-386-4664

New Jersey Division of Travel and Tourism
20 W. State St., CN 826, Dept. TIA
Trenton, NJ 08625
Tel: (609) 292-2470
1-800-JERSEY-7

* New Mexico Department of Tourism
491 Old Santa Fe Trail
Sante Fe, NM 87503
Tel: (505) 827-7400
1-800-545-2040

New York State Division of Tourism, Department of Economic Development
One Commerce Plaza
Albany, NY 12245
Tel: (518) 474-4116
1-800-CALL-NYS

North Carolina Division of Travel and Tourism
430 N. Salisbury St.
Raleigh, NC 27603
Tel: (919) 733-4171
1-800-VISIT-NC

North Dakota Department of Tourism
Liberty Memorial Building,
604 E. Blvd.
Bismarck, ND 58505
Tel: (701) 224-2525
1-800-435-5663

Ohio Division of Travel and Tourism
P.O. Box 1001
Columbus, OH 43266-0101
Tel: (614) 466-8844
1-800-BUCKEYE
(continental U.S. and all of Canada)

Oklahoma Tourism and Recreation Department, Travel and Tourism Division
500 Will Rogers Building, DA92
Oklahoma City, OK 73105-4492
Tel: (405) 521-3981
1-800-652-6552
(information requests only)

Oregon Economic Development Department, Tourism Division
775 Summer St. N.E.
Salem, OR 97310
Tel: (503) 373-1270
1-800-547-7842

Pennsylvania Office of Travel Marketing
Room 453, Forum Building
Harrisburg, PA 17120
Tel: (717) 787-5453
1-800-VISIT-PA

Rhode Island Tourism Division
7 Jackson Walkway, Dept. TIA
Providence, RI 02903
Tel: (401) 277-2601
1-800-556-2484

South Carolina Division of Tourism
Box 71

Columbia, SC 29202
Tel: (803) 734-0122
1-800-346-3634

**South Dakota Department
of Tourism**
711 E. Wells Ave.
Pierre, SD 57501-3369
Tel: (605) 773-3301
1-800-DAKOTA

**Tennessee Department of Tourist
Development**
P.O. Box 23170, TNDA
Nashville, TN 37202
Tel: (615) 741-2158
1-800-836-6200

**Texas Department of Commerce,
Tourism Division**
P.O. Box 12728
Austin, TX 78711-2728
Tel: (512) 462-9191
1-800-88-88-TEX

Utah Travel Council
Council Hall/Capitol Hill, Dept.
TIA
Salt Lake City, UT 84114
Tel: (801) 538-1030
1-800-200-1160

**Vermont Department of Travel
and Tourism**
134 State St.
Montpelier, VT 05602

Tel: (802) 828-3236
1-800-338-0189, 1-800-837-6668

Virginia Division of Tourism
1021 E. Cary St., Dept. VT
Richmond, VA 23219
Tel: (804) 786-4484
1-800-VISIT-VA

**Washington State Tourism
Development Division**
P.O. Box 42500
Olympia, WA 98504-2500
Tel: (206) 586-2088, 586-2012
1-800-544-1800

**West Virginia Division of Tourism
and Parks**
2101 Washington St. E.
Charleston, WV 25305
Tel: (304) 348-2286
1-800-225-5982

Wisconsin Division of Tourism
P.O. Box 7606
Madison, WI 53707
Tel: (608) 266-2161
1-800-372-2737 (in-state)
1-800-432-TRIP (out-of-state)

Wyoming Division of Tourism
I-25 at College Dr., Dept. WY
Cheyenne, WY 82002
Tel: (307) 777-7777
1-800-225-5996

27. State Travel Parks Associations

These associations are for the owners of travel parks, including the larger parks
catering to Snowbirds who have extended stays (for example, up to six
months). As a result, they tend to offer extensive services and amenities. Write
to them for a directory of members. Just the most popular Sunbelt states are
listed. If you want associations in other states, contact **The National
Association of RV Parks and Campgrounds**, 8605 Westwood Center Drive,
#201, Vienna, VA, 22182. Tel: (703) 720-2791.

Arizona Travel Parks Association
8164 E. Jenan Drive
Scottsdale, AZ 85260
Tel: (602) 991-8781
Fax: (602) 991-8781

Florida Association of RV Parks and Campgrounds
1340 Vickers Dr.
Tallahassee, FL 32303-3041
Tel: (904) 562-7151
Fax: (904) 562-7179

California Travel Parks Association
P.O. Box 5648
Auburn, CA 95604
Tel: (916) 885-1624
Fax: (916) 823-6331

Texas Association of Campground Owners
7009 S. I-35
Austin, TX 787744
Tel: (512) 444-6322
Fax: (512) 444-8719

28. Associations of Mobile Home Owners

Many U.S. states have associations of people who own manufactured homes or "mobile" homes. These homeowners tend to live in their homes all year long, or if they are Snowbirds, up to six months a year. Benefits of membership in these associations include group rates for mobile home insurance, a regular newsletter or magazine, and government lobbying efforts on behalf of members. Contact numbers for the key Sunbelt state associations follow. There is no state association for Texas at this time.

Arizona Association of Manufactured Homeowners
2334 S. McClintock Drive
Tempe, AZ 85201
Tel: (602) 966-9566

California Mobile Home Resource and Action Association
3381 Stevens Creek Rd., Suite 210
San Jose, CA 95117
Tel: (408) 244-8134

Federation of Mobile Homeowners of Florida
4020 Portsmouth Rd.
Largo, FL 34641-3399
Tel: (727) 530-7539

National Association of Manufactured Homeowners
62 Hawthorne Circle
Willow Street
PA 17584
Tel: (717) 284-4520

29. National Seniors' Organizations

The following national organizations provide helpful contacts and networking for seniors. Many of these organizations offer Snowbird out-of-country health insurance; discounts on purchases such as medication and on lodgings; meetings; newsletters; advocacy efforts in lobbying various levels of government; and other member benefits. Fees tend to be nominal. Contact the organizations directly for further information. The three organizations noted with an asterisk (*) offer out-of-country insurance to Canadian Snowbirds.

Canada

* Canadian Association of
Retired Persons
27 Queen St. E., Suite 1304
Toronto, ON M5C 2M6
Tel: (416) 363-8748
1-800-363-9736
Fax: (416) 363-8747

Canadian Pensioners Concerned
7071 Bayses Rd., #302
Halifax, NS B3L 2C2
Tel: (902) 455-7684
Fax: (902) 455-1825

Federal Superannuates'
National Association
233 Gilmour St., Suite 401
Ottawa, ON K2P 0P2
Tel: (613) 234-9663
Fax: (613) 234-2314

National Pensioners' and Senior
Citizens' Federation
3033 Lakeshore Blvd. W.
Toronto, ON M8V 1K5
Tel: (416) 251-7042
Fax: (416) 252-5770

One Voice—The Canadian
Seniors Network
350 Sparks St., Suite 1005
Ottawa, ON K1R 7S8
Tel: (613) 238-7624
Fax: (613) 235-4497

U.S.

American Association of Retired
Persons
601 E Street N.W.
Washington, DC 20049-0002
Tel: (202) 434-2277
1-800-424-3410 (U.S. only)
Fax: (202) 434-6483

30. Companies Providing Travel Services

Airlines	Toll-free Number	Number Available from
Air Canada	(800) 776-3000	Canada/U.S.
Air Transat	(800) 471-1011	Canada/U.S.
American Airlines	(800) 433-7300	Canada/U.S.
Canada 3000	(888) 241-1997	Canada/U.S.
Canadian Airlines	(800) 363-7530	Canada/U.S.
Continental Airlines	(800) 231-0856	Canada/U.S.
Delta Airlines	(800) 241-4141	Canada/U.S.
Mexicana Airlines	(800) 531-7923	Canada/U.S.
Northwest Airlines	(800) 225-2525	Canada/U.S.
Royal Airlines	(800) 361-6674	Canada/U.S.
U.S. Air	(800) 428-4322	Canada/U.S.
United Airlines	(800) 241-6522	Canada/U.S.

Car Rentals		
Alamo	(800) 327-9633	Canada/U.S.

Avis	(800) 831-2847	Canada/U.S.
Budget	(800) 268-9800	Canada/U.S.
Dollar	(800) 800-4000	Canada/U.S.
Enterprise	(800) 325-8007	Canada/U.S.
Hertz	(800) 654-3131	Canada
	(800) 527-6700	U.S.
Thrifty	(800) 367-2277	Canada/U.S.

Trains
Amtrak	(800) 872-7245	Canada/U.S.

31. Newspapers for Canadian Snowbirds

To keep current on Canadian events, news, and information, as well as on issues that affect Snowbirds, subscribe to one or both of the publications below. They are published weekly during the Snowbird season (November 1 — April 30), and monthly from June through October. Although both papers are owned by the same parent company, each has different content and a unique style and format. Ask for a complimentary copy.

Canada News and
The Sun Times of Canada
Both c/o P.O. Box 1729
Auburndale, FL 33823-1729
Tel: (813) 967-6450
1-800-535-6788

32. News for Canadian Snowbirds on Sunbelt Radio Stations

There are various radio programs containing news specifically for Canadian Snowbirds. The news program with the greatest coverage is called *Canadian News with Prior Smith* and is heard in Florida, Arizona and The Bahamas each weekday. Most Florida stations also air the news magazine *Canada This Week* each Sunday. Consult stations for scheduling.

Prior Smith has been hosting this radio program for Canadians wintering in the South, for over 22 years, and the program has aired for over 46 years. If you have access to the Internet, you can find his web site at *http://www.canadacalling.com.* You will find the current schedules plus copies of weekly columns that he writes for various daily newspapers in Canada during the fall and spring each year. The papers are *Toronto Star, Ottawa Citizen, Montreal Gazette* and *Halifax Chronicle Herald.*

There are also radio news programs for Canadian Snowbirds heard in various communities in Southern California. Refer to the radio station list below. Stations, coverage, and scheduling may change. Most programs are on AM stations, some on FM, and others on both.

Florida

Station	Region	Dial Position	Broadcast Time(s) (Mon–Fri)
WGUL	Tampa Bay	860	10:30 A.M. 3:30 P.M.
WGUL FM	New Port Richey, Dunedin, Clearwater, Largo	96.1	10:30 A.M. 3:30 P.M.
WBRD	Bradenton	1420	2:30 P.M.
WTMY	Sarasota	1280	8:50 A.M.
WENG	Englewood, Venice	1530	8:30 A.M.
WZZS FM	Arcadia Sebring	106.9	9:00 A.M.
WKII	Port Charlotte, Punta Gorda, Southwest Gulf Coast	1070	9:30 A.M.
WODX	Marco Island	1480	12:00 P.M.
WFTL	Fort Lauderdale, North Miami to Pompano Beach	1400	11:30 A.M.
WPBR	Palm Beaches, Boca Raton, Bahamas	1340	9:00 A.M.
WPSL	Port St. Lucie, Fort Pierce, Stuart	1590	8:50 A.M.
WOKC	Lake Okeechobee	1570	8:30 A.M.
WTTB	Vero Beach	1490	11:30 A.M.
WGYL FM	Vero Beach (Sunday only)	93.7	7:30 A.M.
WMEL	Melbourne, Cocoa Beach, Titusville	920	9:00 A.M.
WSBB	New Smyrna Beach	1230	9:00 A.M. 5:00 P.M.
WROD	Daytona Beach	1340	11:55 A.M.
WAOC	St. Augustine	1420	12:50 P.M.
WDCF	Dade City	1350	8:30 A.M.
WZHR	Zephyrhills	1400	8:30 A.M.
WITS	Sebring, Avon Park, South Central Florida	1340	10:05 A.M. 1:05 P.M.
WWBF	Bartow, Lake Wales, Lakeland	1130	8:30 A.M.
WLBE	Leesburg, Orlando, Central Florida	790	12:15 P.M.
WINV	Inverness, Central Florida	1560	10:30 A.M. 3:30 P.M.
WOCA	Ocala, Silver Springs	1370	11:50 A.M.
WWJB	Brooksville	1450	9:10 A.M.
WXCV FM	Crystal River, Homosassa Springs	95.3	9:30 A.M.
WEBZ FM	Panama City, Florida Panhandle	93.5	9:04 A.M. 3:04 P.M.
WDIZ	Panama City, Florida Panhandle	590	9:04 A.M. 3:04 P.M.

Arizona

Station	Region	Dial Position	Broadcast Time(s) (Mon-Fri)
KXAM	Phoenix, Mesa, Scottsdale, Sun City	1310	10:00 A.M.

California

Station	Region	Dial Position	Broadcast Time(s) (Mon-Fri)
KWXY	Palm Springs, Rancho Mirage, Palm Desert, Indian Wells,	1340 or 98.5	9:15 A.M. 3.15 P.M.

33. Two-day Activity Schedule of a Sample Mobile Home/RV Park

Day/Time	Activity	Location
SUNDAY		
11:00 am	Chapel - nondenominational	Activity Hall
1:00 pm	Solo Potluck (1st Sunday)	All Purpose Room
5:30 pm	Organ Music	Activity Hall
6:00 pm	Ice Cream	Activity Hall
7:00 pm	Entertainment	Activity Hall
7:00 pm	Euchre	All Purpose Room
MONDAY		
7:00 am	Richard Simmons Coed Aerobics	Social Hall
7:50 am	Bend & Stretch (Coed)	Social Hall
8:00 am	Aqua Trims	Pool
8:00 am	Oil Painting	Paint Room
8:00 am	Golf	Golf Course
8:00 am	Line Dancing - Country & Western	Activity Hall
8:30 am	Jackpot Shuffle-board	Court
8:45 am	Coffee	Patio
8:45 am	Piano Practice	Social Hall
9:00 am	Woodworking (9 to 12, 1 to 4)	Shop
9:00 am	Lapidary (closed 12 to 1)	Shop
9:00 am	Silversmithing (closed 11 to 1)	Shop
10:00 am	Round Dance (Phase 3 to 4 workshop)	Activity Hall
10:00 am	Ceramics	Ceramics Room
10:00 am	Friendship Bible Studies	All Purpose Room
10:15 am	Jackpot Shuffle-board	Court
1:00 pm	Craft Class	Paint Room
1:00 pm	Square Dance (A-2 workshop)	Activity Hall

1:00	pm	Round Dance (basic beginners)	Social Hall
3:00	pm	Little Theatre	Activity Hall
3:15	pm	Ladies Barbershop	Social Hall
4:00	pm	Cabaret Meeting - (1st Monday)	All Purpose Room
5:30	pm	Potluck	Activity Hall
6:00	pm	Ladies' Pool	Pool Room
6:30	pm	Water Aerobics	East Pool
7:00	pm	Jackpot Nickel	Social Hall
7:00	pm	Cribbage	All Purpose Room
7:00	pm	Chapel Committee (2nd Monday)	Paint Room

34. Web Sites on the Internet of Interest to Snowbirds

Refer back to Chapter 1 for a brief discussion on the Internet.

Name of site	**Location address**

Tax Information

Canadian Snowbird Institute Inc.	*http://www.snowbird.ca*
Revenue Canada (taxation and customs)	*http://www.revcan.ca*
Internal Revenue Service (IRS)—U.S.	*http://www.irs.ustreas.gov*
U.S. Customs	*http://www.customs.ustreas.gov/index.html*
Arthur Andersen Accounting Firm	*http://www.arthurandersen.com*
BDO Dunwoody Accounting Firm	*http://www.bdo.ca*
Deloitte Touche Accounting Firm	*http://www.deloitte.ca*
Ernst & Young Accounting Firm	*http://www.eycan.com*
KPMG Accounting Firm	*http://www.kpmg.ca*
PriceWaterhouseCoopers Accounting Firm	*http://www.pricewaterhouse coopers.ca*

Financial Institutions

Bank of Montreal	*http://www.mbanx.com*
Bank of Nova Scotia	*http://www.scotiabank.ca*
Canada Trust	*http://www.canadatrust.com*
Canadian Imperial Bank of Commerce	*http://www.cibc.com*
Royal Bank of Canada	*http://www.royalbank.com*
Toronto-Dominion Bank	*http://www.tdbank.ca*

Finance

Canada Stockwatch (Canadian stock quotes)	*http://www.canada-stockwatch.com/main.htm*
TD Greenline (Canadian stock quotes)	*http://www.tdbank.ca/greenline*
Money (U.S. stock quotes)	*http://www.pathfinder.com/money/rtq/index.html*

Money Management and Estate Planning

Canadian Snowbird Institute Inc.	*http://www.snowbird.ca*

**Federal Government Programs
for Seniors**
Health Canada   *http://www.hwc.ca*

**Federal Government Pensions
and Benefits Information**
Human Resources and   *http://www.hrdc-drhc.gc.ca*
Development Canada

Newspapers
Canada
Calgary Herald   *http://www.southam.com/
                                       calgaryherald*
Edmonton Journal   *http://www.southam.com/
                                       edmontonjournal*
National Post   *http://www.nationalpost.com*
Globe and Mail   *http://www.globeandmail.ca*
Halifax Daily News   *http://www.hfxnews.southam.ca*
Montréal Gazette   *http://www.montrealgazette.com*
Ottawa Citizen   *http://www.ottawacitizen.com*
Regina Leader-Post   *http://www.leader-post.sk.ca*
Saskatoon Star Phoenix   *http://www.saskstar.sk.ca*
Southam Press   *http://www.canada.com*
Toronto Star   *http://www.thestar.com*
Toronto Sun   *http://www.canoe.ca/torontosun/
                                       home.html*
Vancouver Sun   *http://www.vancouversun.com*
Winnipeg Free Press   *http://www.mbnet.mb.ca/freepress*

United States
New York Times   *http://www.nytimes.com*
USA Today   *http://www.usatoday.com*
Washington Post   *http://www.washingtonpost.com*

Magazines and News Services
Chatelaine   *http://www.chatelaine.com*
Canadian Broadcasting   *http://www.cbc.ca*
Company (CBC)
Florida Living   *http://www.floridaliving.org*
Maclean's   *http://www.canoe.ca/macleans*
Time   *http://www.pathfinder.com/time*

**Information on Travel, Health,
Visa and Safety Tips**
Canadian Snowbird Institute Inc.   *http://www.snowbird.ca*

Canadian Department of Foreign Affairs and International Trade	*http://www.dfait-maeci.gc.ca*
Canadian Society for International Health	*http://www.csih.org/trav_inf.html*
Laboratory Centre for Disease Control (Health Canada)	*http://www.hc-sc.gc.ca*
Center for Disease Control (U.S.)	*http://www.cdc.org*

Information on Mexico

Mexican Government Tourism	*http://www.mexico-travel.com*
Virtual Mexico	*http://www.virtualmex.com*
Mexico Online	*http://www.mexonline.com*
Mexico Connect	*http://www.mexconnect.com*
Mexico Travel Guide	*http://www.go2mexico.com*
Sanborns	*http://www.hiline.net/sanborns*
Information Mexico	*http://www.mexicosi.com*
Mexican Mike	*http://www.mexicomike.com*
Mexican Travel Information	*http://www.mpsnet.com.mx/ mexico*

Information on Costa Rica

Government of Costa Rica	*http://www.tourism-costarica.com*

Housing Information

Canadian Snowbird Institute Inc.	*http://www.snowbird.ca*
Canada Mortgage and Housing Corporation (CMHC)	*http://www.cmhc-schl.gc.ca*

Information for Seniors/Snowbirds

Canadian Snowbird Institute Inc.	*http://www.snowbird.ca*
Seniors Computer Information Project	*http://www.crm.mb.ca/scip*
Canadian Association of Retired Persons	*http://www.fifty-plus.net*
American Association of Retired Persons	*http://www.aarp.org*
Canada News/Sun Times of Canada	*http://www.canadianmedias.com*
Canada Calling (with Prior Smith)	*http://www.canadacalling.com*
Federal Superannuates National Association	*http://www.fsna.com*

Living Wills

Canadian Snowbird Institute	*http://www.snowbird.ca*

Joint Centre for Bioethics,   *http://www.utoronto.ca/jcb*
   University of Toronto
Choice in Dying (U.S.)   *http://www.choices.org*

Financial Planning
Canadian Snowbird Institute   *http://www.snowbird.ca*
Canadian Association of   *http://www.cafp.org*
   Financial Planners

Sports News
ESPN   *http://www.espnet.sportszone.com*
TSN   *http://www.tsn.ca*
The Sporting News   *http://www.tsn.com*
CNNSI   *http://www.cnnsi.com*

Information on Health Issues
Canadian Snowbird Institute   *http://www.snowbird.ca*
Index of Telemedical   *http://www.telemedical.comm/*
                                 telemedical
Medsite Navigator   *http://www.medsitenavigator.com*
New England Journal of Medicine *http://www.nejm.org*
Rx List - The Internet Drug Index *http://www.rxlist.com*
Medscope   *http://www.medscope.com*
CNN Health   *http://www.cnn.com*
Berkeley Wellness Letter   *http://www.enews.com/*
                                 magazines/ucbwl/
Association of Ontario Health   *http://www.aohc.org/links.html*
   Centres Community Health Links
Health Gate   *http://www.healthgate.com*
National Institute of Nutrition   *http://www.nin*

Weather News
Weather Forecast   *http://www.cnn.com/weather*
National Weather Service   *http://www.nws.noaa.gov*
National Hurricane Centre   *http://www.nhc.noaa.gov*

Travel
Canadian Snowbird Institute   *http://www.snowbird.ca*
Centre for Disease Control   *http://www.cdc.gov/travel/travel.html*
World Travel Guide   *http://www.wtgonline.com*
Lonely Planet   *http://www.lonelyplanet.com*
CNN Weather News   *http://www.cnn.com*
Amtrak   *http://www.amtrak.com*
American Automobile Association *http://www.aaa.com*
   (AAA)

Canadian Automobile Association (CAA)	*http://www.caa.ca*
Detailed Road Maps for North America	*http://www.mapquest.com*
Toronto Driveaway Service	*http://www.torontodriveaway.com*
Travel Magazine	*http://www.pathfinder.com/travel*

Airlines

Air Canada	*http://www.aircanada.ca*
Air Transat	*http://www.airtransat.com*
American Airlines	*http://www.americanair.com*
Canada 3000	*http://www.canada3000.com*
Canadian Airlines	*http://www.cdnair.ca*
Continental Airlines	*http://www.continental.com*
Delta Airlines	*http://www.delta-air.com*
Mexicana Airlines	*http://www.mexicana.com*
Northwest Airlines	*http://www.nwa.com*
Royal Airlines	*http://www.royal.ca*
USAir	*http://www.usair.com*
United Airlines	*http://www.united.com*

Car Rentals

Alamo	*http://www.goalamo.com*
Avis	*http://www.avis.com*
Budget	*http://www.budgetrentacar.com*
Dollar	*http://www.dollarcar.com*
Enterprise	*http://www.pickenterprise.com*
Hertz	*http://www.hertz.com*
Thrifty	*http://www.thrifty.com*

Importing Vehicles from the U.S. to Canada

Registrar of Imported Vehicles	*http://www.riv.com*

Other Federal Government Departments

Veterans Affairs	*http://www.vac-acc.gc.ca*
Citizenship and Immigration Canada	*http://www.cicnet.ingenia.com*
Canadian Government Information	*http://www.canada.gc.ca*
Elections Canada	*http://www.elections.ca*
Canada Deposit Insurance Corporation	*http://www.cdic.ca*

Provincial Governments

Government of British Columbia	*http://www.gov.bc.ca*
Government of Alberta	*http://www.gov.ab.ca*
Government of Saskatchewan	*http://www.gov.sk.ca*
Government of Manitoba	*http://www.gov.mb.ca*
Government of Ontario	*http://www.gov.on.ca*

Government of Quebec   *http://www.gouv.qc.ca*
Government of New Brunswick   *http://www.gov.nb.ca*
Government of Newfoundland   *http://www.gov.nf.ca*
Government of Prince Edward Island   *http://www.gov.pe.ca*
Government of Nova Scotia   *http://www.gov.ns.ca*

Companies Providing Health Insurance for Expatriates

Canada
Expat Financial (Can)   *http://www.expatfinancial.com*
Canadian Residents Abroad (Can)   *http://www.cdnresabroad.com*
Ingle Health (Can)   *http://www.ingle-health.com*
Norfolk Group (Can)   *http://www.norfolkgrp.com*
Telfer Insurance (Can)   *http://www.telferinsurance.com*
Compass International (Can)   *http://www.wrightmogg.com*

United States of America
International Health Care Portal (US)   *http://www.healthcarecity.net*
International Expat Health   *http://www.travelsecure.com*
  Insurance (US)
Expatriate Health(US)   *http://www.escapeartist.com*
International Medical Group (US)   *http://www.imglobal.com*

United Kingdom
Expat Health Insurance (UK)   *http://www.pih-expathealthdirect.com*
Good Health Worldwide (UK)   *http://www.goodhealth.com*
PPP Health Care (UK)   *http://www.ppphc.com*
Bupa International (UK)   *http://www.bupa.com*
Expacare Insurance Services (UK)   *http://www.expacare.com*
International Health Insurance   *http://www.ihi.dk*
  Danmark (UK)

35. Local Chambers of Commerce

To obtain information from a local Chamber of Commerce about a community you are considering, phone the directory assistance operator in that community or contact the appropriate state Chamber of Commerce listed below:

Arizona Chamber of Commerce
1221 E. Osborn Road, #100
Phoenix, AZ 85014
Tel: (602) 248-9172
Fax: (602) 265-1262

**California State Chamber
  of Commerce**
1201 K St., 12th Floor
P.O. Box 1736
Sacramento, CA 95812
Tel: (916) 444-6670
Fax: (916) 444-6685

Florida Chamber of Commerce
136 S. Bronough St.
P.O. Box 11309
Tallahasee, FL 23202-3309
Tel: (904) 425-1200
Fax: (904) 425-1260

Texas State Chamber of Commerce
900 Congress Ave., Suite 501
Austin, TX 98701
Tel: (512) 472-1594
Fax: (512) 320-0280

36. CAA Clubs and Branches

There are many benefits to becoming a member of a local CAA Club that will also help you as a Snowbird. These include out-of-country insurance protection, travel books, and assistance with car problems in the United States and Canada. Contact the office closest to you for detailed information.

British Columbia

Head Office
British Columbia Automobile Association
4567 Canada Way
Burnaby, BC V5G 4T1
Tel: (604) 268-5000
1-800-663-1956
Abbotsford
Tel: (604) 855-0530
Chilliwack
Tel: (604) 792-4664
Delta
Tel: (604) 599-1616
Kamloops
Tel: (250) 372-9577
Kelowna
Tel: (250) 861-4554
Langley
Tel: (604) 268-5950

Nanaimo
Tel: (250) 390-3533
Nelson
Tel: (250) 352-3535
New Westminster
Tel: (604) 268-5700
Penticton
Tel: (250) 492-7016
Port Coquitlam
Tel: (604) 944-7745
Prince George
Tel: (250) 563-0417
Richmond
Tel: (604) 272-5930
Vancouver
Tel: (604) 268-5600, 268-5800
Vernon
Tel: (250) 542-1022
Victoria
Tel: (250) 389-6700, (604) 744-2202
West Vancouver
Tel: (604) 268-5650

ALBERTA

Head Office
Alberta Motor Association
10310 G.A. MacDonald Ave.
Edmonton, AB T6J 6R7
Tel: (780) 430-5555
1-800-642-3810

Banff
Tel: (403) 762-2266
Calgary
Tel: (403) 590-0001, 278-3530, 262-2345, 240-5300, 239-6644
Camrose
Tel: (780) 672-3391

Edmonton
Tel: (780) 473-3112, 474-8601, 484-1221
Fort McMurray
Tel: (780) 743-2433
Grande Prairie
Tel: (780) 532-4421

SASKATCHEWAN

Head Office
CAA Saskatchewan
200 Albert St. N.
Regina, SK S4R 5E2
Tel: (306) 791-4321
Moose Jaw
Tel: (306) 693-5195
North Battleford
Tel: (306) 445-9451

MANITOBA

Head Office
CAA Manitoba Motor League
870 Empress St.
Winnipeg, MB R3C 2Z3
Tel: (204) 987-6161
1-800-222-4357

ONTARIO

Barrie
Tel: (705) 726-1803
Belleville
Tel: (613) 968-9832
Brampton
Tel: (905) 793-4911
Brantford
Tel: (519) 756-6321
Brockville
Tel: (613) 498-1105
Burlington
Tel: (905) 632-6772

Lethbridge
Tel: (403) 328-1181
Medicine Hat
Tel: (403) 527-1166
Red Deer
Tel: (403) 342-6633

Prince Albert
Tel: (306) 764-6818
Regina
Tel: (306) 791-4322, 791-4323
Saskatoon
Tel: (306) 955-4484, 653-1833
Swift Current
Tel: (306) 773-3193
Weyburn
Tel: (306) 842-6651
Yorkton
Tel: (306) 783-6536

Altona
Tel: (204) 324-8474
Brandon
Tel: (204) 727-0561
Portage La Prairie
Tel: (204) 857-3453
Winnipeg
Tel: (204) 987-6202, 987-6226

Cambridge
Tel: (519) 622-2620
Chatham
Tel: (519) 351-2222
Cobourg
Tel: (905) 372-8777
Don Mills
Tel: (416) 449-9993
Dundas
Tel: (905) 627-7777
Espanola
Tel: (705) 869-3611
Gloucester
Tel: (613) 741-2235

Grimsby
Tel: (905) 945-5555
Guelph
Tel: (519) 821-9940
Hamilton
Tel: (905) 525-1210, 385-8500
Islington
Tel: (416) 231-9967
Kingston
Tel: (613) 546-2596
Kitchener
Tel: (519) 894-2582, 741-1160,
1-800-265-8975
Leamington
Tel: (519) 322-2356
London
Tel: (519) 685-3140, 473-3055
Mississauga
Tel: (905) 275-2501, 823-6800
Newmarket
Tel: (905) 836-5171
North Bay
Tel: (705) 474-8230
Oakville
Tel: (905) 845-9680
Orangeville
Tel: (519) 941-8360
Orillia
Tel: (705) 325-7211
Oshawa
Tel: (905) 723-5203
Ottawa
Tel: (613) 820-1890, 736-9696
Owen Sound
Tel: (519) 376-1940
Parry Sound
Tel: (705) 746-9305
Peterborough
Tel: (705) 743-4343,
1-800-461-7622

Pickering
Tel: (905) 831-5252
St. Catharines
Tel: (905) 688-0321
St. Thomas
Tel: (519) 631-6490,
1-800-265-4343
Sarnia
Tel: (519) 542-3493
Sault Ste. Marie
Tel: (705) 942-4600
Scarborough
Tel: (416) 439-6370, 752-9080
Simcoe
Tel: (519) 426-7230
Stoney Creek
Tel: (905) 664-8000
Sudbury
Tel: (705) 522-0000,
1-800-461-7111
Thornhill
Tel: (905) 771-3255,
1-800-268-3750
Thorold
Tel: (905) 984-8585,
1-800-263-7272
Thunder Bay
Tel: (807) 345-1261
Timmins
Tel: (705) 264-1021
Toronto
Tel: (416) 593-7360, 789-7466
Welland
Tel: (905) 735-1100
Willowdale
Tel: (416) 495-1802, 223-1751
Windsor
Tel: (519) 255-1212,
1-800-265-5681
Woodstock
Tel: (519) 539-5676

QUEBEC

Head Office
CAA Quebec
444 Bouvier St.
Quebec, QC G2J 1E2
Tel: (418) 624-0708
Brossard
Tel: (514) 861-7575
Charlesbourg
Tel: (418) 624-0708
Chicoutimi
Tel: (418) 545-8686
Hull
Tel: (819) 778-2225

Laval
Tel: (514) 861-7575
Montréal
Tel: (514) 861-7575
Pointe-Claire
Tel: (514) 861-7575
St-Leonard
Tel: (514) 861-7575
Ste-Foy
Tel: (418) 624-0708
Sherbrooke
Tel: (819) 566-5132
Trois-Rivieres
Tel: (819) 376-9393

NEW BRUNSWICK

Head Office
CAA Maritimes
737 Rothesay Ave.
Saint John, NB E2H 2H6
Tel: (506) 634-1400
1-800-561-8807

Fredericton
Tel: (506) 452-1987
Moncton
Tel: (506) 857-8225

PRINCE EDWARD ISLAND

Charlottetown
Tel: (902) 892-1612

NOVA SCOTIA

Dartmouth
Tel: (902) 468-6306

Halifax
Tel: (902) 443-5530

37. Canadian Corps of Commissionaires
If you need a reliable person to check on your home regularly during your absence, you may wish to contact the Corps of Commissionaires at the offices below.

National Headquarters
100 rue Gloucester St., Suite 503
Ottawa, ON K2P 0A4
Tel: (613) 236-4936
Fax: (613) 563-8508

Victoria and Vancouver Island
4248 Glanford Ave., 2nd Floor
Victoria, BC V8Z 4B8

Tel: (250) 727-7755
Fax: (250) 727-7355

British Columbia
404 - 198 W. Hastings St.
Vancouver, BC V6B 1H2
Tel: (604) 681-9207
Fax: (604) 681-9864

Northern Alberta
1730 - 10405 Jasper Ave.
Edmonton, AB T5J 3N4
Tel: (709) 428-0321
Fax: (709) 426-6573

Southern Alberta
#710, Alberta Pl., 1520 - 4th St. S.W.
Calgary, AB T2R 1H5
Tel: (403) 244-4664
Fax: (403) 228-0623

Northern Saskatchewan
493 - 2nd Ave. N.
Saskatoon, SK S7K 2C1
Tel: (306) 244-6588
Fax: (306) 244-6191

Southern Saskatchewan
Alpine Village Mall
122 Albert St.
Regina, SK S4R 2N2
Tel: (306) 757-0998
Fax: (306) 352-5494

Manitoba
301 One Wesley Ave.
Winnipeg, MB R3C 4C6
Tel: (204) 942-5993
Fax: (204) 942-6702

Ottawa
108 Lisgar St.
Ottawa, ON K2P 0C2
Tel: (613) 231-6462
Fax: (613) 567-1517

Kingston
614 Norris Court, Unit #9
Kingston, ON K7P 2R9
Tel: (613) 634-4432
Fax: (613) 634-4436

Toronto and Region
80 Church St.
Toronto, ON M5C 2G1

Tel: (416) 364-4496
Fax: (416) 364-3361

Hamilton
#609 Imperial Building
25 Hughson St. S.
Hamilton, ON L8N 2A5
Tel: (905) 522-7584
Fax: (905) 522-8011

London
815 Commissioners Rd. E.
(Western Counties Rd.)
P.O. Box 22066
London, ON N6C 4N0
Tel: (519) 681-8440
Fax: (519) 681-3465

Windsor
3381 Walker Rd.
Windsor, ON N8W 3R9
Tel: (519) 966-9651
Fax: (519) 966-9651

Quebec
2323 boul du Versant Nord,
Suite 208
Ste-Foy, QC G1N 4P4
Tel: (418) 681-0609
Fax: (418) 682-6532

Montréal
Plaza Laurier, Suite 400
5115 ave. de Gaspé
Montréal, QC H2T 3B7
Tel: (514) 273-8578
Fax: (514) 277-1922

New Brunswick and P.E.I.
111 Prince William St.
Saint John, NB E2L 2B2
Tel: (506) 634-8000
Fax: (506) 634-8657

Nova Scotia
1472 Hollis St.

Halifax, NS B3J 1V2
Tel: (902) 429-8101
Fax: (902) 423-6317

Newfoundland
3rd Floor
Terrace on the Square

(Churchill Square)
8-10 Rowan St.
St. John's, NF A1B 2X3
Tel: (709) 754-0757
Fax: (709) 754-0116

38. Canadian Banks Offering Services to Snowbirds

Many Canadian banks provide services and products to Snowbirds. A list of the correspondent banks in the United States, as well as trust and estate management and investor services, are noted. Contact the institutions directly to ask about the following: Snowbird services, programs for seniors, U.S. dollar chequing/savings accounts, U.S. dollar credit cards, mortgage loans for purchase of a U.S. residence, ATM access from U.S. to Canadian accounts, and so forth.

- **AMEX Bank of Canada**
1-800-654-2042 (Canada and the U.S.)

- **Bank of Montreal**
1-800-555-3000 (Canada and the U.S.)
Internet address: *http://www.mbanx.com*

Correspondent Banks (e.g., have an associated business relationship)
Arizona:
　Bank of America, Bank One, First Interstate
California:
　Bank of America, First Interstate, Union Bank, U.S. Bank, Wells Fargo
Florida:
　Barnett, First Union, NationsBank, Sun Bank
Texas:
　Bank of America, Bank One, First Interstate, NationsBank, Texas Commerce

Trust and Estate Management
　Through the Trust Company of the Bank of Montreal.

Investor Services
Through subsidiaries Nesbitt Burns and InvestorLine Service.

- **Bank of Nova Scotia**
1-800-387-6556 (Canada and the U.S.)
Internet address: *http://www.scotiabank.ca*

Correspondent Banks
Arizona:
　Bank of America, Bank One, First Interstate
California:
　Bank of America, Bank of California, Bank of Nova Scotia, Standard Chartered Bank, Union Bank, Wells Fargo

Florida:
   Barnett, NationsBank, Sun Bank
Texas:
   Bank One, NationsBank, Texas Commerce

Trust and Estate Management
Through subsidiaries Scotiatrust and Montreal Trust.

Investor Services
Full brokerage service through subsidiary ScotiaMcLeod; discount brokerage
with Scotia Securities.

- **Canada Trust**
1-800-668-8888 (Canada and the U.S.)

Correspondent Bank
Owns First Federal Savings & Loans of Rochester, New York.
Internet address: *http://www.canadatrust.com*

Trust and Estate Management
Full range of services.

Investor Services
Mutual funds through subsidiary CT Fund Services.

- **Canadian Imperial Bank of Commerce**
1-800-465-2422 (Canada and the U.S.)
Internet address: *http://www.cibc.com*

Correspondent Banks
Arizona:
   Bank of America, First Interstate
California:
   Bank of America, First Interstate
Florida:
   Barnett, First Union, NationsBank, Sun Bank
Texas:
   NationsBank, Texas Commerce

Trust and Estate Management
Through subsidiary CIBC Trust Corp.

Investor Services
Through subsidiary Wood Gundy.

- **Royal Bank of Canada**
1-800-263-9191 (English)
1-800-363-3967 (French)
Internet address: *http://www.royalbank.com*

Correspondent Banks
Arizona:
   Bank One, Citibank
California:
   Bank of America, Bank of California, City National Bank, First Interstate
   Bank of California, Union Bank
Florida:
   NationsBank, Royal Bank of Canada, Sun Bank
Texas:
   Texas Commerce

Trust and Estate Management
Through subsidiary Royal Trust.

Investor Services
Through subsidiary RBC Dominion Securities; discount brokerage through
Royal Bank Investor Trading.

- **Toronto-Dominion Bank**
1-800-465-2265 (Canada and the U.S.)
Internet address: *http://www.tdbank.ca*

Correspondent Banks
Arizona:
   Bank One, First Interstate
California:
   Bank of America, First Interstate, Wells Fargo
Florida:
   Barnett, Sun Bank
Texas:
   Bank One, Texas Commerce

Trust and Estate Management
Through subsidiary TD Trust.

Investor Services
Through subsidiaries TD Asset Management and Evergreen Investment
Services; discount brokerage through Green Line Investor Services; Green
Line Mutual Funds.

39. U.S. Banks Offering Services to Snowbirds

Many U.S. banks in Sunbelt states offer Canadians such services as: seniors'
programs, investment services, U.S. dollar credit cards (to winter residents),
mortgage loans for a U.S. residence, personal loans and lines of credit, and
estate and tax planning. Contact the institutions below for more detail.

Bank Atlantic
Tel: (305) 764-3111
1-800-741-1700

Bank One
Tel: (602) 248-0608
1-800-366-BANK (2265)

Barnett Bank
1-800-441-2299 (from U.S.)
1-800-553-9024 (from Canada)

Citibank
1-800-374-9800

Dean Witter
Arizona:
    Tel: (602) 945-4331
    (collect from Canada)
    1-800-347-5107 (from U.S.)

Florida:
    Tel: (407) 394-8632
    1-800-473-2020

Desjardins Federal Savings Bank
(subsidiary of Desjardins in Quebec)
Hallendale, Florida
    Tel: (305) 454-1001

Natbank
(subsidiary of National Bank in Quebec)
Hollywood, Florida
    Tel: (954) 922-9992
Pompano Beach, Florida
    Tel: (954) 781-4005

Republic Bank
Tel: (813) 796-2900

Sun Bank
1-800-382-3232 (from Florida)
1-800-458-4984 (from Canada)

40. Elderhostel

Elderhostel is an international nonprofit organization offering programs which serve the educational needs of older adults. Participants are usually retired or planning retirement and in their mid-to-late fifties and beyond. There are approximately 600,000 members in the United States and 70,000 in Canada. Membership and program catalogues are free.

Elderhostel U.S.
75 Federal St.
Boston, MA 02110-1941
Tel: (617) 426-7788
Fax: (617) 426-8351

The international programs offered include those for people with RVs. Note, the Canadian programs offered through this office in Boston are *different* ones than those offered by Elderhostel Canada. Elderhostel U.S. produces 12 catalogues a year: 4 for the United States and Canada (combined), 4 for international programs, and 4 supplemental catalogues. To be placed on the mailing list for all 12 catalogues, send a cheque for $14 in Canadian funds to cover postage costs. Programs through Elderhostel U.S. are paid in U.S. dollars. Canadians who wish to participate in programs through Elderhostel U.S. must meet U.S. age eligibility requirements. At present the age minimum is 60 for one person and the spouse must be at least 50 years old. There is a different age requirement for Canada (see below).

Elderhostel Canada
308 Wellington St.
Kingston, ON K7K 7A7
Tel: (613) 530-2222
Fax: (613) 530-2096

Elderhostel Canada offers programs in Canada and internationally, and produces four catalogues a year. There is no fee to cover postage costs within Canada. Programs through Elderhostel Canada are paid in Canadian dollars. The age requirement in Canada is a minimum of 55 years for one person and at least 50 years for the spouse.

41. RV Buyers' and Users' Guides

When you begin shopping for your RV, buyers' guides and users' guides are invaluable sources of information. Buyers' guides categorize RVs by type, and provide model and manufacturer names, features, photos, and prices. Users' guides provide information to help you get the most from your RV. Many of these publications can be found at local bookstores and libraries. They can also be purchased directly from the publishers listed here.

Chevy Outdoors
Practical Guide to RVs
The Aegis Group
30400 Van Dyke
Warren, MI 48093
(313) 575-9400
US$3.00

RV How-To Guide
Woodall Publishing Co.
28167 N. Keith Dr.
Lake Forest, IL 60045
(708) 362-6700
US$6.95 plus $2.50 postage

Woodall's RV Owner's Handbook
Woodall Publishing Co.
28167 N. Keith Dr.
Lake Forest, IL 60045
(708) 362-6700

RV Repair and Maintenance
Manual
T.L. Enterprises
3601 Calle Tecate
Camarillo, CA 93012
(805) 389-0300
US$19.95 plus postage

Woodall's RV Buyer's Guide
Woodall Publishing Co.
28167 N. Keith Dr.
Lake Forest, IL 60045
(708) 362-6700
US$5.50 plus $2.75 postage

Vol. 1: Illustrated introduction to RV basics, US$7.95 plus $2 postage

Vol. 2: Illustrations on the operation of major RV systems, US$7.95 plus $2 postage

Vol. 3: Emergency and money-saving repairs and preventive maintenance, US$7.95 plus $2 postage

42. RV Dealers'Associations

United States

To find out more about U.S. RV dealers or rental agencies in your area or at your destination, contact the RV dealers' associations below for information about their members.

Florida RV Trade Association
401 N. Parsons Ave., Suite 107
Brandon, FL 33510-4538
(813) 684-7882

**Recreation Vehicle Dealers'
Association (National)**
3930 University Dr.
Fairfax, VA 22030
(703) 591-7130

**Recreation Vehicle Industry
Association**
P.O. Box 2999, Dept. SL

Reston, VA 22090-0999
(703) 620-6003

**Southern California RV Dealers'
Association**
One Capital Mall, #320
Sacremento, CA 95814
(916) 658-0260

Texas RV Association
3355 Bee Caves Rd., Suite 104
Austin, TX 78746-6751
(512) 327-4514

Canada

Contact the recreation vehicle dealers' association (RVDA) in your province to obtain information on RV dealers, clubs, magazines, and shows.

RVDA of British Columbia, Langley. Tel: (604) 533-4200
RVDA of Alberta, Edmonton. Tel: (709) 455-8562
RVDA of Saskatchewan, Regina. Tel: (306) 525-5666
RVDA of Manitoba, Winnipeg. Tel: (204) 256-6119
Ontario RVDA, Brechin. Tel: (705) 484-0295
RVDA of Quebec, Montréal. Tel: (514) 338-1471
RVDA of Nova Scotia, New Glasgow. Tel: (902) 752-3164

43. RV Rental Sources

The growing popularity of RVs means outlets nationwide now rent motorhomes, folding camping trailers, and other vehicles. Many offer packages that include airline and railway connections for fly-drive and rail-drive plans. One-way and off-season rates are also available from some dealers.

Check your Yellow Pages under "Recreation Vehicles—Renting and Leasing" for local sources or try the following contacts for locations nationwide.

Cruise America
11 Westhampton Ave.
Mesa, AZ 85210
Tel: (602) 464-7300
1-800-327-7799
Nationwide motorhome rentals.

Recreation Vehicle Rental Association
3930 University Dr.
Fairfax, VA 22030
Tel: (703) 591-7130
1-800-336-0355 (U.S. only)
Rental Ventures, a 32-page brochure including a free copy of *Who's Who in RV Rentals,* is available for US$7.50 first class, US$6.50 third class prepaid.

44. U.S. Campground Directories

Campground directories provide comparative information on camping locations across the United States, and their fees and facilities. Directories are available at local bookstores, public libraries, or directly from the publishers listed here. In addition, the National Association of RV Parks and Campgrounds, also listed below, has individual state directories of its members for a nominal handling charge of $1 per state.

AAA Campbooks
(11 regional U.S./Canada editions)
Contact a local CAA or AAA chapter for information.

KOA Directory/Road Atlas/Camping Guide
Kampgrounds of America, Inc.
P.O. Box 30558
Billings, MT 59114
Tel: (406) 248-7444
US$3 by mail or free at any KOA campground in North America.

National Association of RV Parks and Campgrounds
8605 Westwood Centre Drive, #201
Vienna, VA 22182
Tel: (703) 734-3000

Trailer Life Campground & RV Services Directory
TL Enterprises
P.O. Box 6888
Englewood, CO 80155-6888
US$19.95

Wheelers Recreational Vehicle Resort & Campground Guide
Print Media Services
1310 Jarvis Ave.
Elk Grove Village, IL 60007
Tel: (708) 981-0100
US$12.95 plUS$2.50 postage

Woodall's Campground Directories
Woodall Publishing Co.
28167 N. Keith Dr.

Lake Forest, IL 60045
Tel: (708) 362-6700
North American Edition, US$16.95
plus US$3.75 postage
Eastern edition, US$10.95
plus US$2.75 postage
Western edition, US $10.95
plus US$2.75 postage

Woodall's Camping Guides
Woodall Publishing Co.
28167 N. Keith Dr.

Lake Forest, IL 60045
Tel: (708) 362-6700
Eight regional editions:
each US$6.95 plus $2.50 postage

Yogi Bear's Jellystone Park Campground Directory
Leisure Systems, Inc.
6201 Kellogg Ave.
Cincinnati, OH 45230
Tel: 1-800-558-2954

45. Campground Chains

Several well-known companies operate U.S.-wide chains of campgrounds with dependable standards of quality and service. Properties range from safe, convenient places to spend a travel night to full-service family resorts. Contact their national headquarters for information.

Best Holiday Trav-L-Park Association
1310 Jarvis Ave.
Elk Grove Village, IL 60007
Tel: (708) 981-0100

Kampgrounds of America (KOA)
P.O. Box 30558
Billings, MT 59114
Tel: (406) 248-7444

Leisure Systems, Inc.
Yogi Bear's Jellystone Park
Camp-Resorts
6201 Kellogg Ave.
Cincinnati, OH 45230
Tel: 1-800-558-2954

46. Camping on Public Lands

Camping facilities on public lands are generally simple and rustic but set amidst some of the most spectacular scenery in the United States.

Thousands of campsites can be found on lands supervised by U.S. federal agencies including the National Park Service, USDA Forest Service, Bureau of Land Management, and U.S. Army Corps of Engineers. These sites are convenient to scenic byways, waterways, trails, and numerous outdoor recreation activities. Parks managed by state and local governments also offer a wealth of camping opportunities. Contact the agencies listed here to request specific information and publications.

Bureau of Land Management
For camping information, write: Bureau of Land Management, 1849 C Street N.W., Room 5600, Washington, DC 20240.

National Park Service
For a "National Park Camping Guide" send $4 to the U.S. Government Printing Office, Superintendent of Documents, Washington, DC 20402-3925. Request #024-005-01080-7. For campground reservations call 1-800-452-1111.

U.S. Army Corps of Engineers
For camping information, write: Department of the Army, U.S.A.C.E., Regional Brochures, IM-MV-N, 3909 Halls Ferry Rd., Vicksburg, MS 39180-6199.

USDA Forest Service
For a free list of national forests, write: USDA Forest Service, Office of Information, P.O. Box 96090, Washington, DC 20090. For campground reservations call 1-800-283-CAMP.

47. Camping Clubs

Camping clubs let people share good times while exploring the country and enjoying a great way of life. National and brand-name camping clubs listed below sponsor fun-filled rallies and caravans, led by experienced "wagon-masters" who act as escorts and tour guides.

Clubs also offer travel services like mail forwarding and provide camping information through club magazines and newsletters (shown in italics). Club members are part of a network of friends who enjoy the camaraderie and social atmosphere at campgrounds and RV parks across the United States. For a list of Canadian RV clubs, contact a provincial RV dealers' association. Refer to item 42 in Appendix A.

Escapee Club
100 Rainbow Dr.
Livingston, TX 77351
Tel: (409) 327-8873

Family Campers and RVers
4804 Transit Rd., Building 2
Depew, NY 14043
Tel: (716) 668-6242
Camping Today

Family Motor Coach Association
8291 Clough Pike
Cincinnati, OH 45244
Tel: (513) 474-3622
1-800-543-3622
Family Motor Coaching
(Motorhome owners only)

The Good Sam Club
P.O. Box 6060
Camarillo, CA 93011
Tel: (805) 389-0300
1-800-234-3450 (U.S. only)

The International Family Recreation Association
P.O. Box 6279
Pensacola, FL 32503-0279
Tel: (904) 944-7864
The Recreation Advisor

Loners of America
Rt. 2, Box 85E
Ellsinore, MO 63937-9520
Tel: (314) 322-5548
Loners of America News

Loners on Wheels
P.O. Box 1355
Poplar Bluff, MO 63902
Fax: (314) 785-2420

The National RV Owners' Club
P.O. Drawer 17148
Pensacola, FL 32522-7148
Tel: (904) 944-7864

North American Family Campers Association Inc.
P.O. Box 2701

Springfield, MA 01101
Tel: (413) 283-4742
Campfire Chatter

RV Elderhostel
75 Federal St.
Boston, MA 02110-1941
Tel: (617) 426-7788

RVing Women
21413 W. Lost Lake Rd.
Snohomish, WA 98290
1-800-333-9992, ext. 90050

48. Publications for RV Owners and Campers

There are a host of publications dedicated to RV travel and camping. Several cater exclusively to the RV lifestyle, offering destination tips, product reviews, and RV cooking recipes. They also include RV rally and show information so RVers can keep up with the latest news from their favourite RV vehicle or camping club. Ask to be sent a complimentary copy. For a list of Canadian RV publications, contact a provincial RV dealers' association. Refer to item 42 in Appendix A.

Campers Monthly
(Mid-Atlantic and Northeast editions)
P.O. Box 260
Quakertown, PA 18951
Tel: (215) 361-7255
(11 issues) $10/year

Camperways
Woodall Publishing Co.
28167 N. Keith Dr.
Lake Forest, IL 60045
Tel: (708) 362-6700
(monthly) $15/year

Camping and RV Magazine
P.O. Box 458
Washburn, WI 54891
Tel: (715) 373-5556
(monthly) $17.95/year

Camp-orama
Woodall Publishing Co.

28167 N. Keith Dr.
Lake Forest, IL 60045
Tel: (708) 362-6700
(monthly) $15/year

Chevy Outdoors
P.O. Box 2063
Warren, MI 48090
Tel: (313) 575-9400
(4 issues) $8/year

Disabled Outdoors
2052 W. 23rd St.
Chicago, IL 60608
Tel: (312) 358-4160
(4 issues) $10/year

Family Motor Coaching
8291 Clough Pike
Cincinnati, OH 45244
Tel: (513) 474-3622
1-800-543-3622
(monthly) $24/year

Go Camping America
P.O. Box 2669, Dept. 23
Reston, VA 22090
Free vacation planner on request.
Lists many helpful sources of information.

Highways
TL Enterprises, Inc.
3601 Calle Tecate
Camarillo, CA 93012
Tel: (805) 389-0300
(monthly) $6/year

Midwest Outdoors
111 Shore Dr.
Hinsdale, IL 60521
Tel: (708) 887-7722
(monthly) $11.95/year

Motorhome
TL Enterprises, Inc.
3601 Calle Tecate
Camarillo, CA 93012
Tel: (805) 389-0300
(monthly) $24/year

Northeast Outdoors
70 Edwin Ave., Box 2180
Waterbury, CT 06722
Tel: (203) 755-0158
(monthly) $8/year

*"Plan-It-Pack-It-Go"
Camping Guide*
Woodall Publishing Co.
28167 N. Keith Dr.
Lake Forest, IL 60045
Tel: (708) 362-6700
504 pages; $11.95 plus $2.75
postage

The Recreation Advisor
Recreation World Services, Inc.
P.O. Box 6279, Dept. 5N
Pensacola, FL 32503-0279

Tel: (904) 477-7992
(10 issues) $15/year

RV Lifestyle Publications Catalog
Recreation Vehicle Industry
Association
P.O. Box 2999, Dept. POF
Reston, VA 22090-0999
Free with self-addressed stamped
($.52 postage) long envelope.
(Lists many helpful RV/camping
publications that can be ordered by
mail.)

RV Times
Royal Productions Inc.
P.O. Box 6294
Richmond, VA 23230
Tel: (804) 288-5653
(11 issues) $15/year

RV Today
4005 - 20th Ave. W., Suite 110
Fisherman's Terminal
Seattle, WA 98199
Tel: (206) 282-7545
(monthly) $12/year

RV West
4133 Mohr Ave., Suite 1
Pleasanton, CA 94566
Tel: (510) 426-3200
(monthly) $12/year

Southern RV
Woodall Publishing Co.
28167 N. Keith Dr.
Lake Forest, IL 60045
Tel: (708) 362-6700
(monthly) $15/year

Trailer Life
TL Enterprises, Inc.
3601 Calle Tecate
Camarillo, CA 93012
Tel: (805) 389-0300
(monthly) $22/year

Trails-A-Way
Woodall Publishing Co.
28167 N. Keith Dr.
Lake Forest, IL 60045
Tel: (708) 362-6700
(monthly) $15/year

Western RV News
1350 S.W. Upland Dr., Suite B

Portland, OR 97221
Tel: (503) 222-1255
(monthly) $8/year

Workamper News
201 Hiram Rd., HCR 34, Box 125
Heber Springs, AR 72543
Tel: (501) 362-2637
(6 issues) $18/year

49. Membership and Ownership Type of RV Resorts

A unique form of travel option is available through several networks of membership and ownership camping and RV resorts across the United States. Fees and privileges vary, but all membership and ownership resorts allow members to stay at "home" campgrounds and affiliated member resorts. Free or nominal-cost stays are available for prospective members to try out the concept.

These properties are generally open only to members and owners, but some have rental sites, park trailers, and cabins available, making them an ideal vacation spot for those who don't own an RV. There are numerous amenities and activities, including golf, health clubs, and social events.

Contact the following companies for information on locations, membership, sales, and rental availability:

Coast to Coast Resorts
64 Inverness Dr. E.
Englewood, CO 80112
Tel: (303) 790-2267
1-800-368-5721

Outdoor Resorts of America, Inc.
2400 Crestmoor Road
Nashville, TN 37215
Tel: (615) 244-5237
1-800-541-2582

Leisure Systems, Inc.
Safari/Jellystone Parks
6201 Kellogg Avenue
Cincinnati, OH 45230
1-800-558-2954

Resort Parks International
P.O. Box 7738
Long Beach, CA 90807
1-800-635-8498

50. Selecting a Tow Vehicle

Matching the right tow vehicle with an appropriate RV is easier now than ever. Today's van conversions, 4 x 4s, light trucks, most full-size cars, and many mid-size cars come with engines that offer the horsepower and fuel economy to make them choice vehicles. For further information on which vehicles are suitable for RV towing, consult the auto manufacturers' towing guide available from the companies listed below, or visit your local auto dealer.

Ford Motor Company
300 Ren Cen, P.O. Box 43306
Detroit, MI 48243
Toyota Motor Sales U.S.A., Inc.
19001 S. Western Ave.
Torrance, CA 90509

GMC Truck
General Motors Corp.
Customer Service Division
31 Judson St.
Pontiac, MI 48058

Chevrolet vehicle information is available through their computerized system "Spec Manager" at local dealers. The "Dodge Trailer Towing Guide" is also available through local dealers.

51. RV Retail Shows

Recreation vehicle retail shows, often sponsored by local dealerships, offer you the opportunity to see many makes and models of RVs in one location. This is helpful when comparison-shopping for a vehicle that will fit your travel plans and budget. Shows let you talk in person with RV industry experts who can assist you in finding the right RV.

There are annual RV shows in every region of Canada and the United States. Watch your local television stations and newspapers for notices or contact your closest RV dealer. For a free list of shows in the United States, write to:

Recreational Vehicle Industry Association
P.O. Box 2999, Dept. SL
Reston, VA 22090-0999
Tel: (703) 620-6003

52. Scenic Byways in the United States

If you are planning to travel in your RV or car, you probably wish to select scenic routes wherever possible. In addition to taking you off crowded highways, these networks of "Scenic Byways" offer views of mountains, forests, historical sights, and great waterways. For more information, write to:

Scenic Byways
The American Recreation Coalition
1331 Pennsylvania Ave. N.W., Suite 726
Washington, DC 20004

53. Countries with Tax Treaties with Canada

Canada has treaties with other countries covering various issues relating to taxes. This could include the amount of withholding taxes for CPP and OAS among other matters. The main purpose of a treaty is to avoid the inequity of double taxation by having only one country tax for a specific income or capital gain. In the event of double taxation, you would be entitled to an offsetting foreign tax credit. Check with your tax advisor. Also, speak with the International Tax Services Office of Revenue Canada. Contact them at 1-800-267-5177, Fax: (613) 941-9776.

In Force (65 in total):

Argentina	France	Luxembourg	Sri Lanka
Australia	Germany	Malaysia	Sweden
Austria	Guyana	Malta	Switzerland
Bangladesh	Hungary	Mexico	Tanzania
Barbados	Iceland	Morocco	Thailand
Belgium	India	Netherlands	Trinidad &
Brazil	Indonesia	New Zealand	Tobago
Cameroon	Ireland	Norway	Tunisia
China, People's	Israel	Pakistan	Ukraine
Republic of	Italy	Papua New	United Kingdom
Cyprus	Ivory Coast	Guinea	United States
Czechoslovakia	Jamaica	Philippines	USSR
Denmark	Japan	Poland	Vietnam
Dominican	Kazakhstan	Romania	Zambia
Republic	Kenya	Russia	Zimbabwe
Egypt	Korea	Singapore	
Estonia	Latvia	South Africa	
Finland	Lithuania	Spain	

Signed But Not Yet In Force (11 in total)*:

Algeria	Chile	Kyrgyzstan	Portugal
Austria	Croatia	Lebanon	Uzbekistan
Bulgaria	Japan	Nigeria	

*Countries which appear in this category may also appear in the category corresponding to those with tax treaties in force, if a *new* agreement has been signed but is not yet in force.

Under Negotiation or Re-Negotiation (29 in total):

Australia	Germany	Mexico	Turkey
Barbados	Greece	Moldova	United Arab
Belgium	Ireland	Norway	Emirate
Colombia	Italy	Saint Lucia	United Kingdom
Czech Republic	Jordan	Senegal	United States
Ecuador	Kuwait	Singapore	Venezuela
Egypt	Luxembourg	Slovak Republic	
Gabon	Mauritius	Slovenia	

54. Non-Resident Tax Rates

Canada has tax treaties with some countries which affect the amount of non-resident tax withheld on OAS, CPP or QPP payments. See the table below to find the rate of withholding tax by Canada that applies to the country where you might reside. In addition, you could be taxed on other sources of income, either by the country in which you are residing or the country from which you are receiving income or both. Check with your tax advisor, Revenue Canada and Human Resources Development Canada. See chart on pages 285 and 286.

Country of Residence		OAS Benefits	CPP or QPP Benefits	CPP or QPP Death Benefits
Argentina	Indonesia	15%	15%	25%
Barbados	Israel			
Czech Republic	Ivory Coast			
Hungary	Kenya			
Estonia	Malaysia			
Malta	Slovak Republic			
Mexico	Spain			
Netherlands	Sri Lanka			
Papua New Guinea	Zambia			
Poland				
Australia		15%	15%	15%
Brazil		25% or 0%	25% or 0%	25% or 0%

Note: If you are both a resident and a national of Brazil, you are entitled to the lower rate. To get this exemption, you must file the NR5 form and provide evidence of your nationality.

		OAS Benefits	CPP or QPP Benefits	CPP or QPP Death Benefits
Denmark		0%	0%	0%
Finland		20%	20%	25%
Ireland		15%	15% or 0%	15%

Note: The 15% rate applies to any portion of your CPP or QPP periodic benefit payments that relates to self employment earnings. The 0% rate applies to CPP or QPP benefits related to other employment earnings.

		OAS Benefits	CPP or QPP Benefits	CPP or QPP Death Benefits
Italy		15% (see note)	15% (see note)	25% (see note)

Note: You are exempt from tax on CAN$10,000 (or 12 million lire, whichever is higher) of the total of your pensions from Canada. To get this exemption, you must file the NR5 form.

Country of Residence	OAS Benefits	CPP or QPP Benefits	CPP or QPP Death Benefits
New Zealand	15% (see note)	15% (see note)	15% (see note)
Note: You are exempt from tax if the total of your pensions from Canada does not exceed CAN$10,000. To get this exemption, you must file the NR5 form.			
Norway	25%	25% or 0% (see note)	25%
Note: The 25% rate applies to any portion of your CPP or QPP periodic benefit payments that relates to self employment earnings. The 0% rate applies to CPP or QPP benefits related to other employment earnings.			
Philippines	25%	25% (see note)	25%
Note: You are exempt from tax on the first CAN$ 5,000 of the total of all your periodic pensions from Canada. To get this exemption, you must file the NR5 form.			
Romania	25% or 15% (see note)	25% or 15% (see note)	25%
Note: Your OAS and CPP/QPP periodic benefits are taxed at 15% if these benefits are also taxable in Romania. To get this reduced tax rate, you must file the NR5 form and provide evidence that these benefits are also taxable in Romania.			
United Kingdom of Great Britain and Northern Ireland	0%	0%	25%
United States of America	0%	0%	0%
All other countries	25%	25%	25%

APPENDIX B

Suggested Reading

Many excellent books and publications are available to enhance your retirement and Snowbird experience. Most are available at your local library or bookstore. Some booklets are free for the asking. Here is a selected listing of books on lifestyles and leisure time, where to retire, retirement planning, and retirement, tax and money management, travel, senior travel, discount shopping, and running your own business. Check to get the most current edition of these books or publications.

1. Books on Lifestyles, Leisure Time, and Health

Gault, Jan. *Free Time: Making Your Leisure Count.* New York: John Wiley & Sons, 1991.

McCants, Louise, and Robert Cavett. *Retire to Fun and Freedom.* New York: Warner Books, 1990.

Michaels, Joseph. *Prime of Your Life: A Practical Guide to Your Mature Years.* New York: Little, Brown, 1991.

Shephard, Roy J., and Scott G. Thomas. *Fit after Fifty: Feel Better, Live Longer.* Vancouver: Self-Counsel Press, 1989.

Underwood, Richard D., and Brenda Breeden Underwood. *Wise and Healthy Living: A Comprehensive Approach to Aging Well.* Vancouver: Self-Counsel Press, 1989.

2. Books, Newsletters and Newspapers on Where to Retire

United States

Brooks, Mary Lucier. *Retirement Communities in Florida: A Consumer's Guide and Directory to Service-Oriented Facilities.* Sarasota: Pineapple Press, 1992.

Dickinson, Peter. *Sunbelt Retirement: The Complete State-by-State Guide to Retiring in the South and West of the United States.* rev. edition, Washington, DC: Regnery Publishing, 1992.

Giese, Lester J., L. Anne Thornton, and William Kinnaman. *The 99 Best Residential and Recreational Communities in America: For Vacation, Retirement and Investment Planning.* New York: John Wiley & Sons, 1992.

Howells, John. *Where to Retire: America's Best and Most Affordable Places.* 2nd edition, Oakland, CA: Gateway Books, 1995.

Martin, Don W. and Betty Woo Martin. *Coming to Arizona: The Complete Guide for Future Arizonans: Job-Seekers, Retirees and Snowbirds.* Columbia, CA: Pine Cove Press, 1991.

Rosenberg, Lee, and Saralee H. Rosenberg. *50 Fabulous Places to Retire in America.* Hawthorne, NJ: Career Press, 1991.

Savageau, David. *Retirement Places Rated: All You Need to Plan Your Retirement or Select Your Second Home.* 4th edition, New York: Macmillan, 1995.

Warner, Diana. *How to Have a Great Retirement on a Limited Budget.* Cincinnati: Writer's Digest Books, 1992.

Mexico – Books

Bryant, Jane and John Bryant. *Mexico Living and Travel.* Pahrump, NV: Mexico Retirement and Travel Assistance, 1994.

Bryant, John. *Guadalajara: A Great Place to Live or Retire.* Pahrump, NV: Mexico Retirement and Travel Assistance, 1995.

Conway, Stephen C. *Mexican Real Estate.* Kelowna, BC: Wind Dancer Publishing, 1996.

Emling, Shelley. *Your Guide to Retiring to Mexico, Costa Rica and Beyond.* New York: Avery Pub. Group, 1996.

Howells, John. *Choose Mexico: Live Well on $600 a Month.* 5th edition, Oakland, CA: Gateway Books, 1997.

Howells, John. *RV Travel in Mexico.* San Francisco, CA: Gateway Books, 1989.

Nelson, Mike. *Central America by Car,* McAllen, TX: Wanderlust Publications, 1997.

Nelson, Mike. *Live Better South of the Border,* McAllen, TX: Roads Scholar Press, 1996.

Nelson, Mike. *Mexico from the Driver's Seat,* McAllen, TX: Wanderlust Publications, 1995.

Nelson, Mike. *Mexico's Colonial Heart,* McAllen, TX: Wanderlust Publications, 1995.

Nelson, Mike. *Mexico's Gulf Coast and Costa Esmeralda,* McAllen, TX: Wanderlust Publications, 1997.

Nelson, Mike. *Sanborn's RV Guide to Mexico,* McAllen, TX: Wanderlust Publications, 1997.

Newman, R. Emil. *Paradise Found*. Leucadia, CA: United Research Publishers, 1989.

Peyton, Dennis J. *How to Buy Real Estate in Mexico*. San Diego, CA: Law Mexico Publishing, 1997.

Schlundt, Hayes C. *Living Easy in Mexico*. Encinitas, CA: United Research Publishers, 1996.

Symons, Allene and Jane Parker. *Adventures Abroad: Exploring the Travel/Retirement Option*, Oakland, CA: Gateway Books, 1994.

Mexico – Newsletters

Aim (bi-monthly)
Adpo Postal 31-70, 45050 Guadalajara
JAL, Mexico

Canadian Residents Abroad—Update Newsletter (quarterly)
Canadian Residents Abroad Inc.
305 Lakeshore Road East, Oakville, ON L6J 1J3

El Ojo Del Lago (monthly)
(English language newspaper covering Guadalajara and Lake Chapala area)
Apdo. Postal #279
Chapala, Jalisca
45900 Mexico

International Living, Canadian edition (12 times a year)
105 W. Monument Street
Baltimore, MD. US 21201

Living in Mexico (quarterly)
40 Fourth Street, #103
Petaluma, CA. US 94952

Mexico Real Estate and Travel (10 times a year)
325 West Franklin Street, #113
Tuscon, AZ. US 85701

MRTA Mexico Living and Travel Newsletter, The (quarterly)
Mexico Retirement and Travel Assistance
P.O. Box 2190-23, Pahrump, NV. US 89041-2190

Travelmex (8 times a year)
Apdo Postal 31-750, 45050 Guadalajara
JAL, Mexico

Costa Rica – Books

Baker, Christopher. *Costa Rica Handbook*, Chico, CA: Moon Publications, 1995.

Blake, Beatrice. *The New Key to Costa Rica*, Berkeley, CA: Ulysses Press, 1996.

Brooks, Guy and Victoria Brooks. *Costa Rica: A Kick Start for Business Travellers*. Vancouver: Self-Counsel Press, 1996.

Costa Rican Record Guidebook, Miami, FL: Costa Rican Record, 1996.

Exploring Costa Rica: The Tico Times Guide, San Jose, Costa Rica: Tico Times, 1996.

Howard, Christopher. *The Golden Door to Retirement and Living in Costa Rica*, Thousand Oaks, CA: Costa Rica Books, 1996.

Howells, John. *Choose Costa Rica: A Guide to Retirement and Investment.* Oakland, CA: Gateway Books, 1996.

Howells, John. *Choose Latin America: A Guide to Seasonal and Retirement Living.* Oakland, CA: Gateway Books, 1994.

Rackowiecki, Rob. *Costa Rica—A Travel Survival Kit*, Berkeley, CA. Lonely Planet Publications, 1997.

Searby, Ellen. *The Costa Rica Traveller*, Occidental, CA: Windham Bay Press, 1995.

Sheck, Ree Strange. *Costa Rica: A Natural Destination*, Sante Fe, NM: John Muir Publications, 1996.

Symons, Allene and Jane Parker. *Adventures Abroad: Exploring the Travel/Retirement Option*, Oakland, CA: Gateway Books, 1994.

Costa Rica – Newsletters or Newspapers

Canadian Residents Abroad — Update Newsletter (quarterly newsletter)
Canadian Residents Abroad Inc.
305 Lakeshore Road East, Oakville, ON L6J 1J3

Costa Rica Today (weekly newspaper)
117, P.O. Box 0025216
Miami, FL. US 33102

Costa Rican Outlook (bi-monthly newsletter)
P.O. Box 5573, Chula Vista, CA. US 91912-5573

Costa Rican Record, The (monthly magazine)
SJO 956, P.O. Box 025216, Miami, FL. US 33102-5216
(*Note*: This company also publishes *The Costa Rican Record Guidebook*.)

Reach-Out Telephone Directory, The
(lists services in Costa Rica where English is spoken, e.g. doctors, dentists, taxis)
Apartado 6426-1000, San José, Costa Rica

Tico Times (weekly newspaper)
Apdo. 4362
San José, Costa Rica

3. Books, Booklets and Pamplets on Retirement Planning and Retirement

Bolles, Richard N. *The Three Boxes of Life and How to Get out of Them: An Introduction to Life/Work Planning.* Berkeley, CA: Ten Speed Press, 1978.

Danilov, Dan P. and Howard David Deutsch. *Immigrating to the U.S.A.: Who Is Allowed? What is Required? How to Do It!* 6th edition, Vancouver: Self-Counsel Press, 1993.

Duncan, Garry R. and Elizabeth J. Peck. *Canadian Residents Abroad.* Scarborough, ON: Carswell, 1995.

Fyock, Catherine Dorton, and Anne Marrs Dorton. *Unretirement: A Career Guide for the Retired, the Soon to Be Retired, and the Never Want to be Retired.* New York: AMACOM Publishing, 1994.

Gray, Douglas A., et al. *Risk-Free Retirement: The Complete Canadian Planning Guide.* Whitby, ON: McGraw-Hill Ryerson, 1993.

Gray, Douglas A., and John Budd. *The Canadian Guide to Will and Estate Planning.* Whitby, ON: McGraw-Hill Ryerson, 1999.

Howells, John. *Retirement on a Shoestring.* Oakland, CA: Gateway Books, 1992.

Hunnisett, Henry S. *Retirement Guide for Canadians: An Overall Plan for a Comfortable Future.* 12th edition, Vancouver: Self-Counsel Press, 1993.

Wilson, Jim. *Housing Options for Older Canadians.* Vancouver: Self-Counsel Press, 1991.

Wyman, Jack. *Retired? Get Back in the Game: 37 Stories of Vibrant Men and Women Who Are Joyously Productive.* Scottsdale, AZ: Doer Publications, 1994.

Free Booklets and Pamphlets

- Published by the Canadian Bankers' Association:
  – *Steps to Retirement*
  Available through any bank.

- Published by the Canadian Life and Health Insurance Association:
  – *Planning for a Successful Retirement*
  – *Planning for Success: Taking Charge of Your Financial Future*
  – *Retirement: As You'd Like It*
  All available by phoning 1-800-268-8099.

- Published by the Royal Bank of Canada:
  – *Retirement*
  Available from any Royal Bank.

- Published by Canada Deposit Insurance Corporation:
  – *CDIC: We Have a Lot of Answers about Deposit Insurance*
  Available from any bank or credit union.

- Published by Canada Mortgage and Housing Corporation:

  – Housing for Older Canadians: New Financial and Tenure Options
  Available by contacting your closest CMHC office.
* Published by the Department of Foreign Affairs and International Trade
  Canada
  – Retirement Abroad - Seeing the Sunsets
  – Her Own Way: Advice for the Woman Traveller
  – A Guide for Canadians Imprisoned Abroad
  – Working Abroad: Unravelling the Maze
  – México Qué Pasa? A Guide for Canadian Visitors
  – Country Travel Report: These reports offer travellers current information
    on conditions in over 170 countries, including safety, health and passport
    requirements. Services are available 24 hours a day, 7 days a week.
    All available by phoning 1-800-267-8376.

4. Books on Tax and Money Management

Books on Canadian tax planning and pointers, as well as tips, strategies, or
issues to consider when living, investing, working, or operating a business in
the United States are noted below. Check your local library or bookstore.

Budd, John S. *Second Property Strategies: Tax Saving Tips and Estate
Planning Techniques for Canadians.* 2nd edition, Whitby, ON: McGraw-
Hill Ryerson, 1994.

Cohen, Bruce and Alyssa Diamond. *The Money Adviser: The Canadian Guide
to Successful Financial Planning.* rev. edition, Toronto: Stoddart
Publishing, 1995.

Deloitte and Touche. *How to Reduce the Tax You Pay.* Toronto: Key Porter
Books. Annual.

Gray, Douglas A. and John Budd. *The Canadian Guide to Will and Estate
Planning.* Whitby, ON: McGraw-Hill Ryerson, 1999.

Jacks, Evelyn. *Jacks on Tax Savings.* Whitby, ON: McGraw-Hill Ryerson. Annual.

Jacks, Evelyn. *Jacks' 201 Easy Ways to Reduce Your Taxes.* Whitby, ON:
McGraw-Hill Ryerson. Annual.

McCarley, Bruce D. *Retirement Planning: A Guide for Canadians.* Toronto:
Key Porter Books, 1993.

Turner, Mary. *Deloitte & Touche Canadian Guide to Personal Financial
Management.* Annual.

5. Books on Travel

Many travel books can help maximize your travelling enjoyment and experience. Check with your local library, bookstore, travel companies, and auto
clubs. Obtain the free tourist kits from each state (refer to item 26 in Appendix
A). Pick up the various books available on travelling in the United States,
Mexico, or other countries published by the AAA. Contact your local branch

of the Canadian Automobile Association (CAA) (see item 36 in Appendix A). Also check the state and local editions of annually updated travel guides published by the following companies. They contain maps, details of interesting sites, history, and information about accommodation and restaurants.

- Berlitz
- Blue Guides
- Fodor
- Frommers
- Insight
- Michelin
- Thomas Cook

Bruns, Rebecca, et al. *Hidden Mexico: The Adventurer's Guide to the Beaches and Coasts.* Berkeley, CA: Ulysses Press, 1994.

Delaney, John F. *Travelwise: A Guide to Safety, Security and Convenience When You Travel.* Vancouver: Self-Counsel Press, 1990.

Eisman, Alberta and Judith Kahn. *Hidden New England: The Adventurer's Guide.* 3rd edition, Berkeley, CA: Ulysses Press, 1994.

Gleasner, Bill, and Diana Gleasner. *Florida off the Beaten Path: A Guide to Unique Places.* Old Saybrook, CT: Globe Pequot Press, 1994.

Gottberg, John, Ray Riegert and Leslie Hendriques. *Hidden Pacific Northwest: The Adventurer's Guide.* 2nd edition, Berkeley, CA: Ulysses Press, 1994.

Harris, Richard, Ray Riegert and Leslie Henriques. *Hidden Southwest: The Adventurer's Guide.* 2nd edition, Berkeley, CA: Ulysses Press, 1994.

Kerr, Robert John. *The Only Retirement Guide You'll Ever Need.* Revised edition, Toronto: Penguin Canada. Annual.

Kling, Sidney and Joseph Levy. *It's Never Too Early: A Guide to Planning and Enjoying Your Retirement Lifestyle.* Toronto: Stoddart, 1985.

Leslie, Candace. *Hidden Florida Keys and Everglades: The Adventurer's Guide.* Berkeley, CA: Ulysses Press, 1994.

McDonald, Lynn P. and Richard A. Wanner. *Retirement in Canada.* Markham, ON: Butterworths, 1990.

Pager, Sean. *Hawaii off the Beaten Path: A Guide to Unique Places.* 2nd edition, Old Saybrook, CT: Globe Pequot Press, 1995.

Riegert, Ray. *Hidden Coast of California: The Adventurer's Guide.* 5th edition, Berkeley, CA: Ulysses Press, 1995.

Riegert, Ray. *Hidden Hawaii: The Adventurer's Guide.* 8th edition, Berkeley, CA: Ulysses press, 1994.

Riegert, Ray. *Hidden San Francisco and Northern California: The Adventurer's Guide.* 6th edition, Berkeley, CA: Ulysses Press, 1994.

Riegert, Ray. *Hidden Southern California: The Adventurer's Guide.* 4th edition, Berkeley, CA: Ulysses Press, 1994.

Rodriguez, June Nayler. *Texas off the Beaten Path: A Guide to Unique Places.* Old Saybrook, CT: Globe Pequot Press, 1994.

Staats, Todd R. *New Mexico off the Beaten Path: A Guide to Unique Places.* 2nd edition, Old Saybrook, CT: Globe Pequot Press, 1994.

6. Books on Senior Travel

Baker, Sunny and Kim Baker. *The RVer's Bible: Everything You Need to Know About Choosing, Using, and Enjoying Your RV.* New York: Fireside, 1997.

Cannon, Shirley, and Robin Cannon. *50 Plus Globetrotting: The World of Senior Adult Travel.* Toronto: Prime Books, 1992.

Hobbs, Pam and Michael Algar. *Free to Travel: A Canadian Guide for 50-Plus Travellers.* Toronto: Doubleday Canada, 1994.

Howells, John. *Choose the Southwest.* Oakland, CA: Gateway Books, 1996.

Howells, John. *RV Travel in Mexico.* Oakland, CA: Gateway Books, 1989.

Malott, Gene, and Adela Malott. *Get Up and Go: A Guide for the Mature Traveller.* San Francisco: Gateway Books, 1989.

Masse, Rollande Dumais. *RV Travel Leisurely Year Round.* New York: Hippcrene, 1991.

Sullivan, Donald L. *A Senior's Guide to Healthy Travel.* Hawthorne, NJ: Career Press/Monarch Books, 1995.

APPENDIX
C

Retirement, Financial, and Estate Planning Checklist

By completing this extensive checklist, you will focus on key points and issues as well as assemble information, all of which will assist you in developing a financial and estate plan. It will help clarify your wishes when you discuss your needs with your lawyer, tax accountant, financial planner, or financial institution. It will also enhance your peace of mind to know your affairs are in order when you head to the United States for an extended stay. This checklist should be dated, and reviewed and updated annually. Keep a copy in your safety deposit box. Some items may not apply to everyone. Although this checklist highlights many key areas, your advisors can suggest additional issues for you to detail in your specific situation.

Index of Topic Headings

A. Personal Information
B. Current Financial Net Worth
C. Current and Projected Retirement or Snowbird Monthly Income and Expenses
D. Projected/Potential Financial Needs
E. Where Your Retirement Income Will Come From
F. Retirement Planning Goals

A. PERSONAL INFORMATION

		You	Your Spouse
1.	Name (full)	_____	_____
	Address (Canadian)	_____	_____
	City/Province	_____	_____
	Postal Code	_____	_____
	Phone Numbers residence	_____	_____
	work	_____	_____

Fax Numbers	residence	_____	_____
	work	_____	_____
Address (U.S.)		_____	_____
City/State		_____	_____
Zip Code		_____	_____
Phone Numbers	residence	_____	_____
	work	_____	_____
Fax Numbers	residence	_____	_____
	work	_____	_____
Date of Birth		_____	_____
Place of Birth		_____	_____
Citizenship		_____	_____
Social Insurance Number		_____	_____
Place of Marriage* (if applicable)		_____	_____

(*Specify whether legal or common-law)

Name of Doctor (Canada)		_____	_____
Name of Doctor (U.S.)		_____	_____

2. **Children** (indicate if by your or your spouse's previous marriage, adopted, or born in a common-law relationship)

Name	Date of Birth	Married?	Telephone Number(s)	Dependent On You?
_____	_____	_____	_____	_____
_____	_____	_____	_____	_____
_____	_____	_____	_____	_____

3. **Grandchildren**

Name	Date of Birth
_____	_____
_____	_____
_____	_____
_____	_____

4. **Other Dependents**

Name	Date of Birth	Telephone Number(s)	Relationship to You
_____	_____	_____	_____
_____	_____	_____	_____
_____	_____	_____	_____
_____	_____	_____	_____

5. Have you entered into a prenuptial or other marriage contract with your spouse? If so, outline a summary of the contract's terms. Where is the document located?

6. If you or your spouse were previously married, describe any remaining financial obligations (e.g., child support, alimony).

Obligations	You	Your Spouse
Name of former spouse		
Address		
City/Province or State		
Postal or Zip Code		
Social Insurance Number		
Phone Numbers residence		
work		

7. If you or your spouse have any prospective inheritances, detail sources, approximate amounts, and possible dates of receipt.

8. Explain any present or potential special support needs (e.g., for a disabled child, spouse, or parent).

9. **Location of Documents and Other Information**

Item	Location
1) Birth certificates	
2) Marriage certificate	
3) Children's birth certificates	
4) Prenuptial agreements or marriage contracts	
5) Maintenance, alimony, or custody orders	
6) Divorce decrees or separation agreements	
7) Husband's latest will and any codicils	

8) Wife's latest will and any codicils   _____

9) Husband's Power of Attorney   _____

10) Wife's Power of Attorney   _____

11) Wills of family members, if pertinent   _____

12) Passports   _____

13) Citizenship papers   _____

14) Cemetery deeds   _____

15) Directions regarding burial   _____

16) List of heirs   _____

17) Medical records   _____

18) Insurance policies   _____

    – Life   _____

    – Disability   _____

    – Out-of-country medical _____

    – Property   _____

    – Automobile   _____

    – Home   _____

    – Other   _____

19) Stocks   _____

20) Bonds   _____

21) Term deposits   _____

22) Investment certificates   _____

23) Notes or mortgages receivable   _____

24) Real estate documents   _____

25) Leases   _____

26) Inventory of assets of estate   _____

27) Appraisals   _____

28) Bank books   _____

29) Financial records   _____

30) Income tax returns
    (personal and business)   _____

31) Valuation day documents
    (value of asset as of 1972, if applicable,   _____
    for taxation value base purposes)

32) If you own a business, balance sheets
    and profit/loss statements for last 5 years   _____

33) Business agreements   _____

34) Employment contracts   _____

35) Employee benefit plan documents   _____

36) Buy-sell agreements if a shareholder   _____
    in a business

37) Partnership or shareholder agreements if in a business   _____

38) Trust agreements   _____

39) Promissory notes (personal and business)   _____

40) Loan documents (personal and business)   _____

41) Automobile ownership documents (personal and business)   _____

42) RRSP/RRIF records   _____

43) Pension plan documentation (government and/or employer)   _____

44) List of bank accounts   _____

45) List of credit card/charge accounts   _____

46) Miscellaneous documents   _____

47) Other (name) _____   _____

10. Advisors

Lawyer   Name   _____
                      Address   _____
                      Phone   _____

Accountant   Name   _____
                      Address   _____
                      Phone   _____

Financial Planner   Name   _____
                      Address   _____
                      Phone   _____

Life and other Insurance Agents
                      Name   _____
                      Address   _____
                      Phone   _____

Financial Institution
                      Name   _____
                      Address   _____
                      Phone   _____

Banker   Name   _____
                      Address   _____
                      Phone   _____

Investment Dealer
                      Name   _____
                      Address   _____
                      Phone   _____

Other (name)	Name	_____
_____	Address	_____
	Phone	_____

B. CURRENT FINANCIAL NET WORTH

Liquid Assets (Can be relatively quickly converted into cash)	**You**	**Your Spouse**
Term deposits/GICs	$ _____	$ _____
Chequing accounts	_____	_____
Savings accounts	_____	_____
Stocks	_____	_____
Bonds	_____	_____
Term deposits (savings)	_____	_____
Pensions (government or employer)	_____	_____
Annuities	_____	_____
RRSPs/RRIFs/LIFs	_____	_____
Life insurance cash surrender value	_____	_____
Demand loans	_____	_____
– family	_____	_____
– other	_____	_____
Automobile	_____	_____
Tax instalments made/withheld	_____	_____
Other (specify)	_____	_____
Subtotal	$ _____	$ _____

Non-Liquid Assets (Take longer to convert into cash or to accrue total financial benefit)	**You**	**Your Spouse**
Business interests	$ _____	$ _____
Long-term receivables, loans	_____	_____
Deferred income plans	_____	_____
Interest in trusts	_____	_____
Tax shelters	_____	_____
Principal residence	_____	_____
Other real estate (e.g., second home, or revenue or investment property)	_____	_____

	You	**Your Spouse**
U.S./foreign assets (e.g., Snowbird mobile home, condo)		
Personal property		
Valuable assets (e.g., art, antiques, jewellery)		
Other (specify)		
Subtotal	$	$
Total Assets (A)	$	$

Current Liabilities (Currently due within 1 year, or on demand)	**You**	**Your Spouse**
Bank loans (Currently due or on line of credit demand, or within 1 year)	$	$
Credit cards/charge accounts		
Income tax owing		
Alimony		
Child support		
Monthly rent		
Other		
Subtotal	$	$

Long-Term Liabilities (Generally not due for over 1 year)	**You**	**Your Spouse**
Term loan	$	$
Mortgages		
– principal residence		
– other property (investment, revenue, recreational, or commercial)		
Other		
Subtotal	$	$
Total Liabilities (B)	$	$
Net worth before tax (A minus B)	$	$
Tax cost if assets liquidated (if any)	$	$
Net worth after tax	$	$

C. CURRENT AND PROJECTED RETIREMENT OR SNOWBIRD MONTHLY INCOME AND EXPENSES

	Current	Projected at Retirement
I. **Income** (Average monthly income, actual or estimated)		
Salary, bonuses, and commissions	$ _____	$ _____
Dividends	$ _____	$ _____
Interest income	$ _____	$ _____
Pension income	$ _____	$ _____
Other (name) _____	$ _____	$ _____
Total Monthly Income	_____ (A)	_____ (X)
II. **Expenses** (In Canada and the United States)		
Regular monthly payments on:		
Rent or mortgage	$ _____	$ _____
Automobile(s)	$ _____	$ _____
Appliances/TV	$ _____	$ _____
Home improvement loan	$ _____	$ _____
Credit cards/charge accounts (not covered elsewhere)	$ _____	$ _____
Personal loans	$ _____	$ _____
Medical plan	$ _____	$ _____
Instalment and other loans	$ _____	$ _____
Life insurance premiums	$ _____	$ _____
House insurance premiums	$ _____	$ _____
Other insurance premiums (auto, extended out-of-country medical, etc.)	$ _____	$ _____
RRSP deductions	$ _____	$ _____
Pension fund (employer)	$ _____	$ _____
Investment plan(s)	$ _____	$ _____
Miscellaneous	$ _____	$ _____
Other (name) _____	$ _____	$ _____
Total Regular Monthly Payments	$ _____	$ _____
Household operating expenses:	$ _____	$ _____
Telephone	$ _____	$ _____
Gas and electricity	$ _____	$ _____
Heat	$ _____	$ _____
Water and garbage	$ _____	$ _____
Other household expenses (repairs, maintenance, etc.)	$ _____	$ _____
Cable	$ _____	$ _____

	Current	Projected at Retirement
Other (name) _____	$ _____	$ _____
Total Household Operating Expenses	$ _____	$ _____
Food expenses:	$ _____	$ _____
At home	$ _____	$ _____
Away from home	$ _____	$ _____
Total Food Expenses	$ _____	$ _____
Personal expenses:	$ _____	$ _____
Clothing, cleaning, laundry	$ _____	$ _____
Drugs	$ _____	$ _____
Transportation (other than auto)	$ _____	$ _____
Medical/dental	$ _____	$ _____
Day care	$ _____	$ _____
Education (self)	$ _____	$ _____
Education (children)	$ _____	$ _____
Dues (e.g., union or association)	$ _____	$ _____
Gifts, donations	$ _____	$ _____
Travel	$ _____	$ _____
Recreation	$ _____	$ _____
Newspapers, magazines, books	$ _____	$ _____
Automobile maintenance, gas, and parking	$ _____	$ _____
Spending money, allowances	$ _____	$ _____
Other (name) _____	$ _____	$ _____
Total Personal Expenses	$ _____	$ _____
Tax expenses:	$ _____	$ _____
Federal and provincial income taxes	$ _____	$ _____
Home property taxes	$ _____	$ _____
Other (name) _____	$ _____	$ _____
Total Tax Expenses	$ _____	$ _____

III. **Summary of Expenses**

	Current	Projected at Retirement
Regular monthly payments	$ _____	$ _____
Household operating expenses	$ _____	$ _____
Food expenses	$ _____	$ _____
Personal expenses	$ _____	$ _____
Tax expenses	$ _____	$ _____
Total Monthly Expenses	$ _____ (B)	$ _____ (Y)

	Current	Projected at Retirement
Total Monthly Disposable Income Available (subtract total monthly expenses from total monthly income)	$_____ (A–B)	$_____ (X–Y)
Total Annual Disposal Income Available (multiply monthly figures above by 12)	$_____	$_____

D. PROJECTED/POTENTIAL FINANCIAL NEEDS

1. At what age do you plan to retire? _____

2. At what age does your spouse plan to retire? _____

3. Are you a citizen, or a resident, of another country? Yes   No
   If so, what country? _____

4. Is your spouse a citizen, or a resident, of another country? Yes   No

5. Do you and your spouse plan to become nonresidents of Canada?
   Yes   No   If so, when? _____

6. Are you planning to reside or are currently residing three to six months a year in the United States? Yes   No   In another country?
   Yes   No   If so, which? _____

7. Have you thoroughly checked out the implications for your pension plan or health plan eligibility by being away an extended period?
   Yes   No

8. Do you or your spouse expect to receive any lump-sum retirement benefits?
   Yes   No   If so, how much?

	You	Your Spouse
	$	$

   From what source? _____

9. Do you or your spouse anticipate any employment after retirement (part-time or full-time) or income from part-time or full-time self-employment in a home-based or small business?
   Yes   No

	You	Your Spouse
Estimated annual earnings	$	$

10. Do you or your spouse anticipate any major changes in your financial situation in the:
    – short term (less than 2 years)?   Yes   No
    – medium term (2 to 5 years)?   Yes   No
    – long term (more than 5 years)?   Yes   No

11. What combined level of income will you require in retirement (current year dollars)?
    _____

12. How many years of retirement have you projected? _____

13. If you or your spouse died or became disabled, what income would be required to maintain your family's current standard of living (current dollars)?

	You	Your Spouse
Until youngest child no longer financially dependent	$	$
Until age 60	$	$

Until age 65	$	$
Over age 65	$	$

14. What level of inflation do you anticipate will prevail during the time periods in #12?

Have you factored that into your projected future financial needs?
Yes   No

E. WHERE YOUR RETIREMENT INCOME WILL COME FROM

	Estimated Monthly Retirement Income	
	You	**Your Spouse**
Employer's pension plan	$_____	$_____
Canada Pension Plan	$_____	$_____
Old Age Security	$_____	$_____
Guaranteed Income Supplement	$_____	$_____
RRSP/RRIF retirement income	$_____	$_____
LIF income	$_____	$_____
Annuity income	$_____	$_____
Profit-sharing fund payout	$_____	$_____
Salary expected from any earned income in retirement	$_____	$_____
Any other fees, payments for services	$_____	$_____
Disability insurance payments	$_____	$_____
Income expected from a business (part-time or full-time, home-based or small business)	$_____	$_____
Income expected from real estate investments or revenue property	$_____	$_____
Income from renting out part of the house (e.g., basement suite/boarders)	$_____	$_____
Savings account interest (credit union, bank, trust company, other)	$_____	$_____
Federal or provincial savings bonds interest, term deposit interest, guaranteed investment certificate interest, other	$_____	$_____
Other investments: stocks, bonds, mutual funds, etc.	$_____	$_____
Investment income from any expected inheritance	$_____	$_____
Income from other investments you expect to create income	$_____	$_____
Other income sources: alimony, social assistance, UIC, etc.	$_____	$_____
Total Expected Monthly Income:	$_____	$_____
Total Annual Income of you and your spouse (Multiply monthly incomes by 12)	$_____	$_____

F. RETIREMENT PLANNING GOALS

	You	Your Spouse

A. Financial Goal

- Have you determined when your children will finish their schooling?   _____   _____
- Have you determined when any other dependents you have will no longer require your financial support?   _____   _____
- Have you determined when your mortgage will be paid off?   _____   _____
- Have you checked up on the company pension you will receive in retirement, when it will be at the maximum, and when you are eligible to commence receiving benefits?   _____   _____
- Have you determined when you can get the maximum income from your RRSPs?   _____   _____
- Have you determined when you will become eligible for Canada Pension Plan and Old Age Security payments?   _____   _____
- Are you working towards supplementing your pension?   _____   _____
- Have you checked out discounts for seniors on transportation, entertainment, prescription drugs, banking services, etc. (in Canada and the U.S.)?   _____   _____
- Have you explored the kind of work you would like to do and where to find it?   _____   _____
- Are you investigating retirement income plans to convert your RRSP into (such as an RRIF or annuity)?   _____   _____
- Have you found out whether your hobby can earn extra cash for you?   _____   _____
- Are you checking out "tax breaks" for seniors and organizing your income to take maximum advantage of them?   _____   _____

B. Residence Goal

- Have you decided whether to live with, or close to, your family?   _____   _____
- Have you decided where you want to live in retirement?   _____   _____
- Have you checked out the adequacy of transportation facilities?   _____   _____
- Have you checked out how to make your home safe from break-ins or accidents?   _____   _____
- Have you decided whether to sell your house or condominium and move to a smaller one, rent an apartment, or live in a retirement community or recreational vehicle park?   _____   _____

C. Activity/Recreational Goal

- Have you determined what you want to do in retirement?   _____   _____

	You	Your Spouse

- Have you researched interesting voluntary work that you might do?   _____   _____

- Have you checked out travel, cruises, or other tours that you might enjoy?   _____   _____

- Have you found out how you can become more active in community affairs?   _____   _____

- Have you checked out educational courses of interest to you?   _____   _____

- Have you assessed your skills, attributes, talents, interests, values, strengths, and weaknesses?   _____   _____

- Have you checked out social activities for yourself and your partner?   _____   _____

D. Health Goal

- Are you doing everything possible to stay in good physical and mental condition?   _____   _____

- Have you investigated the medical facilities available in the community you intend to retire in?   _____   _____

- Have you researched the provincial medical coverage you obtain if you are travelling outside your province within Canada, or travelling outside Canada (U.S. or elsewhere)?   _____   _____

- Are you working out a retirement plan with the active participation of your partner?   _____   _____

- Are you working at maintaining good relationships with family and friends?   _____   _____

- Have you obtained adequate travel medical insurance coverage to supplement your provincial coverage?   _____   _____

E. Estate Goal

- Have you recorded the location of your family assets (property, bank accounts, stocks, bonds, etc.), including documents and related information, and left one copy with your executor and another copy in your safety deposit box?   _____   _____

- Have you made or updated your will and power of attorney, and confirmed the availability, willingness, and suitability of the executor, trustee, and/or guardian?   _____   _____

- Have you checked out the tax implications of transferring specific personal or business assets to your beneficiaries?   _____   _____

- Have you told your family, a trusted friend, and your executor where your records are located?   _____   _____

- Have you consulted a lawyer, tax accountant, and financial advisor?   _____   _____

Index

About the Author

Douglas Gray, LL.B., formerly a practising lawyer, is now a consultant, columnist and Canada's most published business author, with 17 bestselling business and personal finance books. He retired from his law practice at the age of 50 to concentrate on his educational interests of writing and public speaking.

He is an internationally recognized expert on financial and retirement planning and has given seminars to over 250,000 people nationally and internationally in his various areas of expertise. He is a member of the Canadian Association of Professional Speakers and the Canadian Bar Association.

Mr. Gray is frequently interviewed as an authority on financial matters by publications such as the *Financial Times*, *Profit*, and *The Globe and Mail*. He is a regular guest expert on personal finance issues on CBC-TV *Newsworld*. In addition, he has been a regular columnist for *Profit*, *Computer Paper*, *Opportunities Canada*, *Canadian Moneysaver*, *Forever Young*, *Forever Young South*, *CARP News*, *Good Times*, and *Canada News*.

He is the president of the Canadian Retirement Planning Institute Inc. This organization offers objective educational programs nationally on a wide range of issues related to personal finance, tax, estate planning, and retirement planning that are of interest to those planning for, or in retirement, and Snowbirds.

Mr. Gray lives in Vancouver, British Columbia.

Reader Input and Educational Seminars

If you have thoughts or suggestions that you believe would be helpful for future editions of this book, or if you are interested in having the author give a seminar or presentation to your group or association, anywhere in Canada or the United States, please write to:

Canadian Retirement Planning Institute Inc.
#300 – 3665 Kingsway
Vancouver, BC
V5R 5W2
Tel: (604) 436-3337
Fax: (604) 436-9155
Web site: www.snowbird.ca
E-mail: dgray@institute.ca

Ordering Information for Other Bestselling Books and Software Programs by Douglas Gray

Small Business Titles

- *The Complete Canadian Small Business Guide* (with Diana Gray), 2nd edition ISBN 0-07-551661-6
- *Home Inc.: The Canadian Home-Based Business Guide* (with Diana Gray), 2nd edition ISBN 0-07-551558-X
- *So You Want to Buy a Franchise* (with Norm Friend) ISBN 0-07-560419-1

Real Estate Titles

- *Making Money in Real Estate: The Canadian Residential Investment Guide* ISBN 0-07-549596-1
- *Mortgages Made Easy: The Canadian Guide to Home Financing* ISBN 0-07-551344-7
- *Canadian Home Buying Made Easy: The Streetsmart Guide for First-Time Home Buyers* ISBN 0-07-552900-9
- *Condo Buying Made Easy: The Canadian Guide to Apartment and Town-house Condos, Co-ops and Timeshares*, 2nd edition ISBN 0-07-551791-4
- *Mortgage Payment Tables Made Easy* ISBN 0-07-551722-1

Personal Finance / Retirement Planning Titles

- *The Canadian Guide to Will and Estate Planning: Everything You Need to Know Today to Protect Your Wealth and Your Family Tomorrow* (with John Budd) ISBN 0-07-551740-X
- *The Canadian Snowbird Guide: Everything You Need to Know About Living Part-Time in the U.S.A. and Mexico* ISBN 0-07-086047-5

Software Programs (Disk/Manual/Book Albums)

- *Making Money in Real Estate* (jointly developed by Douglas Gray, Phoenix Accrual Corporation and McGraw-Hill Ryerson Limited) ISBN 0-07-551856-2

Available at your local bookstore or by contacting:
McGraw-Hill Ryerson Limited
Trade & Professional Books Division
300 Water Street, Whitby, Ontario L1N 9B6
Phone: 1-800-565-5758 / Fax: 1-800-463-5885 (orders only)
Web site: www.mcgrawhill.com